UNDERSTANDING
JOHN DEWEY

UNDERSTANDING JOHN DEWEY

Nature and Cooperative Intelligence

J A M E S   C A M P B E L L

Open ❖ Court

Chicago and La Salle, Illinois

Selections from *The Collected Works of John Dewey* are reprinted with the permission of The Center for Dewey Studies, Southern Illinois University at Carbondale.

OPEN COURT and the above logo are registered in the U.S. Patent and Trademark Office.

© 1995 by Open Court Publishing Company

First printing 1995
Second printing 1996

Printed and bound in the United States of America.

Library of Congress Cataloging-in-Publication Data

Campbell, James, 1948–
   Understanding John Dewey : nature and cooperative intelligence /
James Campbell.
    p. cm.
   Includes bibliographical references and index.
   ISBN 0-8126-9284-5. — ISBN 0-8126-9285-3 (pbk.)
   1. Dewey, John, 1859–1952.   I. Title.
B945.D4C36 1995
191—dc20   95-1492
                                            CIP

For Linda—
ever in process

Contents

Preface

The thought of John Dewey has been a factor of greater or lesser importance in American intellectual life for over a century. At the present time, his influence is once again growing. There are many reasons for this recovery of stature, not the least of which is the recently completed publication of the critical edition of his work under the direction of Jo Ann Boydston at the Center for Dewey Studies at Southern Illinois University at Carbondale. With the availability of a complete edition of Dewey's writings it is now possible to step back and see his philosophy whole. Also contributing to this rebirth of interest in Dewey is the recent stream of informed and insightful studies of aspects of his life and work by such scholars as: Thomas Alexander, Raymond Boisvert, Larry Hickman, Steven Rockefeller, Ralph Sleeper, James Tiles, and Robert Westbrook. A third, and perhaps the most important, factor in the contemporary reconsideration of Dewey is the growing dissatisfaction with much contemporary philosophizing, with thinking that neither grows out of the problems and issues of our broader society nor is able to offer any assistance to that society as it attempts to address its difficulties. Creating a philosophy that was connected to society in both of these ways was a major concern for Dewey.

I have tried to present the central themes of Dewey's thought in a way that provides ready access to all aspects of his philosophical vision. For him, we humans live our lives as natural and social creatures who have emerged from and must ever interact with our natural and social environment. This world is our past and our future, our challenge and our means. He emphasizes that we interact with this environment much of the time —too much of the time— based on our unthinking desires and our untested beliefs. Yet we have the ability to inquire and evaluate: to move beyond the immediately good to lasting values, to actions and beliefs and goals that make possible human growth and long-term fulfillment. Central to Dewey's vision is the belief that this evaluative power, which he calls intelligence, is not an individual possession but a possession of the group. The efforts of the vibrant community of cooperative inquirers are consequently our best means of addressing our collective problems. Hence my subtitle: *Nature and Cooperative Intelligence*.

In writing this volume, I have attempted to present the mood of a philosophy that addresses all of life and engages itself with the rich and diverse experience of society. Although both of these aspects run counter to the narrowing and isolating tendencies of much of contemporary philosophizing, they are essential to an understanding of Dewey's philosophical vision. I have, for example, gathered together Dewey's ideas on specific topics from various areas in his corpus to suggest the breadth of these topics and the connections that he saw among them. At the cost of some precision, I have also attempted to let him speak for himself whenever possible, rather than offering his ideas through paraphrase. And I have made frequent mention of commentators—not all of whom are philosophers, and none of whom are narrow thinkers—who were contemporaries of Dewey and who approached their work as intellectuals with much the same public engagement that he demonstrated. All of this should help readers to grasp Dewey's thought in its fullness and within its social ground.

There are many individuals at present who are coming to Dewey's thought via another route, following out suggestions by contemporary writers of various sorts that there is value to be found in his work. These writers—including deconstructionists, post modernists, followers of Rorty or Habermas, and so forth—see in Dewey's work careful discussions of vital themes like contingency and fallibilism, process and adaptation, and the building of democratic society in a world that is simultaneously building its own intellectual foundations. In this volume, I have not directly addressed possible connections between Dewey's thought and that of these other contemporary thinkers. Still, my disinclination to discuss their work here should not be taken as an indication of any lack of appreciation for what they are doing.

I have limited myself in this volume to a consideration of Dewey's thought simply because I believe that presenting his position in its fullness and within its social ground is itself a sufficiently complex and demanding job. His understanding of humans as evolved social organisms that use intelligence to address the problems of living, as rooted in a natural place that both supports and tests them, as challenged to find true values among the many possibilities that present themselves, and as striving to advance the common good by cooperative means constitutes a rich and powerful philosophic perspective that cannot be adequately presented or clearly understood if connections with specific contemporary thinkers and problems become too prominent. Presenting an understanding of Dewey's thought in as clear and accurate and full a fashion as possible, however, will help to make it available not only to contemporary readers of all sorts, but also to those who are new to philosophy and social thought or simply to work within the American tradition, as well as to those whose interests are in historical accuracy or in contemporary usefulness.

In attempting to provide the background that is necessary for understanding Dewey's thought and his place in the American context, I have noted without much commentary occasions when his approach is grounded in an interpretation of America's past that we now find in need of reconstruction. I presume, for example, that contemporary readers are more skeptical of claims to 'American Exceptionalism', or the use of 'the American Experience' in the singular, than earlier readers of Dewey were, and I have not felt the need to caution them. Similarly, I have not told readers how to interpret all of the secondary material which I include, or to which I refer, in the notes. With much of this material I am in agreement, with some of it I am not. All of it, however, contributes to an understanding of Dewey's work and its background.

Provided in this way with a solid base for understanding Dewey's work and his place in American philosophy and social thought, careful readers can, I believe, reach out beyond his work to the thought of his contemporaries and of ours, bringing his contribution into discussions of issues of vital social concern. Thus, I am confident that, although this volume may have a certain historical feel, it will not suggest to readers that I think that Dewey is only, or even primarily, a historical figure, or that our own philosophical work should be historical. Rather, I see Dewey's work as offering us a chance to rethink philosophy, its role in society, and how it carries out this role. To grasp his position clearly, however, we must see it in its own context. It is necessary for us to step back to understand; it is also necessary for us to move forward to live.

CHAPTER 1

Introduction

MORRIS COHEN ONCE wrote that "Dewey is essentially one of those philosophers who, like Spinoza, impress the world with their profound simplicity."[1] The soundness of Cohen's characterization ought not to suggest that it is possible to approach Dewey's work, any more than it is possible to approach Spinoza's, in a casual or uninformed manner. Reaching the core of Dewey's position requires serious intellectual effort combined with a sense of the larger intellectual world in which he lived and wrote. Providing this latter background is the task of this chapter.

The philosophical work of John Dewey can best be understood—and perhaps ultimately can only be fully understood—when approached through an evolutionary or processive interpretation of the American Experience. Although the *validity* of this interpretation of American history is something that should concern us as we proceed, the *content* of this interpretation must be our first topic of consideration. Dewey's development to intellectual maturity took place in the context of a society that presented its own development to self-consciousness as occurring in the midst of the challenges of the New World. What America meant, from this perspective, was a chance to start over—to move to the New World from the Old World, or to move on within the New World—a chance to begin again. Contained in this chance was an optimism grounded in real possibilities: we could learn from our mistakes; defeats, however painful, could ultimately mean growth.

The intellectual importance of this life of opportunities was that it presented beliefs, ideas, customs, morals, and so on, as arising within and corresponding to environing conditions and consequently as

---

[1] Morris Cohen, *American Thought,* 293; cf. Cohen, "Later Philosophy," 255. [Full bibliographical information can be found in the list of works cited below.]

themselves being in process relative to changing situations. In particular, the intellectual life of the New World had to develop from the practices of those living this new life, rather than from the continued cultivation of an imported inheritance. The political importance of these opportunities—in terms of freedom and equality—was no less significant. Society itself is a process of interactive changes among people and their various institutions, institutions that over time become outdated and must be changed.

Dewey accepted both the general historical accuracy of this vision of America and the implications that it had for the future of American society in terms of ongoing intellectual and political reconstruction. One specific focus of this spirit of recognizing and acting out the possibilities of experience was, for Dewey, the work of Ralph Waldo Emerson, whose call to the citizens of this New World to live life fully and to break free from inherited doctrines animates Dewey's work throughout. Another focus can be found in the work of Charles Darwin who demonstrated the pervasiveness of transition in life and emphasized the adaptiveness of living forms. With these twin emphases of the democratic spirit and of ongoing attempts to solve problems we find the key elements of Dewey's understanding of the American Experience.

1.1.   The American Experience

One way to demonstrate the uniqueness of American philosophy is to uncover its rootedness within a unique set of historical experiences. The customary place to begin this history is with the Puritans of New England. They were English Calvinists who wanted a sharper break with Roman traditions and practices than the Church of England afforded; and their errand to Massachusetts Bay was an attempt to build what John Winthrop called "a Citty upon a Hill" for their English fellow Protestants to see and then to imitate. The doctrines that the Puritans advanced were complex and their theology was severe: the limitless power of God, the ultimate depravity of human nature, a special covenanted relationship between God and His chosen people, selective salvation independent of personal works, exacting conditions for church membership, and so on. The details of the Puritan Experience, however fascinating and impor-

tant, are better studied elsewhere.[2] For us at present, the importance
of the Puritans is that they were the first large group—the first of
many such groups—who saw in the New World of America a chance
to start over, an opportunity to break free from crippling aspects of
their social inheritance, the possibility to overcome their troubled
lives by beginning again. And, if we broaden our scope to consider
other groups on the early American scene—the Quakers of Philadelphia, the Catholics of Maryland, the Germans of Pennsylvania, the
Scotch-Irish farther south and west—we find the same belief. In spite
of the dangers of the ocean passage and the harshness of the colonial
life, to these (and later) immigrants America meant the opportunity
to start over and the troubles inherent in the process were a small
price to pay.

The sweetness of the idea of starting over itself begins to sour
when we remember other aspects of the story. These overlooked
elements—the extermination of the native population, the kidnap-
ping of the people of Africa and their subjection to the horrors of
human slavery, the unsettledness of a people whose reality could
never reach its dreams,[3] the wasting of the environment by those who
could always move on, the ascription of personal failure to all who
did not prosper in a land of such opportunity—are essential parts of
this story of starting over as well, and they are parts that haunt us
still. In spite of the problematic reality, however, the myth of the
New World represented just that: a chance for the downtrodden and
dissatisfied to start again in a new world. In the New World, there
was a chance to participate in the ideals of freedom and equality.
There was a chance to create a new society unrestrained by the
barriers and restrictions of Europe.

It is possible to go further and consider not just the chance to start
over but also something about the forces that influenced this
opportunity. Dewey writes that "[p]erhaps the most striking idea
evolved in the interpretation of the history of the United States is the

---

[2] No better place to begin could be chosen than the writings of Perry Miller,
especially *Errand into the Wilderness,* and the two volumes of *The New England
Mind.* For a more experiential approach to the spiritual life of New England, see:
David D. Hall, *Worlds of Wonder, Days of Judgment.*

[3] Cf. John J. McDermott: "A dialectic soon set up between the systemic
loneliness of the frontier and a developing sense of possibility, to be realized over the
next hill, across the next river, atop the next mountain" ("Josiah Royce's Philosophy
of the Community," 156).

importance of the frontier" (LW 5:129)[4]; and the most powerful formulation of the importance of the Frontier is offered by Frederick Jackson Turner (1861–1932), who writes that "[t]he existence of an area of free land, its continuous recession, and the advance of American settlement westward, explain American development." Turner continues:

> American democracy was born of no theorist's dream; it was not carried in the [Susan] Constant to Virginia, nor in the Mayflower to Plymouth. It came out of the American forest, and it gained new strength each time it touched a new frontier. Not the constitution, but free land and an abundance of natural resources open to a fit people, made the democratic type of society in America for three centuries while it occupied its empire.

The ideas and values that made democracy a viable way of life in frontier America came not from books and teachings about democracy. They came from living an egalitarian life. With the freedom to move on, people stayed in any one place only so long as they felt that they were being treated fairly. Thus the Frontier, in addition to its obvious connection with freedom, worked indirectly to preserve the equality component of democracy as well. But, largely as a result of this freedom to move on, there developed no tradition of attempting to work out resolutions of serious problems. Frontier democracy did not develop the permanence or the commitment necessary. It was always possible to go west: in Pennsylvania or Massachusetts, to Ohio or Kentucky, to the Great Plains or California. Central to the American Experience was that the free land of the Frontier enabled people to escape from whatever troubles emerged.

The second theme in Turner's Frontier Thesis is that, since the Frontier played such a role in making us what we are, the loss of the Frontier—which the Census Bureau declared to have occurred in 1890—would have a severe social impact. "When we lost our free lands and our isolation from the Old World," Turner writes, "we lost our immunity from the results of mistakes, of waste, of inefficiency,

---

[4] In this volume, I will be quoting passages from Dewey's writings from the Critical Edition of his works edited by Jo Ann Boydston, abbreviated as follows: EW = *The Early Works, 1882–1898*, five volumes; MW = *The Middle Works, 1899–1924*, fifteen volumes; LW = *The Later Works, 1925–1953*, seventeen volumes.

and of inexperience in our government."[5] The American Experience had been rooted in the possibility to start over; and, with the loss of this outlet, came the need to learn new ways to maintain our democracy. In particular, we needed to develop the political means to ensure social peace. We had been lucky up to that point, Dewey writes, because social conflicts were minimized by freedom and opportunity: "When men make their gains by fighting in common a wilderness, they have not the motive for mutual distrust which comes when they get ahead only by fighting one another" (MW 10:207; cf. LW 11:168). But with the loss of the chance to start over, we needed to create institutions of equality directly. As Turner writes, "the frontier has gone, and with its going has closed the first period of American history." The second period of American history, whatever it was to be, would have to evolve a new way to ensure democracy.[6]

The adequacy of the Frontier Thesis, as a specific cluster of historical claims, is an important issue; but it is one that I wish to leave for another time. My focus of attention here will be, rather, on a more general form of the environmental thesis that emphasizes the relationship between experience and the life of ideas. Ideas must fit their situations, the environmental thesis maintains; the test of a view is whether it *works*. In the words of that great spokesman of American practicality, Benjamin Franklin, "opinions should be judged of by their influences and effects."[7] The most important implication of this environmentalism is that the experience of an open New World shakes out the inherited and transported doctrines, and those that

---

[5] *The Frontier in American History*, 1, 293, 357. For some of the background to Turner's Frontier Thesis, see: Frederic L. Paxson, "A Generation of the Frontier Hypothesis"; Lee Benson, "The Historical Background to Turner's Frontier Essay"; Ellen von Nardoff, "The American Frontier as a Safety Valve"; Merle E. Curti, *Probing Our Past*, 32–55; Henry Nash Smith, *Virgin Land*, 250–60; George R. Taylor, ed., *The Turner Thesis*.

[6] *The Frontier in American History*, 38. The need for a reconstruction of our political situation was the basis of Franklin Delano Roosevelt's call for "a new deal for the American people" in his speech accepting the Presidential nomination at the 1932 Democratic National Convention (*The Public Papers and Addresses of Franklin Delano Roosevelt*, vol. 1, 659; cf. 742–56; Curtis Nettels, "Frederick Jackson Turner and the New Deal"; Steven Kesselman, "The Frontier Thesis and the Great Depression"; Walter Prescott Webb, *Divided We Stand*. See also Walter Lippmann, *The Method of Freedom*, 103–10).

[7] Franklin to his father, Josiah Franklin, 13 April 1738, in *The Writings of Benjamin Franklin*, vol. 2, 214; cf. vol. 1, 296; H. S. Thayer, *Meaning and Action*, 7.

cannot prove themselves in the new experience are modified or abandoned. As Dewey writes, "We have imported our language, our laws, our institutions, our morals, and our religion from Europe, and we have adapted them to the new conditions of our life" (LW 2:18–19; cf. 12). The new environment challenged the inheritance of the colonists—their beliefs, their values, their goals—and in the process made them new people.

A clear recognition that the American Experience had created a new people, as well as a call to these people to recognize their new situation, is contained in an 1837 address by Ralph Waldo Emerson (1803–1882) entitled "The American Scholar." In it, Emerson challenges us to live our lives fully by breaking free from our doctrinal inheritance and opening ourselves fully to the experience of the New World. "Our day of dependence, our long apprenticeship to the learning of other lands, draws to a close." We must overcome our longings for distant baubles and come to appreciate, he writes, "the near, the low, the common." That which has been "negligently trodden under foot by those who were harnessing and provisioning themselves for long journeys into far countries" is now recognized to be "richer than all foreign parts." In such appreciation, our lives will grow in meaning and value. "It is a mischievous notion that we are come late into nature; that the world was finished a long time ago," he continues. "As the world was plastic and fluid in the hands of God, so it is ever to so much of his attributes as we bring to it."[8] The simple life of the common person is as valuable as any other, he maintains; but we cannot see this if our standards of evaluation are drawn from the largely incomparable, but not at all superior, life of Europe. The scholar must thus try to break free of the restraints of imported traditions and inherited 'truths' and return to the fullness of experience, and then try to lead his or her listeners to treasure their own lives based upon domestic evaluative categories. In praise of this democratic aspect of Emerson, Dewey writes:

> Against creed and system, convention and institution, Emerson stands for restoring to the common man that which in the name of religion, of philosophy, of art and of morality, has been embezzled from the common store and appropriated to sectarian and class use.

---

[8] *The Complete Works of Ralph Waldo Emerson,* vol. 1, 81, 110–11, 105.

Beyond anyone we know of, Emerson has comprehended and declared how such malversation makes truth decline from its simplicity, and in becoming partial and owned, become a puzzle of and trick for theologian, metaphysician and litterateur. (MW 3:190).

Emerson's point, Dewey maintains, is simple: experience contains the means for its own evaluation, and we need not call on others to tell us what is good and right and true. Dewey's own point, as we shall see, is much the same. The functioning community of engaged and sincere citizens can be trusted to seek and recognize what is good and right and true.

1.2. Dewey's Life and Intellectual Development

The facts of Dewey's life can be stated briefly.[9] Born on October 20, 1859, to Archibald Sprague Dewey, a grocer, and Lucina Rich Dewey, his wife, in Burlington, Vermont, he was one of three surviving children.[10] Dewey graduated from the University of Vermont in 1879 with his brother Davis Rich Dewey, and spent the next three years (1879–1882) as a high school teacher, two years in a school run by his cousin in Oil City, Pennsylvania, and the next year more irregularly back in Vermont. After some private philosophical study with his former professor, Henry Augustus Pearson Torrey, in Burlington, and some further encouragement from the editor of *The Journal of Speculative Philosophy*, William Torrey Harris,[11] Dewey decided to pursue graduate study in philosophy in 1882 at Johns Hopkins University. There he studied logic with Charles Sanders Peirce (1839–1914), whose five years at Hopkins constituted his

---

[9] Further biographical information on Dewey can be found in: George Dykhuizen, *The Life and Mind of John Dewey*; Neil Coughlan, *Young John Dewey*; Robert B. Westbrook, *John Dewey and American Democracy*; Steven C. Rockefeller, *John Dewey: Religious Faith and Democratic Humanism*.

[10] An older brother, John Archibald, had died tragically in January of that same year. See Dykhuizen, *The Life and Mind of John Dewey*, 2, 7, 329 n.28.

[11] Harris published two of Dewey's essays in his journal prior to Dewey's enrollment at Hopkins. See EW 1:3–18.

only real teaching position; psychology with Granville Stanley Hall (1844–1924), an experimental psychologist who had trained with William James at Harvard and Wilhelm Wundt in Leipzig; and the history of philosophy with George Sylvester Morris (1840–1889), who at that time was dividing his teaching between Hopkins and the University of Michigan. Dewey earned his Ph.D. in 1884 with a dissertation on Kant's psychology[12] and began teaching philosophy with Morris at the University of Michigan. He remained in Ann Arbor for the next decade, with the exception of the academic year 1888–1889 that he spent at the University of Minnesota. In 1886, Dewey married Harriet Alice Chipman (1859–1927), a Michigan graduate with a strong concern for philosophy and social issues who greatly influenced Dewey's social interests.[13]

During his years at Michigan, Dewey met a number of philosophers who were to be important in later life. Especially significant among this group were two. The first was James Hayden Tufts (1862–1942), whom Dewey later described as "a lover of knowledge . . . knowledge for the sake of wisdom, and not as an end in itself" (LW 5:425). Dewey taught together with Tufts for twelve years, first at Michigan (1889–1891) and later at the University of Chicago (1894–1904), and they co-authored both editions of *Ethics*.[14] Of equal, or perhaps even greater, importance was George Herbert Mead (1863–1931), with whom Dewey taught at Michigan (1891–1894) and Chicago (1894–1904), and whom he characterized as "a seminal mind of the very first order" (LW 6:310).[15] While at the University of Chicago from 1894–1904, Dewey chaired the Department of Philosophy (which included psychology) and the Department of Pedagogy, and he directed the Laboratory School. He was also socially active, along with his wife, Alice, his colleagues like Tufts and Mead, and social reformers like Jane Addams of Hull

---

[12] The work, entitled "The Psychology of Kant," was never published and has been lost. See Dykhuizen, *The Life and Mind of John Dewey*, 37; EW 1:lxxii, 34–47.

[13] Cf. Jane Dewey (their daughter): Alice was possessed of "a critical attitude toward social conditions and injustices, [and] she was undoubtedly largely responsible for the early widening of Dewey's philosophic interests from the commentative and classical to the field of contemporary life" ("Biography of John Dewey," 21).

[14] The 1908 edition of *Ethics* is MW 5; the 1932 edition is LW 7. For Dewey's evaluation of the importance of Tufts, cf. LW 5:424–25, 15:321–25.

[15] For Dewey's evaluation of the importance of Mead, cf. LW 6:22–28, 307–12; 11:450–53; 12:5.

House, in addressing the educational and political troubles of Chicago. Disputes with the university administration about the process of integrating the Laboratory School into the School of Education, and particularly about the continuing employment of Mrs. Dewey as Principal, led to Dewey's resignation from the university in 1904.[16] Because of his growing prominence as a philosophical figure, Dewey was able to secure a position at Columbia University in New York City, where he taught from 1905–1930 and served in an emeritus status until the end of the decade.

His major published works during his teaching career consisted of the Dewey and Tufts's *Ethics* (1908), and his own *How We Think* (1910), *Democracy and Education* (1916), *Reconstruction in Philosophy* (1920), *Human Nature and Conduct* (1922), *Experience and Nature* (1925), and *The Public and Its Problems* (1927). Toward the end of his active teaching career and during his nine years as emeritus professor beginning in mid-1930, Dewey produced what have become his best-known works: the revised edition of *Experience and Nature* (1929), *The Quest for Certainty* (1929), the revised editions of Dewey and Tufts's *Ethics* (1932) and of his own *How We Think* (1932), and *Art as Experience* (1934), *A Common Faith* (1934), and *Logic: The Theory of Inquiry* (1938). During his Columbia years, Dewey rose to a position of unequalled prominence in the philosophical profession. He was President of the American Philosophical Association (Eastern Division) in 1905, and offered such prestigious lecture series as the Carus Lectures to the American Philosophical Association in New York City (1922), the Gifford Lectures at Edinburgh (1929), the William James Lectures at Harvard (1931), and the Terry Lectures at Yale (1934). Dewey also travelled widely and lectured in such countries as Japan (1919), China (1919–1921), Turkey (1924), Mexico (1926), and the Soviet Union (1928). Throughout his career, but especially after his retirement from teaching, Dewey was a major figure in America's attempts to address its social and political ills. In 1946, after nearly twenty years as a widower, he married Roberta Lowitz Grant (1904–1970). Dewey died in New York City on June 1, 1952.

Dewey himself tells us little about his life and intellectual development. The "Biography of John Dewey," contained in *The Philosophy of John Dewey* in the Library of Living Philosophers Series,

---

[16] Cf. Robert L. McCaul, "Dewey, Harper and the University of Chicago."

was "written by the daughters of its subject from material which he furnished" and edited by his daughter, Jane.[17] With only one exception, Dewey offers us directly only fragments.[18] The exception is a piece that he wrote for the 1930 two-volume set, *Contemporary American Philosophy: Personal Statements,* that he entitled "From Absolutism to Experimentalism" (LW 5:147–60). As background to his intellectual development, this essay offers us a glimpse at higher education in the late 1870s, when the college course was a pre-set array of lectures and recitations that offered career training for the professions—primarily teaching and the ministry—and when philosophy's task in the educational picture was largely apologetic. The sole philosophy course was offered to seniors as part of what Dewey calls "a kind of intellectual coping" or "the keystone" (LW 5:147) in the education of a Christian gentleman.[19]

The higher education system was fundamentally changed over the next decades as a result of two fundamental challenges. The first was the democratic challenge to this older conception of education represented by the Morrill Act of 1862. The aim of this act, named for Dewey's fellow Vermonter, U.S. Senator Justin Smith Morrill (1810–1898), was to authorize the use of Federal resources, through the sale of land, for the advancement of the practical possibilities of higher education—especially agricultural and mechanical. That is to say, its purpose was to connect the schools with the practical lives of the people and to advance the common good in a democracy. As the Act itself states, its aim is "to promote the liberal and practical education of the industrial classes in the several pursuits and professions in life."[20] The second challenge to the older conception of education was the scientific challenge, based on the research model of the German universities. This challenge resulted in the founding

---

[17] The note continues: "In the emphasis on varied influences and in the philosophical portions it may be regarded as an autobiography." (Jane Dewey, "Biography of John Dewey," 3).

[18] See, for example, the credos: "My Pedagogic Creed" (EW 5:84–95); "What I Believe," (LW 5:267–78); and "I Believe" (LW 14:91–97).

[19] Cf. Morton White: It was "a period when philosophers vied with each other to see who could best preserve the sanctity and stability of religious beliefs." (*Origins of Dewey's Instrumentalism,* 5; cf. EW 1:116–21; Paul H. Buck, *Social Sciences at Harvard, 1860–1920: From Inculcation to the Open Mind,* ix–xii, 1–17).

[20] For the text of the Morrill Act, see: 12 *United States Statutes at Large,* 503–5; cf. Earle D. Ross, *Democracy's College;* William Belmont Parker, *The Life and Public Services of Justin Smith Morrill,* 259–84.

of the new research universities in America—for example, Hopkins (1876), Clark (1889), Stanford (1891), and Chicago (1892)—with their emphases upon the discovery of new knowledge through empirical research, and the advancement of graduate study in narrowly defined specialties under recognized authorities.[21]

During his two years of graduate study at Johns Hopkins, Dewey was introduced to the laboratory orientation in psychology through the efforts of G. S. Hall. Dewey later taught numerous courses in psychology, wrote extensively in the burgeoning field—including his *Psychology* of 1887[22]—and served as President of the American Psychological Association (1899–1900). Whatever the eventual importance of this introduction to the new laboratory psychology at Hopkins, however, the real focus of graduate study for Dewey was to further his philosophical understanding of Idealism, particularly of the work of Georg Wilhelm Friedrich Hegel (1770–1831). His mentor here was G. S. Morris[23]; and working with him, both as a student in Baltimore and later as a junior colleague in Ann Arbor, Dewey developed a philosophical position that he later admits was 'absolutistic'. But, at the time, what Dewey found in Hegel's thought was a spiritual salve. It satisfied, he writes,

> a demand for unification that was doubtless an intense emotional craving, and yet was a hunger that only an intellectualized subject-matter could satisfy . . . the sense of divisions and separations that were, I suppose, borne in upon me as a consequence of a heritage of New England culture, divisions by way of isolation of self from the world, of soul from body, of nature from God, brought a painful oppression—or, rather, they were an inward laceration.

And, whereas his earlier philosophical study had been "an intellectual gymnastic," he writes that Hegel's synthesizing philosophy "oper-

---

[21] Cf. Charles F. Thwing, *The American and the German University,* 40–77; Jurgen Herbst, *The German Historical School in American Scholarship,* 1–22; Daniel J. Wilson, *Science, Community and the Transformation of American Philosophy,* 76–80, 98–102.

[22] Revised versions of the *Psychology* appeared in 1889 and 1891. Cf. EW 2:xlix–liv.

[23] For Dewey's tribute to Morris, see MW 10:109–15; cf. Westbrook, *John Dewey and American Democracy,* 14–22; Rockefeller, *John Dewey,* 77–89; Morton G. White, *The Origins of Dewey's Instrumentalism,* 5–33, 150; Raymond D. Boisvert, *Dewey's Metaphysics,* 21, 24–28.

ated as an immense release, a liberation" by offering a "dissolution of hard-and-fast dividing walls." (LW 5:153). Dewey later became convinced of the superiority of the Darwinian model of naturalized processes to the Hegelian model of ideational process. As he writes, "[g]radually I came to realize that what the principles actually stood for could be better understood and stated when completely emancipated from Hegelian garb."[24] Still, he admits, "that acquaintance with Hegel has left a permanent deposit in my thinking" (LW 5:154). An examination of Dewey's philosophical perspective will be the focus of Part One of this study.

In the essay "From Absolutism to Experimentalism," Dewey also discusses a concern with social problems that had for him "the intellectual appeal and provided the intellectual sustenance that many seem to have found primarily in religious questions" (LW 5:154). He grew to consciousness in an era of enormous social growth—urbanization, industrialization and economic centralization, immigration—and numberless social troubles.[25] For Dewey, as for many other progressive figures, the job of the American intellectual was to attempt to address these ills with the tools of research and publication that were becoming increasingly available. For Dewey, addressing these ills also meant the application of philosophical wisdom to the intelligent conduct of the affairs of social life. His social philosophy is an attempt to lay out in a complete and coherent form a perspective that sees democratic society as a cooperative undertaking of interrelated efforts to advance the common good, that sees institutions as social habits that are more or less adequate to our situations, and that sees social reconstruction as the process of attempting to recognize the current institutionalized ills and to correct them. The goal of life is to live more fully; the goal of

---

[24] Jane M. Dewey, "Biography of John Dewey," 18. Cf. Gail Kennedy: "The fusion of this evolutionary conception of the function of intelligence with the Hegelian view, which Dewey already held, that the workings of the mind are objectively expressed in social traditions and institutions, is the matrix out of which Dewey's subsequent philosophy develops" ("Science and the Transformation of Common Sense," 313; cf. Sidney Hook, *John Dewey: An Intellectual Portrait,* 13–14; Richard Bernstein, *Praxis and Action,* 165–73; James Edwin Creighton, "Darwin and Logic," 171–74).

[25] Cf. Harold Underwood Faulkner: "To many thoughtful men in the opening years of the twentieth century it seemed that America in making her fortune was in peril of losing her soul" (*The Quest for Social Justice, 1898–1914,* 81).

democracy is to increase the number of full lives. Underlying this perspective are two basic assumptions. The first is a melioristic belief that, although there cannot be guarantees that our efforts will make our situation better, the improvement of our situation is a real possibility. The second is an assumption of the possibility of growth: we can learn from our mistaken efforts. We live both now and in the future, and with current defeat can come wisdom for the future. Dewey's social and political thought will be the focus of Part Two of this study.

1.3. Pragmatism

Although Pragmatism is often seen as a practical new philosophy for the New World,[26] it is a philosophy that bears a name from the Greek by way of Kant. "The term 'pragmatic'," Dewey notes, "was suggested to [Peirce] by the study of Kant," who distinguished sharply between *praktisch* and *pragmatisch* (LW 2:3); and Peirce sharply rejected the former because of its *apriori* associations in Kant. As Peirce himself writes, "for one who has learned philosophy out of Kant . . . *praktisch* and *pragmatisch* were as far apart as the two poles, the former belonging in a region of thought where no mind of the experimentalist type can ever make sure of solid ground under his feet, the latter expressing relation to some definite human purpose."[27] Peirce's Kantian terminological distinction could not prevent more idiomatic uses of the term 'practical'; and explicating the nature of the relationship between thinking and practical activity found in Pragmatism—what Peirce called "its recognition of an inseparable connection between rational cognition and rational purpose"[28]—became a central task of its proponents. While this might seem to be an unlikely base upon which to build a philosophical movement, Pragmatism became a powerful force within philo-

---

[26] While Pragmatism may have prospered primarily in America, it was not a purely American creation. Peirce, James and Dewey all discuss its roots in the history of Western philosophy. See: Charles Sanders Peirce, *Collected Papers*, 5.11–5.12; William James, *Pragmatism*, 30, 268–70; LW 2:18–20; Thayer, *Meaning and Action*, 10–65.

[27] *Collected Papers*, 5.412; cf. Thayer, *Meaning and Action*, 7–8, 136–41.

[28] *Collected Papers*, 5.412.

sophical circles and a tremendously popular topic of discussion outside of them.

Pragmatism, as a philosophical movement, was continuous with the rest of the developing American society and needs to be distinguished from at least two other 'pragmatic' strains. One of these is rooted in the practicality and simplicity of the American lifestyle. In part, this admitted 'pragmatism' reflects a popular anti-intellectualism—action being more important than 'useless' speculation—and, in part, it reflects the immense felt task of 'subduing' the American continent.[29] A second pragmatic strain in American society, more or less strong in all societies, is the shallow opportunism of the self-styled 'pragmatists' in many fields of endeavor, individuals whose exclusive concern with personal victory is condemned by William James as "the exclusive worship of the bitch-goddess SUCCESS."[30] Distinct from these two strains is philosophical Pragmatism—the work of Peirce, James, Dewey, and others —that developed a theory of meaning and a theory of truth, grounded in a vision of an adequate human existence. The "fundamental idea" of the various strands of this Pragmatic movement, Dewey writes, is "that action and opportunity justify themselves only to the degree in which they render life more reasonable and increase its value" (LW 2:19). These strands come to a kind of flowering in the work of Dewey and the other members of the Chicago School. This developing philosophical view includes: a metaphysics that emphasizes processes and relations; a naturalistic and evolutionary understanding of human existence; an analysis of intellectual activity as problem-oriented and as benefitting from historically developed methods; and an emphasis upon the democratic reconstruction of society through educational and other institutions.[31] Dewey's two

---

[29] The difference between this sort of pragmatism and that of the philosophical movement is nicely shown in the following statement of Addison Webster Moore: "We insist that [Pragmatism] does not call upon the scientist to turn out every week a new flying machine or a new breakfast food. It has nothing but approval for the investigator who shuts himself up with his 'biophors,' his 'ions' and 'electrons,' provided only he *finally* emerge with *some* connection established between these 'idols of the den' and the problems of life and death, of growth and decay, and of social interaction" (*Pragmatism and Its Critics,* 10).

[30] *The Letters of William James,* vol. 2, 260; cf. LW 2:5, 13, 19; 7:202–3.

[31] Cf. George Herbert Mead, *Movements of Thought in the Nineteenth Century,* 351–52; Charles W. Morris, *The Pragmatic Movement in American Philosophy,* 5–9;

main predecessors in this Pragmatic movement were Charles Sanders Peirce and William James.

Charles Sanders Peirce (1839–1914) was a mathematical and scientific genius of the first order[32] who, for both personal and social reasons, came late to the recognition of the philosophical and broader intellectual community.[33] At one point, Peirce describes his own work as "the attempt of a physicist to make such conjecture as to the constitution of the universe as the methods of science may permit, with the aid of all that has been done by previous philosophers." His hope is not for demonstrable truths but for likely hypotheses, hypotheses that grow out of the past efforts of the sciences and that would be "capable of being verified or refuted by future observers."[34] These future observers are, of course, us; and, for Peirce, we humans are at our best when we engage in cooperative attempts to overcome our intellectual problems.

Dewey was strongly influenced by Peirce's emphasis upon the importance of cooperative inquiry. "C. S. Peirce is notable among writers on logical theory for his explicit recognition of the necessity of the social factor in the determination of evidence and its probative force," he writes; "he was the first writer on logic to make inquiry and its methods the primary and ultimate source of logical subject-matter" (LW 12:484, 17).[35] Building upon this base of ongoing social inquiry, Dewey writes that truth is to be "defined, following Peirce, as the ideal limit of indefinitely continued inquiry" (LW

Darnell Rucker, *The Chicago Pragmatists*, 28–56; Campbell, *The Community Reconstructs: The Meaning of Pragmatic Social Thought*.

[32] Cf. Max H. Fisch: Peirce is "the most original philosopher our country has so far produced, and . . . no university in the country would have him as a *professor* of philosophy" (*Peirce, Semeiotic and Pragmatism*, 309).

[33] As just one indicator of Peirce's lack of stature within the philosophical community prior to the digestion of the eight volumes of his *Collected Papers* (1931–1958), we can consider the index of the first thirty-five years of *The Philosophical Review*, published in 1927, that contains only one mention of Peirce—listed as 'C. A. Peirce'—but dozens of listings for both James and Dewey (*Philosophical Review: Index to Volumes I–XXXV*, 37–38, 81–82, 124). A similar conclusion must be drawn from an examination of the index of the first fifty years of the *Journal of Philosophy* which, except for an initial flurry of interest just after Peirce's death in 1914, does not mention him again until the 1930s (*Journal of Philosophy: Fifty-Year Index, 1904–1953*, 76–77, 264).

[34] *Collected Papers*, 1.7.

[35] Cf. LW 12:3, 464–65; 14:56–58.

14:56).[36] And, because Peirce writes that "[t]he opinion which is fated to be ultimately agreed to by all who investigate, is what we mean by the truth,"[37] at any particular point in this process of cooperative inquiry the individual is admonished by Peirce to maintain an attitude of doubt and openness. "Do not block the way of inquiry," he writes.[38] In our lives as inquirers, we are to live by the cautious attitude that he calls "fallibilism." The following assumptions are among its tenets: no questions are unanswerable; no answers are absolutely true; no formulations are final; no level of examination is ultimate; and so on. In inquiry, there is always more that can be done; and even a failed experiment is an advance, for all possibilities must be considered. The human weakness against which we must be ever on guard is our often-demonstrated willingness to settle issues too soon by acquiescing to inadequate methods for the fixation of belief.[39]

Dewey was also strongly influenced by Peirce's belief that we could develop more precision in our philosophical formulations if we could develop a more adequate theory of meaning. The focus of Peirce's efforts here was in clarifying our use of "intellectual concepts" or "of hard words and of abstract concepts" like 'hard', 'weight', 'force', and 'reality'.[40] He writes:

> a *conception,* that is, the rational purport of a word or other expression, lies exclusively in its conceivable bearing upon the conduct of life; so that, since obviously nothing that might not result from experiment can have any direct bearing upon conduct, if one can define accurately all the conceivable experimental

---

[36] While Dewey describes this understanding of inquiry in 1939 as "our [i.e. Peirce's and his] view" (LW 14:57), Peirce, thirty-five years earlier at least, had expressed serious doubts about the way in which inquiry was conceived of and carried out by Dewey and the other members of the Chicago School. See *Collected Papers,* 8.239–8.244.

[37] *Collected Papers,* 5.407—a passage that Dewey describes as "[t]he best definition of *truth* from the logical standpoint which is known to me" (LW 12:343; cf. Peirce, *Collected Papers,* 5.565–5.573).

[38] *Collected Papers,* 1.135.

[39] Cf. *Collected Papers,* 1.13, 5.358; LW 12:46–47; Justus Buchler, *Charles Peirce's Empiricism,* 74–78; Wilson, *Science, Community and the Transformation of American Philosophy,* 31–36.

[40] *Collected Papers,* 5.467, 5.464, 5.403–5.410.

phenomena which the affirmation or denial of a concept could imply, one will have therein a complete definition of the concept.[41]

The important points in this theory of meaning, in addition to its connection to long-term, group inquiry, are that Peirce is interested in applying it only to certain words or concepts and that he requires a consideration of all effects. The weaknesses that this version of Pragmatism displays, from James's point of view, follow directly from Peirce's emphases: it focusses too narrowly on the issues of the natural sciences, mathematics and formal logic, and it emphasizes too strongly the public forum of verification.

William James (1842–1910) saw himself as carrying forward Peirce's Pragmatism, although he formulated it more broadly. James wanted to develop Pragmatism into a tool for overcoming apparently insoluble philosophical controversies. "The pragmatic method," he writes, "is primarily a method of settling metaphysical disputes that otherwise might be interminable."[42] Although the example that he uses is the homey one of the squirrel on the trunk of the tree, the issues to which he would apply the method are matters of larger human concern, like the questions of substance and attributes, materialism versus theism, and freedom versus determinism.[43] "The pragmatic method in such cases is to try to interpret each notion by tracing its respective practical consequences," he continues. "What difference would it practically make to anyone if this notion rather than that notion were true?"[44] While his concern with results is continuous with the work of Peirce, the change is fundamental. James, maintaining that "the principle of pragmatism . . . should be expressed more broadly than Mr. Peirce expresses it,"[45] eliminates the concern with long-term effects for the group of inquirers and with the full spectrum of effects. And, perhaps most importantly, James moves beyond Peirce's tightly focussed concern with only certain words and ideas to consider the meaning of broad philosophical doctrines. James thus revises what he calls "Peirce's principle" to

---

[41] *Collected Papers,* 5.412; cf. LW 2:4.

[42] *Pragmatism,* 28.

[43] Cf. Dewey: "it lies in the nature of pragmatism that it should be applied as widely as possible." (MW 4:101; cf. LW 2:7–8).

[44] *Pragmatism,* 28; cf. 259–62.

[45] *Pragmatism,* 259; cf. 28–30.

allow for both broader application and narrower verification. As James writes, for example, "the effective meaning of any philosophic proposition can always be brought down to some particular consequence, in our future practical experience."[46]

In addition, James went still further and brought into a central position in his Pragmatism the topic of truth. For James, Pragmatism should have something to say about not only the *meaning* but also about the *meaningfulness* and ultimately about the truth or falsity of philosophic positions.[47] Once we are able to move beyond idle controversies to the real ones—that is, controversies about which we can "show some practical difference that must follow from one side or the other's being right"[48]—James believes that we can use the Pragmatic method to decide truth and falsity. For example, the conflicting answers to the question of materialism versus theism yield what he calls "opposite outlooks of experience": "Materialism means simply the denial that the moral order is eternal, and the cutting off of ultimate hopes; theism means the affirmation of an eternal moral order and the letting loose of hope."[49] Peirce's emphasis upon what in the long-run is fated to be agreed upon by the limitless group of belief-suspending inquirers is of little help deciding this question.[50] James, as we might surmise from his emphasis on hope,[51] maintains that a position may be considered to be true as the result of a different kind of test: "Any idea upon which we can ride, so to speak; any idea that will carry us prosperously from any one part of our experience to any other part, linking things satisfactorily, working securely, simplifying, saving labor; is true for just so much, true in so far forth, true *instrumentally*."[52] For James, an idea or a philosophical position is true if it satisfies this test of workability. Using as an example a matter close to James's heart, if the theistic

---

[46] *Pragmatism*, 259; cf. LW 2:6–7.

[47] Cf. MW 6:46; LW 2:7–8; Thayer, *Meaning and Action*, 135.

[48] *Pragmatism*, 28.

[49] *Pragmatism*, 263–64.

[50] Cf. Herbert W. Schneider: "Peirce was wary of fixing belief this side of infinity; he reveled in doubt. James, on the contrary, reveled in emotional convictions and assertions of will" ("William James as a Moralist," 135).

[51] Cf. James: " 'God or no God?' means 'promise or no promise?' " (*The Meaning of Truth*, 6).

[52] *Pragmatism*, 34; cf. 96–97; *The Meaning of Truth*, 3–10.

viewpoint provides what he calls *"a value for concrete life,"* it will be true, he writes, *"in the sense of being good for so much."*[53]

Because of his enthusiastic public championing of these unorthodox views, James became the center of the storm over Pragmatism. Peirce himself thought James's changes were harmful; and he rechristened his own, narrower position "pragmaticism," a name he thought would be "ugly enough to be safe from kidnappers."[54] But James's position, however startling it may initially seem, contains many valuable aspects. One of the values of his view is that, as might be expected from an understanding of human nature that grounds the activities of mind in the problems of living, it connects truth with other human goods. As James writes, "truth is *one species of good.*"[55] A second value of James's Pragmatism is that, as with Peirce's, it is forward-looking rather than backward-looking. Pragmatism exemplifies, James writes, *"[t]he attitude of looking away from first things, principles, 'categories,' supposed necessities; and of looking towards last things, fruits, consequences, facts."*[56] This means, for James, that truth is a process. While *"for rationalism reality is ready-made and complete from all eternity,"* James writes, *"for pragmatism it is still in the making, and awaits part of its complexion from the future."*[57] A third value of James's view is his emphasis on the importance of the practical over the purely intellectual. Rather than being satisfied with terms like 'God' or 'Reason' as what he calls "solving names," James requires us to "bring out of each word its practical cash-value, set it at work within the stream of [our] experience." Purely intellectual solutions are not to be tolerated. "The earth of things, long thrown into shadow by the glories of the upper ether, must resume its rights."[58]

James's position on the nature and possibilities of Pragmatism has problematic aspects as well, especially related to the topic of truth. Before I consider what I believe is the central problem here, there are several side issues—points that are frequently seen to be

---

[53] *Pragmatism*, 40.

[54] *Collected Papers*, 5.414.

[55] *Pragmatism*, 42.

[56] *Pragmatism*, 32; cf. 107; Peirce, *Collected Papers*, 5.427; MW 10:9–11, 45; LW 2:4, 12–16; 4:227; 11:82.

[57] *Pragmatism*, 123.

[58] *Pragmatism*, 31–32, 62.

troublesome—that need to be cleared away. The first is James's claim, unsettling to some, that truth lives in large measure "on a credit system." As a result, most of our lives are spent engaged with truths like the realities of locations and events whose verification we never perform. "We trade on each other's truth," he writes.[59] Allowing for James's idiosyncratic use of the term 'truth', this is precisely the point made by Peirce when he writes "our knowledge is never absolute but always swims, as it were, in a continuum of uncertainty and of indeterminacy."[60] A second side issue that I do not think is problematic is his belief that truth *"happens* to an idea." Rather than focussing upon abstracted propositions or upon static relationships of unchanging validity, his concern is with a particular belief or idea that *"becomes* true, is *made* true by events."[61] Thirdly, it is not the case that James believes that any delusion whatever can be true. *" 'Reality' is in general what truths have to take account of,"* he writes. "Woe to him whose beliefs play fast and loose with the order which realities follow in his experience: they will lead him nowhere or else make false connexions."[62] The central difficulty that I see with James's position on truth is the problem that, in Peircean terms, it would allow people to 'fix belief' too soon, based upon limited evidence or only individual confirmation.[63] As an example of James's impulsiveness, we can consider the following: "A new opinion counts as 'true' just in proportion as it gratifies the individual's desire to assimilate the novel in his experience to his beliefs in stock."[64] The weakness of James's approach here—one explicitly addressed by Dewey in his elaboration of the pattern of inquiry, as we shall see in 2.4—is that it does not take the time necessary to refine the felt problem sufficiently or to evaluate the proposed solution adequately. Even recognizing the accuracy of the vernacular expression that many ideas 'contain a little truth' should not lead us to accept such troublesome phrases as James's "true in so far forth," "truest," or

---

[59] *Pragmatism,* 100; cf. *Essays in Radical Empiricism,* 33–37, 42–44.

[60] *Collected Papers,* 1.171.

[61] *Pragmatism,* 97; cf. 34; *The Meaning of Truth,* 3–4.

[62] *Pragmatism,* 117, 99; cf. 111–13.

[63] Cf. Joseph L. Blau: For James, "[a]s long as an idea has agreeable consequences in the particular experience of some individual, somewhere, the idea has truth-value" (*Men and Movements in American Philosophy,* 256).

[64] *Pragmatism,* 36.

"true for *me*."[65] We need to be more hesitant and skeptical; we need to test our new opinion in different contexts and consult with other inquirers. But, as Peirce writes, all too often "as soon as a firm belief is reached we are entirely satisfied, whether the belief be true or false."[66] James's weakness here is not that he would have us call the false 'true', but that he would allow us to call the initially workable 'true' without sufficient testing.

There are reasons for this aspect of James's Pragmatism, just as there are for the differing aspect of Peirce's. Whereas Peirce was interested in advancing scientific methods and practice, James was interested in preventing what he saw as science's potential destruction of all human meaning. Dewey explores this aspect of James's work when he notes that James remarks that "every philosopher is motivated by some bogey in the background that he wants to destroy," and that *"his* bogey is *dessication"* (LW 11:470).[67] James's fear is that the rigors of scientific verification will strangle the beliefs necessary to live. As evidence of the reality of this danger, James cites the maxim of William Kingdon Clifford: "It is wrong always, everywhere and for anyone, to believe anything upon insufficient evidence."[68] The key issue here is that of sufficiency of evidence, and James's position differs sharply from Clifford's. As Dewey writes, James "maintained the thesis that the greater part of philosophic problems and especially those which touch on religious fields are of such a nature that they are not susceptible of decisive evidence one way or the other" (LW 2:10). Thus, James writes that at least in certain contexts, not limited only to the religious, "we have the right to believe at our own risk any hypothesis that is live enough to tempt our will."[69]

Dewey recognizes that James, ever the moralist in a broad

---

[65] *Pragmatism,* 34, 36; *Some Problems of Philosophy,* 113.

[66] *Collected Papers,* 5.375.

[67] Cf. LW 11:473–78; Ralph Barton Perry, *The Thought and Character of William James,* vol. 2, 246; Wilson, *Science, Community and the Transformation of American Philosophy,* 36–38, 59–64.

[68] *The Will to Believe,* 18.

[69] *The Will to Believe,* 32; cf. 20. For a fuller development of this analysis of James's understanding of truth, see my "Ayer and Pragmatism." For different analyses, see: Thayer, *Meaning and Action,* 527–56; Gail Kennedy, "Pragmatism, Pragmaticism and the Will to Believe"; Ellen Kappy Suckiel, *The Pragmatic Philosophy of William James,* 91–121.

humanistic sense,[70] is attempting to develop the ethical possibilities of the Pragmatic approach. Seen in the light of this broad humanism, all of James's changes to Peirce's approach appear to be deliberate.[71] Dewey followed James's interests without losing sight of the Peircean social controls. His own version of Pragmatism, a version that he called Instrumentalism,[72] is thus, as we shall see throughout this study, a combination of the inquiring and critical spirit of Peirce with a focus on the issues of general and direct human concern that interested James.[73] Dewey's methods were critical and cooperative, like those of Peirce; but his interests were moral, esthetic, educational, and social, like those of James. This generally scientific approach to generally moral issues offers a kind of logic of practical activity, and Dewey hopes to use this Instrumentalism as a means to foster social reconstruction. By means of this Instrumentalism, Dewey attempts to recast the 'truth' question that entangled James to emphasize inquiry, focussing on "warranted assertion" rather than 'belief' or 'knowledge'.[74] But, at the same time, Dewey emphasizes the broad application of this Instrumentalism, and attempts to address such topics as economic policy, legal practice, educational theorizing, and political organization.

---

[70] "James did not need to write a separate treatise on ethics, because in its larger sense he was everywhere and always the moralist" (MW 6:92; cf. LW 2:14; 14:101).

[71] I am rejecting here the view of Ralph Barton Perry: "Perhaps it would be correct, and just to all parties, to say that the modern movement known as pragmatism is largely the result of James's misunderstanding of Peirce" (*The Thought and Character of William James,* vol. 2, 409).

[72] Cf. LW 2:14; 4:30; 5:156–57.

[73] Cf. H. S. Thayer: "In turning to Dewey we witness the coalescence of the critical and scientific motives of Peirce's pragmatism with the moral implications and ideals of James" (*Meaning and Action,* 165; cf. xviii; Rucker, *The Chicago Pragmatists,* vi, 5; Ralph W. Sleeper, *The Necessity of Pragmatism,* 44–56, 201–6; Cornel West, *The American Evasion of Philosophy,* 6, 69, 71).

[74] Cf. LW 12:15–16; 14:168–88; Thayer, *Meaning and Action,* 193–94; George R. Geiger, *John Dewey in Perspective,* 75–76.

PART ONE

DEWEY'S GENERAL PHILOSOPHICAL PERSPECTIVE

CHAPTER 2

Human Nature

O NE PLACE THAT we can enter into Dewey's philosophical perspective is through sketching out aspects of his understanding of human nature, especially as this human nature was understood by the 'new psychology'. After abandoning his early attempts at psychologizing through speculations about the nature of consciousness, he adopted the Darwinian insights gathered and presented by William James in his masterpiece, *The Principles of Psychology*. Working with other compatible thinkers at the Universities of Michigan and Chicago, Dewey considered the implications that being a self-conscious animal has for humanity. Of primary import was the recognition that there is a coordinated continuity of the live creature that enables it to address the temporary disintegrations of normal living by the reconstitution of the situation. No less important to Dewey's understanding of human nature is his belief that we are social creatures whose identities and fulfillment are grounded in communal participation. He considers also the rising of thought and the relation of thinking to the nonthinking habits of much of our lives. Although he is clearly cognizant of the constant flowering of ideas and images in the mind, in his numerous explorations of the pattern of inquiry he emphasized the reactive nature of deliberative thinking: its arising in the recognition in particular situations that all is not well. In their attempts to determine what is the matter and how it might be addressed, humans use inquiry and hypothetical thinking, testing and revision. And, throughout his discussions of problem-solving, Dewey emphasized that the nature of wisdom is fundamentally moral. Humans are problem-solvers who can use the warranting of careful inquiry in their attempts to address their shared problems even without guarantees of ultimate success, and who should as a result get involved in these activities in their communities.

2.1. Darwinian Roots

What is the fundamental nature of existence? Is ours a world of permanence or a world of process, a world of order or a world of flux? In spite of occasional suggestions that favored the latter alternatives, the answer that has dominated in the West is that ours is a world of ordered permanence. It has been an Aristotelian world in which there are no breaks or jumps, in which nothing happens in vain, a world that is fundamentally unchanging. Dewey captures the flavor of this Aristotelian tradition when he writes of "the facts of life" by means of which seeds, although "inert and passive," suddenly, when conditions are right, "begin to change, to change rapidly in size, form, and qualities." He continues:

> the changes in the living things are orderly; they are cumulative; they tend constantly in one direction; they do not, like other changes, destroy or consume, or pass fruitless into wandering flux; they realize and fulfil. . . . In living beings, changes do not happen as they seem to happen elsewhere, any which way; the earlier changes are regulated in view of later results.

Aristotelian nature made sense: changes were directional and orderly. What appeared to be flux could in fact be explained if we could grasp the organizing principle—named *eidos* and *species*—running through the changes. It was this principle "which operates throughout a series of changes and holds them to a single course," Dewey writes, "which, leaping the boundaries of space and time, keeps individuals distant in space and remote in time to a uniform type of structure and function" (MW 4:5).

The Judeo-Christian tradition was comfortable with an understanding of reality as a Great Chain, continuous and complete from top to bottom in a geocentric universe of divine making. The tradition of classificatory science was comfortable as well, busy with the analysis and placing of the many links of this chain. Change was recognized within this essentially static view; but it was seen primarily as a matter of the existence of *recurrent cycles*—as in the seasons, or in the lives of individual organisms, both of which proved to be bounded by the larger order. There were occasional 'monsters', of course, demonstrating the inherent costs of 'violating' these laws of nature. By and large, however, these laws prevailed and their prevalence was important. Unless there was more than flux, there could be no meaning to existence. Dewey writes: "Change as change is mere flux and lapse; it insults intelligence. Genuinely to know is to grasp a permanent end that realizes itself through changes, holding them thereby within the metes and bounds of fixed truth. Completely to know is to relate all special forms to their one single end and good: pure contemplative intelligence." The basic job of science was to try to understand the principles, the "realities lying behind and beyond the processes of nature, and to carry on its search for these realities by means of rational forms transcending ordinary modes of perception and inference" (MW 4:6). And the generally accepted conclusion of these searchings was that our world was young and orderly and at the center of the universe.[1]

There began to develop much evidence to undermine the inherited view; but the counterevidence long remained isolated and fragmentary. And the individuals whom we now regard as the founding heroes of celestial science—Copernicus and Tycho Brahe and Galileo and others—were publicly regarded as mistaken and dangerous. The contradictory information, however, continued to grow. More people learned that the heavens did not move around a stationary earth in perfectly circular orbits. New planets, and other celestial bodies, were discovered. The moon had craters, and the earth was old and complicated. Geology gave evidence of a rich past: volcanoes and earthquakes, mountains that had grown, and lakes that had died. Paleontology gave evidence of presently nonexisting creatures whose remains were found in unlikely places. In addition, the initial attempts at the objective study of other peoples gave evidence of different cultures and different scriptures and different cosmologies, and thereby undermined the claims of the West to exclusive theological grounding. This accumulating body of evidence meant that the older view was doomed; but, without an

---

[1] Eugene Fontinell portrays this inherited world view as follows: "the world is a cosmos or an ordered world; it possesses this order independently of man; this world is structured by absolute and unchanging principles or essences; this world or reality is permeated by mind or reason of which human reason is a particularized expression; the task of human knowledge—scientific knowledge—is to discover and thereby mirror or correspond to those universal essences by which reality is structured; hence, knowledge is concerned with that which is universal and unchanging rather than the particular and changing" (*Toward a Reconstruction of Religion*, 38–39; cf. Morris Eames, *Pragmatic Naturalism*, 3–4).

adequate theory to challenge it, it lived on. The early critics of the older view knew that change was fundamental and ongoing. They were unable, however, to develop an evolutionary theory adequate to the full range of facts.

Charles Robert Darwin (1809–1882), the author of *The Origin of Species* (1859) and *The Descent of Man* (1871), gave the critics of the static world view, in addition to a great deal more data, this theory. The central aspects of his view of natural selection were: first of all, the prodigality of life, the production of living creatures in numbers higher than can be maintained by their environment; second, the random process of minute, fortuitous variations by means of which, for example, each litter of mammals has a fastest and a slowest, and each clutch of birds one with the longest beak and one with the shortest; third, the fact of differential survival rates that can result from a combination of the first two points in any given environment; fourth, the ongoing process of environmental change that transforms over time what is advantageous; and fifth, a length of time sufficient to enable these minute changes to accumulate, resulting in (in Darwin's words) "the formation of new species."[2] Dewey overestimated the successful impact of Darwin's work and underestimated ongoing opposition to his view; but this is not the core of Dewey's emphasis upon Darwin. That emphasis is rather upon the fact that, although Darwin himself may have been reluctant to part with the Designer, his account of the *origin* of *species* completely undermined the Argument from Design and replaced what Dewey calls its "assumption of the superiority of the fixed and final" and its "treating change and origin as signs of defect and unreality" (MW 4:3; cf. LW 12:97) with a view grounded in the assumption of change and growth and process and evolution and emergence. The Darwinian world was a world that was processive to its core. "The influence of Darwin upon philosophy," Dewey writes, "resides in his having conquered the phenomena of life for the principle of transi-

---

[2] Charles Darwin, *The Autobiography of Charles Darwin, 1809–1882,* 120; cf. Darwin, *The Origin of Species,* esp. Chapter III, "Struggle for Existence"; Chapter IV, "Natural Selection; Or the Survival of the Fittest"; *The Descent of Man,* Chapter XXI, "General Summary and Conclusion." For background material on Darwin and the other individuals who developed the evolutionary perspective, see: John C. Greene, *The Death of Man: Evolution and Its Impact on Western Thought;* Loren Eiseley, *Darwin's Century;* Michael Ruse, *The Darwinian Revolution;* Philip P. Wiener, *Evolution and the Founders of Pragmatism.*

tion, and thereby freed the new logic for application to mind and morals and life" (MW 4:7-8).

In this new perspective, we humans are creatures of eons of evolution. Our bodies and our minds have evolved, and our institutions and our values have evolved as well. The impact of Darwin's work on philosophy was to enable us to redirect our thinking to reflect this evolutionary reality. Dewey points to three aspects. First of all, he writes, philosophy abandons inquiry after "absolute origins and absolute finalities" and searches rather for "specific values and the specific conditions that generate them" (MW 4:10). The search for the absolutely 'correct' form of government, or for the eternally 'proper' type of education, is futile. After Darwin, Dewey continues, our interest

> shifts from the wholesale essence back of special changes to the question of how special changes serve and defeat concrete purposes; shifts from an intelligence that shaped things once for all to the particular intelligences which things are even now shaping; shifts from an ultimate goal of good to the direct increments of justice and happiness that intelligent administration of existent conditions may beget and that present carelessness or stupidity will destroy or forego (MW 4:11).

Second, Darwin's impact compels philosophy to abandon efforts to prove that "life *must* have certain qualities and values—no matter how experience presents the matter—because of some remote cause and eventual goal." In the place of this quest for, say, the 'correct' understanding of sexuality in life or the 'proper' relationship between the sexes, philosophy would now foster "our looking the facts of experience in the face" (MW 4:12). Third, Dewey writes, as a consequence, "logic introduces responsibility into the intellectual life." Concern with analysis of "the universe at large" betrays an inability to control specific problems that are nearer to us. On the other hand, he continues, "if insight into specific conditions of value and into specific consequences of ideas is possible, philosophy must in time become a method of locating and interpreting the more serious of the conflicts that occur in life, and a method of projecting ways for dealing with them: a method of moral and political diagnosis and prognosis" (MW 4:13). All three of these Darwinian points are essential elements in Dewey's conception of Pragmatism.

Some evolutionary themes, themes that are often understood today as being at the core of Darwin's message, appear only as side issues in Dewey's work. One of these themes is what is called 'Social Darwinism'. The theme itself is more prominent in the works of the British social theorist, Herbert Spencer (1820–1903)—who advocated social policies that favored "the survival of the fittest"[3]—and his American champion, William Graham Sumner (1840–1910)—who wrote, "This is a world in which the rule is, 'Root, hog, or die' "[4]—rather than in Darwin himself.[5] Dewey rejects both the claim that Social Darwinism is a legitimate extrapolation of Darwin's view and the content of the position itself, the claim that "this scene of rapine and slaughter" will result in "progress, advance, [and] everything that we regard as noble and fair" (MW 5:333).[6] The second theme of contemporary importance that appears as a side issue, given Dewey's analysis of the meaning of Darwinism, is the ongoing circus of religious protests over the teaching of evolutionary thought. Dewey recognizes, of course, the possibility of serious trouble in a society in which "one-half of the pupils in the last years of the high school think that the first chapters of the Hebrew Scriptures give a more accurate account of the origin and early history of man than does science" (LW 5:47).[7] He recognizes as well that for some the main impact of the evolutionary hypothesis is its denial of our inherited religious faith, leaving the individual, in the words of Loren Eiseley, "increasingly a homeless orphan lost in the vast abysses of space and time."[8] As Dewey writes, there

---

[3] A phrase Darwin later borrowed from Spencer, cf. *The Origin of Species*, 52.

[4] Sumner, *The Challenge of Facts and Other Essays*, 59.

[5] For more on Social Darwinism, see: Richard Hofstadter, *Social Darwinism in American Thought*; Robert C. Bannister, *Social Darwinism: Science and Myth in Anglo-American Social Thought*.

[6] Cf. EW 5:34–53; MW 3:205–9; 5:333–37.

[7] Cf. MW 2:56; 13:301–6; 15:3–5; LW 2:312–13.

[8] Eiseley, *The Unexpected Universe*, 41. Cf., for example, William Jennings Bryan: "God may be a matter of indifference to the evolutionists, and a life beyond may have no charm for them, but the mass of mankind will continue to worship their Creator and continue to find comfort in the promise of their Savior that He has gone to prepare a place for them. Christ has made of death a narrow, starlit stripe between the companionship of yesterday and the reunion of tomorrow; evolution strikes out the stars and deepens the gloom that enshrouds the tomb" (cited in Genevieve Forbes Herrick and John Origen Herrick, *The Life of William Jennings Bryan*, 392; cf. Ray Ginger, *Six Days or Forever? Tennessee v. John Thomas Scopes*).

were those for whom the conception of "a wide open universe, a universe without bounds in time or space, without final limits of origin or destiny, a universe with the lid off, was a menace" (MW 4:45).

For Dewey, however, regardless of the antiscientific activities of various religious groups, the controversy itself is not a matter of science *versus* religion in the first place. "Religious considerations lent fervor to the controversy," he writes, "but they did not provoke it. Intellectually, religious emotions are not creative but conservative. They attach themselves readily to the current view of the world and consecrate it." It is simply a matter of the nature of justification in our intellectual life. "Although the ideas that rose up like armed men against Darwinism owed their intensity to religious associations," he writes, "their origin and meaning are to be sought in science and philosophy, not in religion" (MW 4:4). What he sees in the growth of fundamentalist thinking is "an assertion of a type of philosophic knowing distinct from that of the sciences, one which opens to us another kind of reality from that to which the sciences give access; an appeal through experience to something that essentially goes beyond experience" (MW 4:13–14). But, as Dewey writes in 1924, the persistence of this bifurcation is the result of "the comparative failure of schooling up to the present time to instil even the rudiments of the scientific attitude in vast numbers of persons" (MW 15:49). With improvements in our systems of education and communication, we could reach a point at which process and emergence are accepted—and even championed—as essential elements of human life. At that point, we would be able to recognize that the values that we hold dear—such as equality, democracy, and justice—are not externally derived eternal ideals that pre-existed humans. They are rather goods that we are creating as we go along, failing and learning, testing and rethinking, in our attempts to build better lives for ourselves and for our children.

2.2. The Live Organism

Darwin's answer to the question of the descent of humanity has an impact on more than the evolutionary origins of human life. It brings to the center of consideration the questions of embodiment, of a naturalistic understanding of mind, and of the importance of humans' organic place in nature. "The biological point of view," Dewey writes with regard to all three of these questions, "commits us to the conviction that mind, whatever else it may be, is at least an organ of service for the control of environment in relation to the ends of the life process" (MW 2:41). This essentially embodied understanding of human existence in a natural world, and its consequent re-interpretation of mind, developed in the late nineteenth century into what was called 'The New Psychology'. This new psychology was a move away from the speculative and armchair understanding of mind through introspection upon aspects of consciousness, and away from the traditional psychological work of Locke and his followers in the British Empirical tradition. It was a move toward animal life in which sensations are not seen as "the units or elements of knowledge" but rather as "the occasions for adaptive adjustments to the environment" (MW 7:346), and toward physiology and experimentation as made available in the setting of the developing laboratory.[9]

The new psychology was clearly more than a new way of doing the same sorts of things that had been done before. It was a way of doing *new* things. To understand this, we need only consider the impact of the increasingly more precise equipment on our knowledge of physiology, as demonstrated in the contemporary flood of empirical studies of reaction time and threshold levels.[10] These experimental studies of bodily capabilities had, admittedly, little if anything to do with 'thinking' or with 'the mind' as thinking and the mind had been understood in prior psychological work; but they were central to the

---

[9] Cf. Edwin G. Boring: "By 1900 the characteristics of American psychology were well defined. It inherited its physical body from German experimentalism, but it got its mind from Darwin" (*A History of Experimental Psychology*, 494; cf. 657).

[10] Consider, for example, the level of technical sophistication necessary to justify Dewey's discussion of light intensity: "The minimum amount of objective energy necessary to occasion sensation (threshold value) is stated at $1/300$ of the light of the full moon reflected from white paper. The difference threshold varies with different colors. For white light, it is about $1/100$, for red $1/14$, and the ratio necessary decreases until it reaches the violet end of the spectrum, where it is only $1/268$" (EW 2:66). For another example, we can consider his assertion that "$1/2000000$ of a milligramme" of musk is able to excite a sensation of smell (EW 2:56; cf. James, *The Principles of Psychology*, vol. 1, 88–108; James Rowland Angell and Addison Webster Moore, "Reaction-Time: A Study in Attention and Habit").

new psychology. Why such studies were being undertaken—and, in fact, driving the practice of the quickly developing field of professionalized academic psychology—requires a complex answer. Part of the answer is, as I have suggested, that such studies had become technically possible. Another part, no doubt, was the influence of what we now call 'careerism' on young academics. But most importantly, and at its best, this new psychological research was being undertaken because it was increasingly believed that the physiological knowledge being gained would enable us to better understand our humanity.[11]

Dewey's own early work in psychology—the early essays and the *Psychology* of 1887—shows the effects of his diremptive education at the hands of the speculative Morris and the experimentalist, Hall. He was in between old and new, uncomfortable in the armchair but not yet fully acculturated to the spirit of the laboratory, open to physiological work yet still maintaining that introspection or "internal perception . . . must *ultimately* be the sole source of the *material* of psychology" (EW 2:12).[12] His eventual turn to complete acceptance of the new psychology shows the importance of the influence of William James, especially the biological James of *The Principles of Psychology* of 1890.[13] It was James's influence, Dewey writes, that was the "one specific philosophic factor which entered into my thinking so as to give it a new direction and quality." The Jamesian idea of the

---

[11] For a general introduction to the historical development of the 'New Psychology', see: Boring, *A History of Experimental Psychology;* Gardner Murphy, *An Historical Introduction to Modern Psychology;* Jay Wharton Fay, *American Psychology before William James;* Rand B. Evans, "The Origins of American Academic Psychology." For a sketch of the history of functional psychology at the University of Chicago, see: Rucker, *The Chicago Pragmatists,* 57–82.

[12] See Rucker, *The Chicago Pragmatists,* 57–58; Wilson, *Science, Community and the Transformation of American Philosophy,* 85–86; Rockefeller, *John Dewey,* 98–124, 198–99.

[13] Writing to James in 1903 to request his permission to dedicate to him the edited volume, *Studies in Logical Theory,* Dewey writes: "so far as I am concerned your *Psychology* is the spiritual *progenitor* of the whole industry." (Perry, *Thought and Character of William James,* vol. 2, 521). For discussions of the importance of *The Principles,* see: Perry, *The Thought and Character of William James,* vol. 2, 34–137; Sheldon M. Stern, "William James and the New Psychology"; Gerald E. Myers, *William James: His Life and Thought;* Myers, "Introduction: The Intellectual Context," and Rand B. Evans, "Introduction: The Historical Context," in the critical edition of *The Principles;* William R. Woodward, "William James's Psychology of Will."

active biological organism to be studied through the methods of physiological psychology "worked its way more and more into all my ideas and acted as a ferment to transform old beliefs" (LW 5:157).[14]

Much of the early work of this new psychology centered on what had come to be called 'the reflex arc'. Dewey sees the term to be equally applicable to simple reflexes and to "every unified action, or completed portion of conduct." The value of studying the human from the vantage point of instances of the reflex arc, he writes, is that "each is an *expression,* more or less direct, more or less explicit, of the whole of life" (EW 3:212). Dewey explored the topic most fully in his seminal 1896 essay, "The Reflex Arc Concept in Psychology."[15] Dewey's initial discussion of the child and the candle, drawn from the second chapter of James's *Psychology,* is a simple, nonlaboratory example of the adaptiveness of an organism to the environment. The situation is that of a small child who, upon seeing a burning candle for the first time, reaches out to touch the flame and is burned. Dewey offers as an initial account of the situation the following: "The ordinary interpretation would say the sensation of light is a stimulus to the grasping as a response, the burn resulting is a stimulus to withdrawing the hand as response and so on. There is, of course, no doubt that is a rough practical way of representing the process" (EW 5:97). Dewey's dissatisfaction with this "ordinary" interpretation was due in large part to his belief that interest had been misdirected from the real issue of trying to understand the integrated process of the action to a focus upon the parts or stages of the action. This sort of fragmented and fragmenting analysis offers a picture of human action that fits a machine better than an organism.[16]

---

[14] Cf. Gail Kennedy: "What Dewey discovered in James was the naturalistic basis for the practical idealism that was coming, increasingly, to dominate his thinking" ("Science and the Transformation of Common Sense," 313; cf. Kennedy, "The Hidden Link in Dewey's Theory of Evaluation," 85; Jane M. Dewey, "Biography of John Dewey," 23; MW 1:321; Perry, *The Thought and Character of William James,* vol. 2, 514–33; Andrew J. Reck, "The Influence of William James on John Dewey in Psychology"; Rockefeller, *John Dewey,* 198–99).

[15] Cf. Gordon W. Allport's evaluation: "the most important psychological paper of the nineties and probably, so far as psychology is concerned, Dewey's most influential essay." ("Dewey's Individual and Social Psychology," 269; cf. Andrew Feffer, *The Chicago Pragmatists and American Progressivism,* 147–58).

[16] See Michael M. Sokal's discussion of the anti-organic, mechanistic aspects of reaction-time studies in his "Introduction" to the critical edition of James's *Psychology: Briefer Course,* xxiv–xxv.

Returning to the example of the child and the candle, Dewey offers what he takes to be a more adequate analysis:

Upon analysis, we find that we begin not with a sensory stimulus, but with a sensori-motor co-ordination, the optical-ocular, and that in a certain sense it is the movement which is primary, and the sensation which is secondary, the movement of body, head and eye muscles determining the quality of what is experienced. In other words, the real beginning is with the act of seeing; it is looking, and not a sensation of light (EW 5:97).[17]

If this act of looking stimulates the child to the act of reaching, Dewey suggests, the reason is that both of these acts are part of the "larger co-ordination" of the live creature: "the act is seeing no less than before, but it is now seeing-for-reaching purposes." Continuing on to the next stage, the burning of the child's fingers, he emphasizes that the child is able to learn to avoid the experience in the future only because the pain is "simply the completion, or fulfillment, of the previous eye-arm-hand co-ordination and not an entirely new occurrence" (EW 5:98). In opposition to this analysis, Dewey writes, the ordinary analysis of the reflex arc "proceeds upon the more or less tacit assumption that the outcome of the response is a totally new experience; that it is, say, the substitution of a burn sensation for a light sensation through the intervention of motion." But, as he reaffirms, "the sole meaning of the intervening movement is to maintain, reinforce or transform (as the case may be) the original quale" (EW 5:99).[18] The unity of the overall action, however, the coordinated action of a human organism, is what must be emphasized.

Dewey's analysis of a different case is similar. This is his criticism of a discussion of what James Mark Baldwin calls "reactive consciousness" in the situation of a person who hears and responds to a loud and unexpected sound. Dewey criticizes Baldwin's mechanical

---

[17] Cf. Mead, *Mind, Self, and Society*, 1–13; *Movements of Thought in the Nineteenth Century*, 386–90.

[18] Cf. MW 9:29; LW 7:289–90; 10:105–6, 221–22, 259–60; 12:36–38; Elizabeth Flower and Murray G. Murphey, *A History of Philosophy in America*, vol. 2, 829–32; H. S. Thayer, *Meaning and Action*, 183–90; Thayer, "John Dewey, 1859–1952," 75–77; J. E. Tiles, *Dewey*, 45–48.

analysis of this form of consciousness into three sequential elements: "the receiving consciousness," "the registering element," and "the muscular reaction following upon the sound."[19] Dewey writes: "If one is reading a book, if one is hunting, if one is watching in a dark place on a lonely night, if one is performing a chemical experiment, in each case, the noise has a very different psychical value; it is a different experience" (EW 5:100).[20] Each of these is a situation of a human organism who, in the course of a coordinated activity, is affected—impinged upon, warned, startled, vindicated—by a sound that becomes integrated as an element in the ongoing activity.

Dewey's point is thus that the ordinary analysis of the reflex arc cripples the possibility of our adequately understanding either it or its larger meaning. The reflex arc, as it is usually understood, is still dualistic. "The older dualism between sensation and idea is repeated in the current dualism of peripheral and central structures and functions," he writes; "the older dualism of body and soul finds a distinct echo in the current dualism of stimulus and response" (EW 5:96; cf. 104). As a consequence the reflex arc, which should appear as "a comprehensive, or organic unity," is seen rather as "a patch-work of disjointed parts, a mechanical conjunction of unallied processes." What is necessary, on the contrary, is to develop an analysis that emphasizes that "sensory stimulus, central connections and motor responses shall be viewed, not as separate and complete entities in themselves," he writes, "but as divisions of labor, functioning factors, within the single concrete whole, now designated the reflex arc" (EW 5:97).[21]

Under the analysis that Dewey is proposing, distinctions remain recognizable; but they are distinctions of a particular sort. "The fact is that stimulus and response are not distinctions of existence," he writes, "but teleological distinctions, that is, distinctions of function, of part played, with reference to reaching or maintaining an end." Moreover, he continues, "it is only the assumed common

---

[19] Baldwin, *Handbook for Psychology*, vol. 2: *Feeling and Will*, 60.

[20] Dewey applies this same line of criticism in his 1930 discussion of the failure of behaviorism to deal adequately with "the *context* of the experiment" (LW 5:221; cf. Mead, *Mind, Self, and Society*, 106, 121). For more on Dewey's criticism of Behaviorism, see: LW 3:45; 5:227; 6:27; 14:185. See also: Mead, *Mind, Self, and Society*, 1–41.

[21] Cf. EW 1:98; 5:99; Angell & Moore, "Reaction-Time," 253.

reference to an inclusive end which marks each member off as stimulus and response, that apart from such reference we have only antecedent and consequent" (EW 5:104–5). Our emphasis throughout, however, should be on the active and integrated living organism in its environment. Instead of discussing just the reflex *arc,* we should be discussing the whole *circuit* of living of which the arc is only a part. When part of the situation comes into conflict with another part, and this disintegration calls for reconstruction, we can distinguish the stimulus and the response. He writes:

> The stimulus is that phase of the forming co-ordination which represents the conditions which have to be met in bringing it to a successful issue; the response is that phase of one and the same forming co-ordination which gives the key to meeting these conditions, which serves as instrument in effecting the successful co-ordination (EW 5:109).

We must never forget, however, the larger unity. "Behavior is serial," he writes, "not mere succession"; and, while it may be separated into discrete acts, "no act can be understood apart from the series to which it belongs" (LW 5:221). The aim of psychological study is to grasp this ongoing process, to try to understand the integrated life of the evolved intellect in its natural environment as it attempts to meet and overcome problems.

"Action is response; it is adaptation, adjustment," writes Dewey (MW 2:290). Actions are attempts to redress situations in the animal's favor. In this, humans are like the other animals. When hungry the animal seeks food; when tired, rest; when cold, warmth. "The significance of evolutionary method in biology and social history," he continues, is that the organs and structures of all living things, humans included, are to be treated as instruments "of adjustment or adaptation to a particular environing situation" (MW 2:310). This adjustment "is no timeless state; it is a continuing process" (MW 10:9) in which the human organism responds to encountered situations throughout life.

> The successful activities of the organism, those within which environmental assistance is incorporated, react upon the environment to bring about modifications favorable to their own future. The human being has upon his hands the problem of responding to

what is going on around him so that these changes will take one turn rather than another, namely, that required by its own further functioning (MW 10:7; cf. 6:437–40).

Embodied creatures cannot afford to forget the environing natural conditions that their minds enable them, at least sometimes and to some extent, to modify.

2.3.   The Social Individual

Our survey of some of the aspects of Dewey's discussion of human nature comes now to the third aspect of four. We have already considered his analysis of the evolutionary origins of human life and of our physical embodiment as living organisms in nature. The final aspect to be examined in this chapter will be our lives as problem-solvers. In this section, we will consider Dewey's discussion of humans as social creatures who, if they are "not bound together in associations, whether domestic, economic, religious, political, artistic or educational, are monstrosities" (LW 5:80–81). This social analysis of human nature is related to his often-considered, larger theme that "[a]ssociation in the sense of connection and combination is a 'law' of everything known to exist." Within the system of nature, all that exists is bound in relations. "Nothing has been discovered," he writes, "which acts in entire isolation" (LW 2:250).[22] Among the various types of association that can be explored, however, "the social, in its human sense, is the richest, fullest and most delicately subtle of any mode actually experienced" (LW 3:44).

Dewey's interest in the social conception of the self is present in his writings from the earliest years. He writes in 1884, for example, that "man is somewhat more than a neatly dovetailed psychical machine who may be taken as an isolated individual, laid on the dissecting table of analysis and duly anatomized." The biological aspect of the new psychology, he writes, needs to be considered together with "the other great influence" at work there: "those vast and as yet undefined topics of inquiry which may be vaguely

---

[22] Cf. LW 1:138; 2:330; 3:41; 4:195; 7:323; 12:138; 13:176.

designated as the social and historical sciences." (EW 1:48–49; 56–57).[23] Consideration of the findings of these new inquiries suggests that "men are not isolated non-social atoms, but are men only when in intrinsic relations to men" (EW 1:231).[24] Dewey later writes that humans are associated in such an essential manner that it is not even "an intelligible question" to ask "how individuals or singular beings come to be connected." The question we need to ask is rather "how they come to be connected in just those ways which give human communities traits so different from those which mark assemblies of electrons, unions of trees in forests, swarms of insects, herds of sheep, and constellations of stars" (LW 2:250).

In considering the question of the essential sociability of humans, we can explore three topics in order: the origin of sociability, its relationship to action, and the implications that Dewey draws from this sociability. His discussions of the origins of the social self consider the topic from an ontogenetic rather than a phylogenetic point of view, more concerned with the origin of the individual in his or her current social situation than with the rise of humans as creatures with selves.[25] His point in examining the process of the individual's life is more than the obvious physical one that the individual is born "in dependence on others" and would "miserably perish" without intensive and ongoing assistance (LW 7:227; cf. 323). The focus of his interest is, rather, the more fundamental point that we need to "conceive individual mind as a function of social life." In this way, we will come to understand mind "as not capable of operating or developing by itself, but as requiring continual stimulus from social agencies, and finding its nutrition in social supplies." For Dewey, then, the mind—broadly conceived to mean the embodied human self or the growing person or the social

---

[23] Cf. MW 14:60; LW 12:48–49.

[24] Cf. EW 5:86; LW 7:227, 253. See also James Hayden Tufts: *"There is no individual man* for ethics, for psychology, for logic, or for sociology, except by abstraction,—that is if by individual man we mean a being not influenced by social forces,—*nor are there any feelings, thoughts or volitions in any man which are independent of such forces"* ("Recent Sociological Tendencies in France," 455; cf. Hofstadter, *Social Darwinism in American Thought,* 159).

[25] In his *Mind, Self, and Society,* Mead attempts to achieve the dual task of ontogenetic and phylogenetic analysis, although he has far greater success with the former task of explaining the origin of individual selves as encultured beings than with the latter task of explaining the origin of human consciousness.

individual—"is developed in an environment which is social as well as physical" (MW 1:69).[26]

The mention of the "development" of the individual mind introduces Dewey's belief that we do not start as selves—we *become* selves in the process of social living: "individuality is not originally given but is created under the influences of associated life" (MW 12:193).[27] Dewey's point is not just that what was potential becomes actual when provided with the proper conditions, as, for example, the growth of a seed into a plant is sometimes understood (Cf. LW 9:195–96). His point is rather that persons are incomplete without a social component and develop into what they are—individual members of groups, socially grounded selves—in the ongoing process of living in a social environment. We need to recognize, Dewey writes, that as part of this social environment, our various institutions are both "means and agencies of human welfare and progress" and "means of *creating* individuals" (MW 12:191). The moral and educational implications that result from aspects of this understanding of institutions—for example, the importance of the educational environment, the need for ongoing avenues of growth, the importance of fostering an egalitarian culture—will be of concern in chapter 5. Our concern here is simply to get a sense of the fundamental importance that society and its institutions play in the development of the human self.

In this process of development, Dewey maintains that there is an intimate and reciprocal relationship between the ability to use language and the ability to develop a self.[28] Considering this process from the point of view of language, we see that speech makes available to the developing person the opportunity to enter imaginatively into potential modes of action. "Through speech a person dramatically identifies himself with potential acts and deeds; he plays many roles, not in successive stages of life but in a contemporaneously enacted drama. Thus mind emerges" (LW 1:135). Another version of the same position is contained in the following passage: "Through social intercourse, through sharing in the activities em-

---

[26] Cf. EW 4:343; LW 10:274–75; 12:26.

[27] Cf. MW 7:340; 9:304; LW 2:251; James Gouinlock, *John Dewey's Philosophy of Value*, 113–15.

[28] Dewey nowhere attempts to work out this relationship in any way as thoroughly as Mead does. See *Mind, Self, and Society*, 90–100, 125–52.

bodying beliefs, he gradually acquires a mind of his own" (MW 9:304; cf. LW 2:332). Dewey's meaning is clear: the growing child becomes a person by means of developing a sense of his or her self in the process of interaction with others, and this social self then structures and colors the child's subsequent experience. "Even when a person is alone," Dewey writes, "he thinks with language that is derived from association with others, and thinks about questions and issues that have been born in intercourse" (LW 7:227).[29] Moreover, once individuals have developed this gift of the group, they take it with them into contexts that are often mistakenly interpreted as completely 'isolated' or nonsocial:

> Even the hermit and Robinson Crusoe, as far as they live on a plane higher than that of the brutes, continue even in physical isolation to be what they are, to think the thoughts which go through their minds, to entertain their characteristic aspirations, because of social connections which existed in the past and which still persist in their imagination and emotions (LW 7:323).[30]

The social aspect of the self, essential to the make-up of the individual, remains operative as long as that individual remains who he or she is.

Because the development of the self is through social processes, Dewey maintains that we become familiar with our developing selves indirectly. "Apart from the social medium, the individual would never 'know himself'; he would never become acquainted with his own needs and capacities" (MW 5:388). We understand ourselves as part of larger processes; we adopt others' aspirations and spurnings; we judge success and failure relative to some social context. We understand ourselves in the light of our understanding of our social context; and this means that we understand ourselves, in part, in the light of others' evaluations of us. Dewey writes, "our sense of our own personality is largely a looking-glass phenomenon. It is a reflex

---

[29] Cf. George Herbert Mead: "That . . . a consciousness of a self as an object would ever have arisen in man if he had not had the mechanism of talking to himself, I think there is every reason to doubt" (*Selected Writings*, 140).

[30] Cf. George Herbert Mead: After a self has arisen, "we can think of a person in solitary confinement for the rest of his life, but who still has himself as a companion, and is able to think and to converse with himself as he had communicated with others" (*Mind, Self, and Society*, 140; cf. MW 12:198; 15:178–79; LW 1:135).

thing. We form our ideas, our estimates of ourselves and of our self-respect in terms of what others think of us, in terms of the way in which they treat us" (LW 5:239).[31] These others are the large circle of intimates, acquaintances, and passers-by with whom we interact. As we are first developing, our role is largely passive: we accept the evaluations that we receive. As we develop, however, we become more able to select those whose evaluations are to matter to us.

We turn now to a second topic within the larger question of the social nature of humans: the importance of recognizing that we are acting in a social environment. "Every act brings the agent who performs it into association with others, whether he so intends or not," Dewey writes (MW 5:404). "A being connected with other beings cannot perform his own activities without taking the activities of others into account" (MW 9:16). The usual, and obvious, interpretation of such passages is a moral one, focussing on the effects of our actions on others; but his primary concern here is not with the *evaluation* of action. It is, rather, with the *interpretation* of action. Dewey is emphasizing the degree to which human activities cannot be adequately understood if viewed simply as the doings of an individual in isolation. "Conduct is always shared. . . . It *is* social, whether bad or good" (MW 14:16). If we consider some basic examples, his point becomes clearer. Sound and light and fire are in themselves "physical facts," he writes; but humans integrate such facts into their social lives: "The *use* of sound in speech and listening to speech, making and enjoying music; the kindling and tending of fire to cook and to keep warm; the production of light to carry on and regulate occupations and social enjoyments;—these things are repre-sentative of distinctively human activity" (LW 12:48). It is this participation in the larger life of society by means of shared tools and goals and traditions that demonstrates the cultural meanings of our actions. To the extent that we are organized by such practices, our selves are essentially social selves.

Our social environment shapes us. It mandates or encourages

---

[31] Cf. George Herbert Mead: "The individual experiences himself as such, not directly, but only indirectly, from the particular standpoints of other individual members of the same social group as a whole to which he belongs. For he enters his own experience . . . only in so far as he first becomes an object to himself . . . and he becomes an object to himself only by taking the attitudes of other individuals toward himself within a social environment." (*Mind, Self, and Society*, 138; cf. James, *The Principles of Psychology*, vol. 2, 281–83).

some types of behavior; it eliminates or discourages other types. In doing this shaping, our social environment works with the biological bases of human life to direct our development. "Association does not create impulses of affection and dislike, but it furnishes the objects to which they attach themselves," Dewey writes; "an individual's desires take shape under the influence of the human environment" (MW 9:21; LW 10:274). We need only consider, for example, the ways in which our social environment contributes to the 'natural-ness' with which we have endowed slavery, militarism, and capitalism as systems of organizing our social lives (cf. MW 14:76–87). Even the limited amount of experience made available through the study of the few centuries of American history demonstrates the tremen-dous diversity of potential economic and political systems, all of which seemed 'natural' to those engaged in them at the time. They seemed natural because they were grounded in basic human im-pulses; but their diversity resulted from the directive choices of the social environment. "Native human nature supplies the raw materi-al," Dewey writes, "but custom furnishes the machinery and the designs" (MW 14:78).[32]

We can now turn to our third topic within human sociability and consider four significant implications that Dewey draws from the social understanding of the self. The first is the recognition of the dependency upon our social inheritance that we all share. "It is of grace not of ourselves that we lead civilized lives," Dewey writes (MW 14:19). He continues, "the chief difference between savagery and civilization is not in the naked nature which each faces, but the social heredity and social medium" (MW 1:69).[33] Had we been born and raised in a different time and place, we would have been—even though genetically identical—essentially different persons. For Dewey, as we shall see in 7.1, this chance positioning commits us to

---

[32] Cf. James Hayden Tufts: "the child or primitive adult has various impulses,—to eat, to hunt, to attack, to satisfy the opposite sex, to company with others, to assert control. Society, however, by its very organization makes it necessary for the child to eat with others, to live with a family or clan, to hunt with a group, to satisfy sex impulse under certain limits, to company with certain men, to revenge himself only in certain ways" ("On Moral Evolution," 15; cf. MW 5:59–72; LW 7:54–66).

[33] Dewey repeats this 1889 theme thirty-five years later in *Art as Experience*: "Neither the savage nor the civilized man is what he is by native constitution but by the culture in which he participates" (LW 10:347). Happily, the term 'savage'—along with its congeners 'civilized' and 'primitive'—has finally dropped from social discourse.

the recognition of a fundamental social debt to be repaid through our actions toward advancing the common good. The second implication that Dewey draws is the power of the intimate relationship felt to exist between the familiar and the acceptable. As he writes: "The way our group or class does things tends to determine the proper objects of attention, and thus to prescribe the directions and limits of observation and memory. What is strange or foreign (that is to say outside the activities of the groups) tends to be morally forbidden and intellectually suspect" (MW 9:21; cf. 14:54). To the extent that we are held prisoner by our own moral and intellectual customs, we cannot grow; and it thus becomes the job of a progressive society's educational system to prepare future adults to use customs without being overcome by them. The third implication that Dewey draws from his examination of the social aspects of the self is the recognition of the difficulties that we will have when we attempt to challenge the familiar. He writes that customs persist primarily "because individuals form their personal habits under conditions set by prior customs." As a consequence, he continues, a person "usually acquires the morality as he inherits the speech of his social group." And, just as "[t]here is no miracle in the fact that if a child learns any language he learns the language that those about him speak and teach" (MW 14:43), we should not find it in any way surprising that individuals also adopt customs other than the linguistic. The persistence of custom can thus be attributed to the normal process of developing a habituated self by individuals whose "imaginative is thereby limited" (MW 14:43; cf. 6:14); and change will be difficult. "Ways of belief, of expectation, of judgment and attendant emotional dispositions of like and dislike," he writes, "are not easily modified after they have once taken shape" (MW 14:77).

A fourth implication that Dewey draws from the social nature of the self is the need to reject the view that the social element in the human individual is simply an invasion of or an imposition upon us.[34] For Dewey, on the contrary, the social element is an essential part of us. Because sociability is not the only aspect of human nature,

---

[34] Although Dewey does offer, as we shall see below in 4.2, such passages as, "The community without becomes a forum and tribunal within, a judgment-seat of charges, assessments and exculpations" (MW 14:216), his interpretation is totally distinct from positions such as Sigmund Freud's that society masters the individual by means of a super-ego that then watches over thought and deed "like a garrison in a conquered city" (*Civilization and Its Discontents*, 71).

we can and do at times seek diversity and change. Some people often want to, and everybody at least sometimes wants to, act completely independently of the group. Still, Dewey believes that individuals are "chiefly interested upon the whole, in entering into the activities of others and taking part in conjoint and cooperative doings" (MW 9:28). We want to participate because we define ourselves, in large part, through successful contributions to the activities of our groups. There is as well "the desire of every individual for some acknowledgement of himself, of his personality, on the part of others." He thus writes that it is perhaps "the deepest urge of every human being, to feel that he does count for something with other human beings and receives a recognition from them as counting for something" (LW 5:239). Dewey's claim here is not that we want to have the power of the tycoon or the fame of the celebrity. What we want is to be treated fairly by those with whom we interact, and to be able to claim with justification respectability in the eyes of those individuals whose evaluations we cherish. None of this is far from the matters of moral importance that will engage us below in Part Two.

2.4. The Pattern of Inquiry

As we continue on with this exploration of Dewey's discussion of human nature, the final aspect to be considered will be his analysis of the nature of consciousness and reflection as seen from the point of view of a problem-solving creature. While it would be a mistake to expect from him an elaborately delineated phenomenology, we can find in his work a full discussion of our habitual nature and its integration with our conscious and rational lives. The human organism is animal in origin, still infected with "the dumb pluck of the animal" (MW 14:200), an active and engaged creature. "It is not action that needs to be accounted for, but rather the cessation of activity," Dewey writes; "nothing is more intolerable to a healthy human being than enforced passivity over a long period" (LW 7:289).[35] The active individual can perform many simple and complex activities—climbing stairs, driving an automobile, competing in sports, carrying on a conversation, painting and eating and making love—without thought. "We walk and read aloud," he

---

[35] Cf. MW 8:44–45; 14:84–85; LW 8:96.

writes, "we get off and on street cars, we dress and undress, and do a thousand useful acts without thinking of them" (MW 14:124; cf. EW 4:235). In fact, we often find that we perform such actions in a worse fashion when we pay attention to what we are doing. "If each act has to be consciously searched for at the moment and intentionally performed, execution is painful and the product is clumsy and halting" (MW 14:51; cf. 30).[36] We are able to perform these actions without thinking because of the power of habit in our lives. A habit, he writes, is "energy organized in certain channels" (MW 14:54). By means of these learned practices we are able to act without self-conscious attention, to consign the conduct of much of our lives to our past ways. And, although we may not always take advantage of the opportunity, Dewey writes that "the mastery of skill in the form of established habits frees the mind for a higher order of thinking" (MW 9:268). There is as a consequence a kind of inertia that gets us through much, perhaps most, of living without self-conscious intellectual involvement, at least until something goes wrong.

For Dewey, living is a process of overcoming such troubles. It may be more, but it is at least that. "Life itself consists of phases," he writes, "in which the organism falls out of step with the march of surrounding things and then recovers unison with it—either through effort or by some happy chance" (LW 10:19). Problem-solving is thus not all of living; but it is a major part, and a precondition of the rest. As a corollary, Dewey maintains that wisdom is not the intellectual ability to amass knowledge—a view that is itself pre-Darwinian—but rather the use of what we know to make life better by solving our problems. As he writes, "wisdom is knowledge operating in the direction of powers to the better living of life" (MW 6:221 = LW 8:163). The central question of the process of problem-solving is a topic to which Dewey returned again and again in his work. Each version contains essentially the same position, although on each occasion he discusses the various aspects

---

[36] Cf. George Herbert Mead: "A trained body of troops exhibits a set of conditioned reflexes. A certain formation is brought about by means of certain orders. Its success lies in an automatic response when these orders are given. There, of course, one has action without thought. If the soldier thinks under the circumstances he very likely will not act; his action is dependent in a certain sense on the absence of thought" (*Mind, Self, and Society,* 102; cf. James, *The Principles of Psychology,* vol. 1, 119–23).

of the matter with more or less completeness, in cruder or finer detail. And, while the chapter entitled "The Pattern of Inquiry" in *Logic: The Theory of Inquiry* (LW 12:105–22) is probably the most familiar version, all of the various discussions of the "phases, or aspects, of reflective thought" (LW 8:200) are contributory to an adequate understanding of his position. I have integrated a number of them in the following assimilative discussion.[37]

Inquiry itself Dewey defines as the deliberate creation of an orderly and unified situation out of a problematic one: *"Inquiry is the controlled or directed transformation of an indeterminate situation into one that is so determinate in its constituent distinctions and relations as to convert the elements of the original situation into a unified whole"* (LW 12:108).[38] The notion of "situation" that Dewey has in mind here is *"not* a single object or event or set of objects and events." It is rather "a contextual whole." He continues that *"an* object or event is always a special part, phase, or aspect, of an environing experienced world" (LW 12:72). Inquiry deals with the various pieces, but only as parts of situations.

Inquiry in this sense, Dewey writes, can be seen to demonstrate "a common structure or pattern" (LW 12:105) regardless of the specific subject matter under examination at any given time. In the initial or 'pre-problematic' situation of 'security', everything seems to be 'working'. There are no doubts. Life continues on in a habitual manner, on what we might now call 'automatic pilot'. Our actions are essentially thought-less: water, for example, comes from the tap as it is supposed to. We do not think about the availability of the water because it is, and has been, readily available. As Dewey writes, "no problem or difficulty in the quality of the experience presents itself to provoke reflection" (MW 2:307). But then something goes wrong: we turn the tap but no water flows. The resulting situation is one of indeterminacy and obscurity; and, because we were engaged in some activity that is now arrested, this situation will be experienced as one

---

[37] In addition to discussions specifically mentioned here, Dewey also discusses the process of inquiry in: EW 3:83–89; MW 1:151–74; 2:306–7; 3:9; 4:71–75, 82–90; 9:157–58; 13:61–62; LW 10:20–21. Cf. Thayer, *Meaning and Action,* 190–92, 19; Thayer, *The Logic of Pragmatism,* 49–69; Eames, *Pragmatic Naturalism,* 68–71; Flower and Murphey, *A History of Philosophy in America,* vol. 2, 850–54.

[38] Cf. LW 4:183; 12:121.

of confusion and ambiguity. There is, he writes, "perplexity, confusion, doubt, due to the fact that one is implicated in an incomplete situation whose full character is not yet determined." (MW 9:157; cf. LW 12:109). Initially at least, we cannot determine what the situation *means*. Has the water line frozen or sprung a leak? Is the pump broken or the well dry? Has the water bill not been paid or is this tap just defective? We do not understand what has happened. The dry tap is a sign of something; but "we do not as yet know of what it is a sign" (LW 3:63). We find ourselves in "a *forked-road* situation" (MW 6:189 = LW 8:122), where we feel the unsettledness of the confused situation; but we do not know what it means or what to do. There is one point that we do know, however, and this is that it is the situation that is in doubt, not just us. "It is the *situation* that has these traits," Dewey writes. "*We* are doubtful because the situation is inherently doubtful." What it means especially is that it will not be cleared up "by manipulation of our personal states of mind" (LW 12:109–10).[39]

We then attempt to convert this feeling into thought and thereby to specify or formulate tentatively what is actually wrong. What is required here is the "intellectualization of the difficulty or perplexity that has been *felt* (directly experienced) into a *problem* to be solved" (LW 8:200). As Dewey continues, even though tentative, this process of definition involves a modification of the situation: "*A problem represents the partial transformation by inquiry of a problematic situation into a determinate situation.*" Therefore, it is an immensely important step:

> It is a familiar and significant saying that a problem well put is half-solved. To find out *what* the problem and problems are which a problematic situation presents to be inquired into, is to be well along in inquiry. To mis-take the problem involved is to cause subsequent inquiry to be irrelevant or to go astray. (LW 12:111–12)[40]

Because this step is pivotal, we must resist the tendency to act immediately. We should try to *enjoy,* or at least to *work through,* the doubt. "The natural tendency of man is to do something at once," Dewey writes; "there is impatience with suspense, and lust for

---

[39] Cf. Thayer, *The Logic of Pragmatism,* 75–84.
[40] Cf. MW 8:201; LW 15:210.

immediate action" (LW 4:178).[41] The approach that Dewey has in mind, on the contrary—closely allied with his understanding of science that we will consider in 4.1—is one that is "capable of enjoying the doubtful" and that can make "a productive use of doubt by converting it into operations of definite inquiry" (LW 4:182).

We must also be careful not to assume immediately, he writes, that this new situation "so closely resembles former ones that conclusions reached in these earlier cases can be directly carried over" (LW 12:144; cf. MW 13:64). In the dry-tap case introduced above, prior failures to receive water may or may not be relevant this time. The *problem* to be solved involved us in using our experience to conceptualize the nature and likelihood of the various potential failures in our elaborate water-delivery system. The successful process of defining the problem is thus based upon our success at suspending judgment until we can develop a sense of the problem that is grounded in the indeterminate situation and that will guide subsequent inquiry. "Without a problem," Dewey writes, "there is blind groping in the dark" (LW 12:112).

The third stage in this process of inquiry is to further observe and investigate the situation in order to suggest a solution to the problem under examination. This potential solution is, of course, shaped "by the diagnosis that has been made" (LW 8:203). The likely success of our examination of both the potential solution and the assumed nature of the problem upon which it is based will be enhanced if we keep in mind a number of factors. One of these factors is the importance of recognizing those elements in the situation which are stable and determined: "no situation which is *completely* indeterminate can possibly be converted into a problem having definite constituents," Dewey writes. "The first step then is to search out the *constituents* of a given situation which, as constituents, are settled" (LW 12:112; cf. MW 2:338–39). In our dry-tap case, for example, we can safely assume as the basis of our other thinking the continued operation of the normal laws of hydrodynamics. A second factor is the need to try to recognize "[w]hat facts are *evidence* in this case" (LW 8:250; cf. 212–13). Is the availability of water elsewhere in the house a factor to be considered? Does the age of the tap itself matter? A third factor to keep in mind is the fact that both the formulation of

---

[41] Cf. MW 1:151–52; LW 1:374; 8:124.

the problem and the suggested solution are tentative, and it is thus important to keep alternatives available somewhere in the back of our minds (cf. MW 6:239). It is important to keep in mind, Dewey writes, that we are still at "a speculative stage: a period of guessing" (MW 2:307). We attempt to use all of the ideas that "pop into our heads" (LW 12:114) while working towards that analysis that seems to offer the most as "a guiding idea, a working hypothesis" (LW 8:203).

The fourth stage in the process of inquiry Dewey calls "reasoning" or "developing the meaning-contents of ideas in their relations to one another." This stage involves a series of idea-tests of what we have determined so far to assure that no *ad hoc* analyses are accepted. "If such and such a relation of meanings is accepted," he writes, "then we are committed to such and such other relations of meanings because of their membership in the same system" (LW 12:115).[42] How detailed and elaborate our ideational analysis will be depends upon our personal and social resources: our past experience and education, our culture and level of technology (cf. LW 8:204). These intellectual tests, as tests, are of particular value because what is "tried out in imagination is not final or fatal. It is retrievable" whereas "[a]n act overtly tried out is irrevocable, its consequences cannot be blotted out" (MW 14:133).[43] Moreover, these evaluated hypotheses have attained at least that level of verification. A conclusion that is just accepted without such evaluation, Dewey writes, "is not grounded, even if it happens to be correct" (LW 12:115). This process of reasoning will perhaps lead to some modification of the hypothetical solution. The availability of water elsewhere in the house implies a localized blockage, for example, although it does not determine the nature of the blockage. The addition of warm weather conditions would eliminate the possibility of a frozen pipe and suggest the likelihood of a blockage of a mechanical sort.

The final stage in this process is overt experimental testing of the refined hypothetical solution. Dewey writes: "If it is found that the experimental results agree with the theoretical, or rationally deduced, results, and if there is reason to believe that *only* the conditions in question would yield such results, the confirmation is

---

[42] Cf. MW 2:364; LW 8:205.
[43] Cf. LW 7:275; 8:192–93; 12:63.

so strong as to induce a conclusion—at least until contrary facts shall indicate the advisability of its revision" (MW 6:240–41 = LW 8:205–6). Such success thus returns us to the secure, pre-problematic state. We replace the entire tap and find both that upon testing the water flows as it should with the new device and that upon examination the old tap was completely blocked. Experimental failure, on the other hand, does not return us to the pre-problematic state; instead, because for the methodic inquirer "failure is not *mere* failure" (LW 8:206),[44] we would be in a better state than we had been initially. We would know that the blockage could not be attributed to a faulty tap and that it must be sought somewhere further up the water line.

There are a number of questions about Dewey's understanding of the process of inquiry moving from "a perplexed, troubled, or confused situation at the beginning" to "a cleared-up, unified, resolved situation at the close" (LW 8:199–200) that need to be considered here. One of these is the question of whether or not Dewey believes that in our inquiries we always follow exactly the pattern that he has laid out. The response is that his emphasis is upon the *logic of inquiry* rather than the *history of inquiries:* the pattern is intended to represent "only in outline the indispensable traits of reflective thinking" (LW 8:207). In particular cases, he writes, there is no automatic program or protocol to follow: "No cast-iron rules can be laid down" (MW 6:241).[45] He does maintain, however, that the pattern is in general widely used, and efforts are justifiably aimed at increasing the frequency and broadening the range of its use. His sense of the difference between how people do think and how they ought to think is thus "a difference like that between good and bad farming or good and bad medical practice" (LW 12:107; cf. 13:209–10). We must not, of course, read too much into his use of "good": "It does not follow in any of these cases that the 'better' methods are ideally perfect, or that they are regulative or 'normative' because of conformity to some absolute form. They are the methods which experience up to the present time shows to be the best methods

---

[44] Cf. LW 3:105; 10:23.

[45] Dewey emphasizes the difference between *experimental inquiry* and *attempts at proof,* where our goal is to find "the most effective way in which to set forth what has already been concluded, so as to convince others." (LW 8:173; cf. EW 1:149; MW 15:65–77; LW 8:171–76).

available for achieving certain results" (LW 12:108). As such, they deserve to be tried out in the place of those, he writes, that "experience of past inquiries shows are not competent to reach the intended end" (LW 12:107).

A second question has to do with any possible assurances of success should the pattern be followed; and, of course, the answer is negative. "There is no possibility of disguising the fact," Dewey writes, "that an experimental philosophy of life means a hit-and-miss philosophy in the end" (MW 8:202).[46] The claim behind his method is simply that we are more likely to succeed if we understand how we come to recognize problems and how we can best address them. This point is of special importance when we recall our tendency to be more troubled by the doubt than by the problem of which the doubt is an indicator. "The natural tendency of man," Dewey writes, "is not to press home a doubt, but to cut inquiry as short as possible" (MW 1:151). He continues, "One can think reflectively only when one is willing to endure suspense and to undergo the trouble of searching. To many persons both suspense of judgment and intellectual search are disagreeable; they want to get them ended as soon as possible" (LW 8:123–24).[47] Speed in such matters undercuts success. If we can learn, however, "to sustain and protract that state of doubt which is the stimulus to thorough inquiry" (LW 8:124), we will be able to decrease the frequency with which we err due to thoughtless action. We will be able, Dewey believes, "to protect the mind against itself" (MW 12:99). Moreover, if we can develop the social aspects of intelligence, by such means as recognizing the important role of individuals as trouble-spotters and fostering the importance of education for problem-solving rather than for obedience or conformity, we can decrease the frequency further.

A third question is closely tied to Dewey's sense of social intelligence. It is to wonder about the range of applicability of this pattern of inquiry. Dewey believes that it is not only of use to individuals in their particular problems, but that it also, when

---

[46] Cf. Alan Pendleton Grimes: "Pragmatism was only an experiment: but then so indeed was living" (*American Political Thought,* 427).

[47] Cf. C. S. Peirce: "Doubt is an uneasy and dissatisfied state from which we struggle to free ourselves and pass into the state of belief. . . . as soon as a firm belief is reached we are entirely satisfied, whether the belief be true or false" (*Collected Papers,* 5.372, 5.375; cf. MW 9:196–99; 12:160; LW 4:26).

suitably modified, could be of use to groups and societies in their attempts to deal with their social problems. He believes that by the deliberate cultivation of this pattern of inquiry we can make reflective or intelligent reconstruction a greater part of our social praxis. Since this question will be of central concern in chapters 5 and 6, I will postpone consideration of it until that time.

2.5.   Considering Dewey's Understanding of Human Nature

We have been considering in a sequential fashion a series of aspects of human nature: that humans are the products of evolution, that humans are essentially embodied and essentially social creatures, and that humans are problem-solvers. In this section, I would like to step back a bit from Dewey's discussion and explore more critically this understanding of human nature. While I must admit initially that I do not consider the first two aspects—our evolutionary heritage and our embodiment—to be philosophically problematic, the third aspect of human nature that we have considered opens up a serious philosophical issue and is deserving of a considered evaluation. Does Dewey go too far when he writes of the human individual that "[a]part from the ties which bind him to others, he is nothing" (LW 7:323)? The point to be considered is in essence the question of whether under his understanding of human nature he respects human individuality sufficiently.

Responding negatively, George Santayana maintains that in Dewey's work "there is a pervasive quasi-Hegelian tendency to dissolve the individual into his social functions."[48] Robert Wiebe suggests further that Dewey transformed Pragmatism "into a theory that made individuals the plastic stuff of society."[49] Horace Mayer Kallen, to cite a third instance, writes that Dewey was "ambivalent" about "the individuality of individuals," in that he both cherished and fostered the liberation and growth of humans while at the same time he attempted to integrate human behavior into a system of natural explanations. Kallen continues that, as a result, Dewey's

---

[48] Santayana, "Dewey's Naturalistic Metaphysics," 675 [reprinted in LW 3:370].
[49] Wiebe, *The Search for Order,* 151.

philosophy offers a deeply flawed picture of human nature, writing that it:

> evinces a certain blindness to the sheer individuality of individuals, the precipitousness that their "lives of quiet desperation" often manifest, and the never-to-be reconciled evils that beset their struggles to go on struggling, which we call existence. . . . [It] discloses no deep awareness of humanity *in extremis*, the good of one man's existence stretched on the rack of some other man's good and turned thereon to suffering and evil. . . . [It] communicates no deep sensitivity of the evil that flows from the inexpugnable warfare of irreconcilable goods, or of how ultimately evil this evil is.[50]

Readers will have to decide as they go whether Kallen and the others are correct in their analysis of this aspect of Dewey's work. My own view is that his vision of a reconstructed individualism is in no way blind toward or unaware of or insensitive to individuality. Dewey does not overlook the reality of diversity; but his concern is always with how it can contribute to the common good. He does not fail to recognize and appreciate the pains of human living; but his emphasis is always on our potential response to them, on how we might advance the common good.[51]

As we have considered this criticism of Dewey's essentially social analysis of human nature, I hope it has become clear how closely related this criticism is to the fourth one: that he offers an analysis of human nature that is too pragmatic or too instrumental. The relatedness of the criticisms results from his integration of the two themes in his analysis of people as social and as problem-solvers. To Dewey, fulfillment results from active participation in the doings of society, especially reconstructive attempts at overcoming social problems. To his critics, on the other hand, this conception of fulfillment appears both as a misunderstanding and a devaluation of

---

[50] Kallen, "Individuality, Individualism, and John Dewey," 314, 313; cf. Geiger, *John Dewey in Perspective,* 160; Quentin Anderson, "John Dewey's American Democrat."

[51] Cf. Arthur G. Wirth: "Dewey's meliorism led him to concentrate on defining the rational means required to improve men's chances. This focus led him to shy away from depths of experience which all men confront" (*John Dewey as Educator,* 279).

human individuality. From their point of view, following Dewey's analysis would make it impossible for people to understand themselves, or develop their potentialities, or appreciate the fullness of living, because they would be too busy with selfless engagement in social activities.

The question of whether or not Dewey's instrumentalism offers an accurate picture of human nature is the question of whether or not life can be adequately understood and appreciated if it is approached as a series of problems, or as a process of solving problems. There is no doubt that, suitably qualified, this is Dewey's view. He writes, for example, that "living may be regarded as a continual rhythm of disequilibrations and recoveries of equilibrium" (LW 12:34).[52] We live our lives in a constant attempt to stay in balance with our environment, and we cannot hope to ever transcend this reality. He continues:

> No matter what the present success in straightening out difficulties and harmonizing conflicts, it is certain that problems will recur in the future in a new form or on a different plane. Indeed, every genuine accomplishment instead of winding up an affair and enclosing it as a jewel in a casket for future contemplation, complicates the practical situation. . . . From the side of what has gone before achievement settles something. From the side of what comes after, it complicates, introducing new problems, unsettling factors (MW 14:197).

In this ongoing process of addressing problems, he writes, "as special problems are resolved, new ones tend to emerge. There is no such thing as a final settlement, because every settlement introduces the conditions of some degree of a new unsettling" (LW 12:42).

Under Dewey's analysis, much of life that we do not normally see as 'problematic' becomes so.[53] He writes, for example, that "[a]ll friendship is a solution of the problem" of understanding "another person with whom we habitually associate" (LW 10:339). Another aspect of Dewey's instrumentalism is his understanding of the origin

---

[52] Cf. George Herbert Mead: "is not life a continuous solution of problems?" (*Selected Writings*, 331).

[53] Cf. Morris Cohen: "That thought arises because of the desire to get out of trouble is certainly true, if 'desire to get out of trouble' is stretched to include what it does not ordinarily connote." (*American Thought*, 295).

and proper function of thought. He writes, for example, that "thinking would not exist . . . in a world which presented no troubles" (MW 10:331), because we could get by with our habits and our traditional ways of action. "Only a signal flag of distress recalls consciousness to the task of carrying on," he writes (MW 14:121). He continues: "thinking takes its departure from specific conflicts in experience that occasion perplexity and trouble. Men do not, in their natural estate, think when they have no troubles to cope with, no difficulties to overcome. A life of ease, of success without effort, would be a thoughtless life" (MW 12:159–60).[54] Dewey writes further that *"[d]emand for the solution of a perplexity is the steadying and guiding factor in the entire process of reflection"* (MW 6:189 = LW 8:122). Even more strongly, he continues that thought is properly understood as a preparation for action: "ideas are worthless except as they pass into actions which rearrange and reconstruct in some way, be it little or large, the world in which we live" (LW 4:111).

In our attempt to evaluate the significance of these passages, it is important to recognize immediately that Dewey is denying neither the reality nor the richness of our spontaneously changing mental life that James characterizes in "The Stream of Thought" as "a theatre of simultaneous possibilities."[55] As Dewey himself writes:

> All the time we are awake and sometimes when we are asleep, something is, as we say, going through our heads. . . . More of our waking life than most of us would care to admit is whiled away in this inconsequential trifling with mental pictures, random recollections, pleasant but unfounded hopes, flitting, half-developed impressions (LW 8:113–14).[56]

Stronger still, he continues, "the having of ideas is not so much something we do, as it is something that happens to us" (LW 8:145). He goes even further: " 'It thinks' is a truer psychological statement than 'I think.' Thoughts sprout and vegetate; ideas proliferate" (MW

---

[54] Cf. MW 1:93; LW 1:60, 237; 8:193–94; 10:65. Cf. also George Herbert Mead: "Consciousness arises only when our impulses lead us into conflict—conflict that must be solved before conduct can go on effectively" (*Movements of Thought in the Nineteenth Century*, 321); "reasoning conduct appears where impulsive conduct breaks down" (*Mind, Self, and Society*, 348).

[55] *The Principles of Psychology*, vol. 1, 277.

[56] Cf. MW 6:182–83; 12:83.

14:216).[57] While Dewey has no intention of denying this aspect of consciousness, he *is* very interested in denying that we should characterize such casual having-of-ideas as *thinking,* a structured, intellectual undertaking that he characterizes as "the most difficult occupation in which man engages" (LW 3:112).

The difference between the spontaneous coursing of ideas and reflective thought or "thinking in its eulogistic sense" (MW 13:64), Dewey writes, is that reflective thinking is deliberately controlled to be orderly and goal-oriented. It is constituted by *"[a]ctive, persistent, and careful consideration of any belief or supposed form of knowledge in the light of the grounds that support it and the further conclusions to which it tends"* (LW 8:118; cf. MW 6:185–86). The goal of reflective thinking is the pragmatic one of the improvement of life through the solution of problems: *"The function of reflective thought is, therefore, to transform a situation in which there is experienced obscurity, doubt, conflict, disturbance of some sort, into a situation that is clear, coherent, settled, harmonious"* (LW 8:195). Thus Dewey, in terms of the general philosophical viewpoint that he characterizes as Instrumentalism, "assigns a positive function to thought, that of *re*constituting the present stage of things instead of merely knowing it" (LW 2:18). He continues that the function of reflective thought is consequently "not that of copying the objects of the environment, but rather of taking account of the way in which more effective and more profitable relations with these objects may be established in the future" (LW 2:17).

In the face of this strenuous and demanding stance on the nature and role of thinking,[58] it is in no way difficult to muster at least an initial sympathy with those who would maintain that Dewey's analysis of human nature is skewed by what Santayana calls his "sheer fidelity to the task in hand."[59] We can realize how in the midst of the many potential roles for thinking, Dewey's instrumental analysis of human nature can be viewed as offering a role that is too simple an analysis of the meaning of life, too single-minded a concern with the amelioration of human ills, too willing a surrender of private

---

[57] Cf. LW 8:202; 12:114.

[58] Dewey, of course, recognizes the "great esthetic satisfaction" that can result from *"playing with ideas,"* and he recognizes as well that no one could excel "in any field of science or philosophy who did not have an absorbing interest in the relations of ideas for their own sake" (LW 8:262; cf. 4:111).

[59] Santayana, "Dewey's Naturalistic Metaphysics," 676 [reprinted in LW 3:370].

fulfillment. In light of this, Dewey might even be charged with being, in the words of Morris Cohen, "a naturalistic Puritan."[60]

We can begin consideration of Dewey's possible puritanism with C. I. Lewis, who writes that the author of *The Quest for Certainty* was "preoccupied with the forward-looking function of knowledge to the neglect of the backward-looking ground or premises." Dewey was interested, therefore, in only half of the topic of knowledge. Lewis suggests that one reason for Dewey's "preponderant, and almost exclusive, emphasis upon the forward-looking aspect of content and instrumental function, is that the traditional problems of validity do not greatly interest him."[61] We might suggest, contrary to Lewis, that Dewey had an understanding of knowledge and of the role of validity different from Lewis's, one that places validation itself in the future. Dewey points, for example, to the important Jamesian emphasis, implied in 1.3, that "validity is not a matter of origin nor of antecedents, but of consequents," and that as a result "the value of ideas is independent of their origin, that it is a matter of their outcome as they are used in directing new observation and new experiment" (LW 11:82).

In addition to this devaluation of purely prior evidence, we can also point to what is seen as another casualty in Dewey's analysis of the human as a problem-solving animal. This is what Milton Mayerhoff calls "a 'quiet dimension of experience'," a dimension of experience that he believes is best characterized negatively by such qualities as "lack of purpose, lack of doing and manipulating, lack of sharing, and lack of the immediately practical and social." In Dewey's austere and sober-minded analysis of living, Mayerhoff continues, there is little room to appreciate "such quiet and simple experiences as listening to the rain drops outside one's window, or in the stillness watching the snow flakes come down, or looking at the sea."[62] Although the importance of this criticism remains to be decided, there is little room to dispute the accuracy of Mayerhoff's view here.

Santayana continues this vein of criticism of Dewey's problem-

---

[60] Morris Cohen announces in 1916 that he would *not* characterize Dewey in this way (*A Preface to Logic*, 197), although by 1921 he seems to be willing to come pretty close: "Dewey insists with Puritan austerity on the serious responsibility of philosophy" ("Later Philosophy," 256; cf. *American Thought*, 291).

[61] Lewis, review of *The Quest for Certainty*, 17, 20.

[62] Mayerhoff, "A Neglected Aspect of Experience in Dewey's Philosophy," 146, 148.

solving analysis of human nature when he writes that Dewey "is not interested in speculation at all, balks at it, and would avoid it if he could," and that he "is very severe against the imagination, and even the intellect, of mankind for having created figments which usurp the place and authority of the mundane sphere in which daily action goes on."[63] Morris Cohen carries this criticism still further with the suggestion that with Dewey's strictures on thinking goes a lack of evaluation, maintaining, I think mistakenly, that Dewey "places too much emphasis on being continually on the go, without regard to the places whereto it is worth while to go in order to stay rather than merely to pass through."[64] Cohen sums up this attack on Dewey's instrumental understanding of human nature by suggesting that Dewey's overall position is flawed by his excessive concern with practical well-being:

> Dewey is essentially a moralist. His philosophy is full of the sense of responsibility, of tasks to be achieved, and of the possibilities of philosophy in helping us to perform them more efficiently. Everything in this universe has a job or function and ought to be up and doing. The otiose observer,—the one who idly admires the flowers of knowledge for their own sake rather than their consequences,— is the cardinal sinner.[65]

Thus Dewey, by his connection of the contemplative and the idler, the ornamental and the wasteful, offers us a puritan moralism.

To further our evaluation of Dewey's instrumental understanding of human nature, it might be useful at this point to consider briefly a counter-position to his view; and Cohen, who has been so prominent in this criticism of Dewey, offers us a handy and well-developed view. Cohen believes that no one who has a clear sense of the cosmic insignificance of humanity and of the pervasive evils of human life could be as zealous about advancing human good as Dewey is. In this regard, Cohen describes Dewey's Pragmatism as a "compensatory" philosophy that futilely attempts "reconciling man to scientific

---

[63] Santayana, "Dewey's Naturalistic Metaphysics," 676, 674–75 [reprinted in LW 3:370, 369].

[64] Cohen, "Some Difficulties in Dewey's Anthropocentric Naturalism," 227 [reprinted in LW 14:409]; cf. Bertrand Russell, "Dewey's New *Logic*," 156.

[65] Cohen, *American Thought*, 292; cf. 291, 298; "Some Difficulties in Dewey's Anthropocentric Naturalism," 198 [reprinted in LW 14:381].

discoveries which have diminished his dignity as the center of creation."[66] He notes that there is no sense in Dewey's writings "of the loneliness of the individual human soul, facing the indifferent earth, sea, or sky, or the eternal procession of the stars that ever mock man's vain pretension to exalt himself as the master of the universe." He writes in addition that "no philosophy is really humane, and avoids needless cruelty, unless it recognizes the inevitability of human suffering, defeat, death, and destruction and provides some anodyne through wisely cultivated resignation." Philosophy must provide, in other words, "a redemption from deadly worldliness."[67] Thus, according to Cohen, in order to lead adequate human lives we need to step back from the battle to overcome problems and try to appreciate "the dark and unfathomable seas of being, wherein the world of human conduct occupies but an infinitesimal portion of time and space." In this way, Cohen believes, people will be able to rise "above their petty limitations and learn to look upon their passions and achievements with that measure of aloofness which is essential to any vision that can be called philosophic." If we can cultivate this distance, we will be able to appreciate "the Aristotelian view that philosophic knowledge arises from the natural wonder or curiosity, from the desire to know just for the sake of knowing."[68] We would also be better able to appreciate in this way what he calls "the personal consolations of philosophy," and use this philosophy "to build a haven into which he can for a time escape from the suffocating cruelties of every-day life."[69]

In attempting to formulate a Deweyan response to this funda-mental criticism of what is seen as his relentlessly plodding under-standing of human nature, we must first of all remind ourselves that it is not the aim of his philosophical project to offer a comprehensive phenomenology of every aspect of human experience. Rather, throughout his extensive writings, his primary goal at any particular time is to explore some particular cultural or intellectual problem. Out of these explorations, I have teased four central themes of his

---

[66] Cohen, *A Preface to Logic*, 200.

[67] Cohen, *American Thought*, 299–300; cf. 291–92; "Later Philosophy," 257.

[68] Cohen, *American Thought*, 293, 297, 294–95; cf. "Some Difficulties in Dewey's Anthropocentric Naturalism," 199 [reprinted in LW 14:382].

[69] Cohen, "Later Philosophy," 257; *A Preface to Logic*, 202; cf. Paul K. Conkin, *Puritans and Pragmatists*, 347.

understanding of human existence: humans are evolved and engaged creatures whose lives are essentially social and dependent upon adaptive success. His critics in general recognize the admitted instrumentalism of his thought, and no doubt part of their extended criticism is that he did not think that offering a broader phenomenology was worthwhile. But, for Dewey, we find ourselves, as incomplete creatures living in changing social and natural situations, antecedently committed to lifelong attempts at overcoming difficulties. We find our state to be more fortunate than the other animals, however, in that when habitual modes of action fail us we have an alternative mode of response through reflective thinking. The possibility of intelligent action thus compels inquiry; and in defending this stance Dewey embraces the 'forward-looking' charge we saw above. As he writes in one of several such formulations: "we live not in a settled and finished world, but in one which is going on, and where our main task is prospective, and where retrospect—and all knowledge as distinct from thought is retrospect—is of value in the solidity, security, and fertility it affords our dealings with the future" (MW 9:158).[70]

The only dissent that Dewey might offer to the 'forward-looking' charge as formulated above would be to complain that, in its bifurcation of 'forward-' and 'backward-looking', it disregards his emphasis on the continuity of the human process. The function of thinking is to contribute to a life that is forward-moving, carrying with it all that matters from the experiences of the past and the present. We can never hope, moreover, to leave these experiences behind. "The finished and done with," Dewey writes, "is of import as affecting the future, not on its own account: in short, because it is not, really, done with" (MW 10:10). We are moving forward and carrying with us possibilities for improving our future lives. One of these possibilities is intelligent action, a possibility that reflective thought gives us for addressing our new situations. "We do not merely have to repeat the past, or wait for accidents to force change upon us. We *use* our past experiences to construct new and better ones in the future" (MW 12:134).

As we have seen, this instrumental stance implies to some that thinking is just a means to more efficient, but aimless, motion.

---

[70] Cf. MW 9:336; 14:19; LW 12:52.

Dewey's metaphorical response to this charge is to note that "[i]f it is better to travel than to arrive, it is because traveling is a constant arriving, while arrival that precludes further traveling is most easily attained by going to sleep or dying" (MW 14:195). A less figurative statement of this point would be that Dewey is rejecting the suggestion that his pragmatic view implies that action is "the end of life" (LW 2:5; cf. 19). His view is rather that, for the embodied human organism in a changing environment, living is action that will be followed by further action, and that we need to be constantly watchful to see where we are going, to determine the value of the life we are to live. "The value of any changing thing lies in its consequences," he writes (LW 3:134); and these can never be known fully in advance. To point this out, however, does not mean that we do not care about potential ends. It means that, as we shall see in chapter 4, with a self-conscious method of inquiry we can uncover and foster the values necessary for living in the course of living.[71]

To change the metaphor to a slightly different type of motion, we can consider whether this problem-solving understanding of human nature reduces human action to the futile labors of a Sisyphus "who is forever rolling a stone uphill only to have it roll back so that he has to repeat his old task." Dewey admits that in his view of human nature it is futile to hope for "progress made in a control of conditions which shall stay put and which excludes the necessity of future deliberations and reconsiderations." But, from the standpoint of human existence, these solutions yield the meaning of changing activities which remains "alive" and "growing in significance" (MW 14:144–45). He continues that "in a growing life, the recovery is never mere return to a prior state, for it is enriched by the state of disparity and resistance through which it has successfully passed" (LW 10:19; cf. MW 14:195–96).

Life, for Dewey, is a series of problems or a series of disequilibrations and recoveries. Because of our human potential for learning, however, these experiences can also be a process of growing, of

---

[71] Cf. George Herbert Mead: "the human social animal has acquired a mind, and can bring to bear upon the problem his own past experiences and that of others, and can test the solution that arises in his conduct. He does not know what the solution will be, but he does know the method of the solution. We, none of us, know where we are going, but we do know that we are on the way" (*Selected Writings*, 266; cf. *Mind, Self, and Society*, 294; *Movements of Thought in the Nineteenth Century*, 292–94, 509; *The Philosophy of the Act*, 496, 503).

uncovering connections and relationships, of finding more mean-ing.[72] He writes:

> Every reflection leaves behind it a double effect. Its immediate outcome is . . . the direct reorganization of a situation, a recogni-tion which confers upon its contents new increments of intrinsic meaning. Its indirect and intellectual product is the defining of a meaning which (when fixed by a suitable existence) is a resource in subsequent investigations (MW 10:355–56).

It may be, of course, that we never do make use of the indirect consequence(s) of a particular inquiry—but we might. For now, we have the added meaning, a kind of value. In another discussion, Dewey points to three values of thinking. The first two are "of a practical sort; they give increased power of *control.*" These are that thinking "enables us to direct our activities with foresight and to plan according to ends-in-view, or purposes of which we are aware" and also to set up "artificial signs to remind [us] in advance of consequences and of ways of securing and avoiding them." The third value of thinking is that it "confers upon physical events and objects a very different status and value from those which they possess to a being that does not reflect." What thinking makes possible is "an enrichment of meaning apart from added control." As an example of this third class, he suggests an eclipse: "a certain event in the heavens cannot be warded off just because we know it is an eclipse and how it is produced, but it does have a significance for us that it did not have before" (LW 8:125–28).[73] Elsewhere, he writes,

> while reflective knowing is instrumental to gaining control in a troubled situation (and thus has a practical or utilitarian force), it is also instrumental to the enrichment of the immediate significance of subsequent experiences. And it may well be that this by-product, this gift of the gods, is incomparably more valuable for living a life than is the primary and intended result of control, essential as is that control to having a life to live (MW 10:330).

And this added understanding still might be of instrumental use later.

Two further points need to be made about Dewey's understand-

---

[72] The centrality of growth to Dewey's overall view will become apparent in 4.4.
[73] Cf. MW 6:192–95; 9:82.

ing of increased meaning through attempts at problem-solving. The first is that we should not focus exclusively on success or abandon hope at the sight of initial failure. "Such happiness as life is capable of," Dewey writes, "comes from the full participation of all our powers in the endeavor to wrest from each changing situation of experience its own full and unique meaning." But, since his emphasis here is on endeavor rather than on accomplishment, we can understand his point that even if we fail in our attempts at solving problems growth is still possible. Although frequently accused of being an optimist,[74] he writes in a very sober fashion: "the joy of constant discovery and of constant growing . . . is possible even in the midst of trouble and defeat, whenever life-experiences are treated as potential disclosures of meanings and values that are to be used as means to a fuller and more significant future experience" (LW 5:272).[75] The second point is the reminder that the increase in meaning to which Dewey points is not an increase in 'contemplative' meaning that serves only an ornamental function, but rather in meaning that may be of use in future problems. In the face of the pressures of ongoing existence, there is always more to be done; and we need no cosmic justification for any attempts we might make to improve our situation. "Humanity is not, as was once thought, the end for which all things were formed," Dewey writes; "it is but a slight and feeble thing, perhaps an episodic one, in the vast stretch of the universe. But for man, man is the centre of interest and the measure of importance" (LW 2:345).

For Dewey, it is important to emphasize that we can influence our plastic present as it moves into the future. Although his critics are certainly correct that much of life's suffering is inevitable, Dewey is also correct in his essential point that we cannot know in advance what particular sufferings may be ameliorated. And, while the Deweyan may be demonstrating, in Cohen's word, "an unwise obstinacy in refusing to accept our limitations and thus wasting life in efforts that are fruitless if not worse,"[76] Dewey's own analysis is different. For Dewey, when we assume that the reality of evil makes

---

[74] We will consider this charge of optimism in 6.3.

[75] Cf. Dewey: "Progress means increase of present meaning, which involves multiplication of sensed distinctions as well as harmony, unification" (MW 14:196).

[76] Cohen, *American Thought*, 301.

fatalism justifiable,[77] and that in response a contemplative distancing is the least painful option that we have, we are surrendering. Far better for us, he believes, would be to attempt to solve our problems and determine *in action* whether or not success is possible. This is the sense in which "intelligence" means "competent inquiry at work" (LW 15:41). Both Dewey's stance and Cohen's stance are ethically chosen. As we shall see shortly, Dewey believes that philosophy is essentially moral, asserting that at its best it demonstrates "a moral resolution to prize one mode of life more highly than another, and the wish to persuade other men that this [is] the wise way of living" (MW 11:44; cf. LW 8:25). To point this out is not to settle the question of the proper understanding of human nature, of course; but it does indicate how fundamental the choice is. The development of Dewey's instrumentalism, as well as the development of his theme of the social self will continue throughout the book. At some point, each reader will need to make a personal decision.

---

[77] Cf. Morris Cohen: "No sensitive spirit can fail to be stirred by Dewey's eloquent plea that we help our fellow men in the bitter struggle for a better world. But what should philosophy do about it? Must one who cannot swim jump into the whirlpool to save a drowning man?" ("Some Difficulties in Dewey's Anthropocentric Naturalism," 221 [reprinted in LW 14:403–4]).

CHAPTER 3

Experience, Nature, and the Role of Philosophy

A CONSIDERATION OF experience and nature in Dewey's work can best be undertaken through a series of topics that he explores most closely in *Experience and Nature* and *The Quest for Certainty*—the fruits of his Carus Lectures of 1922 and his Gifford Lectures of 1929 respectively. In these two studies that spanned his seventh decade, Dewey explores such topics as the problem of (natural) goods and evils, our strivings for security, and our attempts to ground our values in human experience. Beginning with the thick sense of experience found in James, Dewey discusses our movement into the future as a process in which we are both actors and undergoers. Our experience tunnels into nature and reveals nature to us on two levels. First, we have the normal, everyday, unproblematic, 'primary' experience; secondly, the theorizing, intellectualized, abstracted, 'secondary' experience that itself arises out of and must be evaluated in the light of normal experience. When nature itself is properly understood, we find ourselves just as intellectually troubled by the appearance of good as of evil: nature is precarious as well as stable. In such a world, we need to abandon the posture of supplication that we have traditionally found in the spectator philosophies of acceptance and to adopt the posture of inquiry found in the active philosophies of control. We need to develop a philosophy that would integrate our practical and our theoretical lives and would function as a tool of criticism or evaluation of our inherited culture. The role that Dewey thus sets for philosophy is to participate in the construction of a new society by turning from issues of merely historical import to focus upon contemporary human problems because, for Dewey, the social aspects of morality are never to be forgotten.

3.1.   The Metaphysics of Experience

The central source for Dewey's understanding of metaphysical inquiry is his monumental, although tremendously difficult, *Experience and Nature* of 1925 (revised edition, 1929).[1] Metaphysics, as he sees it, is an area of philosophical inquiry that attempts to carry out "a detection and description of the generic traits of existence" (LW 1:52; cf. 50, 308). This sense of the term 'metaphysics' is an unusual one, perhaps; and, to avoid confusion, Dewey later appears to be willing to surrender the term (cf. LW 16:387–89). His commitment to inquiry into the generic traits of existence, of course, remains undiminished. If we separate existence for the purpose of discussion into experience and nature, and if we delay our consideration of nature, we can begin with a consideration of the generic traits of experience.

Philosophical discussions of the nature of experience are many, and each requires of us some changes in our ways of thinking. Dewey recognizes that any attempt to reconstruct our understanding of such a well-worn term as 'experience' will be problematic[2]; and he himself appears to have decided eventually that this term was hopelessly entwined with undesirable connotations and abandoned attempts to rehabilitate it.[3] In the years since then, however, in part because of his work, we seem to have broken the hold of the narrow empirical interpretation of experience—rooted "in the English psychological tradition" (LW 3:76)—that Dewey was opposing, and we have

---

[1] Cf. Oliver Wendell Holmes, Jr.: "although Dewey's book is incredibly ill written, it seemed to me after several rereadings to have a feeling of intimacy with the inside of the cosmos that I found unequaled. So methought God would have spoken had He been inarticulate but keenly desirous to tell you how it was" (*Holmes-Pollock Letters*, vol. 2, 287; cf. vol. 2, 272; *Justice Oliver Wendell Holmes: His Book Notices and Uncollected Letters and Papers*, 189–94).

[2] Dewey tried such reconstruction with other concepts as well; and our ability to rescue terms from the encrustations of years of philosophical (ab)use will be a topic for discussion in 5.2 below.

[3] Dewey writes in 1951: "Were I to write (or rewrite) *Experience and Nature* today I would entitle the book *Culture and Nature* and the treatment of specific subject-matters would be correspondingly modified. I would abandon the term 'experience' because of my growing realization that the historical obstacles which prevented understanding of my use of 'experience' are, for all practical purposes, insurmountable. I would substitute the term 'culture' because with its meanings as now firmly established it can fully and freely carry my philosophy of experience" (LW 1:361; cf. 16:263).

moved toward an interpretation closer to his sense of experience as "the complex of all which is distinctively human" (LW 1:331). It would thus seem unnecessary and unadvisable to surrender the term at present, without at least an attempt to examine its contemporary value.

For Dewey, as for James, 'experience' is a "double-barrelled" word that can emphasize either the *process* or the *content* of the interaction of human organism and environment. Dewey writes:

> "experience" is what James called a double-barrelled word.[4] Like its congeners, life and history, it includes *what* men do and suffer, *what* they strive for, love, believe and endure, and also *how* men act and are acted upon, the ways in which they do and suffer, desire and enjoy, see, believe, imagine—in short, processes of *experiencing* (LW 1:18).

In his consideration of experience as both process and content, Dewey immediately rejects two views that fail to correctly incorporate the Darwinian themes considered in 2.1. On the one hand, Dewey makes it clear that his sense of experience is not the equivalent of knowledge. Experience, he writes, is "not primarily cognitive" (MW 9:147), especially when knowledge is identified "with the reception and association of sensory impressions" (MW 9:276). A more accurate analysis recognizes that "knowing is one mode of experiencing" (MW 3:159).[5] The denial of the identification of experience and knowledge, however, ought not to suggest a denial that thinking is an important aspect of much of experience. On the contrary, Dewey maintains that when experience is properly understood, we see that it "is full of inference. There is, apparently, no conscious experience without inference; reflection is native and constant" (MW 10:6).[6] Still, much of what is experienced is

---

[4] See James, *Essays in Radical Empiricism*, 7.

[5] Cf. EW 2:75, 192; LW 1:74–75; 3:79; 11:76–81.

[6] The apparent conflict between this statement that "reflection is native and constant" and Dewey's claim that we just saw in 2.5 that reflective thinking, or "thinking in its eulogistic sense," needs to be contrasted with large amounts of time "whiled away in this inconsequential trifling with mental pictures" can be eliminated if we remember the moral tone of his earlier emphasis upon using our rational abilities to solve problems and his more narrow philosophical emphasis here that opposes traditional empiricism's attempt to separate experiencing and thinking. For Dewey there are aspects of all experience that can form the basis of reflective thinking, if we are willing to put forth the effort.

confused or fleeting or episodic and does not attain the status of knowledge.

The second view of experience that Dewey sets aside immediately is the view that would understand experience as the equivalent of random encounter or transient passage, a view that would overemphasize humans' preconscious ancestry. Mere activity, activity that he describes as "dispersive, centrifugal, dissipating" (MW 9:146), does not qualify as experience for Dewey. Neither does he include "[d]isconnected doing" or "disconnected suffering" (MW 12:129; cf. LW 10:50–51). There is here neither process nor content of human interaction with the environment. As an example of what he intends, Dewey recurs to a theme we examined in 2.2 and offers an incident in which a boy is burned by sticking his finger into a flame. Such a case, he writes, would not necessarily constitute experience. "Being burned is a mere physical change, like the burning of a stick of wood, if it is not perceived as a consequence of some other action." A burning becomes an experience only "when the movement [into the flame] is connected with the pain which he undergoes in consequence" (MW 9:146). While we may dispute Dewey's choice of an example of a particular suffering that might have no recognized impact on the child, his point is less controversial: to be an experience, the interaction must be an interaction from which we learn something, although it need not give rise to knowledge.

Operating within this as yet vaguely delineated center between nonimpact and knowledge, the experiencer is a human organism living in a natural environment whose life includes both active and passive elements. "When we experience something we act upon it, we do something with it; then we suffer or undergo the consequences" (MW 9:146). Dewey sometimes stresses the *undergoing* aspect of experience (cf. MW 10:8–9) and sometimes the *doing* aspect (cf. MW 12:129); but in all cases his discussion includes the dual relationship of organism and environment. Experience, he writes, "is a matter of *simultaneous* doings and sufferings" (MW 10:9; cf. LW 10:50). In one of his most revealing formulations, he notes:

> Experiencing like breathing is a rhythm of intakings and outgivings
> . . . William James aptly compared the course of a conscious

experience to the alternate flights and perchings of a bird.[7] . . .
Each resting place in experience is an undergoing in which is
absorbed and taken home the consequences of prior doing, and,
unless the doing is that of utter caprice or sheer routine, each doing
carries in itself meaning that has been extracted and conserved (LW
10:62).

Besides considering the doing and undergoing of experience, this
passage also makes clear the forward-moving life of the experiencer.
True to his Pragmatic roots, as we saw in 2.5, Dewey maintains that
experience "is characterized by projection, by reaching forward into
the unknown; connexion with a future is its salient trait" (MW
10:6).[8] Experience is thus to be understood in the sense of the
cumulative process of interactions between a living organism and its
environment, a process that finds the organism undergoing change
and striving for control.

If there is a particular moment in the flow of experience that
Dewey considers to be worthy of special consideration, it is what he
calls "*an* experience." What makes such moments of special importance is first of all their internal integrity. "In such experiences, every
successive part flows freely, without seam and without unfilled
blanks, into what ensues," he writes; "there are no holes, mechanical
junctions, and dead centres when we have *an* experience" (LW
10:43).[9] The second significant aspect of these experiences is their
successful alignment with the rest of experience: "we have *an*
experience when the material experienced runs its course to fulfillment" and becomes "integrated within and demarcated in the
general stream of experience from other experiences" (LW 10:42).
As examples of some experiences that could qualify, Dewey offers the
following:

---

[7] Cf. James: "As we take, in fact, a general view of the wonderful stream of our
consciousness, what strikes us first is this different pace of its parts. Like a bird's life,
it seems to be made of an alternation of flights and perchings" (*The Principles of
Psychology,* vol. 1, 236).

[8] Cf. "Pragmatism, thus, presents itself as an extension of historical empiricism,
but with this fundamental difference, that it does not insist upon antecedent
phenomena but upon consequent phenomena; not upon the precedents but upon
the possibilities of action" (LW 2:12; cf. 4:227).

[9] Cf. LW 1:270; cf. 10:278.

> A piece of work is finished in a way that is satisfactory; a problem
> receives its solution; a game that is played through; a situation,
> whether that of eating a meal, playing a game of chess, carrying on a
> conversation, writing a book, or taking part in a political campaign,
> is so rounded out that its close is a consummation and not a
> cessation (LW 10:42).

The distinction between successful consummation and mere cessation introduces a third aspect of these experiences. Dewey suggests
that consummation is present in "those courses of action in which
through successive deeds there runs a sense of growing meaning
conserved and accumulating toward an end that is felt as accomplishment of a process" (LW 10:45).[10] This kind of meaning is a value
that becomes for Dewey a goal in such areas of experience as
education, working, and political life.

Continuing on in our examination of Dewey's understanding of
experience, we see that it is possible to distinguish within experience
two 'levels' that he calls "primary" experience and "secondary or
reflective" experience (LW 1:15–16). The contrast that he has in
mind is that "between gross, macroscopic, crude subject-matters in
primary experience and the refined, derived objects of reflection."
The distinction between primary and secondary experience, he
continues, "is one between what is experienced as the result of a
minimum of incidental reflection and what is experienced in consequence of continued and regulated reflective inquiry. For derived
and refined products are experienced only because of the intervention of systematic thinking" (LW 1:15). As examples of secondary
experience, Dewey offers the "objects of both science and philosophy," objects like theories, equations and intellecutal conventions.
Having made this fundamental distinction, he emphasizes that it is
not to be seen as an attempted bifurcation of experience. Rather, the
two levels to which he points should be united in the integrated
endeavor of understanding by means of which we are to not only
draw our material "from primary experience" but also to "refer it
back again for test" (LW 1:15).[11] Scientists, Dewey believes, confident in their integration of experience and nature, do this routinely

---

[10] Cf. Thomas M. Alexander, *John Dewey's Theory of Art, Experience and Nature,*
198–213.

[11] Cf. MW 2:299; LW 4:159.

and without questioning. They start their inquiries in everyday experience and return there for public testing and revision. Philosophers, on the other hand, often do not return to primary experience from their theorizing; sometimes they even reject the test of coarse experience as a relevant criterion, as when the promiscuous jumble of its 'apparent' complexity has been analyzed down to its constitutive simples.

The ordinary role of secondary experience is to clarify the meaning of primary experience: the objects we develop in secondary experience *"explain* the primary objects, they enable us to grasp them with *understanding,* instead of just having sense-contact with them" (LW 1:16; cf. 39). If we consider a few situations in which individuals lack understanding because they do not comprehend the meaning of events they are witnessing—"[t]he countryman in the crowded city street, the landlubber at sea, the ignoramus in sport at a contest between experts in a complicated game" (MW 6:275 = LW 8:229)[12]—we can get a hint of the nature of these explanations of primary experience. These objects of secondary experience offer us a means of uncovering "the meaning, the significant content, of what is experienced," Dewey writes.

> Directly, in immediate contact it may be just what it was before—hard, colored, odorous, etc. But when the secondary objects, the refined objects, are employed as a method or road for coming at them, these qualities cease to be isolated details; they get the meaning contained in a whole system of related objects; they are rendered continuous with the rest of nature and take on the import of the things they are now seen to be continuous with (LW 1:16).

It is in such a fashion that our understanding of the sonata form in music, or of a particular card game, or of the programming of a computer, develops. We begin with the things of "gross everyday experience." They are initially "fragmentary, casual, unregulated by purpose, full of frustrations and barriers" (LW 4:174). But, by slowly and carefully focussing upon one aspect after another, often in artificial isolation from the larger situation, we gain some sense of the operation of the whole. "By ignoring for a time their concrete and qualitative fullness, by making abstractions and generalizations," we

---

[12] See Geiger, *John Dewey in Perspective,* 42–43.

learn about the things of ordinary experience and we can then "return from abstractive thought to experience of them with added meaning and with increased power to regulate our relations to them" (LW 4:174–75).

The relationship between primary and secondary experience is not a simple one-way relationship, however. Not only do the objects of secondary experience explain the objects of primary experience, but the objects of primary experience work as a test on the theorizing that has occurred. If we forget the importance of attaching "the vine of pendant theory . . . at both ends to the pillars of observed subject-matter" (LW 1:11), we will find our inquiries failing. The most common kind of failing is a kind of hyper-intellectualism that equates the 'real' with the idealized or the known, and consigns the merely experienced to an epistemological limbo. As Dewey writes, "the standing temptation of philosophy, as its course abundantly demonstrates, is to regard the results of reflection as having, in and of themselves, a reality superior to that of the material of any other mode of experience" (LW 1:26). His continued emphasis is on the need to return from the calm distillation of reflective experience to the rushing fullness of primary experience.

Perhaps a more familiar way to phrase this distinction between primary and secondary experience—but one that can introduce many unnecessary troubles against which we must remain on guard—would be to suggest that the clouded interactions of primary experience and the clearer graspings of secondary experience are distinguishable as cases respectively, of the lack of, and of the presence of, knowledge. Both are instances of experience, Dewey writes.

> Both kinds are *had;* they are undergone, enjoyed or suffered. The first are not known; they are not understood; they are dispensations of fortune or providence. The second have, as they are experienced, meanings that present the funded outcome of operations that substitute definite continuity for experienced discontinuity and for the fragmentary quality due to isolation (LW 4:194).

In the process of inquiry, we attempt to resolve felt problems that are present in experience. The tentative knowledge gained in this process of inquiry is then tested through a return to the problematic situation. When inquiry is carried on to fruition, primary and secondary experience become integrated, and we understand by means of this knowledge the meanings of the various aspects of the situation. "In knowledge," Dewey writes, "causes become means and effects become consequences, and thereby things have meanings" (LW 4:236).

One final point is to consider whether Dewey intends this distinction between primary and secondary experience to be an absolute or a relative distinction. He writes at one point in apparent support of the latter alternative, suggesting that there is "a general line of cleavage that decides upon the whole what things fall within, and what fall without, the limits of familiar acquaintance. This line accordingly marks off the concrete and the abstract in a fairly permanent way. *The limits are fixed mainly by the demands of practical life.*" As examples of familiar objects that would be relegated here to primary experience, Dewey points to "[t]hings such as sticks and stones, meat and potatoes, houses and trees . . . constant features of the environment of which we have to take account in order to live" (LW 8:294). We recall, however, that even these familiar objects were once experienced without familiarity or understanding. Moreover, in the same paragraph that he allows for a "fairly permanent" separation between primary and secondary experience, Dewey indicates that the distinction is "purely relative to the intellectual progress of an individual; what is abstract at one period of growth is concrete at another" (LW 8:295; cf. MW 6:287). It is thus sensible to see the primary/secondary distinction within experience to be a relative distinction, of special importance in educational or pedagogic contexts. The teacher's task, Dewey writes, is to begin with "materials which at the outset fall within the scope of ordinary life-experience" of the students. The next step is to bring about "the progressive development of what is already experienced into a fuller and richer and also more organized form, a form that gradually approximates that in which subject-matter is presented to the skilled, mature person" (LW 13:48). The teacher's goal here, at whatever level of instruction, is to move the student from the initial situation of merely having an experience to being able to understand what the situation means. "The world as we experience it is a real world. But it is not in its primary phases a world that is known, a world that is understood, and is intellectually coherent and secure" (LW 4:235). Such a world is a goal, not a given.

3.2. Experience and Nature

I would like to turn now to the theme of the relationship between experience and nature. While Dewey admits that the attempt to discuss the two together seems to some like discussing "a round square," since the notion of their separation is so fundamentally engrained in familiar thinking (LW 1:10), he believes that understanding their relationship properly is vital to understanding either one of them fully. A good deal of philosophical inquiry misses the important point of the close interaction of experience and nature. He maintains that his contemporary science, especially natural science, on the other hand, in spite of all its other failures, does not overlook this interaction.[13] Philosophy needs to develop such a unifying approach and overcome what has been, in the course of the history of philosophy, a stream of mistaken formulations.

One general tendency has been for philosophers to overemphasize the nature side of the relationship to the denigration of the experience side. Dewey writes:

> Experience, they say, is important for those beings who have it, but is too casual and sporadic in its occurrence to carry with it any important implications regarding the nature of Nature. Nature, on the other hand, is said to be complete apart from experience. Indeed, according to some thinkers the case is even in worse plight: Experience to them is not only something extraneous which is occasionally superimposed upon nature, but it forms a veil or screen which shuts us off from nature, unless in some way it can be "transcended" (LW 1:10).

The most prominent difficulty that results from this understanding of the relationship of experience and nature is that, with the divorce of humans and nature, experience is declared to be something "non-natural" or "supra-empirical" (LW 1:10). Dewey rejects this denigration of experience and the claims of its isolation from nature, asserting that experience is not "a veil that shuts man off from nature; it is a means of penetrating continually further into the heart of nature" (LW 1:5). Experience "reaches down into," it "tunnels" into, nature (LW 1:13, 11; cf. 3:76). He continues: "experience is *of*

---

[13] Cf. LW 1:11, 14–15.

as well as *in* nature. It is not experience which is experienced, but nature—stones, plants, animals, diseases, health, temperature, electricity, and so on" (LW 1:12). This conception of the role of experience within nature means that "human affairs, associative and personal, are projections, continuations, complications of the nature which exists in the physical and prehuman world," Dewey writes. "There is no gulf, no two spheres of existence, no 'bifurcation'" (LW 3:74). All is part of one larger and integrated system.

Dewey thus rejects the position that nature is somehow 'superior to' or 'better than' our mere human experience and that we are only guests or trespassers in nature, intruders who should adopt as our stance "a kneeling, before the unknowable and an adjuration of all that is human" (LW 3:74).[14] He rejects as well the other extreme position that we, as self-conscious humans, are 'above' or 'better than' mere nature. He writes: "According to an opposite school experience fares as badly, nature being thought to signify something wholly material and mechanistic; to frame a theory of experience in naturalistic terms is, accordingly, to degrade and deny the noble and ideal values that characterize experience" (LW 1:10). Instead of this 'noble' and 'ideal' understanding of experience, we need to consider the rootedness of human experience in our natural situation—a rootedness that applies to all aspects of human experience. "If experience actually presents esthetic and moral traits," he writes, "then these traits may also be supposed to reach down into nature" (LW 1:13). It does not diminish the importance of experience to recognize its natural rootedness any more that it denigrates, or at least any more than it should denigrate, humans to see them as emergent creatures.[15] For Dewey, neither experience nor nature is primary in itself, and neither can be understood fully without the other.

Experience is "the manifestation of interactions of organism and

---

[14] In a note on LW 3:74, Dewey cites Santayana's comment on the need for falling "in love with the greatness of nature" and sinking "speechless before the infinite" (Santayana, "Dewey's Naturalistic Metaphysics," 679 [reprinted in LW 3:374]).

[15] Cf. H. S. Thayer: "Experience is located in [the] reticulate and interacting movement of events; experiencing animals are thereby able to awaken what powers of reason they may have from the slumber of non-being. . . . If the roots and tendrils of reason are lodged in the restless seed-ground of experience and nature, its flowering is in human inquiry" (*The Logic of Pragmatism,* 32).

environment," Dewey writes (LW 14:16); and when we say that a human being *exists* or *lives* or *is* in the natural world, the meaning of the pivotal term 'in' is of extreme importance. Dewey's suggested sense is "not as marbles are in a box" or as "pennies are 'in' a pocket or paint is 'in' a can" (LW 1:224; 13:25). Such a sense would be adequate for a thing, perhaps, but not for a live creature. The sense of 'in' that is necessary for such a creature, he continues, is a sense of 'in' that could satisfy a usage like: "a plant is in the sunlight and soil" (MW 14:204). The sense of 'in' implies more than simple location. It implies a transactional place where only "by analysis and selective abstraction" (LW 5:220) can the organism and environment be distinguished.[16] "An organism does not live *in* an environment; it lives by means of an environment," he continues. When we say that "a fish lives *in* the water and a bird *in* the air," we mean that "the characteristic functions of these animals are what they are because of the special way in which water and air enter into their respective activities" (LW 12:32; cf. 10:19–20). Terms like 'environment' and 'medium' thus denote, for Dewey, more than just the external encompassment of an individual. They point to "the specific *continuity* of the surroundings with his own active tendencies" (MW 9:15).[17] This continuity involves a process of phases in which, as we have seen, the organism loses and then recovers its integration with the environment. There is an ever-present danger here, of course. "If the gap between organism and environment is too wide, the creature dies." But for Dewey, in this process of slippage and recovery lies the possibility of growth: "Life grows when a temporary falling out is a transition to a more extensive balance of the energies of the organism with those of the conditions under which it lives" (LW 10:19–20).

With this consideration of the experiencing creatures still in mind, we can turn now to an explicit consideration of the topic of nature. We do not find in Dewey a celebration of nature, "an esthetic enjoyment of the properties of nature regarded as a work of divine art" (LW 4:81), as is often present in Emerson or Thoreau or John Muir. For Dewey, nature is not to be seen as a healing rhapsody of

---

[16] For Dewey's further development of the concept of 'transaction', in part with Arthur F. Bentley, see: LW 1:155–56; 13:25; 14:118; 16:3–4, 66–68, 71, 96–130, 242–44, 272, 472–73. See also Dewey and Bentley, *A Philosophical Correspondence, 1932–1951;* Thayer, *The Logic of Pragmatism,* 26–31.

[17] Cf. MW 6:437–40; LW 16:244.

fields and forests and lakes and mountains that nourishes our souls and liberates our spirits. While recognizing the "congruity of nature with man" that makes human life possible, he is quite cognizant at the same time of the "indifference and hostility of nature to human interests" (LW 10:190; cf. 34). Nature is for Dewey the totality of existence that both *supports* and *frustrates* us as embodied creatures, that both allows for melioristic transactions and imposes limitations on what is possible. As he writes, "to exist is to be in process, in change" (LW 5:271). We live in a changing world, in a world where process is ceaseless. "We constantly talk about things coming or drawing to a close; getting ended, finished, done with, over with. It is commonplace that no *thing* lasts forever. . . . nature is an affair *of* affairs" (LW 1:82–83). Some of these affairs benefit humans, others do not; some lead to the life of an individual, others to that individual's death.

The problem of human suffering in the course of natural processes, the problem of natural evil, is a problem of importance for all humans, not only for those who have endured an earthquake or buried a child. Dewey chooses to begin his consideration of natural evil, however, with an indication that he sees natural goods to be equally problematic. He begins this way because he believe that, in spite of the facts that nature is "an indefinite congeries of changes" (MW 4:47) and that in a Darwinian world both evils and goods come without reason, we do not often treat them equally. We choose to see goods as more appropriate elements of our world. "Goods we take for granted," he writes; "they are as they should be; they are natural and proper" (LW 1:45).[18] In what is certainly a deliberately dual usage, Dewey writes: "man finds it natural that nature should support his activities, and unnatural that the burden of continued and hard endeavor should be placed upon him" (LW 1:100). To attempt to uncover the origins of this understanding of nature, Dewey takes a closer look at the actions of humankind over the centuries of our existence. He believes that philosophical inquiry and what might be described more accurately as anthropological inquiry can complement each other in this endeavor. His reasoning here is that, in an examination of cultures where the attempts of people "to formulate the things of experience to which they are most deeply and

---

[18] Cf. MW 14:174; LW 6:18–19.

passionately attached" (MW 12:94) had not yet diverged into religion, history, art, and philosophy, our attempts at understanding must be equally broad. Dewey intends these anthropological speculations not as an invidious commentary on the beliefs and actions of those who lived simpler, less technologically-advanced lives. His intention is rather to offer this examination as a criticism, rooted in history, of contemporary analyses of nature.

Nature as these earlier humans understood it, perhaps more clearly than we often do, was both *precarious and changing* and *stable and secure*. "Man finds himself living in an aleatory world," Dewey writes; "his existence involves, to put it baldly, a gamble." He continues:

> The world is a scene of risk; it is uncertain, unstable, uncannily unstable. Its dangers are irregular, inconstant, not to be counted upon as to their times and seasons. Although persistent, they are sporadic, episodic. . . . Plague, famine, failure of crops, disease, death, defeat in battle, are always just around the corner, and so are abundance, strength, victory, festival and song (LW 1:43).[19]

Living in this fearful and awful world, our distant ancestors found themselves without the various means of protection that we have inherited from their descendants or fashioned for ourselves. Facing a world that offered a "peculiar intermixture of support and frustration" (LW 1:314), that demonstrated "no preference for good things over bad things" (LW 1:93), our ancestors created intellectual solutions: they "snatched at whatever, by any stretch of imagination, could be regarded as a source of help in time of trouble" (LW 4:8–9). They convinced themselves that the system of nature must make sense in terms of human weal, and set out to uncover what that sense was. Dewey writes: "The attention, interest and care which now go to acquiring skill in the use of appliances and to the invention of means for better service of ends, were devoted to noting omens, making irrelevant prognostications, performing ritualistic ceremonies and manipulating objects possessed of magical power over natural events" (LW 4:9). People separated the processes of existence into the mysterious and the mundane on the basis of their

---

[19] Cf. MW 8:139; 10:16; LW 4:194; 9:17–19; 14:98–99.

degree of direct control. Based upon this criterion, the mysterious processes of birth and death, of famine and plenty, "testified to the presence and operation of powers beyond the scope of everyday and mundane things" (LW 4:11) and implied a realm superior to the natural.

Whether or not Dewey's anthropological presentation is now seen as being too speculative, there do seem to be two fundamentally different modes of response to nature available to people, then and now. One of these modes of response is attempted control through art or technology. This mode was initially limited and crude, of course; but, because it contains procedures for self-correction—in the sense of ongoing improvement, not eventual perfection— through inventive interactions with the processes of nature, this 'scientific' mode has grown more sophisticated.[20] The second mode is the respose generally associated with mystery or religion: resorting to some form of supplication or magic. This latter mode, given the modest level of technological achievement in many cultures, was often seen as the 'proper' one. As Dewey writes, in some cultural settings human actions amount to "trespasses upon the domain of the unknown; and hence atonement, if offered in season, may ward off direful consequences that haunt even the moment of prosperity." Individuals in such settings recognize that they cannot sustain their own natural well-being, and they consider any individual "who will not gratefully acknowledge by means of free-will offerings the help that sustains him" to be "a dangerous churl" (LW 1:44; cf. 9:17). While this mode of response may be appropriate under such circumstances, it is not appropriate under all: because it condemns inquiry and invention, it precludes attempts at material change. Moreover, Dewey continues, it is a sad commentary on how little confidence even we have developed in "the method of changing the world through action" that our attempts at controlling natural processes, however modest and realistic, can still be seen to be arrogance or hubris, as manifestations of "dangerous pride, even defiance of the powers which be" (LW 4:3).

An alternate response to our human situation, one that while no less inadequate is perhaps more familiar to us at present, is to go to the opposite extreme and to claim that we are now in full control of

---

[20] This theme of the self-correctability of science will return in 4.1.

goods and evils, or that we are nearly in control, or at least that we soon will be. This claim of (imminent) mastery over nature we should all recognize to be both false and dangerous. It is a false claim, Dewey writes, even though he admits that "[t]hrough science we have secured a degree of power of prediction and of control; through tools, machinery and an accompanying technique we have made the world more comfortable to our needs, a more secure abode." The claim of mastery is false because "when all is said and done, the fundamentally hazardous character of the world is not seriously modified, much less eliminated" (LW 1:45). As an ultimate indication of this reality, Dewey reminds us that a living world must include death, since "[q]ualities have defects as necessary conditions of their excellencies" (LW 1:47). Such a comment on the power and pervasiveness of natural evil by the decidedly nonoptimistic Dewey indicates both his sense of the limits of our control and his recognition that these evils are indeed evil.[21] Secondly, the claims of imminent mastery over nature are dangerous because they can lead us to carelessness and inaction in a world that is increasingly crowded and hungry, polluted and warming, and depleted in resources and options. We need to adopt in the place of these two extreme stances a balanced stance, one that fosters neither surrender nor arrogance. This new stance would see both natural goods and natural evils as problematic and offer thereby a richer understanding of nature.

3.3. Psychological Certainty or Material Security

If we move from this broad anthropological understanding of the human situation to a more narrow consideration of how this situation has been filtered through the history of philosophy, we find in Dewey's discussion the belief that this history contains a series of philosophies of acceptance, "[p]hilosophies of escape . . . philosophies of compensation for the ills and sufferings of the experienced world" (LW 5:268). These philosophies, because they are *intellectual* endeavors, do not busy themselves with the omens and rituals of religious practice. Their focus is rather on finding some

---

[21] The nature and the importance of Dewey's meliorism is examined in 6.4.

aspect of our natural situation that could serve as an intellectual basis of acceptance. This is why he cautions us against "the transformation effected by philosophers of the traits they find good (simplicity, certainty, nobility, permanence, etc.) into fixed traits of real Being" (LW 1:33). While recognizing the inevitability of such selectivity in living, Dewey reminds us to recognize it for what it is. "Deception comes," he writes, "only when the presence and operation of choice is concealed, disguised, denied" (LW 1:34), or, in terms of our consideration in 3.1, for whatever reason our theorizing in secondary experience is not returned to primary experience.

Dewey maintains that philosophy historically has been engaged in "the quest for a certainty which shall be absolute and unshakeable" (LW 4:5). *The Quest for Certainty,* the second volume of particular importance in this chapter, demonstrates the fact that this certainty cannot be found in the realm of practical activity where all action involves "peril, the risk of misadventure, frustration and failure" (LW 4:17). Because practical action "deals with individualized and unique situations which are never exactly duplicable," he continues, "no complete assurance is possible" (LW 4:6). Our chance of attaining certainty is completely different if we move to the realm of ideas. He writes: "The intellect, however, according to the traditional doctrine, may grasp universal Being, and Being which is universal is fixed and immutable. . . . Man's distrust of himself has caused him to desire to get beyond and above himself; in pure knowledge he has thought he could attain this self-transcendence" (LW 4:6; cf. 17). As a result, a fundamental intellectual bifurcation developed, one that remained a powerful element in philosophical thinking in the West to his day. Dewey opposes this bifurcation with the conviction that material security attained by control of natural conditions is of far more value than psychological certainty.

Dewey offers the genetic criticism that classical Greek society, with its social classes and its denigration of physical labor, was predisposed to this type of bifurcation.[22] Later philosophers, with or without a clear recognition of the origins of this separation, continued to build upon the work of the Greeks in their attempts to

---

[22] Cf. Dewey: "The genetic standpoint makes us aware that the systems of the past are neither fraudulent impostures nor absolute revelations; but are the products of political, economic and scientific conditions whose change carries with it change of theoretical formulation" (MW 4:44; cf. 5:8–10; 12:93).

construct a rational explanation for existence that eliminated doubt and disorder. By teasing out philosophic strands from those of art and religion, the historical course of philosophy developed the inherited frameworks to a much higher level of intellectual sophistication. Philosophers took the emotional and mystical formulations of the Greek quest for certainty and gave them a new logical purity grounded in its intellectual pursuit of purer objects of knowledge. They were then able to construct, Dewey maintains, a purer reality out of their perilous and fearful world. The rejected world then became 'appearance'. He writes: " 'reality' becomes what we wish experience to be, after we have analyzed its defects and decided upon what would remove them; 'reality' is what existence would be if our reasonably justified preferences were so completely established in nature as to exhaust and define its entire being and thereby render search and struggle unnecessary" (LW 1:51).[23] This simplified and purified reality would explain away experienced evils and yield a sense of calm based upon the certain knowledge of the true character of existence. "The quest for certainty," Dewey writes, "is a quest for a peace which is assured, an object which is unqualified by risk and the shadow of fear which action casts" (LW 4:7).

A key requirement for attaining such certainty was the development of philosophical positions that denied the "precarious, uncertain nature of existence" and offered in its place a selective emphasis upon the stable in its various forms. He writes:

> If classic philosophy says so much about unity and so little about unreconciled diversity, so much about the eternal and permanent, and so little about change . . . so much about necessity and so little about contingency, so much about the comprehending universal and so little about the recalcitrant particular, it may well be because the ambiguousness and ambivalence of reality are actually so pervasive.

Dewey suggests that the core of our philosophical tradition can then be seen to consist of different attempts at "supplying recipes for denying to the universe the character of contingency which it possesses," attempts that differ only because of accidental factors of

---

[23] Cf. MW 12:140; LW 4:11–12.

"temperament, interest and local surroundings" (LW 1:46).[24] This tradition of denying contingency remains significant in philosophy in no small degree because we still find the craving for certainty powerful. In particular, although we have advanced a long way toward a beneficial cooperation with nature, the contingent and partial character of this advance does not offer complete satisfaction to those who want certain answers to the questions of the meaning of life and who are willing to pay for this certainty even the cost of having life treated "as a preparation for something outside of it and after it" (LW 5:268).

We have inherited, Dewey writes, as part of the legacy of this quest for certainty, two different and frequently conflicting sources of guidance for living our lives. On the one hand, we have information about how to perform what are seen as the proper tasks of living, information that comes from collective human experience and that is often interpreted through the more-or-less scientific expertise of physicians, engineers, historians, plumbers, farmers, and others. On the other hand, we have information about what the proper tasks of living are, information that comes only from such sources as religious codes and patriotic traditions. For Dewey, the conflict results from the traditional assumption that, while what he calls philosophies of control may suggest *means,* only what he calls philosophies of acceptance may suggest *ends.* Such ends, if they are to be immutable and therefore justifiable, must remain cordoned off from facts. In response to our fearful world of danger and change, we create a realm of permanence and certain knowledge; and, to guarantee the correctness of the values that shape our lives, we place values within the latter realm. Once these eternal values are safely in place as *ends,* we can surrender the contingent physical world "to matter and mechanism" (LW 4:33) without endangering anything of lasting importance. The result is the bifurcation of existence into a contingent realm where empirical science has a say in the choice of

---

[24] Cf. Ralph W. Sleeper: "The traditional task of metaphysics had been to provide a cosmic context in which the vicissitudes of everyday existence could be seen in the broader perspective of a stable order of ultimate reality and truth, in which the precariousness of ordinary life could be mitigated by reference to a more secure order than is immediately apparent in the foreground of experience. . . . the role of metaphysics had been to disclose an order of reality hidden from ordinary experience" (*The Necessity of Pragmatism,* 110).

means and an unchanging realm of ends where science is irrelevant. Dewey believes, as we shall see in 4.3, that this split between values and facts could exist without causing severe intellectual problems in society only as long as traditional ends were clearly dominant; but, when they themselves came into question, the need for grounding value choices in terms of human goods would be necessary.

Until this had happened, however, people were able to accept an "incompatibility between the conclusions of natural science about the world in which we live and the realm of higher values, of ideal and spiritual qualities, which get no support from natural science," Dewey writes (LW 4:33). We accepted this split because of the power of traditional values and our strong craving for certainty. We accepted this split even at the cost of rendering the practical realm, the realm of empirical science, devoid of fundamental meaning or lasting value. Dewey writes:

> Instead of being extended to cover all forms of action by means of which all the values of life are extended and rendered more secure, including the diffusion of the fine arts and the cultivation of taste, the processes of education and all activities which are concerned with rendering human relationships more significant and worthy, the meaning of "practical" is limited to matters of ease, comfort, riches, bodily security and police order, possibly health, etc., things which in their isolation from other goods can only lay claim to restricted and narrow value. In consequence, these subjects are handed over to technical sciences and arts (LW 4:25–26).

As matters for such practical techniques, these matters are concerns for "a world of low grade reality" (LW 4:28). Philosophy, on the other hand, is concerned with the eternal questions of values and ends.

The split between means and ends, between facts and values, was tolerable at one time. It might even have been an aspect valuable for mental well-being when our means of control of nature were more primitive. But this is true no longer. Now we should be pursuing security rather than certainty. "The thing which concerns all of us as human beings," Dewey writes, "is precisely the greatest attainable security of values in concrete existence." He continues:

> The thought that the values which are unstable and wavering in the world in which we live are eternally secure in a higher realm . . .

may give consolation to the depressed. But it does not change the existential situation in the least. The separation that has been instituted between theory and practice, with its consequent substitution of cognitive quest for absolute assurance for practical endeavor to make the existence of good more secure in experience, has had the effect of distracting attention and diverting energy from a task whose performance would yield definite results (LW 4:28–29).

The quest for certainty, he continues, has led us away from effective action: "The depreciation of action, of doing and making, has been cultivated by philosophers" (LW 4:4). We can, however, do something about this split. We are able to address it in part because we recognize that the problem is cultural rather than cosmic or non-natural. The philosophies of acceptance are human creations. We are thus responsible for continuing the selective emphasis upon the permanent and the certain, and for the consequence that the changing and the uncertain remain always just beyond our focus. But, we are also able to overcome this split because we are now more able to supplant the hunger for certainty with the desire for solutions and control. We now have the means to recognize and defend as values such goods as human growth and increasing self-consciousness, goods that promote "a respect for concrete human experience and its potentialities" (LW 1:41). In this process, we will make use of the advances made possible by the scientific approach.

3.4. The Role of Philosophy

As would seem appropriate to the perspective that has thus far developed, Dewey offers a broad cultural understanding of philosophy. Rather than seeing philosophies as narrow and academic endeavors, of interest to the erudite few, he writes that they are "significant cultural phenomena and demand treatment from that point of view" (LW 8:29). The evaluation of a philosophy is thus to be carried out in public rather than in internal or academic categories. He suggests the following as

a first-rate test of the value of any philosophy which is offered us: Does it end in conclusions which, when they are referred back to ordinary life-experiences and their predicaments, render them more significant, more luminous to us, and make our dealings with them more fruitful? Or does it terminate in rendering the things of ordinary experience more opaque than they were before, and in depriving them of having in "reality" even the significance they had previously seemed to have? (LW 1:18).[25]

Seen as being of interest to the broader public, "philosophy, like politics, literature, and the plastic arts, is itself a phenomenon of human culture," he continues. "Its connection with social history, with civilization, is intrinsic" (LW 3:3).[26] The connection that he sees existing between philosophy and culture is that philosophical inquiry attempts to address questions of fundamental cultural concern.

"From one point of view," Dewey writes, "the chief role of philosophy is to bring to consciousness, in an intellectualized form, or in the form of problems, the most important shocks and inherent troubles of complex and changing societies since these have to do with conflicts of value" (LW 8:30). Sometimes he emphasizes the natural grounding of philosophical inquiry, as when he writes that "it is the intricate mixture of the stable and the precarious, the fixed and the unpredictably novel, the assured and the uncertain, in existence which sets mankind upon that love of wisdom which forms philosophy" (LW 1:55). At other times his emphasis is on the social grounding of philosophical inquiry: "philosophical problems arise because of widespread and widely felt difficulties in social practice" (MW 9:338). But, in either case, philosophical inquirers, at their best, are attempting to address the fundamental questions of culture's response to problems. Because of this basic relationship between philosophy and culture, Dewey maintains that philosophical activity is "particularly active in periods of marked social change," at least when the individuals undergoing change have been afforded educations that free their minds "to undertake the task of abstraction and generalization" (LW 8:30).[27]

Initially, Western philosophy came into existence, Dewey maintains, "as an attempt to find an intelligent substitute for blind custom and blind impulse as guides to life and conduct" (MW 12:152).

---

[25] Cf. MW 3:188; LW 1:17, 391.
[26] Cf. LW 3:115; 5:162–63; 6:17–18.
[27] Cf. EW 1:34; MW 2:314; 3:73; 9:333; LW 1:61; 6:19.

Greek culture found itself with a crumbling system of belief and value, torn between outmoded conventions and unjustifiable innovations; and it enlisted the intellectual prestige of philosophy to buttress the old ways, to resecure the road to certainty. In this context, he writes, the new philosophical inquiry "had a mission to perform": "It had to extract the essential moral kernel out of the threatened traditional beliefs of the past," and it was to do so "in a spirit congenial to the spirit of past beliefs." A second bias of developing philosophical inquiry was that its intellectual eminence became a practical drawback as the idolization of logic grew. "Since it aimed at a rational justification of things that had been previously accepted because of their emotional congeniality and social prestige, it had to make much of the apparatus of reason and proof," Dewey writes; "it leaned over backward, so to speak, in parade of logical form." A third bias that philosophy carried from its origins was that it saw its task as attempting to replace the "pervasive and comprehensive" poetic systems of the ancients with equally grand speculative systems. "It was then probably inevitable," he writes, "that the rival principle, reflective thought, should aim at a similar universality and comprehensiveness" (MW 12:89–92; cf. LW 4:11–14). In all three of these areas—philosophy's acceptance of traditional values, its overemphasis upon logical formalism, and its fascination with exhaustiveness—historical philosophy shows the biases of its origins; but, Dewey maintains, in all three areas reconstruction in current philosophy was possible.

It is thus important to recognize that, while Dewey's discussion is often historical, his opponents are not the ancients but rather his contemporaries. As he writes, "the adverse criticisms of philosophies of the past are not directed at these systems with respect to their connection with intellectual and moral issues of their own time and place, but with respect to their relevancy in a much changed human situation" (MW 12:257; cf. LW 16:382). The question that he wants to keep ever before our minds is a question of the proper role for the life of the mind: what role should philosophy play in our contemporary society? Should it continue its inherited role as an explanatory system, a means of better understanding and more easily accepting existence? Or, should we attempt to cultivate a philosophy that would foster a more active stance, one that aimed not at just understanding our situation but at responsible control? Because the focus of the former group of philosophies is acceptance rather than control, they can live with—and perhaps even require—"a spectator theory of knowledge" (LW 4:19).[28] This is Dewey's name for an approach to knowing that maintains that "the office of knowledge is to uncover the antecedently real, rather than, as is the case with our practical judgments, to gain the kind of understanding which is necessary to deal with problems as they arise" (LW 4:14). Using this "spectator" approach, the aim of knowing is to display antecedent reality, preferably an antecedent reality that offers Truth(s) of a necessary sort that can be grasped with certainty and 'proven' through the workings of logical machinery. Such an understanding of knowledge severs it from the class of mere beliefs that lack such demonstrable necessity. Belief understood in this way, Dewey writes, "is only opinion; in its uncertainty and mere probability, it relates to the world of change as knowledge corresponds to the realm of true reality" (LW 4:15). From the point of view of this understanding of knowledge, belief is an instance of failure. "We *believe* in the absence of knowledge or complete assurance," Dewey writes, "the quest for certainty has always been an effort to transcend belief" (LW 4:21).

For Dewey, on the other hand, the cultural role of the intellect is to attempt some sort of rational control. In his analysis, knowing is continuous with belief; and, far from being a spectator matter, knowing is the result of inquiry. The struggle to gain what he calls "warranted assertability" (LW 12:15) starts, as we have seen in 2.4, with the arising of a particular problem:

> reflective thinking transforms confusion, ambiguity and discrepancy into illumination, definiteness and consistency. But it also points to the contextual situation in which thinking occurs. It notes that the starting point is the actually *problematic,* and that the problematic phase resides in some actual and specifiable situation. . . . thinking is a continuous process of temporal re-organization within one and the same world of experienced things, not a jump from the latter world into one of objects constituted once for all by thought (LW 1:61; cf. 12:15–17).

This transforming aspect of knowing is emphasized in Dewey's reminder that the solution is the solution to a problem and can only be fully understood as the culmination of the process of inquiry. That is, although "it is the intricate mixture of the stable and the

---

[28] Cf. MW 2:306; 9:131; 12:150; LW 4:195.

precarious" that gives rise to philosophical inquiry, too often "the result of the search is converted into a metaphysics which denies or conceals from acknowledgement the very characters of existence which initiated it, and which give significance to its conclusions." Thus, instead of a recognition of the intermixture of the settled and the novel, we too often have found in the history of philosophy the bifurcation of existence, "that striking division into a superior true realm of being and [a] lower illusory, insignificant or phenomenal realm" (LW 1:55). This sort of bifurcation may be quite acceptable if our goal is constructing a philosophy of acceptance; but it is not if our goal is a philosophy of control.

Rejecting the historical philosophies of acceptance in which the good found in natural existence is transformed into "a refuge, an asylum for contemplation, or a theme for dialectical elaboration," Dewey calls for a philosophy that uses the found good as "an ideal to inspire and guide conduct" (LW 1:51). He writes that "the task of future philosophy is to clarify men's ideas as to the social and moral strifes of their own day" (MW 12:94).[29] Elsewhere he continues: "Unless philosophies are to be Edens of compensatory refuge, reached through an exercise of dialectical ingenuity, they must face the situation which is there. It is their business to bring intellectual order out of the confusion of beliefs" (LW 3:127–28; cf. 14:89). And, while this may seem to some a risky task for philosophy to undertake, fraught with the potential for misunderstandings and failures, Dewey believes that to continue in our current fashion would be worse. "Better it is for philosophy to err in active participation in the living struggles and issues of its own age and times," he writes, "than to maintain an immune monastic impeccability, without relevancy and bearing in the generating ideas of its contemporary present" (MW 4:142).

Dewey is at times vehement in his condemnations of what he sees as intellectual waste. He laments, for example, the diversion of intelligence "from the critical consideration of the natural sources and social consequences of better and worse into the channel of metaphysical subtleties and systems" (MW 4:36; cf. LW 13:274). At other times, he is strident in his rejection of merely academic criteria of philosophical success: "If philosophy declines to observe and interpret the new and characteristic scene, it may achieve scholarship;

---

[29] Cf. MW 10:47; 12:260, 266, 273–77; LW 3:115–16.

it may erect a well equipped gymnasium wherein to engage in dialectical exercises; it may clothe itself in fine literary art. But it will not afford illumination or direction to our confused civilization" (LW 3:131–32). When philosophical activity becomes a reflection upon the history of philosophy, he continues, instead of being a reflection "upon experience saturated with the colors of the social life in which it originated," it ceases to be philosophy and becomes "academic scholarship" (LW 5:163).[30] Our goals as philosophers should always be, not "a study of philosophy," but rather "a study, by means of philosophy, of life-experience" (LW 1:40). Dewey does not maintain, of course, that philosophical scholarship is an endeavor completely without value. It is just a *relatively* less important endeavor for those who hold a conception of philosophy that connects it with the broader life of the society. Philosophy for philosophers is, to Dewey's mind, a mistake: "philosophy recovers itself when it ceases to be a device for dealing with the problems of philosophers and becomes a method, cultivated by philosophers, for dealing with the problems of men" (MW 10:46).[31]

Adopting such an attitude toward inherited philosophies, and toward the ongoing task of philosophic inquiry, will not be without cost. In his moral call for a socially engaged philosophy, Dewey is neither deaf to the "music of ideas" nor anesthetized to the "emotional satisfaction from an imaginative play synthesis of ideas" (LW 8:38). He recognizes that some aspect of "spiritual impoverishment" will take place in our lives from the "neglect of the traditions of the past"; but, in the place of these potential goods, he offers others. "The future as well as the past can be a source of interest and consolation and give meaning to the present," he writes. If we can come to see ourselves as operating on the pivot of past and future—"the world is re-commencing and being re-made under our eyes" (LW 2:20)—and if we can gain confidence in our philosophi-

---

[30] Dewey writes that philosophy is itself "unusually conservative" and that its association "with academic teaching has reinforced this intrinsic conservatism" (MW 10:3).

[31] Cf. Arthur E. Murphy's paraphrase: "a philosophy worth having must justify itself not merely controversially and dialectically, in its quarrel with opposing doctrines, but in its capacity to clarify fundamental issues, to enable men to understand the meaning of what they are doing and of the primary choices that confront them, and thus to raise experience to the level of philosophic wisdom" ("Dewey's Theory of the Nature and Function of Philosophy," 33).

cal efforts to guide the future toward human betterment, then philosophy will be willing to pay the cost. "Nothing but the best, the richest and fullest experience possible, is good enough for man," Dewey writes (LW 1:308); and, to the extent that philosophy helps people to approach this level, the cost will not seem high.

Philosophy, thus understood, becomes a tool of evaluation or criticism. By criticism Dewey means "taking thought as to what is better and worse in any field at any time, with some consciousness of *why* the better is better and *why* the worse is worse" (LW 5:133–34). Philosophical criticism is thus "not a special road to something alien to ordinary beliefs, knowledge, action, enjoyment, and suffering. It is rather a criticism, a critical viewing, of just these familiar things" (LW 5:141). In another formulation, he writes that philosophy is "a generalized theory of criticism. Its ultimate value for life-experience is that it continuously provides instruments for the criticism of those values—whether of beliefs, institutions, actions or products—that are found in all aspects of experience" (LW 1:9). Two factors make philosophical criticism different from other sorts of intellectual criticism. The first of these, Dewey writes, is the importance of the objects of its evaluation. Philosophy is "a critique of basic and widely shared beliefs" (LW 8:29), "of the influential beliefs that underlie culture" (LW 6:19), "of beliefs that are so widely current socially as to be dominant factors in culture" (LW 5:164). The second factor in philosophical criticism is the persistence of its efforts. Philosophical criticism is criticism "which traces the beliefs to their generating conditions as far as may be, which tracks them to their results, which considers the mutual compatibility of the elements of the total structure of beliefs" (LW 6:19; cf. 5:141). Thus, philosophical criticism is a persistent attempt to uncover and evaluate, and replace if necessary, the basic assumptions of culture.

Dewey's understanding of the cultural role of philosophical inquiry grants it a kind of intellectual primacy. He writes, for example, that "philosophy is inherently criticism, having its distinctive position among various modes of criticism in its generality; a criticism of criticism, as it were" (LW 1:298). But this primacy that he sees for philosophy is one based solely upon its potential for broad service to society, not one based on the supposed superiority of philosophy as an activity or way of knowing. In the process of criticism, he writes, philosophy has the task of becoming "in effect a messenger, a liaison officer, making reciprocally intelligible voices speaking provincial tongues, and thereby enlarging as well as rectifying the meanings with which they are charged" (LW 1:306).[32] Performing this job requires philosophical openness and personal humility on the part of philosophers who must always guard against the tendencies towards intellectual arrogance and perspectival imperialism.[33] We also need to remember that, for Dewey, this critical task of philosophical inquiry is not necessarily the work of individuals with chairs in philosophy departments. There are individuals who are now engaged in the philosophical process of cultural criticism; but only some of them are academic philosophers.

There is, as Dewey clearly recognizes, a need to address at some point the propriety of his activist understanding of philosophy, an understanding that Morris Cohen, our representative critic from 2.5, characterizes as Dewey's "too ardent desire to make philosophy a means to improve the world."[34] Dewey's defense is straightforward: "in some sense all philosophy is a branch of morals" (LW 1:387). He writes in 1940 that he has "consistently insisted" that, because it "contains value-considerations within itself, indispensable to its existence as philosophy," philosophy "has a 'practical,' that is a *moral* function" (LW 14:148). The wisdom for which philosophy searches is not based upon the mastery of knowledge of antecedent reality, he noted earlier. "Wisdom is a moral term, and like every moral term refers not to the constitution of things already in existence." Rather, "it refers to a choice about something to be done, a preference for living this sort of life rather than that . . . to a desired future which our desires, when translated into articulate conviction, may help bring into existence" (MW 11:44).[35] As seekers of wisdom, we must thus think and evaluate and act. Dewey continues:

---

[32] Cf. MW 9:339; LW 4:248.

[33] Cf. Richard Rorty: "Philosophy as a discipline thus sees itself as the attempt to underwrite or debunk claims to knowledge made by science, morality, art, or religion . . . in the position . . . of judging other areas of culture on the basis of its special knowledge of the 'foundations' of these areas . . . keeping the other disciplines honest, limiting their claims to what can be properly 'grounded' " (*Philosophy and the Mirror of Nature*, 3, 8, 162; cf. *The Consequences of Pragmatism*, 87–88). For an attempt to evaluate Rorty's overall understanding of Dewey's work, see my "Rorty's Use of Dewey."

[34] *A Preface to Logic*, 202; cf. Brand Blanshard, "Can the Philosopher Influence Social Change?" 750–51.

[35] Cf. LW 15:157; 16:365, 389.

as human beings interested in good and bad things in their connection with human conduct, thinkers are concerned to mitigate the instability of life, to introduce moderation, temper and economy, and when worst comes to worst to suggest consolations and compensations. They are concerned with rendering more stable good things, and more unstable bad things (LW 1:51).

Philosophical inquiry is thus a demonstrably moral activity. This is a conception of philosophy that is, of course, not provable—no conceptions of philosophy are provable—but it is a conception of philosophy that is justifiable given the analysis of the human condition that we have been examining.

It will perhaps be advantageous for our understanding of Dewey to return at this point to the theme of metaphysics with which I began this chapter, and the relation that Dewey sees existing between it and philosophy in general. The former is an area of inquiry that he characterizes as "cognizance of the generic traits of existence" (LW 1:50). In his attempt to explore these generic traits, Dewey resists the spectatorial temptation to treat his inquiry as simply one of "analysis and definition." He maintains, on the contrary, that because the traits of existence themselves—such traits as need and contingency, movement and arrest, precariousness and stability—both generate values and place them at risk, "[a]ny theory that detects and defines these traits is therefore but a ground-map of the province of criticism" (LW 1:308–9), a preparation for action. Metaphysics is thus a valuable tool in our attempts to understand our natural situation, a tool to be used in philosophical criticism rather than as a contemplative end in itself. Metaphysical knowledge, the clear understanding of the generic traits of existence, remains for Dewey a means to gaining some level of active security.[36] Failure to remember this, Dewey writes, can result in our philosophical efforts becoming attempted escapes from the world of change and suffering. It can lead as well to the isolation and abandonment of philosophy as something "arbitrary, aloof . . . 'abstract' " (LW 1:17). Remembering it, on the other hand, makes philosophy "an intellectualized wish, an aspiration subjected to rational discriminations and tests, a social hope reduced to a working program of action, a prophecy of the future, but one disciplined by serious thought and knowledge" (MW

---

[36] Cf. LW 1:50, 67; 13:281.

11:43). Metaphysics contributes to this task of philosophical criticism. "A true wisdom," Dewey continues, "discovers in thoughtful observation and experiment the method of administering the unfinished processes of existence so that frail goods shall be substantiated, secure goods be extended, and the precarious promises of good that haunt experienced things be more liberally fulfilled" (LW 1:67–68; cf. 305).

PART TWO

DEWEY'S SOCIAL VISION

CHAPTER 4
Designating the Good

IT IS POSSIBLE to distinguish in the work of anyone interested in social change three separate endeavors. The first is the call for improvement itself, the criticism of the current social situation, found alike in the work of critics as diverse as Henry David Thoreau and B. F. Skinner, William Graham Sumner and Jane Addams. The third endeavor is the introduction and evaluation of the reform proposals themselves, the specific changes that need to be enacted. In between these two, and justifying each, is a fundamental discussion of the nature of a fulfilled life. This second endeavor of social critics, the one that leads to the deep conflicts among them, is the specification of the 'good'. In this chapter, we will consider Dewey's position on this question. Negatively, we know that for him the 'good' is not likely to be uncovered through Scriptural study or be attained by obedience to authorities. We also know that the 'good' is not simply equivalent to either the pleasurable or the exciting. Positively, the search for the 'good' entails for Dewey a turn from the past to the future, from authority to results. In a word, he calls this 'intelligence'. The morality that is to grow out of this stance, intelligent or scientific ethics, will need to be explicitly naturalistic rather than supernatural. It will also need to turn away from egoism and narrow individualism. The necessity for the cooperative searching for the 'good' also involves a great deal of toleration for those of differing perspectives and the fostering of all of these points in our social interactions and ultimately in our educational systems.

4.1. The Scientific Spirit

The understanding of Dewey's analysis of the nature and importance of science is somewhat complicated in our 'postscientific' age by our own distance from the flush of the spirit of Progress.[1] We all

---

[1] Cf. John J. McDermott: "We have come to distrust science as the guarantor of

recognize, however, that there was a time not that long ago when few would have been even slightly troubled by a proposal for the 'scientific' study of religion or juvenile crime or political corruption, or by a discussion of 'scientific' business management or charity or parenting.[2] Science then functioned as a kind of icon whose eventual beneficial transformation of the human realm was thought to be simply a matter of time. Dewey, while never falling victim to this sort of science-worship, still pressed for its use across the broad scope of human conduct. The goal of an increased role for science, as he understood it, was not the reduction of matters of conduct to "physical or even quasi-mathematical form" (MW 3:5), but the attempt to bring new and systematized approaches to bear in our evaluation of our actions in these various areas. Thus, even when he gilds science as "experience becoming rational" (MW 9:233), what he intends is the quite modest point that science is "the method of emancipating us from enslavement to customary ends, the ends established in the past" (MW 8:81). The essence of his emphasis was thus to suggest a turning away from the traditional analyses based in deduction from fixed truths toward self-reflective inquiry based upon broad historical and cross-cultural studies, introduction of research methods and controls, evaluation of results, and so on.[3]

When we try to formulate a bit more precisely the positive aspects of Dewey's conception of 'science', we see first of all his belief that we too often overemphasize the finished material—the facts, the conclusions, the discoveries and inventions—that science has pro-

---

salvation and with the advent of this distrust, have become decidedly skeptical of the inevitability of progress. . . . In the past, the assessment of our immediate situation, especially in its negative import, was diluted by the confidence we had in a healing and fruitful future" (*The Culture of Experience,* 119–20.)

[2] Dewey himself discusses, for example, "the scientific method of ethics" (EW 4:55) and "the philosophical sciences" (EW 4:132; cf. 1:158), and such activities as the "scientific mobilization of school children" (MW 10:298) and making "taxation scientific" (MW 11:117).

[3] Cf. Morton White: "In 1938 Dewey's *Logic* appeared, and there for the first time he tried to deal intensively with difficult questions like probability, measurement, and classification. But when he spoke of scientific method to the politicians of the twenties, he meant nothing more pretentious than observation, deduction, and experiment" (*Social Thought in America,* 239; cf. Joseph Blau, "John Dewey and American Social Thought," 123–24; Sidney Hook, *Pragmatism and the Tragic Sense of Life,* x–xiii; Richard Bernstein, *Philosophical Profiles: Essays in a Pragmatic Mode,* 264–65; Daniel J. Wilson, *Science, Community and the Transformation of American Philosophy,* 128–30, 175–78).

duced. In doing so, we neglect what he takes to be the essential factor: "the inherent logic" of the process of inquiry, the "methods of control of formation of judgments" (MW 3:4, 37).[4] He writes that "the value of any cognitive conclusion depends upon the *method* by which it is reached" (LW 4:160). He thus places "the emphasis in using the term 'scientific' first upon methods, and then upon results through reference to methods" (MW 3:3). He continues that the term is better understood to signify "the existence of systematic methods of inquiry, which, when they are brought to bear on a range of facts, enable us to understand them better and to control them more intelligently, less haphazardly and with less routine" (LW 5:4).[5]

These methods of inquiry, pieces of the larger pattern we examined above in 2.4, include, for example, careful and objective observation and the interim suspension of judgment. If a person is "scientifically-trained," he writes, that individual "suspends—postpones—reaching a conclusion in order that he may not be led by superficial occurrences into a snap judgment" (LW 8:252; cf. 5:8). Also included in methodic inquiry is the heightened ability to deal constructively with uncertainty. As Dewey writes, "scientific method is, in one aspect, a technique for making a productive use of doubt by converting it into operations of definite inquiry" (LW 4:182). The doubt can thus be channelled into a stance of hypothetical flexibility that furthers inquiry.

As might be anticipated, there is a close connection between this method, that Dewey calls at one point "the scientific technique," and "the scientific temper" (LW 11:457). Consequently, without pretending to have fully distinguished these two parallel concerns, I can begin to characterize the scientific attitude. Negatively, he sees the scientific attitude as "freedom from control by routine, prejudice, dogma, unexamined tradition, sheer self-interest." Positively, the scientific attitude is "the will to inquire, to examine, to discriminate, to draw conclusions only on the basis of evidence after taking pains to gather all available evidence" (LW 13:273). It is in this sense that

---

[4] Dewey believes that this failing is particularly prominent in our schools, where science has been regarded "too much as an accumulation of ready-made material with which students are to be made familiar . . . rather than as the effective method of inquiry into any subject-matter" (MW 6:70, 74).

[5] Cf. LW 2:337; 9:27.

Dewey offers the characterization of the scientific attitude as "that which is capable of enjoying the doubtful" (LW 4:182). He recognizes, as we saw in 2.4, that the enjoyment of doubt is a challenge to normal human living. "To hold theories and principles in solution, awaiting confirmation," he writes, "goes contrary to the grain" (LW 13:166); and acquiring this ability offers a challenge to self-development and to education.[6] In another passage, he summarizes the stance of the scientific inquirer as one of:

> willingness to hold belief in suspense, ability to doubt until evidence is obtained; willingness to go where evidence points instead of putting first a personally preferred conclusion; ability to hold ideas in solution and use them as hypotheses to be tested instead of as dogmas to be asserted; and (possibly the most distinctive of all) enjoyment of new fields for inquiry and of new problems (LW 13:166).

Included as well in the scientific attitude are such traits as the primary emphasis upon the importance of accuracy in observing and reporting, and the completely sincere search for troubles with one's own work.[7]

Dewey writes that "the scientific attitude and method are at bottom but the method of free and effective intelligence" (LW 13:279), thus emphasizing the connection between science and what is often referred to as 'common sense'. He thus rejects the attempt to treat science as something esoteric or more properly operating on a plane removed from normal living (cf. LW 1:344–45). There is a difference between "these two distinctive modes of inquiry," of course; but this difference should not obliterate their "community of pattern" (LW 12:118). The difference is one of purpose of inquiry: whether the inquiry is attempting to settle some particular problem —"some issue of use or enjoyment" (LW 12:66–67)—or attempting to advance knowledge. "In commonsense knowing the knowing is for the sake of the *faciendum;* in scientific knowing the reverse is the case" (LW 1:342). That is, while in our normal lives knowledge

---

[6] With regard to education, Dewey writes: "it should be axiomatic that the development of scientific attitudes of thought, observation, and inquiry is the chief business of study and learning" (LW 6:60).

[7] Cf. MW 6:179; 7:335–39; LW 8:109.

serves action, in scientific knowing we act so that we can find out. Or, as he phrases it elsewhere, "[s]cientific knowing is that particular form of *practical* human activity which is concerned with the advancement of *knowing* apart from concern with *other* practical affairs" (LW 16:253). From his point of view, then, it is necessary to see common sense and science to interact in a fashion similar to the interaction between primary and secondary experience that we saw in 3.1. "Scientific subject-matter and procedures grow out of the direct problems and methods of common sense, of practical uses and enjoyments," he writes, and "react into the latter in a way that enormously refines, expands and liberates the contents and the agencies at the disposal of common sense" (LW 12:71–72; cf. 16:291–92). It is in such a fashion that Dewey suggests we might most usefully understand, for example, the interaction of everyday water and H_2O (cf. LW 1:343–44; 16:245).[8]

The emphasis upon intelligence also indicates that, for Dewey, entwined with every aspect of this consideration of the scientific method and the scientific attitude is the fundamental importance of publicity that connects him up with Peirce. Both the method of science and its appropriate attitude are inherently communal. The scientific method is based on publicity of experiment and the dissemination of results. "Everything discovered belongs to the community of workers," he writes. "Every new idea and theory has to be submitted to this community for confirmation and test" (LW 5:115). Likewise, the scientific attitude commits the individual to give the viewpoints of others a fair hearing, and to search for such viewpoints as a criticism of his or her own. And ultimately the efforts of cooperative intelligence are aimed at attempts to advance the common good, a standard of evaluation to which we will ever need to aspire.

Dewey believes that science, understood in this way, offers us both "the sole dependable means of disclosing the realities of existence"

---

[8] Cf. John E. Smith: "Science is thus seen as continuous with ordinary experience, at least with respect to the general pattern of inquiry; the inquiry characteristic of the sciences represents a refinement of those rudimentary trial-and-error operations everyone engages in when confronted with an obstacle which can be removed only when the grounds of the difficulty have been discovered" (*Purpose and Thought*, 97; cf. Kennedy, "Science and the Transformation of Common Sense," 315–18; Thayer, *The Logic of Pragmatism*, 34–49).

and open-ended possibilities of success that yield "a new morale of confidence, control, and security" (LW 5:269–70). It is "the agency of progress in action" he writes (MW 9:231); "the scientific method of experimentation" generates "faith in progress through the intelligent regulation of existing conditions" (MW 6:299–300 = LW 8:275). It is the one means of organizing cooperative attempts to break free of the customary and the assumed. "There is but one sure road of access to truth—the road of patient, cooperative inquiry operating by means of observation, experiment, record and controlled reflection" (LW 9:23; cf. MW 6:78).

If the scientific approach is "sure" in the sense of being *trustworthy*, however, it is in no way "sure" in the sense of being *guaranteed*. Science can offer no assured answers to specific problems.[9] Dewey writes that we too often make the mistake of viewing science as "a stamp of final approval upon this and that specific procedure . . . as a guarantee that goes with the sale of goods rather than as a light to the eyes and a lamp to the feet" (LW 5:7). There cannot be any such guarantees in the practical realm of human action—in part because the results of scientific activity are always complex and ambiguous. "There is probably no case," he writes, "in which the good achieved by the intervention of science has not been offset by some evil" (LW 16:373; cf. 364–65). In addition, with many practical problems there is the difficulty of forced response, whether or not we are fully prepared to act.[10]

Moreover, he continues, we cannot even assume that science will address our real problems. This fundamental limitation results from the fact that science is a neutral method, a passive tool. Science is "strictly impersonal," Dewey writes.

> It owes its operation and its consequences to the human beings who use it. It adapts itself passively to the purposes and desires which animate these human beings. It lends itself with equal impartiality to the kindly offices of medicine and hygiene and the destructive deeds of war. It elevates some through opening new horizons; it

---

[9] Cf. John Herman Randall, Jr., and Justus Buchler: "The scientific method lays no claim to infallibility, and in this respect differs most strikingly from the other methods" (*Philosophy: An Introduction*, 60).

[10] Cf. George Herbert Mead: "In problems of conduct we must act, however inadequate our plan of action may be. The research problem may be left because of our inability to find a satisfactory hypothesis" (*Selected Writings*, 257).

depresses others by making them slaves of machines operated for the pecuniary gain of owners (LW 6:54).[11]

The ends to which the power of science is put are not to be found in science itself, and this fact makes ever-important the role of the inquirer. The actual uses to which the power of science is put are based in our choices of fundamental human values. These fundamental values, some positive and some negative, include nationalism, personal freedom, obedience or faithfulness, simplicity, empire, and democracy. To keep the applications of science on the right track, it is these fundamental values that in their various conceptions and instantiations must be evaluated as to their contribution to better lives in ongoing processes of cooperative inquiry, as we shall see in 4.4.

It is important to keep Dewey's caveats about the efficacy of the scientific method in mind because it has not proven difficult for commentators to exaggerate his faith in science,[12] partly with the help of his own formulations. He writes, for example, that the scientific method "is a method of knowing that is self-corrective in operation; that learns from failures as from successes" (MW 12:270).[13] We must be careful, however, not to make too much of this sort of comment. The method of science is "self-corrective and self-developing," perhaps, but only in the limited sense that Dewey intends: over time new inquirers tend to recognize earlier mistakes. "Imperfect and even wrong hypotheses," he writes, "when *acted upon,* brought to light significant phenomena which made improved ideas and improved experimentations possible" (LW 6:66). So, for example, the continued development of the healing arts over the centuries tends

---

[11] Cf. Charles A. Beard and Mary R. Beard: "The chemist, for example, as chemist, was not at all concerned during any of his chemical experiments as to whether his discovery was to be employed in healing the sick or blowing bank safes" (*America in Midpassage,* vol. 2, 832; cf. LW 13:184; 16:254).

[12] Cf. John E. Smith: "One of the most reliable clues to the true status of science in American culture is the strength of the belief that science can be made to do at one stroke the work traditionally performed by ethics and religion. Dewey shared that belief" (*The Spirit of American Philosophy,* 150; cf. Howard B. White, "The Political Faith of John Dewey," 358–59; May Brodbeck, "The Philosophy of John Dewey," 214–15; Wiebe, *The Search for Order,* 151–52).

[13] Cf. Morris Cohen: "The progressive character of science shows that its essence is to be sought not in the content of its specific conclusions but rather in the method whereby its findings are made and constantly corrected" ("Scientific Method," 389; cf. MW 13:316; LW 6:224).

to eliminate unfounded diagnoses and worthless or harmful thera-
pies. These improvements are, however, a matter of what Dewey calls
"the 'long-run' phase of knowledge connected with the self-
developing and self-correcting nature of scientific inquiry" (LW
12:483), an admission that is of little solace to particular patients
who are suffering at intermediate stages along the way. And, even
here, the process of scientific inquiry is not self-directing but depends
on the dedicated research and the fortunate hunches of skilled
practitioners.

Dewey maintains that the potential contribution of the neutral
scientific method has been greatly hampered by the frustrating
limitations brought about by "the essential capture of the technical
resources of the new science: first, by industry controlled by finance-
capital, and then by political nationalism" (LW 11:459). Dewey
writes, for example, of the misdirection of science in capitalist
society, maintaining that, as a result of the deal struck between
"rising capitalism" (LW 6:56) and the inventors and developers of
new technologies, the applications of science have benefitted primarily the antecedently wealthy.[14] By his day, this meant that making
money for individual entrepreneurs and providing dividends to
private investors was taken to be more important than—or even
equivalent to—providing for a better world. As he writes, science has
been "employed primarily for private aggrandizement" rather than
"for the promotion of social well-being" (LW 6:55; cf. 58). Framing
this same point in a manner more like Thorstein Veblen, Dewey
writes: "The engineer has worked in subordination to the business
manager whose primary concern is not with [increasing social] wealth
but with the interests of property as worked out in the feudal and
semi-feudal period" (LW 2:302).[15] Because of these constraints, we
find many of the problems of the modern industrial world—
advertising to enhance consumer 'demand' for unneeded gizmos,

---

[14] Cf. EW 4:17; LW 1:130–31.

[15] Cf. Thorstein Veblen: "The realities of the business world are money-values.
. . . The business man's care is to create needs to be satisfied at a price paid to
himself. The engineer's care is to provide for these needs, so far as the business men
in the background find their advantage in allowing it" (*Absentee Ownership and
Business Enterprise in Recent Times*, 108; cf. *The Engineers and the Price System*,
69–70). For Dewey's evaluation of Veblen, see: LW 5:102; 9:104; 11:28, 271,
278–79; Joseph Dorfman, *Thorstein Veblen and His America*, 450.

secrecy and competition and a concern with short-term profits, mass assembly in spite of worker frustration, planned obsolescence, waste and pollution—to be tolerated and even advocated because of their favorable effect upon private ledger books. The other side to this complex problem of constraints placed upon science is its relationship to the nation-state. Science as we have known it is largely *war* science: scientific results applied through advanced technology, and under the cover of sophisticated propaganda, to the advancement of destruction. In neither of these cases, however, does Dewey believe that the persistence of the misapplications of science are indications of an economic or military combativeness so deeply rooted in an unalterable human nature that science could never be liberated. "A truer psychology," he writes, "shows that the trouble lies in the inertness of established habits" (MW 14:88).[16]

Dewey is similarly critical of those who claim that these two problems are not the result of the particular misapplications of science that we have made but rather are the inherent problems of the modern, technological world. "There is no greater sign of the paralysis of the imagination which custom and involvement in immediate detail can induce," he writes, "than the belief, sedulously propagated by some who pride themselves on superior taste, that the machine is itself the source of our troubles" (LW 5:87).[17] The problem is not the machine, he responds, but what *we* have done with it.

> For machinery means an undreamed-of reservoir of power. If we have harnessed this power to the dollar rather than to the liberation and enrichment of human life, it is because we have been content to stay within the bounds of traditional aims and values although we are in possession of a revolutionary transforming instrument.

The blame here is squarely human and cultural, not technological. As he concludes, "it is hard to think of anything more childish than the animism which puts the blame on machinery" (LW 5:87; cf. 6:58).

---

[16] Cf. LW 6:38–39; 13:288–93.

[17] Cf. C. Wright Mills: " 'science' seems to many less a creative ethos and a manner of orientation than a set of Science Machines, operated by technicians and controlled by economic and military men who neither embody nor understand science as ethos and orientation" (*The Sociological Imagination*, 16).

Instead of this blaming of technology, he maintains that we need to develop a responsible use of the opportunities that have become available to us.[18]

Thus, rather than retreating into a luddite past, we need to bring about the more intelligent evaluation of the uses of our new scientific possibilities. This problem, Dewey maintains, is "the greatest which civilization has ever had to face . . . the most serious issue of contemporary life." He continues:

> Here is the instrumentality, the most powerful, for good and evil, the world has ever known. What are we going to do with it? Shall we leave our underlying aims unaffected by it, treating it merely as a means by which uncooperative individuals may advance their own fortunes? Shall we try to improve the hearts of men without regard to the new methods which science puts at our disposal?

On the contrary, he suggests that we should take "the method of science home into our own controlling attitudes and dispositions" and employ "the new techniques as means of directing our thoughts and efforts to a planned control of social forces" (LW 6:55–56; cf. 4:36). This point about the reconstructive possibilities of science runs throughout Dewey's work. He writes in 1891 that "science has got far enough along to make its negative attitude towards precarious codes of life evident, while its own positive principle of reconstruction is not yet evident" (EW 3:125). Nearly half a century later, he returns to this theme: "A culture which permits science to destroy traditional values but which distrusts its power to create new ones is a culture which is destroying itself" (LW 13:172; cf. MW 6:66). In spite of his efforts, however, the problem continues. He writes: "Science has hardly been used to modify men's fundamental acts and attitudes in social matters. It has been used to extend enormously the scope and power of interests and values which anteceded its rise. Here is the contradiction in our civilization" (LW 6:58; cf. 50–52). Thus, although science is "a potential creator of new values and ends" (LW 5:118)—or, more precisely, although "science is capable of influencing the formation of ends" and although "science has

---

[18] Cf. Larry A. Hickman: "Dewey argued that the failure of progress, when it occurs, is not the result of technology so much as it is the result of lazy reliance on unreconstructed impulses, sentiments, and emotions" (*John Dewey's Pragmatic Technology*, 184).

intrinsic moral potentiality" (LW 13:171)[19]—Dewey maintains that it has been forced to remain "a servant of ends imposed from alien traditions" (MW 6:78). Science has been confined to managing how predetermined ends are to be achieved without having any input into what those ends are to be. And this, he believes, must change. "If ever we are to be governed by intelligence, not by things and by words, science must have something to say about *what* we do, and not merely about *how* we may do it most easily and economically" (MW 6:78–79).[20]

We will be able to apply science to our choices of ends, Dewey maintains, only if we adopt the understanding of the relationship of thought and action that was considered above in 3.3. This understanding renounces "the traditional notion that action is inherently inferior to knowledge," he writes, and it fosters "the conviction that security attained by active control is to be more prized than certainty in theory" (LW 4:29–30). The replacement of the quest for certainty with cooperative efforts at security will be a long and painstaking process, taken in the face of both passive and active opposition. "What stands in the way is a lot of outworn traditions, moth-eaten slogans and catchwords, that do substitute duty for thought, as well as our entrenched predatory self-interest" (LW 6:61). Although he sees science as "the supreme means of the valid determination of all valuations in all aspects of human and social life" (LW 13:250), he repeatedly denies that its possibilities have been put to use. His lament of 1908 that "[o]ur science is still an outward garb more or less awkwardly worn rather than a habit of mind" (MW 4:172) is followed in 1944 with another: the denial that "the scientific method has at the present time been seriously and systematically applied to the problems of human life" (LW 15:256).[21] Later, he denies that the

---

[19] The imprecision in the suggestion that science might "create" new values results both from Dewey's talking in terms of *power* rather than *influence,* and also from his failing to make explicit the various levels of abstractness that are present in his value discussions. This latter theme returns in 4.4.

[20] Cf. LW 6:58; 10:340–43; 15:7.

[21] Cf. James Hayden Tufts: "Most men of science today are glimpsing the possibility of assisting man to take possession of his inheritance. Science has been applied to many processes of manufacture, but in matters of health and disease, of marriage, of education, of economic methods, of social organization, we pursue our course largely by the guide of habit, tradition, or blind impulse. The demand of the scientific spirit is that reason, inquiry, patient investigation, carefully planned experiment, shall take the place of unreasoned advocacy or hasty fervor in all these fields" (*Selected Writings,* 86).

scientific attitude has ever been shared by "the great mass of human beings" (LW 16:393). It is still possible to hope and work for such great changes and developments, Dewey writes, because "science itself is still in its babyhood" (LW 15:161; cf. 16:375–79), and no one can be sure how soon it will mature. "It is a newcomer even in the physical field of inquiry," he writes (MW 12:258). "A very short history has been enjoyed by free scientific method in comparison with the long history enjoyed by forces which have never felt the influence of science" (LW 13:276; cf. 6:56). And here, he believes, with increased efforts on our part we have time on our side.

4.2.   Ethics as Moral Science

In this section, I want to examine Dewey's position on how science as he conceives it might inform the development of a moral science. Because this notion of 'moral science' initially sounds so strange to our ears,[22] it will be necessary to explore its meaning further. In the "Introduction" to both the 1908 and the 1932 editions of *Ethics*, Dewey and Tufts write, "Ethics is the science that deals with conduct, in so far as this is considered as right or wrong, good or bad" (MW 5:7 = LW 7:9). Ethics as moral science is thus understood as the methodical and intentional attempt to discover and foster proper human action. The 'scientific' strain emphasizes in particular a concern with "the inherent logic" of our attempts to solve our moral problems, Dewey writes, and the attempt to establish "an order of judgments such that each one when made is of use in determining other judgments thereby securing control of their formation" (MW 3:4). We need to create "a working theory of morals," he continues (LW 7:176), that would enable us to counterbalance our inherited theories of morality that attempt to display and 'prove' predetermined rights and wrongs. Such a moral science would require the development of "a more adequate science of human nature," he writes, and "a scientific social psychology" to assist us in understanding, for example, "the formation of habits of belief, desire and judgment" (MW 14:221–22).

---

[22] Dewey himself at one point fought the connection between ethics and science. Cf. EW 1:205–26 (esp. 208–9).

Dewey sees the role of science or intelligence in ethics to be of such importance that he maintains that human conduct becomes moral *only* when reflective thought is applied. As he writes, "only deliberate action, conduct into which reflective choice enters, is distinctively moral, for only then does there enter the question of better or worse" (MW 14:193; cf. EW 4:135). Dewey recognizes that there will be dissenters from his attempt to develop a moral science, individuals who believe that "there is something in the very nature of conduct which prevents the use of logical methods in the way they are employed in other recognized spheres of scientific inquiry" (MW 3:5).[23] From his point of view, however, the moral and the scientific or intelligent are intimately related. On the basic technological level, attempts to lead moral lives have throughout history given rise to scientific problems, like obtaining enough food to feed all of the community's people, or forging weapons to defend the community from its enemies. The march of science, similarly, has throughout history given rise to ethical problems, like the challenges of centuries of advancing biomedical possibilities or our increasing responsibility for both damaging and safeguarding our environment. We cannot hope to maintain a dichotomy between morality and science without damage to both sides. From a broader point of view, Dewey maintains that we need to see our problematic lives as requiring a series of important choices that will benefit from scientific attempts to turn them into legitimate judgments. We need, then, to increase the application of the scientific method, the method of intelligence, to matters of moral valuation. The three major themes to be considered in his attempt to develop a moral science are that the resultant morality would be naturalistic, social, and inquiring.

Because ethics is rooted in Dewey's conception of humans as fundamentally organic beings transacting with a natural environment, as we saw in 2.2, ethics is a naturalistic matter, a matter of the happiness and suffering of this world rather than of another. The natural results that conduct has for human living determine which actions are moral and which are not. As Dewey writes, "conse-

---

[23] Cf. Frank H. Knight: "The habit of thinking of life-problems in terms of means and end, power and technique, is necessary in our relations, individual or group, to the physical environment; but it must be *prevented* from carrying over into the social field itself if ethical society—which is to say any true society—is to exist" ("Pragmatism and Social Action," 230–31; cf. Joseph Wood Krutch, *The Measure of Man*, 32–33; Krutch, *The Modern Temper: A Study and a Confession*, 39–57).

quences fix the moral quality of an act" (MW 14:34). He offers a broad consequentialism, evaluating actions by their effects "upon the common welfare, the general well-being" (LW 7:344) and defending, as we shall see in 4.4, growth as the criterion for evaluating the effects. Such a shift in moral interest to purely naturalistic considerations would reconnect our moral efforts with our changing situation and "with the amelioration of the conditions of the common lot in this world" (MW 10:25).

The second theme in our consideration of Dewey's moral science is its social aspect. We have seen in 2.3 his understanding of the social nature of the human organism, with its emphasis upon the origin of the self in a social group and the pervasive influence of the social environment upon human activity. While it was clear from that discussion that for Dewey human conduct is essentially social, we passed over at that time the corollary that moral conduct is not a private matter. "Morals *are* social," he writes; and, joining this second theme with the prior one of naturalism, he continues that morality "is as much a matter of interaction of a person with his social environment as walking is an interaction of legs with a physical environment" (MW 14:219).[24] Dewey does not simply equate the social and the moral, of course, for the terms each carry many related meanings and it seems quite sensible to describe our lives as becoming in some ways 'more social' without becoming at the same time 'more moral' (Cf. MW 11:101). What is clear, however, is that for him immorality is possible only because of our social existence. We can be immoral only because we can do harm to, or fail to do good for, others. He writes: "If a man lived alone in the world there might be some sense in the question 'Why be moral?' were it not for one thing: No such question would then arise. As it is, we live in a world where other persons live too. Our acts affect them. They perceive these effects, and react upon us in consequence" (MW 14:223; cf. 16). Our actions interpenetrate the actions of those around us, and intertwine with the actions of those who have gone before us and with those who are to follow. And, even if we on occasion fail to recognize this, the others do not. Thus, "all morality

---

[24] Cf. George Herbert Mead: "ethical and unethical behavior can be defined essentially in social terms: the former as behavior which is socially beneficial or conducive to the well-being of society, the latter as behavior which is socially harmful or conducive to the disruption of society" (*Mind, Self, and Society,* 320–21).

is social; not because we *ought* to take into account the effects of our acts upon the welfare of others, but because of facts," he writes. "Others *do* take account of what we do, and they respond accordingly to our acts" (MW 14:217).

We hold people accountable for what they do; and, in this way, we hope to develop their sense of responsibility. "The individual is *held* accountable for what he *has* done," Dewey writes, "in order that he may be responsive in what he is *going* to do" (MW 14:217). He recognizes that we all need to be chided on occasion, to be made aware of "thoughtless, self-centered action." There is, he continues, "no one who can be safely trusted to be exempt from immediate reactions of criticism, and there are few who do not need to be braced by occasional expressions of approval." This matter of criticism is, of course, one of degree and emphasis. All too often in our daily lives, he writes,

> these influences are immensely overdone in comparison with the assistance that might be given by the influence of social judgments which operate without accompaniments of praise and blame; which enable an individual to see for himself what he is doing, and which put him in command of a method of analyzing the obscure and usually unavowed forces which move him to act (MW 14:220).

In general, we spend too much of our time praising and blaming, separating the "sheep and goats; the saved and the lost; the elect and the mass" (LW 9:55), thereby undercutting the development of moral science.

"Approach to human problems in terms of moral blame and moral approbation, of wickedness or righteousness," Dewey writes, "is probably the greatest single obstacle now existing to development of competent methods in the field of social subject-matter" (LW 12:489).[25] He maintains, on the contrary, that we must try to come to see morals as "a matter of direction, not of suppression" (MW 5:331). Eventually, with the development of conscience, individuals become conscious of the requirements of responsibility. "Gradually persons learn by dramatic imitation to hold themselves accountable," he writes, "and liability becomes a voluntary deliberate acknowledgment that deeds are our own, that their consequences

---

[25] Cf. MW 14:222; LW 5:119; 9:51.

come from us" (MW 14:217). We become able to evaluate our own conduct:

> In language and imagination we rehearse the responses of others just as we dramatically enact other consequences. We foreknow how others will act, and the foreknowledge is the beginning of judgment passed on action. We know *with* them; there is conscience. An assembly is formed within our breast which discusses and appraises proposed and performed acts. The community without becomes a forum and tribunal within, a judgment-seat of charges, assessments and exculpations (MW 14:216).[26]

In this way, if we emphasize the directive aspects of the social challenge to the self, we can develop individuals who offer and accept guidance without being crippled by blame and guilt.

When we consider the changes that this emphasis upon social ethics will require, we can separate the discussion, as Dewey does on occasion, into two different strands and examine the reconstructed ethical theory "either from the standpoint of what it effects in society as a whole, or with reference to the particular individual concerned" (EW 5:55; cf. 4:234). To begin with the latter strand, we see that the primary change that would result is that morality would lose its anchoring in individual feelings and benefits and focus upon the larger world. "The evangelical Protestant tradition," he writes, "has fostered the tendency to locate morals in personal feelings instead of in the control of social situations" (MW 10:262).[27] Emphasizing changes made "in ourselves," however, instead of those made "in the world in which we live," Dewey maintains, is "the essence of what is objectionable in 'subjectivism'" (LW 4:219). He is not, of course, opposed to the 'internal' changes themselves. His opposition is to solely internal changes, changes that have no corresponding 'external' effect. "It is not in the least implied that change in personal attitudes, in the disposition of the 'subject,' is not of great importance," he writes. "But there is a radical difference between a change

---

[26] Cf. George Herbert Mead: "self-criticism is essentially social criticism, and behavior controlled by self-criticism is essentially behavior controlled socially. Hence social control, so far from tending to crush out the human individual or to obliterate his self-conscious individuality, is, on the contrary, actually constitutive of and inextricably associated with that individuality" (*Mind, Self, and Society,* 255).

[27] Cf. EW 5:75; LW 4:25.

in the self that is cultivated and valued as an end, and one that is a means to alteration, through action, of objective conditions" (LW 4:220). In the place of this ethics of feelings, Dewey maintains that we need to develop an ethics of service. He is not suggesting, as I pointed out in 2.5, that we raise up an army of selfless zombies who have no real interests or lives of their own. Rather, he is advocating efforts to develop the naturally social self. "The child is born," he writes, "with a natural desire to give out, to do, and that means to serve" (EW 5:64; cf. MW 4:275). This natural desire will not thrive, however, if it is neglected or undermined by the social situation. Cultivating the child's natural desire to help, what he describes as "saturating him with the spirit of service" (MW 1:20), is part of what Dewey sees as the justifiable effort to change the emphasis of our ethical theorizing or, as he puts it, "to shift the centre of ethical gravity from an absorption which is selfish to a service which is social" (EW 5:65–66 = MW 4:277). Our aim here is to develop *"a sympathetic imagination for human relations in action"* and "a sense of community life" (EW 4:57; 5:66) that will further the life of service.[28]

We turn now to the former strand of the social theme of moral science. From the point of view of our highly interrelated contemporary society, the emphasis upon personal morality—or, as Dewey writes, "merely personal morality" (MW 10:263)—is no longer enough. Personal ethics, particularly an ethics of personal sin and personal righteousness, has been made inadequate. In this regard, he cites Jane Addams: "To attain personal morality in an age demanding social morality, to pride one's self upon the results of personal effort when the time demands social adjustment is utterly to fail to apprehend the situation" (LW 7:315).[29] At the present time, Dewey continues, "almost all important ethical problems arise out of the conditions of associated life"; and we must change our focus "from 'personal' to 'social' morality" (LW 7:318–19). For example, our conceptions of stealing and justice must be reconstructed: "For many individuals it is not now a question of whether they individually will appropriate property belonging to another, but whether existing large-scale economic arrangements operate to effect an

---

[28] This theme returns in 5.9.

[29] In her text, Addams refers to "individual" morality, not "personal" morality (*Democracy and Social Ethics*, 2–3).

equitable distribution of property; and if not, what they as individuals shall do about it" (LW 7:319; cf. EW 5:72–73).[30] This reconstruction of ethics based in service would lead to a new involvement in social affairs. Dewey is convinced that the prior 'personal' emphasis of ethical theorizing was the result of mistaken assumptions which pushed moral discussion "out of the range of the concrete problems of economic and political inquiry." He continues, "I doubt whether a more momentous *moral* fact can be found in all human history than just this separation of the moral from other human interests and attitudes, especially from the 'economic'" (LW 15:232–33). As a result, we find ourselves with a moral system that is "remote and empty" (LW 4:225), a moral system that is not able either to inspire the individual or to effect the necessary social reconstruction.

To bring about a higher level of human morality, Dewey maintains that a world with higher possibilities must be enacted. This means that the social world must be reconstructed. "Just as physical life cannot exist without the support of a physical environment," he writes, "so moral life cannot go on without the support of a moral environment" (LW 10:347). It is one of the tasks of the moral reformer to call for the creation of this moral environment, and one of the tasks of the moral theorist to integrate discussions of the practical and theoretical phases of life. The failure to rethink the focus of ethical endeavors will result in a continuation of the ethical theorists' concern with purely theoretical matters, while "men of executive habits will . . . regulate the concrete social conditions" and "the coercive restraint of immediate necessity will lay its harsh hand upon the mass of men." Dewey continues: "the vacuum left in practical matters by the remote irrelevancy of transcendental morals has to be filled in somehow. . . . It is filled in with class-codes, class standards, class-approvals" (MW 4:48–49).[31] All of these are examples, he maintains, of the sorts of morality that prevent reforms through social reconstruction.

For Dewey, the third theme in the development of moral science is that morals is a matter of inquiry. As we saw above in 2.4, the

---

[30] Cf. Edward Alsworth Ross: "The modern high-power dealer of woe wears immaculate linen, carries a silk hat and a lighted cigar, sins with a calm countenance and a serene soul, leagues or months from the evil he causes. Upon his gentlemanly presence the eventual blood and tears do not obtrude themselves" (*Sin and Society*, 10–11; cf. James Hayden Tufts, *Ethics* [with Dewey], MW 5:443–44).

[31] Cf. MW 14:17; LW 4:211–12.

human is to be seen as a problem-solver who can use his or her reflective abilities to overcome life's ongoing difficulties through inquiry. When the difficulties under consideration are more narrowly moral, there are a number of specific aspects of moral inquiry that deserve to be made explicit. I will discuss four in order, although because these aspects are distinctions made within an integrated activity their number and ordering are somewhat artificial.

The most obvious change is that a reflective approach to moral action requires the development of a hypothetical stance. In our world of natural transactions and social diversity, Dewey writes, "there are cases when a man literally does not *know* what he likes or what is good to him, or what to take as a good" (MW 13:14).[32] Moreover, in our world of process, new values arise "first in dim and uncertain form" and only if nurtured will "they grow in definiteness and coherence" (LW 9:34). In the face of this sort of uncertainty about the best action to perform, our moral duty remains attempting to embody intelligence in action in order to make the world better. Considered hypothetically, morality emphasizes the present situation and what it is developing into. For Dewey, "the moral issue concerns the future. It is prospective" (MW 14:18; cf. 217). We must focus upon future possibilities, especially the development of the personal habits and social institutions which suggest that they will result in better experiences. "We cannot undo the past; we can affect the future" (LW 7:304). Adopting this hypothetical stance would involve a change from forming ideas and judgments of value "on the basis of conformity to antecedent objects," he writes, "to constructing enjoyable objects directed by knowledge of consequences" (LW 4:217). As a result, no longer are moral rules "formed accidentally or under the pressure of conditions long past" to be "protected from criticism and thus perpetuated" (MW 14:167).[33]

Dewey is not suggesting, of course, "that the experiences of the past, personal and social, are of no importance." He writes, on the contrary, that "past experiences are significant in giving us intellectu-

---

[32] Cf. MW 11:7; 12:176; Kennedy, "The Hidden Link in Dewey's Theory of Evaluation," 88–89.

[33] Cf. Darnell Rucker on the members of the Chicago School: "they fear the constant threat that an end held under a peculiar set of historical circumstances will be erected into The End for man and become with a passing of the circumstances a millstone around men's necks, dragging them away from the demands of new problems" (*The Chicago Pragmatists*, 44).

al instrumentalities. . . . They are tools, not finalities." He continues:

> Reflection upon what we have liked and have enjoyed is a necessity. But it tells us nothing about the *value* of these things until enjoyments are themselves reflectively controlled, or, until, as they are recalled, we form the best judgment possible about what led us to like this sort of thing and what has issued from the fact that we liked it (LW 4:217).

The question is thus not the importance of the past as past, but rather its meaning as a guide to the present action. This is a point, Dewey believes, that is often overlooked when our subject is ethics. There is normally in ethical matters, he writes, "a presumption in favor of principles that have had a long career in the past and that have been endorsed by men of insight" (LW 7:330). Such a presumption is no doubt a good idea, provided it is no more than a presumption. "A moral law," he writes, "is a formula of the way to respond when specified conditions present themselves. Its soundness and pertinence are tested by what happens when it is acted upon" (LW 4:222). Old choices gain whatever status they have as possible-values depending "upon the extent in which the present situation is like the past" and "upon the extent in which *they* were critically made" (MW 8:46). Both of these factors must be determined by a careful examination of particular situations.

This hypothetical stance is to be adopted throughout the entire moral field. So, for example, although Dewey calls into question inherited moral rules, he does not have in mind simply replacing the old rules with new and presumably better ones. In the past, when "Reason was to take the place of custom as a guide to life," it was often mistakenly seen as a new means "to furnish rules as final, as unalterable as those of custom" (MW 4:32). In the sort of ongoing moral inquiry that he has in mind, however, there would be "honest acknowledgement of the uncertainty of the moral situation and of the hypothetical character of all rules of moral mensuration prior to acting upon them" (MW 8:44). Rules would thus be treated "as intellectual instruments to be tested and confirmed—and altered—through consequences effected by acting upon them" (LW 4:221). In a similar fashion, he writes that a moral principle *"is a tool for analyzing a special situation"* (MW 5:302 = LW 7:280), "a formula of the way to respond when specified conditions present themselves" (LW 4:222).[34] Likewise, in moral inquiry "the function of theory is not to furnish a substitute for personal reflective choice but to be an instrument for rendering deliberation more effective and hence choice more intelligent." Moral theory thus should not be expected to yield "a ready-made solution to large moral perplexities" (LW 7:316); but, when it is used properly, it can "uncover the reality, the conditions of the matter, and thus . . . lay bare the circumstances which action has to meet, to synthesize" (EW 3:157).

A second aspect of the development of moral inquiry is that, with this adoption of a hypothetical stance, reflective morality would have to anticipate differences of opinion. We consequently need to foster in individuals a more open mind toward what they see as the moral 'mistakes' of others. Dewey recognizes that this runs against the familiar human stance that "while an open mind may be desirable in respect to physical truths, a completely settled and closed mind is needed in moral matters" (LW 7:329).[35] He maintains, on the contrary, that we must come to anticipate diversity in ethics as in other conduct. A customary morality can rightly expect conformity to some presumably correct code as a result of its method, but a reflective morality cannot. In fact, a reflective morality must assume that variations will occur, and that some of those who cause the variations will challenge the most cherished values of the society, occasionally for the better. "History," he writes, "shows how much of moral progress has been due to those who in their own time were regarded as rebels and treated as criminals" (LW 7:231). We must thus come to anticipate and to accept such moral diversity as our reflective conduct results in.

To live in a world of such moral diversity will require of us a great deal of tolerance; and, within the reconstructed morality of Dewey, tolerance becomes essential. He sees such tolerance to be "not just an attitude of good-humored indifference" but a "positive willingness to permit reflection and inquiry to go on in the faith that the truly right will be rendered more secure through questioning and discussion, while things which have endured merely from custom will be

---

[34] Cf. EW 3:99–103, 157, 158.

[35] Cf. George Santayana: "Moral absolutism is the shadow of moral integrity" (*The Genteel Tradition at Bay*, 27).

amended or done away with" (LW 7:231).[36] We must provisionally accept the sincere moral decisions of others, whether or not they conform to ours. Experimentalism, pluralism, and tolerance go hand-in-hand. The tremendous disparity among ethical claims that now exists is a result, not of too much reflection, but of too little.[37] When we come to be more tolerant of others (and less defensive about our own values), we will be able to stop seeing anyone who differs from us "as a wilful violator of moral principles" and his or her actions as "an expression of self-interest or superior might" (MW 14:59). Rather, we will be able to see these individuals as fellow experimenters and their actions as attempts to solve their moral problems in the best way they can. When we recognize that "without freedom of thought and expression of ideas, moral progress can occur only accidentally and by stealth" (LW 7:231), we will be more willing to live by what Dewey calls "the method of democracy," a method of "positive toleration which amounts to sympathetic regard for the intelligence and personality of others, even if they hold views opposed to ours, and of scientific inquiry into facts and testing of ideas" (LW 7:329; cf. 15:58–59).

A third aspect of moral inquiry that merits special mention is that it would broaden the scope of moral concern to include (potentially, at least) *all* actions, not just those actions that might be singled out in religious commandments or in inherited codes. Rejecting the position that conduct can be divided into "two distinct regions, one of expediency and the other of morality," Dewey writes that moral science "is physical, biological and historic knowledge placed in a human context where it will illuminate and guide the activities of men" (MW 14:146, 204–5). It attempts, in other words, to make use of the results of all available inquiries to help people solve their moral problems. "Morals is not a theme by itself because it is not an episode nor department by itself," he continues. "It marks the issue of all the converging forces of life" (LW 5:275). There is thus no special kind of moral knowledge or moral insight to be sought. There is "no *fixed* line between the morally indifferent and the morally significant," Dewey writes, or between "moral goods, like the

---

[36] Cf. LW 13:152–53, 277, 301; 14:277.

[37] Cf. Robert L. Holmes: "irreconcilable conflicts arise, not in consequence of the approach [Dewey] advocates, but precisely because it has not been implemented" ("John Dewey's Moral Philosophy in Contemporary Perspective," 61).

virtues, and natural goods like health, economic security, art, science and the like" (MW 5:195; 12:178). We must make do, he writes, with "the every-day workings of the same ordinary intelligence that measures dry-goods, drives nails, sells wheat, and invents the telephone" (EW 3:94–95). What we need, he continues, "is that the traditional barriers between science and moral knowledge be broken down, so that there will be organized and consecutive endeavor to use all available scientific knowledge for humane and social ends" (LW 7:283; cf. 4:83).

One part of Dewey's emphasis here is on the continuity of action. As he writes, every action "is, through its consequences, part of a larger whole of behavior" (LW 7:169) and "strengthens or weakens some habit which influences whole classes of judgments" (MW 5:195: cf. 14:193). Another part of his emphasis on increasing our moral scope is our need to recognize the processive nature of our lives, and the relationship between increased knowledge and increased responsibility. "When knowledge of bacteria and germs and their relation to the spread of disease was achieved," he writes, "sanitation, public and private, took on a moral significance it did not have before" (LW 7:282).[38] Still another part of his emphasis upon including all action within moral evaluation is that the inclusion of all action precludes an easy self-satisfaction with our accomplishments up to any point. In this vein, he writes, "morality is a continuing process not a fixed achievement" (MW 14:194) and thus "[t]he bad man is the man who no matter how good he *has* been is beginning to deteriorate, to grow less good. The good man is the man who no matter how morally unworthy he *has* been is moving to become better" (MW 12:180–81; cf. EW 3:374). In a similar fashion, he writes on one occasion, "the better is too often the enemy of the still better" (LW 11:50), and on another, "the better is an enemy of the best" (LW 8:297; cf. 7:272–73). But, under the approach that he is suggesting, the currently accepted 'better' would simply be one option to be compared with all the others.

---

[38] Cf. George Herbert Mead: "If we can control the means we become responsible for the new ends which they enable us to form. And we have come far short of accepting that responsibility. We fashioned the marvelous world of the twentieth century, and then undertook within it to fight an eighteenth-century war. The hands were the hands of Esau, but the voice was the voice of Jacob" ("Bishop Berkeley and His Message," 430).

A fourth aspect of the moral inquiry that Dewey is advocating is the importance of focussing upon the relationship between ends and means. He writes that "the distinction between the instrumental and the final adopted in philosophic tradition as a solving word presents in truth a problem, a problem so deep-seated and far-reaching that it may be said to be *the* problem of experience" (LW 1:277). As a specifically moral topic, as part of his naturalistic theory of morality, Dewey is particularly concerned to prevent any split between 'ideal' ends and 'mere' means. "Means and ends are two names for the same reality," he writes. "The terms denote not a division in reality but a distinction in judgment" (MW 14:28).[39] Together they offer us a chance to control our lives.

> Means-consequences constitute a single undivided situation. Consequently when thought and discussion enter, when theorizing sets in, when there is anything beyond bare immediate enjoyment and suffering, it is the means-consequence relationship that is considered. Thought goes beyond immediate existence to its relationships, the conditions which mediate it and the things to which it is in turn mediatory (LW 1:297).

Ends desired and means used are hence interrelated and interdependent. To achieve an end requires us to concentrate on the means necessary; to bring a means into existence it itself must be treated as "a temporary end until we have attained it" (MW 9:113). When we consider the long flow of life, ends and means both overlap and interpenetrate. "Every condition that has to be brought into existence in order to serve as means is, *in that connection,* an object of desire and an end-in-view, while the end actually reached is a means to future ends as well as a test of valuations previously made" (LW 13:229; cf. 1:297). We must stop thinking of value choices in terms of isolated predetermined ends which are to be arrived at through the use of the most economical means.

For Dewey, there can be no absolute ends the attainment of which is not to be questioned: "ends are determinable only on the ground of the means that are involved in bringing them about" (LW 13:238). As an example of the sort of trouble that a separation of

---

[39] Cf. MW 8:17; 14:27, 160; 13:5.

ends and means can get us into, Dewey suggests that we consider the situation in modern industrial society. He believes that we have mistakenly made a distinction between the "conditions of a worthy life" and the "constituents of it," a distinction that renders the elements of economic well-being "only prerequisites of a good life, not intrinsic elements in it." But because "the life which men, women and children actually lead, the opportunities open to them, the values they are capable of enjoying, their education, their share in all the things of art and science, are mainly determined by economic conditions," any approach to moral theorizing that concentrates exclusively on ends and ignores economic conditions as merely means will be "remote and empty" (LW 4:225). Ends-in-view are developed under conditions of "need, deficit, and conflict" and indicate the solutions to situations. These ends-in-view, when correctly chosen, are "the means of instituting a complete situation or an integrated set of conditions" (LW 13:231–32).

Dewey's advocacy of a moral science thus contains the rejection of the separation of morality from reflection. He writes that "a moral that frames its judgments of value on the basis of consequences must depend in a most intimate manner upon the conclusions of science." And, from what we have seen, it is clear that what Dewey has in mind here is not attempts to reduce human action to the mechanical but rather attempts to uncover and disseminate "the knowledge of the relations between changes which enable us to connect things as antecedents and consequences" (LW 4:218–19). These attempts to link up intelligence and morals should not be seen to contain the assumption that moral choices will become easy, however, or always ultimately successful. Such a reconstruction of morality, Dewey writes, would not "do away with moral struggle and defeat. It would not make the moral life as simple a matter as wending one's way along a well-lighted boulevard" (MW 14:10). It would, however, make the moral life a self-conscious and reflective attempt to create a better life.

4.3 Goods and Values

Dewey maintains that humans are extraordinarily 'plastic' or flexible. We need to feed ourselves and we need to reproduce; but the types of food and the methods of their preparation, and the proprieties of courtship and family structure that have been developed, are without number (Cf. LW 13:287). We need to produce material goods and we need to engage in recreation; but the styles and modes of production, and the arts and games that serve the purpose of recreation, are similarly without number. Our societies organize our unfocussed potentials into significant patterns: "the *meaning* of native activities is not native; it is acquired" (MW 14:65). If we consider developing solutions to these and other human needs to be 'problems', social customs can be seen as shared habitual modes of solving these problems. "Whatever are the native constituents of human nature," he writes, "the culture of a period and group is the determining influence in their arrangement; it is that which determines the patterns of behavior that mark out the activities of any group, family, clan, people, sect, faction, class" (LW 13:75; cf. 3:22–23). These patterns bring order and meaning to our lives. "Custom is for social life what habit is for individual life, namely a principle of organization, continuity, and efficiency" (MW 6:413).

Habits, as we saw in 2.4, give continuity and stability: they enable the live creature to act free from the need to think through and decide on a plan of action at each particular step. Initially, Dewey writes that habits are "the tools which put at our immediate disposal the results of our former experiences, thus economizing force" (EW 4:241). Later, he concludes that the 'tool' metaphor is inadequate, especially since it may cause us to think of habits as "waiting, like tools in a box." Habits are, on the contrary, "active means, means that project themselves, energetic and dominating ways of acting" (MW 14:22; cf. 55). Moreover, a habit is more than just a power: it is a power over us. A habit has this control over us, he writes, "because it is so intimately a part of ourselves. It has a hold upon us because we are the habit" (MW 14:21).[40] More broadly, he maintains that the human being is "a creature of habit, not of reason nor yet of instinct" (MW 14:88). The force of habit, Dewey believes, "is a stronger and deeper part of human nature than is desire for change" (LW 11:133–34). Because of this inertial power, regardless of the specifics of any particular habit, as long as it is functioning at a minimal level of acceptability, we will keep it. "No matter how accidental and

---

[40] Cf. MW 14:29–31; LW 7:304.

irrational the circumstances of its origin, no matter how different the conditions which now exist to those under which the habit was formed," he writes, "the latter persists until the environment obstinately rejects it." He continues: "Habits once formed perpetuate themselves, by acting unremittingly upon the native stock of activities. They stimulate, inhibit, intensify, weaken, select, concentrate and organize the latter into their own likeness. They create out of the formless void of impulses a world made in their own image" (MW 14:88). Because of the essential role played by habit in human life, our goal cannot be some sort of 'liberation' from habits. Our goal is rather the recognition of their general importance to life and of the specific impact of particular habits. Habits "of whose import we are quite unaware," Dewey writes, "possess us, rather than we them. They move us; they control us." And they will continue to do so until such time as "we become aware of what they accomplish, and pass judgment upon the worth of the result" (MW 9:34–35). Thus, he continues, "the real opposition is not between reason and habit but between routine, unintelligent habit, and intelligent habit or art" (MW 14:55).[41]

These personal habits are closely related to the social habits we call customs. "Most of the important habits of the individual," Dewey writes, including "a large part of the content of morality," depend for their origin and growth "upon prior customs in society" (MW 6:413). These customs or traditions are set ways of conduct, ways with which we are in general comfortable and ways that we are for the most part willing to carry forward and defend. Moreover, because of social embellishments these customs are integrally ours. "If social customs are more than uniform external modes of action, it is because they are saturated with story and transmitted meaning," he writes (LW 10:329). So essential and fundamental is the social aspect of the self that we seldom notice how powerfully it shapes our actions. Dewey continues:

> our tendency to ignore the influence of tradition as a controlling factor is itself very largely due to the fact that when we begin to reflect, to invent, and to project new methods and aims, tradition has already done its work so completely that we take it for granted

---

[41] See Flower and Murphey, *A History of Philosophy in America,* vol. 2, 841–43.

without thinking about it, so that we deliberate and project within limits set by custom (MW 6:414).

Again here, as with habits, our goal is not liberation but recognition: "the choice is not between a moral authority outside custom and one within it. It is between adopting more or less intelligent and significant customs" (MW 14:58; cf. LW 1:23).

Dewey writes that people all "require moral sanctions in their conduct: the consent of their kind" (MW 4:49). Most frequently this sanctioning comes indirectly, through custom. The usual or traditional way of doing things—'our' way—carries a special moral status. "In customary society, it does not occur to anyone that there is a difference between what he ought to do, i.e., the moral, and what those about him customarily do, i.e., the social," he writes. "The socially established *is* the moral" (MW 5:387). Even in societies like our own, people often "take their social relations for granted; they are what they are and, in being that, are what they *should* be" (LW 7:314). He continues:

> There are today multitudes of men and women who take their aims from what they observe to be going on around them. They accept the aims provided by religious teachers, by political authorities, by persons in the community who have prestige. Failure to adopt such a course would seem to many persons to be a kind of moral rebellion or anarchy (LW 7:184).[42]

It becomes obvious by this point that Dewey's use of "customary" is not related primarily to some historical or anthropological setting but rather to the nature of moral justification that is being offered, to "the centre of gravity in morality." His intention is to bring about a shift in this center of gravity, from justification through conformity with "ancestral habit" to "conscience, reason, or to some principle which includes thought" (LW 7:162).

The shift Dewey has in mind is a shift from "customary" to "reflective morality" (LW 7:162; cf. MW 12:173); and the most obvious difference between the two, he writes, is that "definite

---

[42] Cf. George Herbert Mead: "As a rule we assume that this general voice of the community is identical with the larger community of the past and the future; we assume that an organized custom represents what we call morality" (*Mind, Self, and Society,* 168).

precepts, rules, definitive injunctions and prohibitions issue from the former, while they cannot proceed from the latter" (LW 7:165). We all recognize that the rules that customary morality generates are not to be taken lightly. Dewey, pointing to the absolutism of these rules, wonders about the motivation of our reliance upon social sanction:

> is there not something strange in the fact that men should consider loyalty to "laws," principles, standards, ideals to be an inherent virtue, accounted unto them for righteousness? It is as if they were making up for some secret sense of weakness by rigidity and intensity of insistent attachment (LW 4:222; cf. MW 14:151–60).

With the absolutism of these rules comes a kind of permanence; and, while science has advanced our knowledge of facts, what are characterized as "values" have been kept separate and unchangeable. As we saw in 3.3, our family systems and our economic organizations, our modes of regulating property accumulation and sexual activity, have successfully managed to resist the challenges of the socially deviant thanks to their presumed eternal validity and their consequent ability to stigmatize such challenges as 'sin' or 'immorality'. Still, the validity of these customs, whether grounded in scriptural command, private revelation or social tradition, continues to be attacked by individuals who respond to the charges of sin and immorality with a counter-charge that the customs are an unnatural restraint on living.

One clear reaction that Dewey sees occurring in response to the absolutism and rigidity of customary moralities is thus the embrace of the kind of antinomianism that he has just characterized as "moral rebellion or anarchy." Whenever a customary morality is firmly in place, there is the ongoing possibility of reaction in the form of an equally extreme ethical position that simply equates *desire* with *value*. He writes of the two views:

> There is either a basic distrust of the capacity of experience to develop its own regulative standards, and an appeal to what philosophers call eternal values, in order to ensure regulation of belief and action; or there is acceptance of enjoyments actually experienced irrespective of the method or operation by which they are brought into existence (LW 4:204).

Under this latter approach, the answer to the question of whether a particular action *'feels* good' is also the answer to the question of whether it '*is* good'. As Dewey writes, "we oscillate between a theory that, in order to save the objectivity of judgments of values, isolates them from experience and nature, and a theory that, in order to save their concrete and human significance, reduces them to mere statements about our own feelings" (LW 4:210; cf. 228). So, for example, if the restrictions imposed upon the conduct of the young by parents and society can be justified only in terms of their successful preservation of custom, then the resultant antinomianism of youth is the reaction to be anticipated. The only way that we will be able to break free from this cycle of calcifying custom and explosive change is through the introduction of what Dewey has characterized as moral science.[43] "If knowledge, even of the most authenticated kind, cannot influence desires and aims, if it cannot determine what is of value and what is not," he writes, "the future outlook as to formation of desires is depressing" (LW 13:162).

It is possible to break free from this cycle of alternating absolutisms and antinomianisms, Dewey believes, by making use of some defensibly grounded distinction between *what is* and *what ought to be*. The is/ought distinction he has in mind appears in his writings under many names, including the following:

"immediate goods . . . and reasonable goods" (LW 1:301);

"the apparent and the real good" (LW 1:319);

"likings" and "values" (LW 1:320);

"the enjoyed and the enjoyable, the desired and the desirable, the satis*fying* and the satis*factory*" (LW 4:207);

"ends that merely seem good and those which are really so . . . specious, deceptive goods, and lasting true goods" (LW 7:181);

"desire and interest" (LW 13:220).

While the criterion of growth that he is using to distinguish between the former *desiderata* and the latter *desideranda* will not be consid-

---

[43] Dewey frequently introduces a problem by suggesting that an apparently irresolvable conflict is actually due to an illegitimate bifurcation. See, for example: EW 2:37; 3:240, 249; 5:117; MW 4:14; 5:218–20; 6:225–26; 12:172, 187, 195, 260; 14:14, 33; 15:237, 240; LW 1:10, 46, 119–20, 295; 2:55–56; 4:18, 88, 157; 7:206; 8:180–83; 9:3; 10:109, 308; 13:141.

ered until 4.4, Dewey views the distinction itself to be completely familiar. "Common sense regards some desires and interests as short-sighted, 'blind,' and others, in contrast, as enlightened, far-sighted"; "some things sweet in the having are bitter in after-taste and in what they lead to" (LW 13:214; 1:298).[44]

In an attempt to understand the nature of this fundamental distinction, we can focus upon Dewey's discussion of the difference between "[t]he *experience* of a good and the *judgment* that something is a value" (MW 8:23).[45] This distinction enables him to recognize the existence or the reality of an experienced good without thereby automatically endorsing it as a value. "To say that something is enjoyed is to make a statement about a fact, something already in existence," he writes; "it is not to judge the value of that fact." Desired things are desired; immediate goods are immediately good. He maintains, moreover, that there is no difference "between such a proposition and one which says that something is sweet or sour, red or black." To go further and call one of the experienced goods a "value," however, is to offer a judgment: "to call an object a value is to assert that it satisfies or fulfills certain conditions" (LW 4:207).[46] Thus, what he calls "a genuine practical judgment" differs from a "mere report" in that a judgment is a claim "as to the importance and need of bringing a fact into existence; or, if it is already there, of sustaining it in existence" (LW 4:208–9). Moreover, as a judgment, a value claim is, even if only implicitly, "a social claim, something

---

[44] Cf. LW 1:311; 7:191, 265; 13:219–20, 325.

[45] Failure to note Dewey's emphasis here upon judgment to resolve particular situations of need led to Morton White's claim that for Dewey "'*a* is desirable' is equivalent to 'For every normal person, *y*, if *y* looks at *a* under normal conditions, then *a* is desired by *y*'" (*Pragmatism and the American Mind,* 160; cf. *Social Thought in America,* 212–19; *Science and Sentiment in America,* 277–80. A better understanding of Dewey's distinction can be found in Sidney Hook, "The Desirable and Emotive in Dewey's Ethics," 200–205; Gail Kennedy, "Science and the Transformation of Common Sense," 322–25; Kennedy, "The Hidden Link in Dewey's Theory of Evaluation," 94; Ralph W. Sleeper, "Dewey's Metaphysical Perspective," 102–8; LW 17:480–84.

[46] Cf. LW 13:207–8; 15:101–6; 16:310–17, 353–57. It should be noted that Dewey himself, on occasion, slips and uses the term 'value' ambiguously for both *desiderata* and *desideranda:* "Values are values, things immediately having certain intrinsic qualities. Of them as values there is accordingly nothing to be said; they are what they are. All that can be said of them concerns their generative conditions and the consequences to which they give rise" (LW 1:297; cf. 301–2; Gouinlock, *John Dewey's Philosophy of Value,* 127–28).

therefore to be tested and confirmed by further trial by others" (LW 7:231).[47] He continues: "To declare something satis*factory* is to assert that it meets specifiable conditions. It is, in effect, a judgment that the thing 'will do'. It involves a prediction; it contemplates a future in which the thing will continue to serve; it *will* do. It asserts a consequence the thing will actively institute; it will *do*" (LW 4:208). In another formulation, he considers the difference between "*priz-ing,* in the sense of holding precious . . . and *appraising* in the sense of *putting* a value upon, *assigning* value to" (LW 13:195).[48] To find an object or an action to be immediately enjoyable, to prize it, simply "poses a problem to judgment." The fact, Dewey writes, "that something is desired only raises the *question* of its desirability[49]; it does not settle it" (LW 4:208).

All things experienced as *goods* are in-so-far *good;* but "intuitions or immediate feelings of what is good and bad are of psychological rather than moral import" (LW 7:267).[50] The immediate, although certainly real, is not trustworthy without further examination. "The *feeling* of good or excellence," Dewey writes, "is as far removed from goodness in fact as a feeling that objects are intellectually thus and so is removed from their being actually so" (LW 4:212; cf. 1:303). Of

---

[47] This is the core of Dewey's rejection of emotivism, a position which maintains that alleged ethical claims are just the expression of wishes without any factual content. On the contrary, Dewey maintains that such exclamations, for example cries for help, are *symbolic* rather than just *expressive,* and indicate: "(i) that there exists a situation that will have obnoxious consequences; (ii) that the person uttering the expressions is unable to cope with the situation; and (iii) that an improved situation is anticipated in case the assistance of others is obtained" (LW 13:201; cf. 196–202). Thus such cries are more than just expressions of desires (Cf. LW 11:462–63; 15:127–40; Gouinlock, *John Dewey's Theory of Value,* 188).

[48] Cf. LW 7:264; 12:174–75.

[49] There is, of course, an ambiguity in the term 'desirable': it can mean either 'capable of being desired' or 'ought to be desired'. There is a similar ambiguity in the term 'valuable': it can mean either 'capable of being valued' or 'ought to be valued'. This ambiguity is also present in Dewey's parallel discussion of 'edible': "Consider the difference between the proposition 'That thing has been eaten', and the judgment 'That thing is edible' " (LW 4:213). Clearly, what he has in mind is not just 'edible' but also 'nutritious'. As he writes elsewhere, there is a difference between "actually eaten" and "nourishing article" (MW 8:27–28). Similarly, 'desirable' or 'valuable' "signifies not that which is capable of being desired," because "experience shows that about everything has been desired by some one at some time," but "that which in the eye of impartial thought *should* be desired" (LW 7:192). 'Valuable' or 'desirable' should then be considered throughout to mean not just 'capable of being valued' or 'capable of being desired' but "satis*factory*" (LW 4:207).

[50] Cf. MW 13:4, 11; LW 7:217; 13:243.

such immediate goods, "which occur and which are possessed and enjoyed, there is no theory at all; they just occur, are enjoyed, possessed; and that is all" (LW 1:301; cf. 4:210). To admit this does not mean, however, that we cannot move from this kind of immediate enjoyment to evaluation. The familiar saying, *de gustibus non disputandum*, may have some value in the elimination of useless factionalism, he writes; but it is "a stupid saying" if we mean by it "that likings cannot be gone behind, or be made subject to inquiry as to their productive causes and consequences" (LW 2:95–96).[51] Throughout the world of ordinary experience, there is the recognition that we can and must go behind immediate likings. "Not stern moralists alone but everyday experience informs us that finding satisfaction in a thing may be a warning, a summons to be on the lookout for consequences" (LW 4:208). Thus, if we distinguish between the enjoyment of goods and their evaluation, we recognize that "[a]ny *theory* of values is perforce entrance into the field of criticism" (LW 1:298), into the field of comparative evaluation. Criticism is necessary, in part, precisely because all immediate goods really are good. The problem, Dewey writes, is that such immediate goods are also "blind and gross"; consequently, the immediate goodness of goods "is both the obstacle to reflective examination and the source of its necessity" (LW 1:320, 304).

This means that moral choices are not necessarily, as is often thought, choices between doing one action that is quite attractive but obviously wrong and another that is less attractive but obviously good, "between something clearly bad and something known to be good" or "between a good which is clear to him and something else which attracts him but which he knows to be wrong" (LW 4:212; 7:165). Quite frequently, deliberation is the result of "an *excess* of preferences" (MW 14:134). We are presented with desirable alternatives "between values each of which is an undoubted good in its place but which now get in each other's way" (LW 7:165). Faced with this need to choose between competing goods, we must stop and deliberate. "We want things that are incompatible with one another; therefore we have to make a choice of what we *really* want." The process of choosing is seen by Dewey as "the emergence of a unified preference out of competing preferences" (MW 14:134). As a consequence, only after deliberation and judgment is Dewey willing

---

[51] Cf. MW 13:13–14; LW 1:303.

to apply the label of *bad:* "the rejected good" is then "the bad of the situation" (MW 14:193; cf. LW 7:187). Up to the point of judgment, however, both the justifiable value and the various pretender-goods are all logically "problematic goods" (LW 4:207).

It is thus necessary to be critical, to evaluate and judge, to reject some immediate goods as nonvalues, for a number of closely related reasons.[52] One of these reasons is that goods are often exclusive. Often to choose one potential good—whether the choice is of a spouse or a career, of a lunch or a movie—is to reject other possibilities. Dewey writes:

> there are always in existence rival claimants for liking. To prefer *this* is to exclude *that*. Any liking is choice, unwittingly performed. There is no selection without rejection; interest and bias are selective, preferential. To take this for a good is to declare in act, though not at first in thought, that it is better than something else.

Thus to choose one "without thought of the other object, and without comparison" is to make a choice that is "arbitrary, capricious, unreasoned" (LW 1:320). In a world of limitations, "[e]njoyment ceases to be a datum and becomes a problem." He continues:

> If values were as plentiful as huckleberries, and if the huckleberry-patch were always at hand, the passage of appreciation into criticism would be a senseless procedure. . . . But values are as unstable as the forms of clouds. The things that possess them are exposed to all the contingencies of existence, and they are indifferent to our likings and tastes (LW 1:298).

A second reason for the necessity of ongoing moral judgment is that we live in a time of rapid change that brings with it "moral unsettlement and tends to destroy many ties which were the chief safeguards of the morals of custom" (LW 7:177). Thus, we need to keep in mind that "in a changing world, old habits must perforce need modification, no matter how good they have been" (MW

---

[52] It is here, as I suggested above in 1.3, that Dewey differs most clearly from William James's noncritical ethics. Cf. James: "Since everything which is demanded is by that fact a good, must not the guiding principle for ethical philosophy (since all demands conjointly cannot be satisfied in this poor world) be simply to satisfy at all times *as many demands as we can?*" (*The Will to Believe,* 155). For a further development of this topic, see my volume, *The Community Reconstructs,* 10–22.

14:41).[53] We cannot casually rely "upon precedent, upon institutions created in the past . . . upon rules of morals that have come to us through unexamined customs, upon uncriticized tradition" (LW 4:217). Neither should we resist attempts at rational reconstruction "till an accumulation of stresses suddenly breaks through the dikes of custom" (MW 14:73). An ongoing process of serious evaluation is necessary. Never before did our human relationships considered broadly and fully require "the unremitting and systematic attention of intelligent thought as they do at present"; in our contemporary situation "the need for reflection and insight is perpetually recurring" (LW 7:177, 212). A final point is that, while Dewey may be charged with severity here, he cannot be accused of asceticism. Our aim is not to avoid contact with goods, or to fail to enjoy them, but rather to enhance their power and range over the long-term. "There is no reason for not enjoying the present," he writes, "but there is every reason for examination of the objective factors of *what* is enjoyed before we translate enjoyment into a belief in excellence" (MW 14:175).

4.4. Human Needs and Moral Growth

We have been exploring in great detail such topics as the role of scientific method in improving moral choices, the move from customary to reflective morality, and the difference between apparent goods and true values. But we have yet to consider the fundamental point underlying all of these topics. In this section, I want to examine the criterion of growth, introduced in 2.5, that is at the basis of Dewey's attempt to develop a moral science. Morris Cohen, among others, complains that Dewey never really offers such a criterion. After recognizing Dewey's call for social reconstruction to advance the common good, Cohen remarks: "Just what constitutes an improvement of man's estate we are not clearly told."[54] Perhaps Cohen's criticism is related not so much to Dewey's alleged lack of a

---

[53] Cf. Jane Addams: "in moments of industrial stress and strain the community is confronted by a moral perplexity which may arise from the mere fact that the good of yesterday is opposed to the good of today, and that which may appear as a choice between virtue and vice is really but a choice between virtue and virtue" (*Democracy and Social Ethics,* 172).

[54] Cohen, "Later Philosophy," 256; cf. *American Thought,* 296.

criterion as to what he sees as the defective nature of the criterion Dewey offered. To use growth as a moral criterion appears to some as vacuous[55] and to others as question-begging;[56] but Dewey believes that growth provides the only legitimate criterion of moral worth. As we proceed, readers will need to determine for themselves both the value of growth as a criterion and the accuracy of Dewey's conception of growth.

At the basis of Dewey's attempt to use growth as a criterion of moral worth is an understanding of human nature and of human needs.[57] His understanding of human nature, as we saw in chapter 2, emphasizes the pervasiveness of our natural, social and problem-solving aspects. Although human life is highly plastic and constantly adapting, there is, he writes, a "basic identity of human nature" (MW 14:230; cf. LW 10:250) that is reflected in human needs. By such needs, he is referring to "the inherent demands that men make because of their constitution," needs that are "so much a part of our being that we cannot imagine any condition under which they would cease to be." Some examples are the needs "for food and drink and for moving about." He continues that there are other, less "physical," needs:

> There are other things not so directly physical that seem to me equally engrained in human nature. I would mention as examples the need for some kind of companionship; the need for exhibiting energy, for bringing one's powers to bear upon surrounding conditions; the need for both cooperation with and emulation of one's fellows for mutual aid and combat alike; the need for some sort of aesthetic expression and satisfaction; the need to lead and to follow; etc. (LW 13:286).[58]

---

[55] Cf. Richard Hofstadter's criticism of the use of *growth* as a criterion of educational success: "The idea that education is growth is at first blush all but irresistible. Certainly education is not a form of shrinkage" (*Anti-intellectualism in American Life,* 373).

[56] Cf. Arthur Bestor: The Pragmatic "system of values was little more than an unexamined acceptance of the preferences that men of good will in America had been expressing for the two or three generations just past" ("John Dewey and American Liberalism," 19; cf. John E. Smith, *The Spirit of American Philosophy,* 149–50; Murphy, "John Dewey and American Liberalism," 427–28, 431).

[57] In spite of his Darwinian grounding of the human organism, Dewey offers no defense of animal rights. Cf. LW 2:98–103; LW 13:333.

[58] Cf. MW 14:45; LW 2:300; 3:22; 6:239; 10:250–51; 13:142–44; 14:260–61.

Although humankind lives in a changing world and changes with it, relative to needs like these Dewey believes that human nature does not change. Such needs as these, he writes, have been human needs "since man became man" and there is no evidence "that they will change as long as man is on the earth" (LW 13:286).

With this understanding of the needs of human nature, it is possible to recognize the task of morality as determining that course of conduct "which satisfies want, craving, which fulfills or makes complete the need which stirs to action" in such a wise way as to "meet the demands of impartial and far-sighted thought as well as satisfy the urgencies of desire" (LW 7:191). Dewey is thus committed to a naturalistic conception of ethical obligation that places that obligation in the fulfillment of human needs. Obligation moves in the progression from the *recognition* that some action is the solution to a problem, to the *judgment* that it is the good of the situation, to the *assertion* that it ought to be done. "The difference between saying, 'This act is the one to be done, this act will meet the situation,' and saying, 'This act *ought* to be done,'" Dewey writes, "is merely verbal." Put more succinctly: "the 'ought' is the 'is' of *action*" (EW 3:108–9). For Dewey, the 'should' emerges as easily in ethics as in nutrition or engineering (cf. LW 13:209–10).[59]

These values must be related to the purpose of human life which, for Dewey, can only be specified as personal growth. We have seen in 2.5 and 3.2 how his emphasis upon growth in the process of addressing life's problems avoids the impasse of seeing life as just a series of problems. In a correct conception of ethics, he writes, "the process of growth, of improvement and progress . . . becomes the significant thing." No fixed or attainable goal can be set up as a moral ideal. "Growth itself is the only moral 'end'," he writes. He is using the term 'end' here in the following sense: "The end is no longer a terminus or limit to be reached. It is the active process of transforming the existent situation. Not perfection as a final goal, but the ever-enduring process of perfecting, maturing, refining is the aim in

---

[59] Cf. Gail Kennedy: "If the question is raised, 'Why this alternative rather than another?' the answer is, 'Because it is a more adequate solution of the problem.' Since what the situation demands—the claim made by it—is the most adequate solution possible, it follows that whichever proposed alternative does seem more adequate is within that context the better—it is the 'good' *of* that situation or it is the 'right' thing to do *in* that situation" ("The Hidden Link in Dewey's Theory of Evaluation," 94).

living" (MW 12:181; cf. 9:55). This indicates the way in which Dewey saw human growth as continuous with nature, with the past, and with the future. This continuity of growth is the 'end' or purpose of life. Life itself is the process. "The reality *is* the growth-process itself" (LW 1:210). The job of value criticism is to simplify, broaden and extend this growth process.

Dewey maintains that "growing, or the continuous reconstruction of experience, is the only end" (MW 12:185). We must consequently attempt to uncover the exact conception of growth that he holds. A firm starting point comes from the realization of what it does *not* mean: growth is not the patterning of life after some "presupposed fixed *schema* or outline" of what it is to be a person (EW 4:43). "No individual or group will be judged by whether they come up to or fall short of some fixed result, but by the direction in which they are moving" (MW 12:180). Moral growth "does not mean, therefore, to act so as to fill up some presupposed ideal self" (EW 4:49).[60] From the positive side, we can see that the prime feature of growth is the recognition that it is a continuous reconstructive process of self-realization. "The dominant vocation of all human beings at all times," he writes, "is living—intellectual and moral growth" (MW 9:320). Growth or self-realization is an endless process in both its aspects. First, in a world where human existence remains precarious, there are always new powers to be gained and new controls to be instituted. Second, in a world amenable to pluralistic understandings, the amount of meaning that is possible is without limit; there are always new insights and fuller conceptions to be sought. "We always live at the time we live and not at some other time," he writes, "and only by extracting at each present time the full meaning of each present experience are we prepared for doing the same thing in the future" (LW 13:29–30).[61]

In our moral lives, we recognize on occasion a possible future self who would have actualized traits and qualities that are at present only possibilities. Growth or movement toward "that ideal self which is

---

[60] The schema approach, Dewey believes, is frequently a problem in education—especially when we see human capacities in fundamentally negative terms, and hence see the job of the educator as filling up the child's emptiness. However, he writes, if educational growth is viewed "intrinsically" rather than "comparatively," we will be able to recognize that "[g]rowth is not something done to them; it is something they do" (MW 9:46–47).

[61] Cf. MW 12:185; 14:183–84; LW 5:272.

presented in aspirations" is a process of reconstruction—"a more or less painful and difficult reconstruction of the habitual self" (MW 5:326; cf. EW 5:47). Dewey maintains that every moral act has an impact on the self. Every choice, he writes, has a double relation to the self: "It reveals the existing self and it forms the future self." As a consequence of the latter point, "it is proper to say that in choosing this object rather than that, one is in reality choosing what kind of person or self one is going to be" (LW 7:286–87; cf. MW 14:150). This is so because by their actions individuals are determining in large measure the direction and amount of growth which is to take place. He continues this same theme when he writes that "some acts tend to narrow the self, to introduce friction into it, to weaken its power, and in various ways to *disintegrate* it, while other acts tend to expand, invigorate, harmonize, and in general organize the self" (EW 4:244). These latter acts are obviously the ones that should be performed. "Every good act realizes the selfhood of the agent who performs it; every bad act tends to the lowering or destruction of selfhood" (MW 5:352). One key matter in moral choice then becomes the relation between "the old, the habitual self" and the "new and moving self" (LW 7:306–7). And, in his continued emphasis upon the development of the self and upon the point that "morality is a continuing process not a fixed achievement" (MW 14:194), we find the same severity that we encountered above in 2.5. The bad person, as we saw in 4.2, is the one who is "beginning to deteriorate, to grow less good"; the good person, the one who is "moving to become better" (MW 12:180–81).

If we wish to evaluate particular experience with regard to personal growth, we must consider two factors: "the principle of continuity of experience" and the principle of "interaction." The former maintains that "every experience both takes up something from those which have gone before and modifies in some way the quality of those which come after." Consequently, those experiences are growth experiences—and, in our present context, those 'immediate likings' are 'real values'—that "create conditions for further growth" and which do not "set up conditions that shut off the person who has grown in this particular direction from the occasions, stimuli, and opportunities for continuing growth in new directions." The latter principle "assigns equal rights to both factors in experience—objective and internal conditions" (LW 13:19, 24), the environmental and individual aspects of the situation. For social

creatures, this latter criterion emphasizes that those experiences—
'likings'—which develop the individual's perception of his or her
place in the ongoing social situation and foster the individual's
ability to take part in and improve such ongoing situations are
growth experiences—'values'. These two principles together constitute "the longitudinal and lateral aspects of experience." When an
individual moves from situation to situation, "something is carried
over from the earlier to the later ones" because of the former; and,
because of the latter, "his world, his environment, expands or
contracts" (LW 13:25).[62] By means of using these two criteria of
experience, Dewey hopes to be able to offer a means of avoiding the
inclusion of 'negative growth'—or what we might better call
'degeneracy'—as a kind of growth. "That a man may grow in
efficiency as a burglar, as a gangster, or as a corrupt politician, cannot
be doubted," he writes (LW 13:19).[63] What can be doubted,
however, is whether this process is properly considered to be "growth
in general" (LW 13:19).[64]

Recognizing that humans are social creatures, the earlier question
of "what sort of self is in the making" also becomes the question of
"what kind of a world is making" (MW 14:150). Moral growth is
necessarily a social process because both phases of growth—greater
control and increased meaning—implicate the individual more
closely with other members of the group. Greater control of disease,
for example, is a social phenomenon which affects all the members of
the community. Increased meaning brings individuals into contact
with others through the sharing of experience, a value that, as we
shall see below in 7.1, Dewey considers to be "the greatest of human
goods" (LW 1:157). This growth continues on, potentially without
end:

> We are not caught in a circle; we traverse a spiral in which social
> customs generate some consciousness of interdependencies, and
> this consciousness is embodied in acts which in improving the

---

[62] See the discussion of the two aspects of *"an* experience" above in 3.1.

[63] Cf. MW 9:88–92, 105; LW 2:328.

[64] Cf. Morris Eames, who explicitly rejects the view that Dewey's position can be
accurately interpreted to allow "that growth could be increase in evil, falsehood, and
ugliness." The correct interpretation, Eames continues, is "growth toward the
intellectual, moral, social, and aesthetic ideals of life" (*Pragmatic Naturalism*,
206–7).

environment generate new perceptions of social ties, and so on forever. The relationships, the interactions are forever there as fact, but they acquire meaning only in the desires, judgments and purposes they awaken (MW 14:225; cf. LW 3:104).

Social growth thus involves bringing to consciousness the "[i]nfinite relationships of man with his fellows and with nature [that] already exist," he writes, a growth that is possible "in the midst of conflict, struggle and defeat" (MW 14:226).

In the attempt to lead a moral life conceived as a life of growth, there are no quick answers, Dewey maintains, no rules or absolutes. The difficulty here is, of course, a difficulty of moral living rather than one of his philosophy. We are all engaged in the process of developing and maintaining a sense of good moral judgment and of living in accordance with it. Oftentimes, we discuss this sense of good judgment in terms of an individual's moral 'character', such that a person of sound moral judgment might be referred to as 'a person of good character.' Dewey's use of this term, however, is more closely allied to the equally familiar descriptive sense of the term that allows for such uses as "a selfish and egoistic character" (MW 5:234). He describes character as "the interpenetration of habits" or "the name given to the working interaction of habits" (MW 14:29, 31; cf. LW 7:173), thus offering a sense of the term that emphasizes an individual's habitual self rather than a reflective moral stance. The term that Dewey prefers to use in relation to good moral judgment is 'taste'. His concern with taste is, as might be expected, not with the arbitrary likings and their accidental origins with which the term is often associated. He writes that we need to overcome our normal sense of contentment "with haphazard beliefs about the qualities of objects that regulate our deepest interests" (LW 4:214) and develop a 'taste' for what is valuable. He continues, "if the word be used in the sense of an appreciation at once cultivated and active, one may say that the formation of taste is the chief matter wherever values enter in, whether intellectual, esthetic or moral." This formation is a matter of the interaction of intelligence and experience—inquiring, testing, correcting, learning—leading to growth. "The formation of a cultivated and effectively operative good judgment or taste," he writes, "is the supreme task set to human beings by the incidents of experience" (LW 4:209).

Undergirding this moral 'taste' or moral 'vision', there will always be a set of fundamental moral values. I am distinguishing here among *fundamental values* (for example, democracy or individualism), the various *specific conceptions* of these values (for example, particular understandings of democracy or individualism), and *instantiations* of these conceptions (for example, in particular customs, laws and evaluations).[65] Dewey's life and writings demonstrate the acceptance of such fundamental values as democracy, equality, freedom, and so on. While the sources of these various fundamental values may be of some biographical interest,[66] as with other questions that we have considered, origins are of less importance to those operating in the Pragmatic spirit than are results. The question of the origin of these values is thus of less importance than that of their possible conceptions and instantiations—how we, for example, define democracy or legislate equality—and their possible justifiability. Attempts at such justification must necessarily be in terms of their impact upon future social experience: Do we want a society that emphasizes equality, or some other value? Do we believe that freedom is best understood in one sense, or in another? Do we think that this law will promote democracy as we conceive it?

In this process Dewey does not believe that he is proving to the skeptic, for example, the ultimate value of democracy, but only that democratic practices are more likely to lead to lives that democratic values see as more worthwhile. "Can we find any reason [why we should prefer democracy] that does not ultimately come down to the belief," he asks, "that democratic social arrangements promote a better quality of human experience, one which is more widely accessible and enjoyed, than do non-democratic and anti-democratic forms of social life?" (LW 13:18). Moreover, he maintains that because of their justifiability in the process of experience such fundamental values as democracy, equality and freedom do not constitute some sort of abstract or rootless ends. On the contrary, he maintains that "common experience is capable of developing from within itself methods which will secure direction for itself and will create inherent standards of judgment and value" (LW 1:41; cf.

---

[65] This tripartite distinction reappears in a slightly different form in the discussion of conceptual reconstruction in 5.2.

[66] Cf. Dewey's discussion of his democratic faith: "I did not invent this faith. I acquired it from my surroundings as far as those surroundings were animated by the democratic spirit" (LW 14:227).

10:41). Initially, of course, the conceptions and instantiations of these fundamental values exist in only an implied form and they are not recognized by all. We are dependent upon the work of the reformer who is driven by such values and who attempts to show the members of the society the possibilities within its grasp.

There is a frequently heard criticism that Pragmatic social thought, and Dewey's work in particular, operated to advance a set of social values like democracy and equality that were not generated by Pragmatism itself.[67] The claim here is true: Dewey's support for values like democracy and equality was not the result of his philosophical method. The values arose within human experience and the purpose of the method being developed was to expand their reach. The fact, however, that this point of the values arising prior to the method is offered as a criticism of Dewey again suggests the importance of distinguishing between the fundamental values and their conceptions and instantiations. In any case, because of this separability of method and value, there is the possibility of the 'misuse' of the method by others who are not always guided by the broad humanistic values that were originally assumed. Such misuse has certainly occurred; and Dewey himself would seem to have been on occasion guilty, as in his support for World War I[68] and on his general deadness to American race problems.[69] But it is not obvious

---

[67] Cf., for example, H. S. Thayer: "It is clear that pragmatic social thought, advanced in its most influential intellectual form by Dewey, operated with certain ulterior moral assumptions never made wholly explicit nor of evident justification. Thus, for Dewey, as for many thinkers, organically related, unified, integrated social conditions are more *desirable* than conflicting ones. This might be true, but it is not pragmatism, or instrumentalism, that assures us of this truth" (*Meaning and Action,* 446; cf. Georges Dicker, "John Dewey: Instrumentalism in Social Action," 225–26; Kenneth Burke, "Liberalism's Family Tree," 115; Howard White, "The Political Faith of John Dewey," 360; Walter Feinberg, "The Conflict between Intelligence and Community in Dewey's Educational Philosophy," 237, 247; Timothy Kaufman-Osborn, "Pragmatism, Policy Science, and the State," 831–35).

[68] Cf. Randolph S. Bourne: "Dewey, of course, always meant his philosophy, when taken as a philosophy of life, to start with values. But there was always that unhappy ambiguity in his doctrine as to just how values were created, and it became easier and easier to assume that just any growth was justified and almost any activity valuable so long as it achieved ends" (*War and the Intellectuals,* 60–61). For a further consideration of Bourne's criticism of Dewey's support of World War I, see: Clarence Karier, "Making the World Safe for Democracy," 26–31; Westbrook, *John Dewey and American Democracy,* 202–12; David W. Levy, *Herbert Croly of 'The New Republic,'* 259–62.

[69] Cf. LW 6:224–30; and my "Du Bois and James," 571–72.

that the possibility of misuse, or the prior origin of the fundamental values, should be seen as a criticism of his philosophical position. Considering the question of misuse, we remember that science may be, as we have seen in 4.1, "strictly impersonal" (LW 6:54); but the applications of scientific method are never 'neutral'. Regrettable actions do not take place because of a lack of values, he maintains, but because of mistaken ones. "It is false that the evils of the situation arise from absence of ideals; they spring from wrong ideals" (MW 12:154). And, it seems to me, criticisms that Dewey is unclear about the origins or the justification of fundamental values should be redirected more to considering the unclearness of fundamental values themselves and the complexity of their justification.

CHAPTER 5

Building a Better Society

W E SAW IN the introduction to chapter 4 that it is possible to distinguish three phases in the activities of all social reformers. The first phase is the lamentation over the present ills, a lament that is the same in form regardless of whether the content comes from William Zebulon Foster or Herbert Hoover, from a Fundamentalist or a Unitarian. The second phase is the development and presentation by each particular critic of criteria for determining what would constitute a fulfilled life. We have just considered Dewey's presentation in terms of growth. We now move on to the third phase: the introduction and evaluation of proposals designed to enable us to build a better society. In Dewey's case, these proposals are of two different sorts. Some of his suggestions are fundamentally intellectual in nature and require us to rethink the ideas that underlie our social practice. For example, what would a fully 'democratic' society be like at any given time or how should we understand a concept like 'individualism' or 'work'. Intellectual reconstruction more broadly involves the integration of the intellectual efforts of the various experts of the community to help mold the indeterminate social situation into an addressable problem. Other of Dewey's suggestions are more practical: institutional reconstruction involves our collective attempts to evaluate and enact the suggestions of our various experts about how we should live our lives. We thus need to decide, for example, whether a system of national electioneering satisfies a full sense of 'democracy'; and, if not, what we need to do to make it more democratic. Similarly, we need to decide how to make possible the attainment of a richer sense of 'individualism' or the creation of a better working situation. The various proposals that Dewey suggested demonstrate the degree to which his understanding of the nature of social inquiry reflects the pattern of inquiry that he developed to analyze the individual's attempts to address the problematic situation. Habits of thought and of action become over time outdated and must be reconstructed. The efforts of the members of the community benefit each other as they attempt, through cooperative inquiry, to address their common ills. It is to Dewey's discussion of building a better society that we now turn.

5.1. The Political Crisis

The Pragmatic philosophy of John Dewey and the other Social Pragmatists, especially George Herbert Mead and James Hayden Tufts, is in its nature a philosophy of social reconstruction.[1] It was developed as a means of contributing to the intelligent resolution of social problems by turning from *the problems of philosophers and other intellectuals* to *the problems of average women and men*. Their basic hope was that we might be able to use our newly found intellectual stance—'science'—to address more adequately the problems of contemporary living. Through careful study we might be able, for example, to determine what aspects of our social problems are the results of outdated habits, to develop new and better habits—better adapted and more adaptive institutions—and to bring these institutions into existence. And while we cannot be unaware of the limitations of the Social Pragmatists and others, both with regard to the range of social problems that their fellow citizens were facing and their recognition of the embeddedness of these problems in the American context,[2] we must recognize the value of what they did accomplish and the potential for further efforts contained in their work.

There is a theme running through the political thought of many

---

[1] The evidence for this claim is all of Part Two of the present volume. For another attempt to flesh out this claim, see my volume, *The Community Reconstructs*.

[2] Cf. Cornel West: "American pragmatism emerges with profound insights and myopic blindnesses, enabling strengths and debilitating weaknesses, all resulting from distinctive features of American civilization: its revolutionary beginning combined with a slave-based economy; its elastic liberal rule of law combined with an entrenched business-dominated status quo; its hybrid culture in combination with a collective self-definition as homogeneously Anglo-American; its obsession with mobility, contingency and pecuniary liquidity combined with a deep moralistic impulse; and its impatience with theories and philosophies alongside ingenious technological innovation, political strategies of compromise, and personal devices for comfort and convenience" (*The American Evasion of Philosophy*, 5).

'progressive' thinkers, Dewey included, that 'things' once worked pretty well, but no longer. Once life was simpler: areas were less densely populated, there was a more manageable technological base, people had free land, open opportunity, and a lesser degree of interdependence, there was greater continuity from generation to generation, and so on. It is this theme—misunderstood as a kind of nostalgia—that has led to the many complaints that these 'progressives' were really attempting to return to the past.[3] Under these simpler circumstances, it seems that our inherited democracy worked. People lived apart, choices were less complex and facts more apparent, people shared values, felt compromises were few, wealth was reasonably equal—or at least no one was dependent without blame—and so on. Dewey writes that our democracy "was won in a more or less external and accidental manner" (LW 13:185) and because of conditions that were "primarily non-political in nature" (LW 2:288; cf. MW 15:151). The political choices and programs developed arose from, and were directed at solving, particular felt problems; and the individuals involved did about as well as could have been expected with these problems. The only serious mistake our predecessors made, he thinks, was of an abstract sort: they failed to see these attempts as responses to particular problems. On the contrary, their subsequent formulations "were uttered and held not as hypotheses with which to direct social experimentation but as final truths, dogmas" (LW 2:326). These individuals thought that they had created what Dewey calls "a machine that solved the problem of perpetual motion in politics" (LW 14:225).[4] After a series of great changes, however, during which "an agricultural and rural people has become an urban industrial population" (LW 13:69), he writes that we must recognize the need for adopting a more hypothetical stance in order "to re-create by deliberate and determined endeavor the kind of democracy which in its origin one hundred and fifty years

---

[3] Cf. Richard Hofstadter: Progressivism's "general theme was the effort to restore a type of economic individualism and political democracy that was widely believed to have existed earlier in America and to have been destroyed by the great corporation and the corrupt political machine; and with that restoration to bring back a kind of morality and civic purity that was also believed to have been lost" (*The Age of Reform*, 5–6, cf. 215–17; cf. Charles Forcey, "Introduction" to Herbert Croly, *The Promise of American Life*, ix; Henry F. May, *The End of American Innocence*, 22; George Novack, *Pragmatism versus Marxism*, 39).

[4] Cf. LW 11:416; 13:87.

ago was largely the product of a fortunate combination of men and circumstances" (LW 14:225; cf. 13:186).

It does not pose a severe challenge to Dewey's presentation to suggest that there never really was a time when 'things' actually did work without problems.[5] It is clear that Dewey postulates no 'golden age.' His point is rather that, as we look back to survey the social actions of the past, we find there a kind of settledness, whereas the social situation that he and others encountered was full of confusion and uncertainty. It was a situation in need of reconstruction. In terms of the pattern of inquiry that we examined in 2.4, we have entered into an indeterminate situation that is obscure in meaning and unsettling in effect. "Individuals are groping their way," he writes, "through situations which they do not direct and which do not give them direction" (LW 5:75).[6] The easy times in which we thought we could rely upon casual and presumably automatic progress were now over; and it was necessary to reject our "policy of drift as far as human intelligence and effort were concerned" (LW 15:253). We could no longer expect "democratic institutions that work successfully" to be produced through a trial-and-error process of the actions of "human nature when left to itself" (LW 13:151). It was now necessary and possible to take control of our lives and to *guide* them deliberately toward the common good. As the conducting of the Great War—however tragic an instance it was—had made clear, "it is possible for human beings to take hold of human affairs and manage them, to see an end which has to be gained, a purpose which must be fulfilled, and deliberately and intelligently to go to work to organize the means, the resources and the methods of accomplishing those results" (MW 11:82; cf. 87–92). By means of intelligent action, we can collectively gain control of our shared historical existence and move it toward the good. "To foresee consequences of existing conditions is to surrender neutrality and

---

[5] Cf. Carl Sandburg: "There are those who speak of confusion today / as though yesterday there was order / rather than confusion" ("Under the Capitol Dome," *The Complete Poems of Carl Sandburg*, 696).

[6] Cf. George Herbert Mead: "We have never been so uncertain as to what are the values which economics undertakes to define, what are the political rights and obligations of citizens, what are the community values of friendship, of passion, of parenthood, of amusement, of beauty, of social solidarity in its unnumbered forms, or of those values which have been gathered under the relations of man to the highest community or to God" (*The Philosophy of the Present*, 167).

drift; it is to take sides in behalf of the consequences that are preferred" (LW 5:109–10).[7]

Dewey grew to consciousness during a process of great changes in American economic and political and ethnic life. His philosophy is essentially and deliberately political. Throughout his writing career, but especially in the turbulent years between the World Wars, he produced books and articles of political import. I have in mind such volumes as *The Public and Its Problems* (1927), an inquiry into whether and how a contemporary society might become a community; *Individualism, Old and New* (1930), a deliberate rethinking of the meaning of the central value of the human individual; *Liberalism and Social Action* (1935), a study of the ends and means of radical change; *Freedom and Culture* (1939), a defense of the need to create institutions for the support of freedom; and his more explicitly political writing for such organs as the *People's Lobby Bulletin,* the *Newsletter of the League for Independent Political Action* and *Common Sense.*[8]

It is possible to uncover in Dewey's political work a fairly well worked out method of social reconstruction. Since the idea of a 'method' of social reconstruction might initially seem troubling, it is perhaps useful at this point to discuss his sense of method, indicating initially what it does *not* mean. First, having a method for social action does not imply having in advance a minutely prepared procedural protocol that can be imposed upon events in the social realm. Similarly, his sense of method should not be understood to include a system of using general principles to generate quick solutions. In none of his discussions of inquiry is there the suggestion that any such method for generating answers could be developed. On the contrary, for Dewey, possible solutions just appear: "suggestions just spring up, flash upon us, occur to us" (LW 12:113–14). So, methodicalness, in the sense intended, implies neither the necessity for some predetermined plan of action nor a

---

[7] Cf. Walter Lippmann: "We can no longer treat life as something that has trickled down to us. We have to deal with it deliberately, devise its social organization, alter its tools, formulate its method, educate and control it. In endless ways we put intention where custom has reigned. . . . This is what mastery means: the substitution of conscious intention for unconscious striving" (*Drift and Mastery,* 267, 269; cf. David E. Price, "Community and Control").

[8] For Dewey's writings in these and similar organs, see volumes 5, 6, 9, 11, 13, 14, and 15 of the *Later Works.*

system for generating quick and easy answers from a general philosophical viewpoint.

Turning to a closer consideration of what Dewey does intend by method, we recognize that there are many procedures or techniques —'methods'—that, if adopted, will yield possible answers to our social problems. We approach still closer to his sense of method when we examine these various methods to discover "why some methods succeed and other methods fail" (LW 12:17). Thus, after finding methodicalness in virtually all procedures for organizing action, Dewey focusses upon evaluating the various methods to determine which are more likely to resolve problematic situations and produce desired results. Bad methods are thus methods that produce "short-cut 'solutions'" that "do not get rid of the conflict and problems; they only get rid of the feeling of it" (MW 12:160). As he notes, "[u]ncertainty is got rid of by fair means or foul" (LW 4:181). On the other hand, a good method would "protect the mind against itself" (MW 12:99) by making sure that the doubt was put to "productive use" (LW 4:182) by the inquirers who recognize that the existence of such problems requires that they make changes through social exploration and evaluation.

Dewey's method can be studied both as a means to better understanding his philosophical work and as a means to assist us in our attempts to deal with such recurring problems as unemployment, health care allocation, farm problems, the production and usage of energy supplies, and so on. This method—to be sketched out in this chapter—is based upon his work on the pattern of inquiry that we considered above in 2.4. In our reasonably well functioning social system something happens and doubts and conflicts arise. Recognition of this trouble results in the development of a self-conscious public and the formulation of the problem. In its attempts to address the problem, the public then proceeds in some organized fashion through a process of social inquiry, hypothesizing and testing. The results of this inquiry, some proposed institutional change involving new laws or modified regulations, are then hypothetically introduced and socially evaluated. And, if all goes well, this hypothetical solution is adopted and works as a solution to the problem.

Dewey's method of social reconstruction operates on two distinguishable 'levels'.[9] The first level is that of the formation of problems and the selection and development of potential solutions. This level of social reconstruction is largely intellectual in nature. For example, we need to address such questions as these: What level of energy will be required by society in the foreseeable future, and how can this level be provided at the least cost to ourselves, our environment and our descendants? Or, what sorts of educational policies should be enacted to ensure the individual development and happiness of our future citizens and the well-being of the larger group, and how can these policies be introduced and managed in our current social situation? Especially in our complex modern world, this level of reconstruction exploits the talents and special skills of intellectual experts. To solve problems like these, it is necessary to *think differently;* and those members of the society with special experience or with special expertise may be particularly helpful in formulating problems and suggesting possible solutions. Individuals like chemists and biologists, engineers and economists, lawyers and historians, poets and philosophers, may—depending upon the particular case —have something to say from the point of view of their particular talents and preparations in the formulating of the problem and in the suggesting of possible solutions. In the cases of our energy and educational policies, for example, each group of experts has a special contribution to make that is relevant to understanding and addressing the particular problem. The work of fundamental social reconstruction, Dewey writes, "can be done only by the resolute, patient, cooperative activities of men and women of good will, drawn from every useful calling, over an indefinitely long period" (MW 12:273).[10]

In 3.4 above, we considered Dewey's understanding of the

---

[9] I use this term to describe the two stages or phases of the ongoing process of social reconstruction, in spite of its potentially adverse spatial connotations, because I think that it successfully captures Dewey's emphasis upon experience penetrating into nature, "reaching down into its depths," tunnelling "in all directions," and bringing "to the surface things at first hidden" (LW 1:11). In just this way, intellectual reconstruction uncovers and carries to the surface for public discussion the facts, ideas, and suggestions that are to play such a central role at the level of institutional reconstruction. See my volume, *The Community Reconstructs,* 46–48.

[10] Cf. Max C. Otto: "The farmer, the laborer, the businessman, the lawyer, the scientist, the doctor, the political leader, the journalist—all these must be enlisted with the clergyman, the teacher, the social worker, the philosopher, in the undertaking that concerns us all" (*The Human Enterprise,* 86).

philosopher's role as interpreter or "messenger" or "liaison officer" (LW 1:306) among the various disciplines. We have also seen his emphasis upon the philosopher's contribution through evaluation and criticism. Here we can see a third aspect of Dewey's understanding of the role of philosophy in society. Philosophers, he believes, have a special expertise with regard to their sense of the historical development and the current implications of our social ideas. He consequently writes that they could make an additional contribution through their careful study of our social ideas. Philosophers would then function as custodians of the full historical life of the terms through the study of the history of ideas, and as testers of contemporary formulations and suggesters of new formulations in the ongoing reconstruction of these terms. He writes, for example, of the needed inquiry into "moral conceptions and doctrines" to see "whether they are intellectually competent to meet the needs of the situation" (MW 15:54), and of philosophy's skill for "clarifying certain of the ideas which enter into the discussion" (MW 10:245; cf. 15:89) and its ability to "sharpen and deepen" our understanding of our problems (LW 14:89). In political contexts, this philosophical expertise is related to political ideas such as 'democracy' and 'justice', 'freedom' and 'equality', and so on. It is also related to other less-studied but politically important ideas such as 'health' and 'security', 'education' and 'science', and so on. Dewey's assumption is that at least one element in all of our social problems is the result of conceptual confusion. "Any significant problem involves conditions that for the moment contradict each other," he writes. "Solution comes only by getting away from the meaning of terms that is already fixed upon and coming to see the conditions from another point of view, and hence in a fresh light" (MW 2:273). We can learn a great deal, even if only negatively, by escaping the merely traditional aspects of ideas.

This contribution to conceptual reconstruction is not the exclusive responsibility of philosophers, of course. There is no "sacred priesthood," Dewey writes (MW 12:273). "The task of revising our words, remaking our tools, even while they are actually at work," he continues, "cannot be confined to those who are professionally and officially 'philosophers'" (LW 3:345).[11] Neither

---

[11] Dewey does maintain, however, that philosophers bear a special burden for "emancipating mankind from the errors which philosophy has itself fostered" by its persistent bifurcation of life into the real and the ideal (MW 12:154; cf. EW 4:62; MW 10:46–47; LW 3:120–21; 5:160).

is it always the supreme or primary aspect of political reconstruction. It is, however, the primary task for philosophers. On one hand, from the point of view of society, it is necessary work and work that philosophers can do, probably better than others. On the other hand, from the point of view of philosophers themselves, "it is a vital matter that they have an active share in developing points of view and outlooks which will further recognition of what is humanly at stake and of how the necessary work may be initiated" (LW 16:380).

On the second level of this method of social reconstruction under which Dewey is operating, we find the public testing and evaluating of ideas and proposals that the experts and others have put forward, and the enactment of those that are found to be effective. We recognize that to solve our problem, it is necessary to begin to *act differently* as well, to create and eliminate and modify institutions. The institutions or social habits by means of which the society carries on its evaluations include both voluntary ones—that is, institutions like customs, clubs, groups, organizations, settlement houses, and so on, that carry no official authority—and governmental ones—that is, institutions like laws, bureaucratic arrangements, and so on, that do carry official authority. All of these institutions on occasion need to be modified. In a democracy, it is the job of the community to determine if the solutions suggested to it by the experts are adequate to solve the problems it recognizes. Thus this two-level process of social reconstruction that Dewey offers to address our social ills includes both expert intellectual attempts to analyze the problem and suggest possible solutions and non-expert, democratic procedures for testing and evaluating the proposals. In the next four sections, we will examine these two levels of social reconstruction in greater detail.

5.2. Conceptual Reconstruction

Let us begin this examination of the philosophers' contribution to intellectual reconstruction with a consideration of the complex nature of positive political terms like 'individualism' or 'community'. Roughly speaking, we can consider such terms in three different contexts of meaning, just as we saw in 4.4 that a person's moral vision can be distinguished into *fundamental values, specifiable concep-*

tions of these values, and particular *instantiations*. With regard to these political terms the first meaning offers what can be called the *ideal* sense of the term. Here, our interest is in emphasizing the importance of fulfilled human individuality or of fulfilling community life. These ideal senses of terms, like other ideals, "are not intended to be themselves realized but are meant to direct our course to realization of potentialities in existent conditions" (LW 12:303).[12] The favorable evaluation of the referent of the term here is counterbalanced by the lack of explicit content. The second meaning context offers what might be called the *conceptual* sense of the term. Here we will find a number of more specific formulations or interpretations or conceptions[13] of what the term specifically means, a set of interpretations that is ultimately inconsistent. We find, for example, early capitalist individualism and the individualism of Walden Pond, monastic community and business community. In many—perhaps most—cases, the conception of the term that is defended, however different from others, is put forward by proponents as the 'proper' interpretation of the term, as 'real' individualism or 'true' community. A third meaning context of a political term offers what might be called the *statutory* sense of the term. This is the sense of the term contained in various laws and regulations designed to advance or defend individualism or community as specifically conceived in a particular way. For example, a law might be enacted to eliminate taxation on estates in the light of a particular conception of individuality that emphasizes inheritance and property rights. Similarly, a zoning regulation might be introduced to constrain the potential uses of a piece of property in line with a particular conception of community that emphasizes public access and facilities held in common. The primary focus of my discussion in this section will be on the conceptual sense of the term, although a brief discussion of his analysis of ideals will set the stage.

For Dewey, ideals like *justice* or *beauty* or *equality* have all the power in human life that the proponents of 'abstract', 'fixed', or 'remote' senses of such ideals claim for them. The problem that he sees is with their interpretation, one that presents ideals as some sort

---

[12] Dewey also renders this point in the following simile: "Ideals are like the stars; we steer by them, not towards them" (EW 4:262; cf. MW 14:156).

[13] For Dewey's uses of the term 'conception', see: LW 8:58, 235, 259; 12:499.

of finished and unchanging Existents placed in a realm other than the natural world of hunger and death, secure from the problems and confusions of day-to-day existence.[14] Dewey writes, on the contrary, that human experience, thick and creative, "reveals" ideals to us (LW 10:325). What he means here is that "[t]he idealizing imagination seizes upon the most precious things found in the climacteric moments of experience and projects them" (LW 9:33). Further, in its dealings with the challenges and frustrations of nature, experience "shatters and remakes" these ideals (LW 10:325).[15] Our ideals are connected to the ongoing processes of living: they are rooted in particular difficulties and draw upon presumptive solutions. We must thus recognize that these ideals are in part the products of human imagination. He writes that "the ideal itself has its roots in natural conditions; it emerges when the imagination idealizes existence by laying hold of the possibilities offered to thought and action" (LW 9:33; cf. 4:86).[16]

Ideals like *democracy* or *justice,* as the imaginative projections of humans facing the problems of social living, are never fully specifiable. The closest we come to specifiability is in the various conceptions of the terms, conceptions that are subject to dispute. There has long been a recognition of the political entanglements that surround what have been called 'essentially contested concepts'.[17] Abraham Lincoln's allegorical example of the fundamental disagreement between the sheep and the wolf over the proper interpretation of the term 'liberty', and his rejection of the Confederate States' version of liberty as coming from "the wolf's dictionary,"[18] offers a nice introduction to the problem of such terms; but this approach also skews later discussion. It skews discussion because it implies, as does much of the other writing on these contested concepts, that at what I

---

[14] Cf. James Hayden Tufts: "the true ethical contrast between the actual and the ideal was thus shifted over into a metaphysical contrast" (*Ethics* [with Dewey] MW 5:129 = LW 7:120).

[15] Cf. MW 12:147; 13:399; LW 9:31.

[16] Cf. Eames, *Pragmatic Naturalism,* 196–97; Alexander, *John Dewey's Theory of Art, Experience, and Nature,* 260–66.

[17] Two recent volumes in this ongoing discussion are: William E. Connolly, *The Terms of Political Discourse;* and Daniel T. Rodgers, *Contested Truths.* See also my volume, *The Community Reconstructs,* 59–70.

[18] "Address at the Sanitary Fair," 18 April 1864, *The Collected Works of Abraham Lincoln,* vol. 7, 302.

am calling the conceptual level these terms have fundamental, correct, and unchanging proper meanings, meanings that can be uncovered and must be preserved in the interest of social well-being.[19] Dewey rejects both of these views; and he suggests that the presumption of immutability inherent in this approach ultimately leads to politically unfortunate actions. This immutability, for example, can feed a reactionary political mood that uses such intellectual views to claim that 'democracy' refers only to political matters devoid of any economic elements, or that 'equality' refers only to opportunity and not to results, or that 'liberty' includes some individuals' rights to control their investments without interference but not the rights of other individuals to a meaningful job. Or such immutability can feed a mood at the other political extreme that claims, for example, that 'democracy' means only the responsiveness of institutions to majority desires, or that 'equality' refers only to results, or that 'liberty' means only the willing acceptance of social obligations. But the key in either case is that the terms are to be understood only in conformity with the 'proper' antecedent and unchanging conception.

For Dewey, rooted in an evolutionary cosmology, it is necessary that we recognize the ongoing nature of change in our social lives. We must ever keep in mind that, although at the abstract *ideal* level the meaning of a term like 'democracy' may never change—that is, it may always stand abstractly for, in Lincoln's formulation, "government of the people, by the people, for the people"[20]—at the other levels, the meaning of 'democracy' is ever in process. On the *conceptual* level, there is the process of ongoing interaction between narrower and broader political understandings, narrower and broad-

---

[19] Cf. Friedrich A. Hayek: "change of meaning of the words describing political ideals is not a single event but a continuous process, a technique employed consciously or unconsciously to direct the people. Gradually, as this process continues, the whole language becomes despoiled, and words become empty shells deprived of any definite meaning, as capable of denoting one thing as its opposite and used solely for the emotional associations which still adhere to them" (*The Road to Serfdom*, 159; cf. George Orwell, "Politics and the English Language," *The Collected Essays, Journalism, and Letters*, vol. 4, 127–40). Dewey was not blind to the problem of the totalitarian abuse of language (see, for example, MW 8:143–44; LW 11:296; 14:275); but the response to totalitarian claims to have the 'correct' meanings of these terms is not the counterclaim that we have the 'correct' meanings or that our traditional meanings must be 'correct'.

[20] Lincoln, "Address Delivered at the Dedication of the Cemetery at Gettysburg," 19 November 1863, *The Collected Works of Abraham Lincoln*, vol. 7, 22.

er economic understandings, understandings that integrate and those that are divorced from religion, understandings that recognize a gender component and those that do not, and so on. On the *statutory* level, there are constant discussions and re-evaluations of who may become a citizen, what matters are to be decided at the polls, how we might rectify past 'mistakes', and so on.

Dewey maintains that one great problem that we face is that, if we are not careful, particular formulations of what I am calling political *conceptions* like 'democracy' have a tendency over time to usurp the place of our more abstract political *ideals*. As a result, for example, our current institutional system is often seen to be, and for many people becomes, the full possibility of 'government of the people, by the people, for the people'. We fail to recognize this shift because we fail to distinguish between, using Dewey's language here, the *"word"* and the *"idea"* (LW 2:43). As he writes, it is possible for words to become "mere counters . . . to be manipulated according to certain rules, or reacted to by certain operations without consciousness of their meaning" (MW 6:320). When this happens, we have stopped thinking about these terms as intellectual tools for opening up and analyzing situations. In such cases, "the words at our disposal are largely such as to *prevent* the communication of ideas," he continues. "The words are so loaded with associations derived from a long past, that instead of being tools for thought, our thoughts become subservient tools of words" (LW 13:323; cf. 5:139).[21] Such fixed conceptions, like other sorts of general answers "do not assist inquiry. They close it" (MW 12:188).

At this point we have forgotten that we, or at least our human predecessors, constructed the conception as an intended response to some problematic situation. As Dewey writes, "the one who uses static meanings is not even aware that they originated and have been elaborated for the sake of dealing with conflicts and problems" (MW 1:152). For example, we see how for so many the 'liberal' or 'bourgeois' *conception* of democracy—although it had a specific beginning in a specific situation as a response to a specific problem of political economy—has usurped the place of the political *ideal* of

---

[21] Cf. Charles Frankel: Dewey believed that "many words we habitually use . . . have quite the wrong [i.e., harmful] meanings attached to them as a result of their historical careers. He wanted to squeeze the wrong meanings out of these words and attach new and better meanings to them" ("John Dewey's Legacy," 315–16).

democracy. Thus it is that the fullness of 'democracy' means, for our average fellow citizen, the cluster of the following particulars: our version of private-property capitalism, our two-party system, the separation of powers in our three branches of government, our Bill of Rights, our fixed periods for elections, and so on. Similarly, for these same people anything else is not an alternative conception of democracy—it is, rather, something much less than democracy.

The problem here is that these outdated conceptions have maintained their position and are diverting the possibilities of social response. Dewey continues that

> the older symbols of ideal life still engage thought and command loyalty. Conditions have changed, but every aspect of life, from religion and education to property and trade, shows that nothing approaching a transformation has taken place in ideas and ideals. Symbols control sentiment and thought, and the new age has no symbols consonant with its activities (LW 2:323).

He maintains that it is necessary to keep the variability of the specific concepts in mind. "Because we live in a world in process, the future, although continuous with the past, is not in its base repetition," Dewey writes. "The very words which must be used are words that have had their meanings fixed in the past to express ideas that are unlike those which they must now convey if they are to express what is intended" (LW 12:46).[22] Our conceptions of 'democracy', 'justice', 'equality', and so on, are tools that should be regarded "as *hypotheses* to be employed in observation and ordering of phenomena, and hence to be tested by the consequences produced by acting upon them" and not "as *truths* already established and therefore unquestionable" (LW 12:499).[23]

---

[22] Cf. C. S. Peirce, who suggests that at this point of emerging novelty we need rather "to coin new terms": "If philosophy is ever to stand in the ranks of the sciences, literary elegance must be sacrificed . . . to the stern requirements of efficiency, and the philosophist must be encouraged—yea, and required—to coin new terms to express such new scientific concepts as he may discover, just as his chemical and biological brethren are expected to do" (*Collected Papers*, 5.13).

[23] Cf. James Hayden Tufts: "Our conceptions of honesty and justice, of rights and duties, got their present shaping largely in an industrial and business order when mine and thine could be easily distinguished . . . when the producer sold to his neighbors, and an employer had also the relations of neighbor to his workmen. . . . Such conceptions are inadequate for the present order" (*Ethics* [with Dewey], MW 5:443–44; cf. Hook, *John Dewey*, 232).

The inherited meanings of these terms are of *historical* importance as solutions to prior problematic situations, of course; but they are not thereby necessarily solutions to our problems. A term's "most specific historical usage," Dewey writes, is not "the only legitimate one" (LW 14:252); we must thus move away from the unthinking defense of accidentally derived conceptions, however valuable they might have been, since the results of their employment might not stand up to the different tests of today. It is thus valuable and necessary to attempt to keep some connection with the term's historical meaning, while at the same time breaking free from the encrustations of the past. It remains the task of philosophers engaged in intellectual reconstruction to engage in ongoing conceptual reconstruction, to advance the continuous reconstruction of such terms as 'individuality' and 'liberty', as Dewey writes, "in their intimate connection with changes in social relations" (LW 11:292).

5.3   'Individualism', Old and New

We can get a better sense of Dewey's understanding of conceptual reconstruction if we consider as examples his discussions of a few of our key political terms. Recognizing that a close integration of various terms will emerge as we proceed, we can enter initially through the term *individualism*. This term is a particularly apt one with which to begin our survey of his work on conceptual reconstruction because, as he writes, the term has no generally recognized meaning: "Individualism is about the most ambiguous word in the entire list of labels in ordinary use. It means anything from egoistically centred conduct to distinction and uniqueness." Moreover, he continues that "[i]t is possible to say that excessive individualism is an outstanding curse of American civilization, and that absence of individualism is our marked deficiency" (MW 13:289).[24] Individuality is clearly one of the most cherished values in Western culture; there are those who would claim that ours is an essentially individualistic culture. Yet, regardless of how important the ideal of individuality may be to our and Dewey's way of thinking, he believes that we are at present hampered by a time-bound conception of its meaning. As

---

[24] In one place, Dewey lists and describes seven separate meanings of the term 'individualism' (see MW 15:242–44).

he puts it, "[t]he idea that human nature is inherently and exclusively individual is itself a product of a cultural individualistic movement" (LW 13:77). This individualistic movement, however, has become in the meantime inadequate: "the individualism of the past has lost its meaning. Individuals will always be the centre and the consummation of experience, but what an individual actually *is* in his life-experience depends upon the nature and movement of associated life" (LW 5:275).

Our inherited and now outdated conception of individualism separates for Dewey upon analysis into a number of interlocking, fundamentally moral assumptions, all of which run counter to his views on human nature examined in Part One above. There is the psychological assumption that there are "ready-made" individuals (LW 11:30) who are the holders of personal rights "prior to political organization of social relations" (LW 11:6–7).[25] There is the political assumption that such individuals, in recognition of the "natural opposition between the individual and organized society" (LW 11:8), should be left alone, free from 'interference', especially that from the state. There is also the economic assumption that these individuals will recognize and pursue their own well-being and thereby "not only best further their own private interests but will also promote social progress and contribute most effectively to the satisfaction of the needs of others and hence to the general happiness" (LW 7:331).

In spite of Dewey's belief that these three assumptions were no longer justifiable, he does not regard the inherited individualism to have always been bankrupt. This claim is, of course, part of his larger evolutionary view: "That which was on the side of moral progress in the eighteenth and early nineteenth centuries may be a morally reactionary doctrine in the twentieth century; that which is serviceable now may prove injurious at a later time" (LW 7:336). As he notes, at its origin the doctrine of individualism "was held by 'progressives', by those who were protesting against the inherited regime of rules of law and administration" (LW 2:318). Individualism emphasized the person's right to determine his or her own destiny: "It sought to release from legal restrictions man's wants and his efforts to satisfy those wants" (LW 5:78). This individualism also "promoted invention, initiative, and individual vigor, as well as

---

[25] Cf. LW 7:332; 11:290.

hastened the industrial development of the country" (LW 11:250; cf. 2:297); the importance of contract as distinct from status was emphasized, and the era of the machine was carried forward "against obstacles of lethargy, skepticism and political obstruction" (LW 5:79; cf. 9:177–78). However, the positive contributions were by Dewey's day, by which time the 'rugged' individual had become "ragged" (LW 5:45), in the distinct minority. "Where is the wilderness," he wonders, "which now beckons creative energy and affords untold opportunity to initiative and vigor?" (LW 5:80).[26] The "orgy" of "waste and destruction" was over, and the "penalties" now had to be paid (LW 11:251). "The period of free lands that seemed boundless in extent has vanished," he continues. "Unused resources are now human rather than material" (LW 14:225). But the older, regnant conception of individualism was not developing these resources.

Part of the trouble with our inherited conception of individualism was its denial of the power of human intelligence to control and direct social action. Under this analysis, as Dewey notes, "human reason is confined to discovering what antecedently exists, the pre-existent system of advantages and disadvantages, resources and obstacles, and then to conforming action strictly to the given scheme." Such confinement resulted in an "abnegation of human intelligence" (MW 7:58) to change, adjust, control, and alter social events and in the acceptance of a policy of passivity and drift. A second troubling aspect of this conception of individualism is that it does not count all individuals equally, and the result is injustice. Our inherited view of individualism, he writes,

> in the very act of asserting that it stood completely and loyally for the principle of individual freedom, was really engaged in justifying the activities of a new form of concentrated power—the economic, which new form, to state the matter moderately, has consistently and persistently denied effective freedom to the economically underpowered and underprivileged (LW 11:136).

As a result of the acceptance of this conception of individualism, Dewey writes, we find "a diminution of the range of decision and

---

[26] Dewey continues: "the children of the pioneers, who live in the midst of surroundings artificially made over by the machine, enjoy pioneer life idly in the vicarious film" (LW 5:80).

activity for the many along with exaggeration of opportunity of personal expression for the few" (LW 5:66). This conception thus failed where failure ought to be most severe for an *individualism*—it failed to recognize that "the full freedom of the human spirit and of individuality can be achieved only as there is effective opportunity to share in the cultural resources of civilization" (LW 11:295; cf. 138).

Perhaps most important in Dewey's mind was the fact that the continued lip service to the inherited individualism resulted in "a submergence of the individual." As he continues, "the loyalties which once held individuals, which gave them support, direction and unity of outlook on life, have well-nigh disappeared. In consequence, individuals are confused and bewildered. . . . Stability of individuality is dependent upon stable objects to which allegiance firmly attaches itself." Our social situation thus does not support individual growth. It is "too diversely crowded and chaotic" to allow people to make sense of their lives. One key aspect of this submergence is that people are lost *economically:* they can find in their working lives neither satisfaction, nor direction, nor security. "Assured and integrated individuality is the product of definite social relationships and publicly acknowledged functions," Dewey writes (LW 5:66–67); but such a stable social place cannot be attained through contributing to our culture. What we have instead is "the inability to find a secure and morally rewarding place in a troubled and tangled economic scene" (LW 5:80).

The few economically favored, whom Dewey describes with such colorful terms as "parasites" (LW 11:158) and "economic overlords" (LW 6:289),[27] reap their rewards "not in what they do, in their social office and function, but in a deflection of social consequences to private gain" (LW 5:67). Further, he maintains that these favored individuals are not truly fulfilled: "Useless display and luxury, the futile attempt to secure happiness through the possession of things, social position, and economic power over others, are manifestations of the restriction of experience that exists among those who seemingly profit by the present order" (LW 5:274). For the vast majority of individuals, however, these contributors to counterfeit fulfillment do not even exist. For these "underpowered and underprivileged" (LW 11:136), there is fundamentally the insecurity of the constant pressure of unemployment that Dewey

---

[27] Cf. MW 11:76; 12:9; LW 6:126, 379–80, 436; 9:64.

describes in 1930 as "millions of men desirous of working . . . recurrently out of employment," and as "a standing army at all times who have no regular work" and who "dread of the oncoming of old age." Under such circumstances, when they recognize that "honest and industrious pursuit of a calling or business will not guarantee any stable level of life" (LW 5:67–68), people can hardly anticipate finding fulfillment through their work lives. And, should there be any suggestion that perhaps something might be done to redress this overall situation, there arises a chorus of Sumnerian complaints about 'interference' with the 'natural' workings of the market place. In response, Dewey maintains that "[a]ny system that cannot provide elementary security for millions has no claim to the title of being organized in behalf of liberty and the development of individuals" (LW 11:287). In fact, in 1946 he concludes, "the movement that goes by the name of *Individualism* is very largely responsible for the chaos now found in human associations—the chaos which is at the root of the present debasement of human beings" (LW 15:212).

Dewey writes that attempts to address this economic mess and challenge its minimization by 'market-oriented' analysts were overcome by "the irrelevant artificiality of the issues" that were at the center of the political arena (LW 2:312)—for example, the evolution circus considered above in 2.1—and by "the meaninglessness of the present political platforms, parties and issues." As a result, people are also lost *politically*. They are confused in the sense that they know neither the meanings of social facts nor where to look for answers. They lack "secure objects of allegiance, without which individuals are lost" (LW 5:70). They lack the loyalties "that once held men together and made them aware of their reciprocal obligations." They are deracinated, rootless, without a social place. To regain such a place, he continues, people need to uncover a fuller understanding of their social situation and then work at developing "new stable relationships in society out of which duties and loyalties will naturally grow" (LW 7:234). Frequently, however, their response is completely different, and they treat the *feeling* of rootlessness itself as the problem.[28] All too often, instead of attempting to regain a place, people try to avoid the feeling of loss of place through the fevered pursuit of pleasure or through the adoption of intellectual uniformity.

---

[28] See the discussion of the uncomfortableness of doubt in 2.4.

Interest in efforts at cooperative social inquiry are undermined as well, Dewey writes, by the fact that there are "too many other interesting things to do and to enjoy" (LW 6:183), things that divert us from our cooperative task. His examples of currently available diversions are far more modest than our own—"the movie, radio, cheap reading matter and motor car"—but he recognizes that they "have come to stay" (LW 2:321).[29] The quest for satisfaction in limitless action, the "unrest, impatience, irritation and hurry" of the life he sees around him, he analyzes as the "inevitable accompaniments of a situation in which individuals do not find support and contentment in the fact that they are sustaining and sustained members of a social whole." This condition, often thought to be the essence of American life, he sees as pathological:

> Only an acute maladjustment between individuals and the social conditions under which they live can account for such widespread pathological phenomena. Feverish love of anything as long as it is a change which is distracting, impatience, unsettlement, nervous discontentment, and desire for excitement, are not native to human nature. They are so abnormal as to demand explanation in some deep-seated cause (LW 5:68).

Human fulfillment for Dewey, on the other hand, is based upon establishing and maintaining a social place, not through the pursuit of exciting diversions.

Further, Dewey finds that, in a society with a virtually limitless number of possibilities for individual diversity and development, there is excessive intellectual uniformity. "In theory, democracy should be a means of stimulating original thought, and of evoking action deliberately adjusted in advance to cope with new forces," he writes. "In fact it is still so immature that its main effect is to multiply occasions for imitation" (MW 14:48). The causes of this uniformity are not hard to find: "The individual cannot remain intellectually in a vacuum. If his ideas and beliefs are not the spontaneous function of a communal life in which he shares, a seeming consensus will be secured as a substitute by artificial and mechanical means." This uniformity is, however, very shallow and in constant and confusing flux. "Conformity is a name for the absence of vital interplay; the

---

[29] Cf. MW 15:167–69; LW 5:61; 6:96, 183; 7:353, 359.

arrest and benumbing of communication"; "it is the artificial substitute used to hold men together in lack of associations that are incorporated into inner dispositions of thought and desire" (LW 5:81–82). Our society, insecure with itself, fails to foster tolerance and "has put a false value upon mere uniformity, and created to some extent jealousy of distinction, fear of the dissenter and non-conformist in social matters, a fear increased as population has become heterogeneous through immigration" (LW 7:355).

Dewey maintains that we have reached the concluding phase of the usability of our inherited conception of individuality. He is emphatic, however, that in spite of the loss of individuality in our frenetic and homogenized situation, we ought not to be abandoning individuality as a value. "Life still centres in individuals," he writes, "and always will" (LW 11:388). In spite of the difficulties in its attainment, individuality is to be cherished. Individuality is, moreover, a means to social progress: "individuals are the finally decisive factors of the nature and movement of associated life" (LW 14:91). The reason why individuals are central is fairly simple. "Every *new* idea," Dewey writes, "every conception of things differing from that authorized by current belief, must have its origin in an individual" (MW 9:305).[30] The individual's mind, "the vehicle of experimental creation" (LW 2:20), is the only means of directing change. "Change is going to occur anyway, and the problem is the control of change in a given direction," he writes. "The direction, the quality of change, is a matter of individuality" (LW 14:113).[31]

It is consequently necessary to reconstruct 'individuality' to make it fit our current situation. To do so does not mean looking backwards. "Traditional ideas are more than irrelevant," Dewey writes. "They are an encumbrance; they are the chief obstacle to the formation of a new individuality integrated within itself and with a liberated function in the society wherein it exists" (LW 5:86). We must discover a new meaning within our experience—so that we can re-establish individuality as a living value. "Individuals will refind

---

[30] Dewey also emphasizes the centrality of the Pragmatic movement for bringing "into prominence the importance of the individual" as "the carrier of creative thought, the author of action, and of its application" (LW 2:20).

[31] Cf. George Herbert Mead: "that which is novel must appear in the experience of an individual as an individual. . . . we are solving problems, and those problems can appear only in the experience of the individual" (*Movements of Thought in the Nineteenth Century*, 405, 411).

themselves," he writes, "only as their ideas and ideals are brought
into harmony with the realities of the age in which they act" (LW
5:75). He thus undertakes the development of at least the initial
stages of "a new individualism as significant for modern conditions
as the old individualism at its best was for its day and place" (LW
5:56–57).

The most striking difference between the two conceptions of
individualism will probably be that our new conception will have to
be social, because individuals are social. "Only in social groups,"
Dewey writes, "does a person have a chance to develop individuality"
(MW 15:176).[32] We will thus have to overcome the suggestion that
there is "some inherent difference amounting to opposition between
what is called the individual and the social," he continues (LW
13:82). Both 'individual' and 'social' are adjectives which describe
"traits and capacities of human beings in the concrete" (LW
15:168).[33] Dewey thus maintains that "there can be no conflict
between *the* individual and *the* social" and "no wholesale opposition
between society and individuals." This does not mean, of course,
that there are no conflicts at all. Rather, what it means is that the
conflicts that occur are conflicts "between *some* individuals and *some*
arrangements in social life; between groups and classes of individuals; between nations and races; between old traditions imbedded in
institutions and new ways of thinking and acting which spring from
those few individuals who depart from and who attack what is
socially accepted" (LW 7:324). Once we can recognize the importance of developing a social place and overcome the attempt to
divorce the individual from society, we can come to see the
individual as being in process, as developing in the course of social
interaction and by means of society's facilities.

Because he recognizes that individuality is neither something
"fixed, given ready-made" nor achieved "in isolation" but rather
something attained "with the aid and support of conditions, cultural
and physical," Dewey emphasizes that we must take "an active
interest in the working of social institutions that have a bearing,
positive or negative, upon the growth of individuals" in order to
advance as much as possible "the positive construction of favorable
institutions, legal, political and economic," and the work of "remov-

---

[32] Cf. EW 3:219, 322.
[33] Cf. LW 15:4–5, 211.

ing abuses and overt oppressions" (LW 11:291).[34] To attain a society of this sort, a society in which neighborliness is possible, in which we can attain "a worthy and rich life for all" (LW 5:98) and the "more genuine development of individuality for the mass of individuals" (LW 9:180), and in which these "individual variations" are used as a means to the society's growth (MW 9:315), we will need to reconstruct our culture. Our citizens must develop "that kind of individuality which is intelligently alive to the common life and sensitively loyal to its common maintenance" (MW 11:57); and, since this individual mind does not come ready-made, we recognize the educational impact of positions like the following: "The only guarantee of impartial, disinterested inquiry is the social sensitiveness of the inquirer to the needs and problems of those with whom he is associated" (MW 12:165).[35] This kind of individuality is "a moving thing, something that is attained only by continuous growth" (LW 11:30).

Certainly, Dewey does not offer a complete picture of what this new individualism is to mean, or how we are to attain it. In part, his reluctance is due to a personal reticence to decree a meaning by adopting the stance of what he calls at one point "a lexicographical autocrat" (LW 3:73). More importantly, however, Dewey is reluctant to attempt to specify the nature of "this emergent individualism" because, as he writes, "I do not see how it can be described until more progress has been made in its production." The key is thus the cooperative attempt to advance both the understanding and the actuality of individuality (in conjunction with the other values yet to be explored). And, as he continues,

> such progress will not be initiated until we cease opposing the socially corporate to the individual, and until we develop a constructively imaginative observation of the role of science and technology in actual society. The greatest obstacle to that vision is, I repeat, the perpetuation of the older individualism now reduced, as I have said, to the utilization of science and technology for ends of private pecuniary gain (LW 5:89).

If we can turn individualism away from the emphases of this older conception of the term, and from the emphasis on privacy that we

---

[34] Cf. LW 2:61; 5:75–76.
[35] Cf. EW 4:57; 5:72–73.

saw in 2.5, Dewey believes that we will be able to move toward completing the new conception of individualism.

This examination of 'individualism' has clearly carried us into areas beyond the term itself; but it demonstrates the various aspects of Dewey's understanding of conceptual reconstruction. There is first of all the philosophical claim that our interpretations or conceptions of the central terms of political discourse are tools for dealing with felt social problems.[36] Those who value the ideal of individuality but who believe that the ideal is not being properly understood develop conceptions of the term different from the one(s) currently ascendent, conceptions that emphasize the aspects of the ideal that they value. Secondly, there is the more historical claim that our inherited conceptions of such terms once fit reasonably well in the situations in which they were applied. In the American context, as we saw in 1.1, on the Frontier of free land and limitless opportunity, the individual—or, better, the individual extended family—could pretty much assume effective responsibility for its own well-being, relying on others and affecting others only minimally. In such a situation, the ruggedness of the older conception of individualism was to a great extent appropriate and beneficial. Thirdly, Dewey offers the political claim that, although such inherited understandings of our key political terms are no longer adequate to our attempts to deal with our problems, they live on in our shared lives causing social problems and preventing social responsiveness. This results from the fact that, as he writes, although the various interpretations of these terms "were themselves historically conditioned, and were relevant only to their own time," they were mistakenly put forward "as immutable truths good at all times and places" (LW 11:26; cf. MW 1:306–7).

5.4.   Rethinking 'Freedom' and 'Community'

The impact of Dewey's understanding of the life of a conception of a political term has a fundamental implication for all of our political discourse. While we cannot examine other key political terms in as

---

[36] Cf. George Herbert Mead: "Abstract individualism and a negative conception of liberty in terms of the freedom from restraints become the working ideas in the community. They have the prestige of battle cries in the fight for freedom against privilege" (*Selected Writings*, 226).

great detail here as we have examined 'individualism', it is still possible to get a better feel for the nature and importance of conceptual reconstruction by examining briefly a few more terms. Let us begin with the term *freedom* or *liberty* or *rights*.[37] "Liberty in the concrete signifies release from the impact of *particular* oppressive forces"; "the conception of liberty is always relative to forces that at a given time and place are increasingly felt to be oppressive" (LW 11:35).[38] He maintains, however, that the historical doctrine of 'natural' or 'absolute' rights developed when various thinkers' attempts to assert their condemnation of certain particular abuses at the hands of others, when their attempts "to get liberation from some specific evil," were " 'rationalized' into a universal struggle of humanity to obtain freedom in the abstract" (LW 13:99–100; cf. 9:301).[39] This "negative and formal" conception of freedom emphasizes too strongly "freedom *from* subjection to the will and control of others" (MW 5:392), especially when those others represented the government,[40] and connects freedom too strongly "with ability to achieve economic success . . . to make money" (LW 11:366). As such, this older sense of freedom as an ultimate personal goal is adequate only in the context of the older sense of individualism. For Dewey, on the other hand, rights, although "individual in residence," are "social in origin and intent" (MW 5:394).

Thus, for Dewey, these rights are 'natural' in some sense, although not in the frequently advocated sense of being a series of fundamental human powers that were inherent in individuals prior to their entry into civil society. While this sense of rights was historically progressive and contributed greatly to the power of the American Declaration of Independence and our Constitution's Bill of Rights, it became a drag on social progress when these specific

---

[37] Dewey writes: "That which, taken at large or in a lump, is called freedom breaks up in detail into a number of specific, concrete abilities to act in particular ways. These are termed *rights*" (MW 5:394).

[38] Cf. George Herbert Mead: "The contents of our so-called natural rights have always been formulated negatively, with reference to restrictions to be overcome" (*Selected Writings*, 159).

[39] Cf. Walter Lippmann: "what every theorist of liberty has meant is that certain types of behavior and classes of opinion hitherto regulated should be somewhat differently regulated in the future" ("Basic Problem of Democracy: I. What Modern Liberty Means," 617).

[40] Cf. James Hayden Tufts: "Oppression by the government was what the men of '76 feared most" (*The Real Business of Living*, 357–58).

formulations were decreed inalienable. In Dewey's view, rights should not be "defined as inherent in an original and native fixed structure, moral or psychological," nor, relatedly, should their definition feed a political stance that "all that is required on the side of institutions and laws is to eliminate the obstructions they offer to the 'free' play of the natural equipment of individuals" (LW 3:99–100; cf. 11:26).[41] Accordingly, Dewey advocates instead a sense of rights as a cluster of fundamental, yet processive, social powers. He believes that the meaning of 'natural' is to be found in examining those fundamental aspects of human nature and living that must be satisfied before a life of personal growth and cooperative fulfillment is possible.[42] The term is thus an ethical one; and, if we hope to grasp its meaning adequately, we need to keep the ethical sense in mind. Writing of Thomas Jefferson, who is often associated with the sense of 'natural' that emphasizes pre-political origins, Dewey writes, "To put ourselves in touch with Jefferson's position we have therefore to translate the word 'natural' into *moral*" (LW 13:174).[43]

Dewey maintains that for a sense of freedom to capture this moral core, it must go beyond freedom as simply release from historically specified controls. Dewey calls this new conception "effective freedom" (MW 5:392) or "effective liberty" (LW 11:27). Liberty, he writes, "is always a *social* question, not an individual one . . . a matter of the *distribution* of power that exists at the time" (LW 11:361–62). He continues that the older analysis of freedom, in asserting "the mutual incompatibility of equality and liberty," fails to realize that "the *actual* liberties of one human being depend upon

---

[41] Cf. James Hayden Tufts: " 'Natural' easily loses the force of an appeal to reason and to social good, and becomes merely an assertion of ancient usage, or precedent, or even a shelter for mere selfish interests. . . . Individualism has been so successful in asserting rights that it is now apt to forget that there are no rights morally except such as express the will of a good *member of society*" (*Ethics* [with Dewey], MW 5:143–44).

[42] Cf. George Herbert Mead: "We find that the term 'natural right' is bound up with another very important conception in the history of political theory, that of natural law. Here the reference to nature does not imply a prior existence, but points rather to the fundamental character of the law, or in the other case to the fundamental character of the right" (*Selected Writings*, 160–61).

[43] Cf. LW 9:301–2; 14:212–13. See also Dewey's changed emphasis in LW 16:401–4.

the powers of action that existing institutional arrangements accord to other individuals" (LW 11:370).[44] The struggle for freedom is thus a struggle for "conditions which will enable an individual to make his own special contribution" to the interests of society (MW 9:310), conditions that will make individuals effective members of the community. Dewey's conception of our goal is thus not *freedom from involvement* but rather *free and full participation.* Our ongoing aim, he writes, must be to create a situation in which "the powers of individuals shall not be merely released from mechanical external constraint but shall be fed, sustained and directed" (LW 11:25).[45]

A free society, then, is one that has a set of institutions—a culture—that operates to achieve full growth and equal participation. Of course, we need to move beyond this formulation to the construction of such a society.

> The problem is to know what kind of culture is so free in itself that it conceives and begets political freedom as its accompaniment and consequence. What about the state of science and knowledge; of the arts, fine and technological; of friendships and family life; of business and finance; of the attitudes and dispositions created in the give and take of ordinary day by day associations? (LW 13:67)

Among these essential institutions is the educational system. "No man and no mind was ever emancipated merely by being left alone," Dewey writes (LW 2:340); and "[f]reedom of mind is not something that spontaneously happens" (MW 15:51).[46] Moreover, this freedom is the keystone: "freedom of the mind is the fundamental and central freedom in maintenance of a free society" (LW 15:175). It is the job of the educational system to help foster freedom by helping individuals to think better, to observe more clearly and to judge more adequately. "Genuine freedom," Dewey writes, "is intellectual; it rests in the trained *power of thought,* in ability to 'turn things over', to look at matters deliberately, to judge whether the amount and kind

---

[44] Cf. James Hayden Tufts: "We are not necessarily tied to the eighteenth century conceptions of freedom. The twentieth century calls for a higher emphasis upon the goods achieved through association. Government is the instrument for securing and protecting these goods" (*America's Social Morality,* 216).

[45] Cf. MW 5:394; 9:270.

[46] Cf. LW 3:104; 15:181–83.

of evidence requisite for decision is at hand, and if not, to tell where and how to seek such evidence" (MW 6:232 = LW 8:186).[47]

This social sense of freedom grounds it neither in individual privilege nor in individual comfort, but in social welfare, the higher good itself. It is in our common interest to live in a free society. "The democratic idea of freedom is not the right of each individual to *do* as he pleases," Dewey writes, "even if it be qualified by adding 'provided he does not interfere with some freedom on the part of others'." The intent is rather "freedom of *mind* and of whatever degree of freedom of action and experience is necessary to produce freedom of intelligence." The various social guarantees offered by our Constitution's Bill of Rights are thus best interpreted in light of the realization that "without them individuals are not free to develop and society is deprived of what they might contribute" (LW 11:220). He defends freedom of speech, for example, as "the best method humanity has discovered for combining conservation of attained values with progress toward new goods" (LW 7:361). Thus, he bases his defense of these freedoms "on the indispensable value of free inquiry and free discussion to the normal development of public welfare, not upon anything inherent in the individual as such" (LW 11:374).

Dewey is quick to assert that to ground freedom in social welfare is not to sacrifice individual freedoms to the whims of the majority. On the contrary, he sees these freedoms as being more secure under his approach than they were previously. Under the older analysis of freedom, since these rights are seen as individual goods and not social goods, they could be sacrificed when necessary to the social good. In our increasingly complex and integrated society, *"merely individual claims,"* because they are always "lightly esteemed when they appear (or can be made to appear) in conflict with the general social welfare" (LW 11:373–74), will have no adequate defense. As an example, we can consider the following: "As long as freedom of thought and speech is claimed as a merely individual right, it will give way, as do other merely personal claims, when it is, or is successfully represented to be, in opposition to the general welfare" (LW 11:47; cf. 15:172–73).

Dewey considers it important to emphasize in addition that this

---

[47] Cf. LW 3:111; 13:39.

reconstructed understanding of freedom should also possess, in addition to its social aspect, an essentially processive aspect.[48] The older approach to rights and freedom is, for him, deficient in that it has no dynamic character. It emphasizes, rather, "protecting individuals in the rights they already have" (LW 2:241). Such an approach cannot be adequate to a changing social situation, and in fact can prevent the expansion of human freedoms through social action. Thus it is the case that when we have a certain specifiable number of rights guaranteed (for example, by the Bill of Rights), this can also mean that we do not have any additional rights, unless we can convincingly extract these presumptive new rights—however laboriously—from the prior set. The ongoing difficulties of Americans to secure areas of sexual freedom under the guise of a right to privacy which is itself of uncertain grounding offer clear evidence of this. Defending an approach to rights that has no dynamic element also means that once a right has been guaranteed it is to remain in effect, regardless of later developments in the society.[49] So, for example, we encounter defenses of continuing rights to hold vast wealth or to amass weapons on purely Constitutional grounds, with no other justification being needed. Dewey maintains, however, that although the dynamic aspect of freedom is primarily a matter of the expansion of rights in range and number it may also require at times specific contractions, because freedom is grounded not in individual preference but in social welfare. In this regard, many other currently accepted rights—like owning an internal-combustion engine automobile or having a large family—may some day have to be reconsidered in the light of new circumstances just as some previously accepted rights—like raising livestock in the backyard or disposing of waste material without any regard for the environment—have had to be.

Human individuals are, as we have seen, inherently social—

---

[48] Cf. George Herbert Mead: "the next struggle for liberty, or our liberties, will arise out of some infraction that will not have reference to the definition which we have formulated of what a man should be and, consequently, of what constitute his liberties. On the contrary, we will find in all probability that the struggle will lead to a quite different definition from the one with which we started" (*Selected Writings*, 159).

[49] Cf. MW 11:101–2; Mead, *Selected Writings*, 165–66; *Movements of Thought*, 362.

creatures for whom association and *community* are essential. For Dewey, communities or "publics"[50] are natural; we need groups to *become* human. We develop our humanity, our individuality, in the midst of community living. "To learn to be human," he writes, "is to develop through the give-and-take of communication an effective sense of being an individually distinctive member of a community; one who understands and appreciates its beliefs, desires and methods, and who contributes to a further conversion of organic powers into human resources and values." This is a process that, as Dewey continues, "is never finished" (LW 2:332). Participation in a community is essential to a fulfilled human life because it makes possible a more diversified and enriching experience for all members. But his claims about the importance of human groups to individual fulfillment should not suggest a belief on his part that all groupings are necessarily beneficial.

Dewey, in fact, uses 'community' alternatively in both descriptive and eulogistic senses. He talks at times of all kinds of "societies, associations, [and] groups" (LW 2:278)—"scattered communities" (LW 2:306), "the business community" (LW 2:354), "political machines" (MW 9:88), "street gangs" and "trade unions" (MW 12:194), and "criminal bands" (LW 2:278)—and at other times, of what we might call 'good' communities—a democratic community (cf. LW 2:328) or a moral community (cf. LW 2:330–32). Dewey does not believe that he is being ambiguous here, but rather recognizing an important point: the ambiguity of the terms themselves. As he writes, terms like "society, community . . . have both a eulogistic or normative sense, and a descriptive sense; a meaning *de jure* and a meaning *de facto*." However, he tells us, although there are these two meanings, "[i]n social philosophy, the former connotation is almost always uppermost" (MW 9:88).[51]

"The gangster is as highly 'social' in one connection," he writes, "as he is anti-social in other connections" (LW 15:221; cf. MW 9:25). There are thus two distinct criteria in operation here, both drawn from Dewey's analysis of growth that we saw in 4.4. The first

---

[50] Dewey frequently chooses the less contested term, 'public', that was brought into current discourse by Walter Lippmann. A brief discussion of Dewey's analysis of Lippmann is to be found below, in 6.1.

[51] I have discussed the question of the *de jure* and *de facto* meanings of 'community' in light of the writings of Justus Buchler in "Buchler's Conception of Community," 326–32.

criterion is *internal:* "How numerous and varied are the interests which are consciously shared?" The second criterion is *external:* "How full and free is the interplay with other forms of association?" (MW 9:89; cf. 105). In the case of a gangsters' mob, Dewey maintains, whatever quality the association might merit under the former criterion would be overridden by its inadequate performance on the latter. "The robber band cannot interact flexibly with other groups; it can act only through isolating itself" (LW 2:328).[52] Consequently, it is important that we do what we can to develop, both separately and in coordination, a presence or 'place' in the public life of our society along with "participation in family life, industry, scientific and artistic associations." These various places are mutually contributory: "fullness of integrated personality is therefore possible of achievement, since the pulls and responses of different groups reenforce one another and their values accord" (LW 2:328).

In addition to his position that it would be mistaken to consider all human groupings to be examples of community, Dewey points to other possible misunderstandings. One such mistake would be to equate community with the state or the government. He is careful to indicate that he does not mean the 'external' or institutional forms of political association: the state is properly and should be maintained as subordinated to the community.[53] He tells us that there are social "agencies that lie deeper than the political" and that "the real needs of the American people must be met by means more fundamental than our traditional political institutions put at our disposal," namely the voluntary agencies of a vital and concerned community (LW 3:135). "We are held together by non-political bonds," he writes, "and the political forms are stretched and legal institutions patched in an *ad hoc* and improvised manner to do the work they have to do" (LW 2:306). He notes further that it is by means of these "social forces" that changes in "our inherited political machinery" will be made (LW 3:135).

In a similar fashion, Dewey also rejects the homogenized and monochromatic sameness with which some critics of community identify it. He recognizes that the community cannot be a community without some degree of shared experience and shared meanings.

---

[52] Cf. MW 9:89; Josiah Royce, *The Philosophy of Loyalty,* 101–46.
[53] Cf. EW 1:238–39; MW 2:81–83; 8:169–70; LW 5:193.

However, this communality implies also a richness, a complexity of possible perspectives to enter into, not the simplicity of identity.[54] The advancement of community does not require, Dewey believes, "a sacrifice of individuality; it would be a poor kind of society whose members were personally undeveloped" (LW 7:345). In particular, Dewey emphasizes the value of the diversity brought to this country through immigration, and the ongoing loss that results from our failure to appreciate what this diversity could mean. He writes, for example:

> The concept of uniformity and unanimity in culture is rather repellent. . . . Variety *is* the spice of life, and the richness and the attractiveness of social institutions depend upon cultural diversity among separate units. In so far as people are all alike, there is no give and take among them. And it is better to give and take (MW 10:288; cf. LW 3:141).

In the American context, "unity cannot be a homogeneous thing like that of the separate states of Europe from which our population is drawn." Our efforts should rather focus on creating a unity "by drawing out and composing into a harmonious whole the best, the most characteristic which each contributing race and people has to offer" (MW 10:204).

In his attempt to develop a conception of the term 'community' adequate for our current situation, Dewey offers three marks. The first of these is *association* or *interaction*. Of course, as he notes, "[e]verything that exists in as far as it is known and knowable is in interaction with other things" (LW 1:138); and consequently, association is just one precondition for community. As he writes, "no amount of aggregated collective action of itself constitutes a community" (LW 2:330). Thus it is that in the modern world this interaction strongly establishes the need for a community, the need for shared activity and common values. Secondly, then, for interaction to result in community, it must become *shared action*. There must be cooperation on the part of individuals for addressing the ills of common life and for the selection and achievement of goals which

---

[54] Cf. George Herbert Mead: "the attainment of that functional differentiation and social participation in the full degree is a sort of ideal which lies before the human community. The present stage of it is presented in the ideal of democracy" (*Mind, Self, and Society*, 326).

are felt to be good. "Wherever there is conjoint activity whose consequences are appreciated as goods by all singular persons who take part in it, and where the realization of the good is such as to effect an energetic desire and effort to sustain it in being just because it is a good shared by all, there is in so far a community" (LW 2:328). As a social activity, as a "partaking," such shared activity is similar to "taking part in a game, in conversation, in a drama, in family life" (LW 7:345). This shared activity makes possible the emergence of *shared values* and thus gives rise to full community. Thirdly, then, he tells us that people live "in a community in virtue of the things"— that is, the "aims, beliefs, aspirations, knowledge"—"which they have in common; and communication is the way in which they come to possess things in common" (MW 9:7; cf. LW 13:176). He continues that "[t]o have the same ideas about things which others have, to be like-minded with them . . . to attach the same meanings to things and to acts which others attach" (MW 9:35; cf. 17), is to live in community with them. For individuals like these, " 'we' is as inevitable as 'I' " (LW 2:330). Before there can be such a community, "there must be values prized in common" (LW 13:71), values which arise in shared activity. "A society that is largely held together by the aim of many individuals to get on as individuals is not really held together at all," Dewey writes (LW 9:179). There must thus be a central core of common felt values which operate as significant values for the community. In a community each individual "feels its success as his success, its failure as his failure" (MW 9:18).

Moving from conceptual analysis to speculative anthropology, Dewey offers an explanation of the origin of communities in the attempts of individuals to solve problems. He writes that "human acts have consequences upon others," and it is the perception of these consequences, when problematic, that leads "to subsequent efforts to control action so as to secure some consequences and avoid others" (LW 2:243). It is this recognition of, and attempts to deal with, the "[i]ndirect, extensive, enduring and serious consequences of conjoint and interactive behavior" that calls into existence a public with "a common interest in controlling these consequences" (LW 2:314). A public is thus "all those who are affected by the indirect consequences of transactions" to such an extent that they realize the existence of the problem and determine it "necessary to have those consequences systematically cared for" (LW 2:245–46). This self-conscious public is vital to the potential problem-solving activities of the community.

Our great problem in the modern world is the nonexistence of an adequately self-conscious public to sift through and evaluate information. Dewey maintains that "the machine age in developing the Great Society has invaded and partially disintegrated the small communities of former times without generating a Great Community" (LW 2:314). As a result, many consequences are "felt rather than perceived"; "they are suffered, but they cannot be said to be known, for they are not, by those who experience them, referred to their origins." Without an adequate public to help us, we do not understand the meaning of the constant stream of events. We can neither comprehend the importance of the facts we uncover nor place the consequences of our actions in understandable future orders. A public that is as yet "inchoate" will be able to organize "only when indirect consequences are perceived, and when it is possible to project agencies which order their occurrence" (LW 2:317; cf. MW 8:443). This perception and projection involves moving from events to meanings. "Events cannot be passed from one to another," he writes, "but meanings may be shared by means of signs." When our wants and impulses are associated with common meanings they are "transformed into desires and purposes, which, since they implicate a common or mutually understood meaning, present new ties, converting a conjoint activity into a community of interest and endeavor." A community, he continues, thus "presents an order of energies transmuted into one of meanings which are appreciated and mutually referred by each to every other on the part of those engaged in combined action" (LW 2:331).

In this way, we could advance the conversion of mere interaction into shared activity and common values, what Dewey refers to as "transforming physical interdependence into moral—into human —interdependence" (LW 13:180). In his opinion, "the greatest experiment of humanity" is that of "living together in ways in which the life of each of us is at once profitable in the deepest sense of the word, profitable to himself and helpful in the building up of the individuality of others" (LW 13:303; cf. MW 10:233). This experiment can be enhanced by the recognition that the well-being of each individual is bound up with the well-being of others within the community and throughout the world. This recognition of common interests can also lead to the improvement of our communities through a development of "the interests which are consciously shared" and a furtherance of "the interplay with other forms of association." In this way, Dewey believes, we can use "the desirable traits of forms of community life which actually exist . . . to criticize undesirable features and suggest improvement" in our current associations (MW 9:89). The draw to expand community is, he believes, part of its nature: "To extend the range and the fullness of sharing in the intellectual and spiritual resources of the community is the very meaning of the community" (MW 2:93).

5.5. Developing a Fuller Sense of 'Democracy'

This discussion of community has presumed the significance of *democracy* to a full community life. We still need to consider, however, what Dewey believed 'democracy' should mean in our contemporary situation. It is, as he writes, "a word of many meanings" (LW 2:286). It carries these many meanings because democratic life "has to be enacted anew in every generation, in every year and day, in the living relations of person to person in all social forms and institutions" (LW 11:416). We need to remember, he continues,

> that every generation has to accomplish democracy over again for itself; that its very nature, its essence, is something that cannot be handed on from one person or one generation to another, but has to be worked out in terms of needs, problems and conditions of the social life of which, as the years go by, we are a part (LW 13:299).[55]

Because of this ongoing social evolution, our conception of democracy "must be continually explored afresh; it has to be constantly discovered, and rediscovered, remade and reorganized" (LW 11:182).

One basic choice we need to make is between focussing broadly upon "democracy as a social idea" or narrowly upon "political democracy as a system of government" (LW 2:325). Dewey's emphasis is on the former, which he calls elsewhere "a mode of associated living, of conjoint communicated experience" as distinct from democracy as "a form of government" (MW 9:93). It is this broader sense of democracy that recognizes "the moral sense of

---

[55] Cf. EW 3:203; LW 13:87.

democracy as a way of living together" (LW 14:79). In defense of this moral emphasis, he writes:

> The idea of democracy is a wider and fuller idea than can be exemplified in the state even at its best. To be realized it must affect all modes of human association, the family, the school, industry, religion. And even as far as political arrangements are concerned, governmental institutions are but a mechanism for securing to an idea channels of effective operation (LW 2:325; cf. 11:217).

It would thus be a mistake to regard democracy as "an alternative to other principles of associated life." More than the simple agnostic claim that no one is likely to have better opinions than the average person, and more than the timorous claim that democracy is simply a device for self-protection from tyranny, democracy should be seen, Dewey writes, as "the idea of community life itself" (LW 2:328).[56]

In line with this broader conception of democracy, we can consider Dewey's analysis of the level of American democracy. In its fullest form, of course, he admits that democracy *"has not been adequately realized in any country at any time"* (LW 11:299). Aside from some early passages extolling America as, for example, "a democratic and progressive society" (EW 5:59 = MW 4:270), Dewey's view on the effective level of American democracy is quite reserved. In 1933, for example, he writes about the need "to restore democracy" that had been wrested from "the nominal government" by those who control "the means of production, exchange, publicity, transportation and communication" (LW 9:76). In 1936, he characterized the United States as only "nominally democratic" (LW 11:373), and three years later he discusses the still to be solved problem of the "creation of genuine democracy" when "the full conditions, economic and legal, for a completely democratic experience have not existed" (LW 13:97, 115). Still, Dewey never suggests any qualms on his part that the American situation had deteriorated to such a point that the people could not retake control. He writes in 1931, for example, that:

> The dominant issue is whether the people of the United States are to control our government, federal, state and municipal, and to use

---

[56] Cf. EW 1:240; James Gouinlock, *Excellence in Public Discourse*, 52–73; Gouinlock, "Dewey," 320–28.

it in behalf of the peace and welfare of society or whether control is
to go on passing into the hands of small powerful economic groups
who use all the machinery of administration and legislation to serve
their own ends (LW 6:149).[57]

The following year he takes the majority to task "for standing
passively by and permitting" evil to occur (LW 7:363), and he writes
a year later that "the forms of representative government are
potentially capable of expressing the public will when that assumes
anything like unification" (LW 11:60). It thus remains in our power,
as he put it in 1940, to make use of our "measure of democratic
institutions" (LW 14:253) to make the necessary changes to preserve
and develop our democracy.

Advocating this broader conception of democracy requires that
Dewey place a great deal of faith in his fellows. "Democracy is a way
of life," he writes, "controlled by a working faith in the possibilities
of human nature" (LW 14:226; cf. 11:219). This democratic faith
includes a faith "in individuality, in uniquely distinctive qualities in
each normal human being" (MW 13:297) and "in the capacity of
human beings for intelligent judgment and action if proper conditions are furnished" (LW 14:227; cf. 17:400). His inclusion of the
importance of 'conditions' reminds us of the centrality to all of his
thought of the social conception of the individual. His faith in
individuality is predicated upon a recognition of the moral efficacy
"of associated living, of conjoint communicated experience" (MW
9:93), "of pooled and cooperative experience" (LW 11:219).
Dewey's work can thus serve as a needed counteractive to the
excessive strain of individualistic freedom in some conceptions of
democracy.[58] "Cooperation," he writes, "is as much a part of the
democratic ideal as is personal initiative" (LW 13:78). He continues,
"the habit of amicable cooperation . . . is itself a priceless addition to
life. . . . Democracy is the faith that the process of experience is more
important than any special result attained, so that special results
achieved are of ultimate value only as they are used to enrich and
order the ongoing process" (LW 14:228–29). And, with democracy,
the possibility of recognizing and overcoming problems in those
results is increased. Moreover, because all of this is grounded in a

---

[57] Cf. LW 6:176, 180, 413.

[58] Dewey does on occasion consider individual opportunities in terms of "social
mobility" (MW 10:138), but his emphasis is clearly upon cooperative interaction.

faith, it can be validated or falsified only in the future success or failure of social action, "in *its* works, its fruits" (MW 13:308).

Democracy as a way of life is tested by interactive living. "From the standpoint of the individual," Dewey writes, the democratic idea

> consists in having a responsible share according to capacity in forming and directing the activities of the groups to which one belongs and in participating according to need in the values which the groups sustain. From the standpoint of the groups, it demands liberation of the potentialities of members of a group in harmony with the interests and goods which are common (LW 2:327–28).[59]

Democracy, because of its emphasis upon engagement in social life, is "the road which places the greatest burden of responsibility upon the greatest number of human beings" (LW 13:154; cf. 7:359). The level of work necessary to fulfill the responsibilities of democracy makes Dewey's democrats active participants in communal life. "The key-note of democracy as a way of life may be expressed," he continues, "as the necessity for the participation of every mature human being in formation of the values that regulate the living of men together" (LW 11:217). Without the chance to participate, individuals cannot grow: "human nature is developed only when its elements take part in directing things which are common, things for the sake of which men and women form groups—families, industrial companies, governments, churches, scientific associations, and so on" (MW 12:199–200). If one is to be a "spectator" rather than a "participant," however, that person will assume the attitude of "a man in a prison cell watching the rain out of the window; it is all the same to him" (MW 9:131). Consequently, Dewey holds up to us the goal of developing "the particular kind of social direction fitted to a democratic society—the direction which comes from heightened emotional appreciation of common interests and from an understanding of social responsibilities" that can be gained "only by experimental and personal participation in the conduct of common affairs" (MW 11:57).

Democracy as a way of life is thus an element in the whole spectrum of human life. Keeping this large scope of democracy in mind, we can briefly consider two particular aspects: the political and the economic. As Dewey writes, "the supreme test of all political

---

[59] Cf. MW 9:129; Moore, *Pragmatism and Its Critics*, 267–68.

institutions and industrial arrangements shall be the contribution they make to the all-around growth of every member of society" (MW 12:186). In the political realm, democracy denotes "a mode of government, a specified practice in selecting officials and regulating their conduct as officials" (LW 2:286). It is a mode of government "which does not esteem the well-being of one individual or class above that of another; a system of laws and administration which ranks the happiness and interests of all as upon the same plane, and before whose law and administration all individuals are alike, or equal" (MW 10:137). In furtherance of these goals several familiar procedures have been developed: "Universal suffrage, recurring elections, responsibility of those who are in political power to the voters, and the other factors of democratic government are means that have been found expedient for realizing democracy as the truly human way of living" (LW 11:218). The political aspect of democracy also includes, at present, a method of integrating and using the knowledge available to experts to help solve our social problems.

The economic side of democracy, in modern industrial society, is equally important because, as Dewey notes in 1932, "political questions are now economic in nature" (LW 7:357). He maintains that it is thus necessary to abandon one of the "eternal" truths of our inherited industrial system, namely "the complete separation of the economic from the political (no government in business)" (LW 11:366). In particular, economic changes since the time of the foundation of our political frameworks have rendered them to a large extent irrelevant because "economic developments which could not possibly have been anticipated when our political forms took shape have created confusion and uncertainty in the working of the agencies of popular government" (LW 13:107; cf. 11:368–371). In the modern world where so many people "have the minimum of control over the conditions of their own subsistence," he writes, "it is a problem of the future of democracy, of how political democracy can be made secure if there is economic insecurity and economic dependence of great sections of the population" (LW 13:300). Consequently, even from his earliest writings, he maintains that at present "democracy is not in reality what it is in name until it is industrial, as well as civil and political." This "democracy of wealth" (EW 1:246) requires an organized effort by the community, acting through its government, to foster both liberty and equality. In this regard, Dewey sees democracy as "an endeavor to unite two ideas which have historically often worked antagonistically: liberation of individuals on one hand and promotion of a common good on the other" (LW 7:349; cf. 9:103).

This emphasis upon industrial democracy can be seen in Dewey's social writings in his advocacy of the democratic management of our economic system. He was emphatic that it was necessary to grant to workers "a responsible share in the management of activities" (MW 12:9). Such "cooperative control of industry" (LW 5:104) might entail, as he writes at one point,

> a kind of conjoined supervision and regulation, with supervisors and arbiters, as it were, to look after the public interests, the interests of the consumer, the interests of the population as a whole, others to represent those who have their capital immediately invested, and others to represent those who have their lives (in the form of work) immediately invested (MW 11:85).

This system could evolve, over time, into "a federation of self-governing industries with the government as adjuster and arbiter rather than as direct owner and manager" (MW 11:105). Or perhaps the cooperative control would entail a larger governmental role under which the people would both own and control: "the socialization of all natural resources and natural monopolies, of ground rent, and of basic industries" (LW 9:289–90). The development of specific circumstances would determine what level of management was appropriate. In Dewey's conception of industrial democracy the outcome itself would have to be shaped by future individuals facing particular situations.

Related to these egalitarian aspects of industrial management, a full sense of the economic element in Dewey's sense of democracy would also require that the kinds of employment that are available to workers have meaning in their lives and involve them as contributing participants. This does not necessarily mean the elimination of authority or the undermining of expertise in the workplace. Dewey writes: "Some are managers and others are subordinates. But the great thing for one as for the other is that each shall have had the education which enables him to see within his daily work all there is in it of large and human significance" (MW 1:16). He recognizes that fundamental changes would be necessary to make this kind of significant work possible; but he recognizes as well that it is impossible that the ways in which activities are carried on for the greater part of the waking hours of the day; and the way in which the shares of individuals are involved in the management of affairs in such a manner as gaining a livelihood and attaining material and social security, can only be a highly important factor in shaping personal dispositions, in short forming character and intelligence (LW 11:221)[60]

The aesthetic and moral aspects of living demand that we attempt to create a situation in which workers would no longer have to engage in pursuits that are "fixed by accident and necessity of circumstance" (MW 9:143), nor be "appendages to the machines they tend" (LW 3:124), nor have jobs in which "[p]ersonal judgment and initiative have no organic place" (LW 5:137; cf. 1:271). Working, he believes, can be a means to human fulfillment if our working is itself a human rather than a robot activity, if our working has continuity and unity, if our jobs in fact have "large and human significance," if we can recognize "the intellectual value of labor" (MW 10:142) and learn through working something of the "doing and undergoing" of human life (LW 10:51). This could be done by aiming at increasing "on the part of every worker his sense of the meaning of the activities that he is carrying on, so that more of his own ideas, thinking, will go into it" (LW 5:240; cf. MW 12:9). Finally, this reconstruction of working must develop the workers' positions, and consciousness of those positions, with regard to the social ends of the community. Our goal, Dewey writes, must be that "every person shall be occupied in something which makes the lives of others better worth living, and which accordingly makes the ties which bind persons together more perceptible" (MW 9:326; cf. LW 5:105). The problems found in working as we know it result not from the nature of work itself but from the devotion of the organizers of our industries to the advancement of the narrowest conception of efficiency in production when "[t]he ultimate problem of production is the production of human beings" (LW 13:320).

Dewey concerned himself during his lifetime with the reconstruction of the full range of political concepts. Throughout his reconstruction of these various terms, he continued to make, as we saw in 5.3, three separable claims. Each of these three claims is fundamental-

---

[60] Cf. MW 14:86–87; LW 1:271–72.

ly pragmatic in nature and stands in need of our ongoing evaluation. The first was that such conceptions are tools to be used in our attempts to settle our social problems, and that they have an 'absolute' or 'final' meaning only in an abstract or definitional sense. Consequently, the requirements of, for example, a full sense of 'democracy' cannot be settled by recourse to traditions or historical documents but must be evaluated in accordance with our particular situations. His second claim was that the various historically bound conceptions of political terms that we have inherited did at one time make reasonable contemporary sense. The third claim that he was making was that at the present time many of these conceptions—like a conception of 'community' that emphasizes sameness rather than the complex interaction of diverse perspectives—no longer 'work'. These outdated conceptions owe their continued existence to the fact that there are individuals in society who are benefitting from their continuance. There are individuals, for example, who make use of the unbridled sense of 'freedom' that we have inherited to take advantage of others who are equally free only in an abstract sense. Dewey's aim in this conceptual reconstruction was to advance the process of social reconstruction by making available new suggestions and tools. For example, we find individuals constantly calling for a fuller sense of 'equality' and a richer sense of 'justice' than is currently present in our accepted conceptions of these terms.

5.6.   Institutional Reconstruction

We now come to the second level of social reconstruction. Institutional reconstruction is the level at which the various philosophers' and others' suggestions for rethinking and reconstructing our situation that were developed at the level of intellectual reconstruction are democratically evaluated and enacted. Some of the suggestions will involve the introduction of bureaucratic changes: new power for the government, new restrictions on the government, new ways to integrate the activities of the citizens and the government. Other of the suggestions will involve the citizens in less 'official' ways: clubs and organizations and neighborhood projects. Our overall purpose in social reconstruction is not simply making "refinements in the general concepts of institution, individuality, state, freedom, law, order, progress, *etc.*" but also in developing "methods concerned with reconstruction of special situations" (MW 12:190). The social institutions in question are, Dewey writes, "organized modes of actions, on the basis of the wants and interests which unite men" (EW 3:347). This position, expressed when he was still at the University of Michigan in 1891, resembles closely that of a number of his later colleagues at the University of Chicago.[61] Some typical Deweyan examples of institutions based upon this broad analysis would be customs, economic systems, political procedures, "[g]overnment, business, art, religion . . . language . . . [f]amily life, property, legal forms, churches and schools, academies of art and science" (MW 12:186; 14:57). Because these institutions are essential to the satisfaction of human needs and are thus so much a part of our shared and changing human existence, we are faced with "the necessity of maintaining the institutions which have come down to us, while we make over these institutions so that they serve under changing conditions," he writes. "To give up the institutions is chaos and anarchy; to maintain the institutions unchanged is death and fossilization" (EW 5:48).[62]

Dewey writes that the purpose of "all social institutions" is "to set free and to develop the capacities of human individuals without respect to race, sex, class or economic status," to "educate every individual into the full stature of his possibility," and to bring about "the all-around growth of every member of society" (MW 12:186).[63] But, as Veblen notes, institutions tend to lag behind: "Institutions are products of the past process, are adapted to past circumstances, and are therefore never in full accord with the requirements of the present." As a consequence, he continues, "the institutions of to-day . . . do not entirely fit the situation of to-day."[64] As Dewey

---

[61] Thorstein Veblen calls institutions "prevalent habits of thought with respect to particular relations and particular functions of the individual and of the community" (*The Theory of the Leisure Class,* 190). George Herbert Mead's view is similar: "The institution represents a common response on the part of all members of the community to a particular situation" (*Mind, Self, and Society,* 261; cf. 211; *Movements of Thought,* 366). James Hayden Tufts writes that the institution "brings a sense of direction and organizes impulses, habits, and collective strength to deal with the situation or conflict" (*Selected Writings,* 331). As we saw in 1.2, both Mead and Tufts had also served with Dewey previously at Michigan.

[62] Cf. MW 14:54; LW 7:227.

[63] Cf. MW 5:431; 9:9.

[64] *The Theory of the Leisure Class,* 191; cf. William Fielding Ogburn, *Social Change with Respect to Culture and Original Nature,* 200–213.

writes, "[t]he force of lag in human life is enormous" (MW 14:77). Religious formulations and business practices, educational systems and family arrangements, all become inappropriate as time passes.

> Change in patterns of belief, desire and purpose has lagged behind the modification of the external conditions under which men associate. Industrial habits have changed most rapidly; there has followed at considerable distance, change in political relations; alterations in legal relations and methods have lagged even more, while changes in the institutions that deal most directly with patterns of thought and belief have taken place to the least extent (LW 11:42).[65]

As Dewey notes with regard to laws, "statutes have never kept up with the variety and subtlety of social change" (MW 15:75). When serious lag develops, the laws and other institutions must be reconstructed, a process which in a democracy of the rich and participatory sort that he advocates requires ongoing debate and discussion to bring the outdated institutions more into line with the social vision by which we choose to live. Our goal, he maintains, "the universal and all-embracing human task," is "the construction of a proper human environment that will serve by its very existence to produce sound and whole human beings, who in turn will maintain a sound and healthy human environment" (LW 13:336). Dewey sees this reconstruction as part of the life of a liberal democratic community; and I will consider his understanding of 'liberalism' in the context of his discussion of how to build such a community.

Dewey notes in 1930 that the term 'liberalism' does not have a precise meaning. It is, he writes, "hardly more than a temper of mind, vaguely called forward-looking, but quite uncertain as to where to look and what to look forward to" (LW 5:70).[66] Part of the problem here was that the earlier heroes of the liberal tradition—individuals like John Locke and Adam Smith and John Stuart Mill—had been canonized by the static, regnant interpretation of 'individualism' and were currently providing "the intellectual justification of the *status quo*" (LW 11:26; cf. MW 15:76). As such, this conception of liberalism was not advancing the "enduring values for

---

[65] Cf. LW 11:54; 12:82–83; 13:97.

[66] In 1935, Dewey writes more strongly: "It is called mealy-mouthed, a milk-and-water doctrine and so on" (LW 11:5).

which earlier liberalism stood." These enduring values, all misinterpreted in ways we have considered by the dominant understanding of individualism, were "liberty, the development of the inherent capacities of individuals made possible through liberty, and the central role of free intelligence in inquiry, discussion and expression" (LW 11:25). More importantly, however, this "degenerate and delusive liberalism" (LW 11:295) had simply failed to carry forward its own message. For Dewey, that aim of the "renascent" or "fighting liberalism" he was attempting to develop was, simply stated, "the liberation of individuals so that realization of their capacities may be the law of their life" (LW 11:41, 48, 41). This liberalism was an aspect of "a new spirit that grew and spread with the rise of democracy." This liberal spirit, he continues, "implied a new interest in the common man and a new sense that the common man, the representative of the great masses of human beings, had possibilities that had been kept under, that had not been allowed to develop, because of institutions and political conditions" (LW 11:364–65). Out of this attempt to set free the possibilities of the great masses of people come three guiding themes of modern liberal democracy.

First of all, in an evolving society where institutions are constantly being strained by their tendency to lag behind, liberalism is committed to "the mediation of social transitions," to "adjusting the old and the new" (LW 11:36, 133). Dewey continues that "liberalism is committed to the idea of historic relativity. It knows that the content of the individual and freedom changes with time" (LW 11:291–92; cf. 26); and it attempts to move out of the currently felt problems toward resolutions that advance the common good. Secondly, he rejects the view that, because liberalism works to adjust and mediate, it is somehow precommitted to limiting the amount of change, usually to the minimum required to prevent open strife. Rather, he believes that liberalism should pursue radical changes in society, changes that reach down to the roots of our problems. He writes that "liberalism must now become radical, meaning by 'radical' perception of the necessity of thoroughgoing changes in the set-up of institutions and corresponding activity to bring the changes to pass" (LW 11:45). Renascent liberalism must seek out "the causes of which inequalities and oppressions are but the symptoms," Dewey writes; and, "instead of using social power to ameliorate the evil consequences of the existing system, it shall use social power to change the system" (LW 11:287). This spirit of fundamental change will require a great deal of organized planning, he believes; and this too would be a change from the traditional planlessness of the liberal:

> the gulf between what the actual situation makes possible and the actual state itself is so great that it cannot be bridged by piecemeal policies undertaken *ad hoc*. The process of producing the changes will be, in any case, a gradual one. But "reforms" that deal now with this abuse and now with that without having a social goal based upon an inclusive plan, differ entirely from efforts at re-forming, in its literal sense, the institutional scheme of things (LW 11:45).

As far as content is concerned, he writes in 1935 that one fundamental change required would be "a radical change in economic institutions and the political arrangements based upon them." This change is required, he writes, because the ends of liberal democracy can be attained "only as control of the means of production and distribution is taken out of the hands of individuals who exercise powers created socially for narrow individual interests" (LW 11:367).

Thirdly, although Dewey admits that "any liberalism which is not also radicalism is irrelevant and doomed" (LW 11:45), he maintains that liberalism must also be committed to carrying out these radical changes by peaceful means. As he writes, "democracy can be served only by the slow day by day adoption and contagious diffusion in every phase of our common life of methods that are identical with the ends to be reached and that recourse to monistic, wholesale, absolutistic procedures is a betrayal of human freedom no matter in what guise it presents itself" (LW 13:187).[67] Those who draw upon a revolutionary interpretation of Marxism and defend the inevitability of violence "as the main method of effecting drastic changes" are wrong, he believes, "in view of the vast scope of changes that are taking place without the use of violence" (LW 11:45, 58). Even admitting as he does that the United States has a "tradition of violence" and that force "is built into the procedures of the existing social system, regularly as coercion, in times of crisis as overt violence" (LW 11:46, 45; cf. 294), he still rejects continued reliance upon violence. Part of the basis of his rejection is his belief that in the highly interrelated contemporary world violent revolutions are likely to fail (cf. LW 11:266) or at best to achieve "only a Pyrrhic victory"

---

[67] Cf. LW 11:218, 298.

(LW 9:94; cf. 11:288). In addition, he maintains that, even assuming that revolution was *once* necessary, those who continue to advocate violence cannot prove that it is *still* necessary, writing that "even if it be admitted to hold of the past, the conclusion that violence is the method now to be depended upon does not follow—unless one is committed to a dogmatic philosophy of history" (LW 11:58).

Here as elsewhere, Dewey resists the easy transition of the past from historical record to prescription. "The question is whether force or intelligence is to be the method upon which we consistently rely and to whose promotion we devote our energies," Dewey writes. "Insistence that the use of violent force is *inevitable* limits the use of available intelligence, for wherever the inevitable reigns intelligence cannot be used" (LW 11:55). Rather than seeing violence as an inherent element in the social process, he writes that "what generates violent strife is failure to bring the conflict into the light of intelligence where the conflicting interests can be adjudicated in behalf of the interest of the great majority" (LW 11:56; cf. 5:415). Such adjudication should make violence unnecessary. "The one exception," he writes,

> to dependence upon organized intelligence as the method for directing social change is found when society through an authorized majority has entered upon the path of social experimentation leading to great social change, and a minority refuses by force to permit the method of intelligent action to go into effect. Then force may be intelligently employed to subdue and disarm the recalcitrant minority (LW 11:61).

But particularly for an individual like Dewey, whose interest in liberalism is primarily in its adjectival form—that is, in liberal democracy—most instances of violence will not prepare us for self-rule; violence will give us new bosses. As he writes, what is accomplished without the growth of democratic participation "will be badly done and much of it will have to be done over" (LW 9:110–11).[68]

Liberal democracy is thus the attempt to apply social intelligence to the process of shared living. Liberalism is committed, Dewey writes, "to the use of freed intelligence as the method of directing

---

[68] For a more complete discussion of Dewey's analysis of these revolutionary themes, see my "Dewey's Understanding of Marx and Marxism."

change" (LW 11:41; cf. 3:178). It offers society the possibility of bringing about, without violence, the kinds of fundamental changes that are necessary. He believes that it is now becoming possible for the members of society to use what he once called their "foreseeing and contriving intelligence" (MW 14:10) to "direct their common life intelligently" (LW 13:54). We need to abandon our tradition of trusting "the direction of human affairs to nature, or Providence, or evolution, or manifest destiny—that is to say, to accident" and turn instead "to a contriving and constructive intelligence" (MW 10:240). Accomplishing this redirection would require a recognition of the fact, Dewey writes, that "a government of and by the people might be a positive and necessary organ for securing and extending the liberties of the individuals who both govern and are governed, instead of being an instrument of oppression" (LW 11:248). It is possible, he maintains, to develop a system of "collective social planning" that would enable us to translate "the general creed of liberalism" into "a concrete program of action" (LW 11:32, 64). Behind these claims is Dewey's belief that "the great weakness" of the historical liberal movement was "its failure to recognize that the true and final source of change has been, and now is, the corporate intelligence embodied in science" (LW 11:144; cf. 51). Thus, if we could come to use our social intelligence to overcome our social conflicts, we could maintain a greater degree of ongoing social reconstruction.

Reliance upon this kind of intelligent social reconstruction follows from a series of assumptions about social action. One such assumption is a belief on Dewey's part that the society to which we belong can legitimately by spoken of in collective terms like 'the people' or 'the common good', and not just in terms of individuals, or of personal or group goods. As he writes, when attempting to address our social conflicts we try to discover "some more compre-hensive point of view from which the divergencies may be brought together" (MW 9:336). By working together in this way, we hope to recognize and advance the common good. This assumption is a crucial one, of course, for if we are not a collective unit with collective goods, then the use of a social focus will disproportionately favor those individuals and groups who are successful in presenting their interests as corresponding with the general welfare. A second assumption is his belief, as we saw in 5.2, that American society is ultimately a democracy—that is, either the people *are presently in control* or at least *can assume control* should they wish to do so through means which presently exist. A third assumption underlying Dewey's method of social reconstruction is of a basic common sense on the part of the members of the democratic community who are able to distinguish and willing to follow sound advice. He clearly believes that there is "a general disposition on the part of people to listen to good advice and, when it has been shown that it is good advice, to follow it" (MW 10:403). Moreover, this third claim is not just that they will be willing to follow explicit courses of action once enumerated, but also that they will be willing to engage in social inquiry along an as yet indeterminate path. This third assumption makes the job of social reconstruction largely an educational rather than a narrowly political undertaking. He writes that the work of liberalism is "first of all education, in the broadest sense of that term" (LW 11:42; cf. 44), suggesting that widespread and time-consuming efforts at education and refining public opinion are not just misdirected actions that would be better replaced by partisan activities aimed at more 'practical' and immediate results. Thus Dewey denies that many familiar political activities—'stretching' the truth, dwelling upon divisive themes and fostering feelings of fear of, or superiority over, opponents—are necessary parts of any attempt at social reconstruction. "Fair-play, elementary honesty in the representation of facts and especially of the opinions of others" (LW 9:94),[69] and so on, are aspects of the sort of intelligent social inquiry that he is advocating. "The security of democratic ideals depends upon the intelligent use of the method of combined and unified honest effort to come to consciousness of the nature of social and political problems and their causes" (LW 11:515).

Dewey does not believe that the process of democratic life will be without conflict; but he does believe that the cooperative inquiry of the community can be conducted in spite of such oppositions. Because the circumstances within the society will continue to change, conflicts will continue to occur. "Of course, there *are* conflicting interests," he writes, "otherwise there would be no social problems" (LW 11:56; cf. 7:322–28). The hope of eliminating conflict is, he continues, "a hopeless and self-contradictory ideal" (EW 4:210). This admission does not introduce despair, however, because conflict, when controlled, can lead to beneficial results for

---

[69] Cf. LW 13:117; 14:227.

the society. "Conflict is the gadfly of thought," Dewey writes. "It shocks us out of sheep-like passivity, and sets us at noting and contriving" (MW 14:207; cf. LW 13:125). In particular, when it is approached with the attitude of cooperative inquiry, social conflict can help us to "bring to clearer recognition the different interests that are involved and that have to be harmonized in any enduring solution" (LW 13:115). Our purpose then should be, he continues, "the directing of the struggle to reduce waste and to secure its maximum contribution" to ongoing social reconstruction (EW 4:210). This, he maintains, is the method of democratic social reconstruction: "The method of democracy—insofar as it is that of organized intelligence—is to bring these conflicts out into the open where their special claims can be seen and appraised, where they can be discussed and judged in the light of more inclusive interests than are represented by either of them separately" (LW 11:56).[70] True democrats, Dewey claims, have faith that the disputes which are "bound to arise" in society can be settled through "cooperative undertakings in which both parties learn." Through the fostering of "the habit of amicable cooperation" conflicts can be ameliorated (LW 14:228).[71]

Dewey's position is in essence that attempts at intelligent social reconstruction can be compared to a kind of cooperative experiment. Those involved are seeking the common good in a democratic way. The amount of time and effort required of us to deal with our problems is an irrelevant matter; we must do whatever is necessary to address these ills, and take as long as it takes. In the building and furtherance of community, the process of developing shared activity and values held in common is what matters. Our social groups need to develop, he maintains, the kind of long-term focus that he demonstrates in statements like the following: "the aim is not limited to effecting a decision on some particular restricted issue, but is rather concerned with securing such decisions on special points as will deepen interest, create a more intelligent outlook on all similar questions, and secure a more personal response from all concerned in

---

[70] Cf. MW 9:226; 12:189–90.

[71] Cf. George Herbert Mead: "Any such social reconstruction, if it is to be at all far-reaching, presupposes a basis of common social interests shared by all the individual members of the given human society in which that reconstruction occurs" (*Mind, Self, and Society*, 308).

the future" (LW 5:413–14). Disagreements will occur and mistakes are to be expected; and they must be tolerated because we trust the sincerity and the commitment of our fellows to the common good. The political process could then be seen as an educative one in which we all hope to grow in our ability to address social problems and in our appreciation of our shared existence. This kind of cooperative learning would be, Dewey asserts, "precisely the type of education a democracy most needs" (LW 5:416).

5.7. Social Inquiry as Inquiry

There are, certainly, fundamental questions to be considered in relation to this conception of our social life as a form of cooperative inquiry. It is more important initially, however, to consider how this view fits in with the larger Deweyan picture we have been exploring so far. In particular, we need to examine just how this view of social action as cooperative inquiry fits in with the overall understanding of the pattern of inquiry. Then, in the two following chapters we will be able to concentrate on the two main lines of criticism to Dewey's view on social inquiry: the tactical question of whether or not his approach to social action through cooperative community is likely to succeed, and the moral question of whether or not the goal of fulfillment through community is the proper human end.

Based on our earlier consideration of Dewey's pattern of inquiry in 2.4, we can approach instances of social problems as situations in which we have moved out of a state of security or quiet. Our habitual modes of social organization have failed. There is a breakdown of the social process; indeterminacy and ambiguity fill the situation, and those involved become confused and frustrated. Next come some attempts on our part to formulate the problem through thinking. Without a reasonably well formulated problem, Dewey writes, "there is blind groping in the dark" (LW 12:112). In the course of carrying forward this process of social inquiry, we must then experiment with alternative explanations, test various hypotheses to see what success or failure might offer us, and offer some tentative solution to be itself tried out and evaluated.

Dewey considered this kind of social inquiry, when done properly, to be a form of scientific inquiry. To understand this claim better, we can examine his discussion from the "Social Inquiry" chapter of

Logic: The Theory of Inquiry (LW 12:481–505). Beginning with a consideration of the similarities among all scientific inquiries— whether physical or biological or social—we find first that social science must be seen as a 'natural' science, rather than a 'supernatural' science. The interests of social science are in human behavior; and inquiries into this area do demonstrate the possibility of developing, through ongoing self-conscious endeavor, scientific quality. As Dewey writes: "The question is not whether the subject-matter of human relations is or can ever become a science in the sense in which physics is now a science, but whether it is such as to permit of the development of methods which, as far as they go, satisfy the logical conditions that have to be satisfied in other branches of inquiry" (LW 12:481).[72] Consequently, in this broad conception of 'natural' science, inquiries into human behavior have the potential for being just as scientific as those into physics. A second similarity is that all inquiry—not just social inquiry—"proceeds within a cultural matrix." All of our actual inquiries are shaped and modified by the "social relations," the ideas, traditions, prejudices and possibilities of our situations. "When we look back at earlier periods, it is evident that certain problems could not have arisen in the context of institutions, customs, occupations, and interests that then existed," Dewey observes, "and that even if, *per impossibile,* they had been capable of detection and formulation, there were no means available for solving them" (LW 12:481–82). Thus it is that only in a world that has 'unlocked the secrets of the atom' do nuclear problems arise, and that only within a context of mass communication can the curse of mass dictatorship unleash itself. Contemporary neonatology and gerontology as medical disciplines are not possible without a certain level of technological sophistication, and worries about the destruction of the ozone layer will not emerge unless a social situation is capable of both the destruction and its recognition. Another aspect of this second similarity—that all scientific inquiry, physical and social, takes place within a social context—we saw in 4.1: An inquirer in any specific field "appeals to the experiences of the community of his fellow workers for confirmation and correction of his results" (LW 12:484).[73]

---

[72] Cf. LW 3:44–46; 5:115–16; 9:108; 12:433.

[73] Dewey explicitly points to Peirce's valuable contributions to scientific inquiry on this point (see 1.3).

A third similarity is that all scientific inquiry aims at the settling of problems. Whether in the social field or not, inquiry attempts, as we saw in 2.4, to transform "a problematic situation (which involves confusion and conflict) into a unified one." Although, as Dewey admits, it is "much more difficult to accomplish this end in social inquiry than in the restricted field of physical inquiry," the greater difficulty ought not to suggest that there is "an inherent logical or theoretical difference between the two kinds of inquiry" (LW 12:484–85; cf. 108). A fourth similarity is that all scientific inquiries must integrate theory and practice. We need to develop interrelated procedures for gathering and organizing our data and for testing our ideas, he writes, in order to be able "to satisfy the requirement of institution of factual and conceptual subject-matter in conjugate correspondence with each other" (LW 12:485). The fact that social inquiry has so far not achieved this, Dewey writes, is obvious: "The immature state of social inquiry may thus be measured by the extent to which these two operations of fact-finding and of setting up theoretical ends are carried on independently of each other" (LW 12:500).

Before we consider a fifth similarity between social and other inquiries, we can consider three significant differences between social and physical science to which Dewey points. The first of these is one that has been touched upon already: social problems are fundamentally more complex. The workings of the various physical conditions that underlie our social problems—for examples, disease or famine or poverty—must be understood before we can address the problems themselves. Inquiry into social problems, "with respect both to data that are significant and to their relations or proper ordering, is conditioned upon extensive prior knowledge of physical phenomena and their laws." So, if we consider a social problem like alcoholism, for example, we need to consider it in the context of the antecedent uncovering of the scientific data on human chemical dependency. "Only recently has there been sufficient understanding of physical relations," Dewey continues, "to provide the necessary intellectual instrumentalities for effective intellectual attack upon social phenomena" (LW 12:486). A second difference between social and other inquiry is that inquiries into social phenomena are more deeply rooted in history than are the others, especially physical inquiries. The phenomena of social inquiry, Dewey writes, are "inherently historical." As a consequence, "taking facts as finished and over with is more serious in inquiry into social phenomena than it is with respect to physical objects." The result of doing so is to cut the facts off from their meaning: any "fact isolated from the history of which it is a moving constituent loses the qualities that make it distinctively social." So, for example, an attempted account of the assassination of Julius Caesar purely in terms of general conceptions like "assassination, conspiracy, political ambition, [and] human beings," would result in a treatment of it as "just and merely a case" and prevent understanding of it as "a social fact" (LW 12:494–95).

A third difference between social inquiry and physical or biological inquiry is that social inquiry 'lags behind' or develops more slowly than the other branches of inquiry. However, unlike the two just considered, this is a difference about which Dewey believes we can do more than limit ourselves to recognition. We can and must work to minimize this lag. One aspect of this lag is that social policies are too often adopted and carried out in a nonhypothetical fashion because they are consonant with our social inheritance. The conception of 'law' in capitalist individualism or marxian communism, or in biblical christianity or koranic islam, all give rise to public policy choices that are not derived from social inquiry. Each of them, moreover, suggests that there is no need for social *inquiry* in the case of many problems since the proper solution to the issue has already been determined. Dewey maintains, however, that policy proposals are better seen as suggestions being put forward with the hope of offering part of the solution for complex social problems. So, for example, proposals for generating additional revenues or for limiting unwanted pregnancies should be put forward hypothetically. He writes:

> every measure of policy put into operation is, *logically,* and *should* be actually, of the nature of an experiment. For (1) it represents the adoption of one out of a number of alternative conceptions as possible plans of action, and (2) its execution is followed by consequences which, while not as capable of definite or exclusive differentiation as in the case of physical experimentation, are none the less observable within limits, so they may serve as tests of the validity of the conception acted upon (LW 12:502).

Far too often, especially with regard to issues that are seen as vitally important, we are not hypothetical.

Dewey is challenging here the commonly held position that social inquiry is "genuinely scientific only as it deliberately and systematically abstains from all concern with matters of social practice." His hypothetical and experimental view is that "social inquiry, *as inquiry*, involves the necessity of operations which existentially modify actual conditions that, as they exist, are the occasions of genuine inquiry and that provide its subject-matter" (LW 12:486–87). When we approach social practice, as we too frequently do, without the hypothetical and experimental attitude of inquirers, we tend to be controlled by the past. In politics, for example, we hastily accept problems as given antecedently. All too often, we think we know what the welfare problem, or the teen-pregnancy problem, or the drug problem, is. As he writes, we assume that "the problems which exist are already definite in their main features." Our job is simply "to ascertain the best method of solving them." As a consequence, Dewey continues, "the work of analytic discrimination, which is necessary to convert a problematic situation into a set of conditions forming a definite problem, is largely foregone." In this regard, he believes that there is an instructive analogy to be made between our current social practice and "medical practice as it was conducted before the rise of techniques of clinical observation and record." In both cases, he writes,

> there is the assumption that gross observation suffices to ascertain the nature of the trouble. Except in unusually obscure cases, symptoms sufficiently large and coarse to be readily observable sufficed in medical practice to supply the data that were used as means of diagnosis. It is now recognized that choice of remedial measures looking to restoration of health is haphazard until the conditions which constitute the trouble or disease have been determined as completely and accurately as possible (LW 12:487–88).

Our primary requirement is thus to make the shift that medicine has already made: to adopt a hypothetical and experimental stance toward our problems.

Shifting to this type of social inquiry will be especially difficult, Dewey writes, because "[s]erious social troubles tend to be interpreted in *moral* terms." He is not suggesting, of course, that such problems are anything but "profoundly moral in their causes and consequences, in the genuine sense of moral." His point, rather, is that

> conversion of the situations investigated into definite problems, that can be intelligently dealt with, demands objective *intellectual* formulation of conditions; and such a formulation demands in turn complete abstraction from the qualities of sin and righteousness, of vicious and virtuous motives, that are so readily attributed to individuals, groups, classes, nations (LW 12:488).

In light of our need to conduct our social inquiry in such a hypothetical and experimental manner and to admit that we do not antecedently *know* what to do, our usual approach to human problems "in terms of moral blame and moral approbation, of wickedness or righteousness," he writes, "is probably the greatest single obstacle now existing to development of competent methods in the field of social subject-matter" (LW 12:489).

We are now able to consider the fifth similarity that Dewey finds between inquiry into social areas and inquiry into physical or biological areas: if it hopes to be scientific, an inquiry must be evaluative.

> All competent and authentic inquiry demands that out of the complex welter of existential and potentially observable and record-able material, certain material be selected and weighed *as* data or the "facts of the case." This process is one of adjudgment, of appraisal or evaluation. On the other end, there is, as has been just stated, no evaluation when ends are taken to be already given (LW 12:491).

Dewey is here rejecting the claim that all science, including social science, must be non-evaluative. He comments that the belief that "in order to base conclusions upon the facts and only the facts, all *evaluative* procedures must be strictly ruled out" is derived in large part from "the realization of the harm that has been wrought by forming social judgments on the ground of moral preconceptions, conceptions of what is right and wrong, vicious and virtuous" (LW 12:489). The problem, however, is that these moral preconceptions were *preconceptions,* not that they were *moral.* As they are most frequently encountered, moral blame and approval, he writes, are *not* evaluative in any logical sense of evaluation. They are not even judgments in the logical sense of judgment. For they rest upon some preconception of *ends* that *should* or *ought* to be attained. This preconception excludes ends (consequences) from the field of inquiry and reduces inquiry at its very best to the truncated and distorted business of finding out means for realizing objectives already settled upon.

Actual judgment, on the other hand, "institutes means-consequences (ends) in *strict conjugate relation* to each other." Evaluation is thus a process of finding and proclaiming values through the use of scientific inquiry. "In all fields but the social, the notion that the correct solution is already given and that it only remains to find the facts that prove it" has been thoroughly discredited. "But in social matters," Dewey continues, "those who claim that they are in possession of the one sure solution of social problems often set themselves up as being peculiarly scientific while others are floundering around in an 'empirical' morass" (LW 12:490).

In summary then, Dewey maintains that those who would deny the scientific possibilities of social inquiry are overlooking five clear continuities among all inquiries that are scientific. For him all scientific inquiries, regardless of their field of focus, are natural, situational, grounded in problems, integrations of theory and practice, and evaluative. And, while social inquiries are admittedly at the more complex end of the spectrum of scientific inquiries, these five qualities allow for cooperation within social inquiry. The ultimate effectiveness of cooperative inquiry, for Dewey, depends upon our ability to carry over into social inquiry the attitudes and techniques that have helped us in other inquiries. Central among these attitudes is the willingness to listen. The integration of particular, non-expert, experience, fostered by the establishment of interaction and discussion, enables the community to better use the unique insights of its individuals who are attempting to fill the role of "moral prophet" (LW 7:343).[74] We have seen in 5.3 the importance that he places in

---

[74] Cf. Eugene Fontinell: "The prophet . . . is the one who at a particular moment in history is the best expression of the community inasmuch as he illuminates the community's self-betrayal and urges it to be faithful to those ideals which give the community its meaning and identity" (*Toward a Reconstruction of Religion,* 132).

individuals. "Every *new* idea," he writes, "every conception of things differing from that authorized by current belief, must have its origin in an individual" (MW 9:305; cf. 5:433). And, as he writes, "social institutions as they exist can be bettered only through the deliberate interventions of those who free their minds from the standards of the order which obtains" (LW 1:169). These individuals, whose non-conformity is "not for the sake of private advantage, but for the sake of an object which will serve more amply and consistently the welfare of all" (LW 7:230–31), function, through their "social sensitive-ness" to the needs and problems of others (MW 12:165), as social critics and moral prophets. These individuals working alone, or more successfully in voluntary groups, are the initiating means of social reconstruction. "The question of whether there is hope in and for politics is," he continues, "finally a question whether there is a minority having the requisite courage, conviction, and readiness for sacrificial work" (LW 6:189). By means of making public their particular insights in the community of tolerant fellow citizens, Dewey believes that these individuals will be able to initiate processes of intelligent social reconstruction.

5.8. Democracy as a Cooperative Experiment

The process of living in democratic community requires a recogni-tion that our political life "is essentially a cooperative undertaking, one which rests upon persuasion, upon ability to convince and be convinced by reason; or, in ordinary language, upon public opinion" (MW 10:404). Effective democracy is thus rooted in "back-and-forth give-and-take discussion" (MW 8:443). Dewey has a particularly high regard for such discussion.[75] He praises "the role of consulta-tion, of conference, of persuasion, of discussion, in formation of

---

[75] Cf. John Herman Randall, Jr.: "This respect for the experience of other men, this willingness to learn from them what they have found out, above all, to learn by working with them, is the very core of John Dewey the man, and it is the core of his philosophy as well. From the point of view of the assorted absolutists—chancellors, commissars, or cardinals—who already know all the answers, this has been Dewey's unforgivable sin. He hadn't found The Truth, and he actually thought that other men were as likely to discover more of it as he or you or I. He had a curious, faintly old-fashioned faith, that men can really hope to learn something of wisdom by working together on their common problems" ("John Dewey, 1959–1952," 12).

public opinion, which in the long run is self-corrective" (LW 14:227).[76] His point here, as we saw in 4.1, is that through publicity and reflection we can learn from our social mistakes. Equally important to effective democracy is the nature of the relationships among the citizens. "Democracy must begin at home, and its home is the neighborly community" (LW 2:368). It is here that discussion can yield a public opinion capable of rising above mere information. As Dewey writes, "the heart and final guarantee of democracy is in free gatherings of neighbors on the street corner to discuss back and forth what is read in uncensored news of the day, and in gatherings of friends in the living rooms of houses and apartments to converse freely with one another" (LW 14:227; cf. 13:153). He continues that, through its concentration upon "face-to-face associations" (LW 13:176), "the method of democracy" develops "a positive toleration which amounts to sympathetic regard for the intelligence and personality of others, even if they hold views opposed to ours, and of scientific inquiry into facts and testing of ideas" (LW 7:329). Dewey's emphasis upon public opinion as the directive force in our society is reinforced by his concern over how this public opinion is formed. While the notion of the 'formation' of public opinion may perhaps suggest manipulation to some, when Dewey uses the phrase he intends no such connotation. He writes, for example, "I am a great believer in the power of public opinion. In this country nothing stands against it. But to act, it must exist." And, more importantly for Dewey, "[t]o act wisely, it must be intelligently formed." And, "[t]o be intelligently formed, it must be the result of deliberate inquiry and discussion" (MW 8:100).

The process of developing an informed public opinion used to be simpler, Dewey believes, because, as we saw in 5.1, the social life with which it was concerned was far simpler. Social decisions were made by people whose judgment "was exercised upon things within the range of their activities and their contacts." However limited their information might have been about the wider questions, he writes

they knew more about the things that affected their own lives than the city dweller of today is likely to know about the causes of his affairs. They did not possess nearly as many separate items of

---

[76] Cf. MW 13:316; LW 12:483.

information, but they were compelled to know, in the sense of *understanding,* the conditions that bore upon the conduct of their own affairs.

Although "they knew infinitely less concerning what the world at large was doing," Dewey continues, "they knew better what they themselves were about" (LW 13:94–95). The citizens of whom Dewey writes, on the other hand, find themselves awash in a sea of unorganized information. The modest means of assembling information of which Dewey writes in 1927—"[t]elegraph, telephone, and now the radio, cheap and quick mails, the printing press"—had even by that time "far outrun the intellectual phase of inquiry and organization of its results." Information could be gathered but it was unlikely to be understood. He continues:

> "News" signifies something which has just happened, and which is new just because it deviates from the old and regular. But its *meaning* depends upon relation to what it imports, to what its social consequences are. This import cannot be determined unless the new is placed in relation to the old, to what has happened and been integrated into the course of events. Without coordination and consecutiveness, events are not events, but mere occurrences, intrusions; an event implies that out of which a happening proceeds (LW 2:347).

To form public opinion that is more than " 'opinion' in its derogatory sense," Dewey writes, it will be necessary to uncover the meaning of this information, and to do this will require inquiry. This inquiry will make possible the kinds of comparisons and evaluations that do not result from casual encounters with facts but are necessary if our actions are to be justified. "Public opinion, even if it happens to be correct, is intermittent when it is not the product of methods of investigation and reporting constantly at work" (LW 2:346). Moreover, he believes that this ongoing inquiry is necessary to uncover and interpret some of this information itself: "The prime condition of a democratically organized public is a kind of knowledge and insight which does not yet exist" (LW 2:339).[77]

---

[77] Cf. Herbert Croly's call for a school designed to address this weakness: the School of Social Research was to "contribute to the social education of the American

We can consequently see that, although Dewey accepts the Lincolnesque view "that no man or limited set of men is wise enough or good enough to rule others without their consent" (LW 11:218),[78] he clearly does not believe that democracy could be satisfied with anything like the simple counting of heads. Nor does Dewey believe that we can be casual about mistakes, even if they reflect the majority's wishes.[79] Rather, he maintains that such mistakes can and should be avoided. Moreover, he maintains that such avoidance is possible if we are not slavish followers of unimproved public opinion. "Majority rule, just as majority rule, is as foolish as its critics charge it with being" (LW 2:365).[80]

We need to recognize that carrying over the legitimate flight from unjustified authority inherent in the old understandings of individualism and freedom into situations with possibly justifiable authorities would "deprive individuals of the direction and support that are universally indispensable both for the organic freedom of individuals and for social stability" (LW 11:136). The proper uses of influence and persuasion are thus essential aspects of a democracy that recognizes that intelligence is social; and such means of influencing should be interpreted as mutual *guidance* rather than *manipulation*. From social interaction and discussion, individuals receive both "a support, a reenforcement" for their views and actions and, secondly, the "enjoyment of new meanings, new values." Thus, he maintains that "in a genuine conversation . . . what is confirmed is not the previous notions, which may have been narrow and ill-informed, but

---

people and to the better realization of the social ideal, implicit in American democracy, by promoting the disinterested investigation of the subject matter of modern society and by deriving therefrom more serviceable social disciplines. It will study society . . . to make social research of immediate assistance to a bewildered and groping American democracy" ("A School for Social Research," 167; cf. Levy, *Herbert Croly*, 269–71). For Dewey's involvement with the New School, see: Dykhuizen, *The Life and Mind of John Dewey*, 172, 269–70; as well as LW 11:155–57, 303–5, 563–66; 15:9–17; 17:147–48, 442–50.

[78] Cf. Abraham Lincoln: "no man is good enough to govern another man, *without that other's consent*" ("Speech at Peoria, Illinois," 16 October 1854, *The Collected Works of Abraham Lincoln*, vol. 2, 266; cf. LW 13:295, 403).

[79] This casualness is present, for example, in the following remarks by Jerome Nathanson: "democracy . . . rests on the belief that people living together this way, no matter what fool mistakes they may make, are in the long run better off than if they live any other way" (*John Dewey: The Reconstruction of the Democratic Life*, 94).

[80] Cf. Walter Lippmann, *Men of Destiny*, 45–60.

his capacity to judge wisely" (LW 7:345–46). In this social process of rethinking and reshaping of viewpoints, we have mutual guidance, not manipulation.

Seeing cooperative inquiry in this way results from Dewey's prior analysis of human nature and social interaction. If, on the contrary, individuals know in advance what they need, and if attempts to change their minds are 'infringements', and if there is nothing more to act upon than each person's opinion, then Dewey's conception of democracy *is* manipulative. Manipulative as well, of course, are all other conceptions of democracy that contain a sense of the human good that is not reducible to pure individual freedom and the simple tallying of expressed preferences.[81] If, on the other hand, we follow Dewey and understand manipulation more narrowly as the secretive use of unauthorized power,[82] then his formulation suggests an adjuvant conception of democracy which may or may not function manipulatively depending on factors present within the social situation. All attempts at guidance by a teacher, for example, would not then be seen as manipulative.

In his examination of legitimate persuasion, Dewey emphasizes the importance of integrating experts into the cooperative inquiry of democracy. In large measure, the use of experts is simply a recognition of the complexity and integration of the modern world and our consequent need for help in clarifying our social problems. Thus he writes:

> The questions of most concern at present may be said to be matters like sanitation, public health, healthful and adequate housing, transportation, planning of cities, regulation and distribution of immigrants, selection and management of personnel, right methods of instruction and preparation of competent teachers, scientific adjustment of taxation, efficient management of funds, and so on (LW 2:313).[83]

---

[81] See, for example, the conception of democracy presented by C. Wright Mills, *The Sociological Imagination*, 166–76.

[82] Cf. C. Wright Mills: "Manipulation becomes a problem wherever men have power that is concentrated and willful but do not have authority, or when, for any reason, they do not wish to use their power openly. Then the powerful seek to rule without showing their powerfulness. They want to rule, as it were, secretly, without publicized legitimation" (*The Power Elite*, 317).

[83] Cf. MW 10:406–7; LW 5:135.

In matters like these, the experts' viewpoint plays a major role; and, to the extent that these problems "are to be settled by inquiry into facts," the experts' decision should have great weight—perhaps as much as being "the final umpire and arbiter" of these matters. One such case which Dewey offers is "the construction of an efficient engine for purposes of traction or locomotion" (LW 2:313). There are other, very different, questions which must also be faced. There are, for example, the socially more important questions like what places transportation facilities should connect, how quickly and how often, the method adopted to finance them, and their administration. These questions, and others like them, must be faced on the second level of political reconstruction.[84]

Dewey is careful to point out here that he is not advocating a "government by experts." Recognizing that "[t]he world has suffered more from leaders and authorities than from the masses," he emphasizes that "their expertness is not shown in framing and executing policies, but in discovering and making known the facts upon which the former depend" (LW 2:365). These experts may properly research and hypothesize and advocate; but they may not properly determine or dictate (cf. MW 10:406–7). Nor is Dewey advocating a privileged status for experts, as some sort of brain trust that is to advise on general matters about which they have no particular expertise. "It is a matter of common notice," he writes, "that men who are expert thinkers in their own special fields adopt views on other matters without doing the inquiring that they know to be necessary for substantiating simpler facts that fall within their own specialties" (LW 8:135; cf. 13:272–73). Nor are the experts

---

[84] There remains, of course, the serious problem of deciding which level of political discourse is involved at any given time, and who should decide *this* highly controversial aspect of social reconstruction. Consider, for example, the case of the educational material that led up to the Scopes trial. Here, scientific experts maintained that what should be taught in the schools was an expert-issue; but much of the general populace acting through their elected representatives decided otherwise.

Dewey's position of the primacy of the (ideal) community would seem to force him to side with the majority against the experts, although his support of the educators against the (actual) communities (cf. MW 2:56; 15:47–52, 162; LW 2:312–13; 9:161–62) is not incomprehensible, given his faith in education to improve the abilities for social inquiry in the various communities. Here, as elsewhere, Dewey's criterion is advancing the common good, not simple majoritarianism (cf. Joseph G. Metz, "Democracy and the Scientific Method in the Philosophy of John Dewey," 258).

usually able to evaluate the social importance of their own contributions.[85] The diverse experts are greatly useful to us on the first level of social reconstruction. They can often understand and think and propose alternatives in ways that the rest of us cannot. But this special role is limited to the first level, to problem formation. On the second level of social reconstruction, the level of testing and evaluation of suggested institutional changes, there is no special role for experts as there was on the prior level. The experts' role in clarifying and coordinating the indeterminate social situation is for the process of the formulation of problems; and there their particular expertise serves them, and us, well. However, in the task of enacting solutions, of making the value choices from among the possibilities which we have before us, of deciding which possible solutions are most nearly adequate, there is no expertise. The individuals of the society may be at present part of a "submerged mass" and they "may not be very wise," Dewey notes facetiously. "But there is one thing they are wiser about than anybody else can be, and that is where the shoe pinches, the troubles they suffer from" (LW 11:219; cf. 2:364). He thus believes that for this process of social reconstruction to be democratic—as well as effective—the step of institutional reconstruction can allow for no special role for experts.

Because of his hypothetical and experimental approach to social reconstruction, Dewey is frequently criticized for being without a plan or for leaving his readers lost in generalities.[86] In light of this and similar criticisms, it is initially puzzling to find in his work the same condemnation of what he calls "planlessness" (LW 5:97). He writes, for example, that the earlier attempts at thorough social reconstruction "failed because they were the expression of temporary sentiment and because their bond of union was so largely negative" (LW 5:347). In a similar fashion, he condemns more contemporary attempts to meet social ills "with ideas improvised for the occasion"

---

[85] For example, only highly qualified experts could solve the problem of infertility by *in vitro* fertilization; but this possible solution still needs to be socially evaluated.

[86] Cf. Charles Frankel: "in his writing he regularly stopped at just the point where we are anxious to see, if only in outline, the kind of practical, positive program he thought his ideas implied" ("John Dewey's Legacy," 317–18 cf. John Herman Randall, Jr., "Dewey's Interpretation of the History of Philosophy," 90–91). Elsewhere I have attempted to demonstrate the inaccuracy of criticisms like these. See my volume, *The Community Reconstructs*, 39–43.

(LW 5:86). For Dewey, more is required. "Experimental method is not just messing around nor doing a little of this and a little of that in the hope that things will improve" (LW 11:292–93; cf. MW 13:326). On the contrary, it is the attempt to uncover and rectify our social ills. It is in the spirit of such attempts that he offers in 1933 one possible version of how he would like to see the future turn out:

> I should want to see politics used to forward the formation of a genuinely cooperative society, where workers are in control of industry and finance as directly as possible through the economic organization of society itself rather than through any form of superimposed state socialism, and where work ensures not only security, leisure and opportunity for cultural development, but also such a share in control as will contribute directly to intellectual and moral realization of personality (LW 9:72).

We must recognize, Dewey maintains, that "[t]hose who suppose that with a little patching up here and there" (LW 6:180) conditions will rectify themselves are mistaken: "'reforms' that deal now with this abuse and now with that without having a social goal based upon an inclusive plan, differ entirely from effort at re-forming, in its literal sense, the institutional scheme of things" (LW 11:45; cf. 13:109).

The key here seems to be a difference between Dewey and the critics charging him with planlessness over what is to count as a *program*. At least some of the critics seem to want machinery for generating answers that are quick, sweeping, and final. Dewey's conception of a program for a political unit, on the contrary, is drawn directly from his understanding of the nature of such units. A program must be, first of all, *situational*. The program that we devise must satisfy social needs that are not being met, and social possibilities that are not being realized; and the "actual social conditions and needs suffice to determine the direction political action should take" (LW 9:67). There can be no general rules or formulae: "No single formula signifies the same thing, in its consequences, or in practical meaning under different social conditions" (LW 7:336). Our program must secondly be presented in a *flexible* or *hypothetical* manner. The program should thus be "partial and tentative, experimental and not rigid" (LW 9:67). Dewey thus maintains that all policy measures should be envisioned as experiments to be tested in future consequences. As a result of this testing, the program will undergo *ongoing revision.* He writes in this regard that "an immense difference divides the plann*ed* society from a *continuously* plann*ing* society" (LW 13:321; cf. 8:70). Third, a social plan must be derived by cooperative evaluation. "The attempt to *plan* social organization and association without the freest possible play of intelligence contradicts the very idea in *social* plann*ing*" (LW 13:321). This final point reflects Dewey's caution in putting forward proposals, lest they be taken as pronouncements rather than as suggestions.

Dewey believes that society had finally developed an effective method of intelligent social reconstruction. Social intelligence, he writes, "after millions of years of errancy has found itself as a method." He believes that we had developed a new kind of method that was appropriate to the modern, processive world, a method "of cooperative and experimental science" (LW 11:65, 58), a method "which proceeds on the basis of the interrelations of observable acts and their results" (LW 2:258). It is important to recognize, however, that for Dewey the notion of a method is better understood as a *framework* or an *outline* for approaching and dealing with problems than a *protocol* for setting out in advance our responses to possible conditions. Dewey offers no predetermined path of reform, no claim that individual reformers can be made irrelevant, and no guarantees of success. He believes moreover that the methodicalness of a method is not based simply on the ready production of answers or conclusions, but on the way in which they are justified after production. What sets this method off from other possible methods — "authority, imitation, caprice and ignorance, prejudice and passion . . . [h]abit, custom and tradition . . . routine, prejudice, dogma, unexamined tradition, sheer self-interest . . . custom, external authority, force, so-called absolute ideals and standards" (LW 1:326; 9:107; 13:273; 14:74)[87] — is the nature of its justificatory process. Dewey writes, for example, that "the worth of any object that lays claim to being an object of knowledge is dependent upon the intelligence employed in reaching it" and that "the value of any cognitive conclusion depends upon the *method* by which it is reached" (LW 4:160). So too in matters of social policy, reaching proposed solutions is not difficult. What is difficult is demonstrating the intelligence of a particular proposal, demonstrating that it is the best option available.

---

[87] Cf. LW 6:146; 7:185; 8:87, 117–18.

Dewey believes that we are now able to abandon these other methods of problem-solving, methods which "originated when the practice of knowing was in its infancy" (LW 4:164; cf. 13:276). He writes that the reconstruction of society involves carrying over "into any inquiry into human and moral subjects the kinds of method (the method of observation, theory as hypothesis, and experimental test) by which understanding of physical nature has been brought to its present pitch" (MW 12:258). He writes in 1931 moreover that "the great scientific revolution is still to come." What this revolution will entail is the adoption of the cooperative inquiry model of science in our social lives. This revolution will ensue "when men collectively and cooperatively organize their knowledge for application to achieve and make secure social values; when they systematically use scientific procedures for the control of human relationships and the direction of the social effects of our vast technological machinery." The issue is, Dewey tells us, "between chaos and order, chance and control: the haphazard use and the planned use of scientific techniques" (LW 6:62, 61). We must end the "state of imbalance, of profoundly disturbed equilibrium between our physical knowledge and our social-moral knowledge," that leaves our knowledge of human social existence far behind the progress made in our knowledge of the physical world. And, in our social choice between chance and control, "the chief opportunity and chief responsibility of those who call themselves philosophers are to make clear the intrinsic kinship of democracy with the methods of directing change that have revolutionized science" (LW 15:254, 274).

Dewey does not believe that the necessary reconstruction of social institutions is likely to result from foreseeable developments in our current two-party political system. The two parties themselves he describes as "secondary political agencies, not contemplated by the framers of our constitutions, agencies which have become primary in political matters" (MW 5:427)[88]; and the adversarial operations of these two parties he sees as ineffectual for addressing our social ills. "The idea that the conflict of parties will, by means of public discussion, bring out necessary public truths," he writes, "is a kind of

---

[88] The fact that the two parties are not aboriginal is, of course, not really a criticism from Dewey's reconstructive perspective. His criticism of the two parties is aimed at their sense of their own permanence and the conservatism of their practices that undermines a popular recognition of the fundamentally processive nature of social and political life.

political watered-down version of the Hegelian dialectic, with its synthesis arrived at by a union of antithetical conceptions" (LW 11:51).[89]

His current process of party politics could never lead to adequate social reconstruction, Dewey writes, because both parties are "the servants of the same dominant railway, banking, and corporate industrial forces" (LW 6:186). Consequently, whenever there is a "clash between property interests and human interests, all their habits of thought and action fatally impel them to side with the former" (LW 6:159). Because of the parties' indentured status, necessary policies do not get adopted, while ineffectual or harmful ones do. In addition, because the majority of the populace recognizes the dependency of the two parties upon more powerful forces, they respond to the parties' stranglehold on the political system with indifference to politics. The people are convinced, he writes, "that there is no important difference between the two old parties and that accordingly a vote for one or the other signifies little" (LW 6:185). As a consequence, interest falls and political control continues in the hands of "professionals who are interested not in principles or issues, but in keeping or getting power by winning elections, and who use the spoils of office to strengthen their own machines and not for public ends" (LW 7:353–54).

Dewey also maintains, as we saw in 5.4, that it is the indirect consequences of social interactions that give rise to the public and its efforts at control. Consequently, for him, the size and shape of the government at any given time should reflect the jobs that are then required of it: to serve the public in its attempts to deal with the indirect consequences of social interaction. As he notes, "at one time and place a large measure of state activity may be indicated and at another time a policy of quiescence and *laissez-faire*" (LW 2:281).[90] The point is adaptability to the processive nature of social interaction.[91] He writes that he was raised with "the conviction that governments were like the houses we live in, made to contribute to

---

[89] Cf. LW 2:309–11; 13:111.

[90] Cf. LW 2:254–55; 7:335–37. See also Dewey's earlier, less activist, view: MW 12:196–97.

[91] Cf. Ralph Henry Gabriel: the typical American farmer of the 1850s "saw the State engaged in no collectivist activity beyond the carrying of mail" (*The Course of American Democratic Thought*, 6).

human welfare, and that those who lived in them were as free to change and extend the one as they were the other when developing needs of the human family called for such alternations and modifications" (LW 5:194).[92] Thus, whether the public should act through its government to provide public transportation or medical care or employment, to subsidize children's day care or clothing expenses, or to control alcohol or pornography, are all questions that must be determined by cooperative inquiry. To accomplish the task of the reconstruction of the political framework of our society into a system that would be more effective, Dewey also believes it will be necessary to establish voluntary associations that would help educate and organize the members of the community and that would make possible the eventual establishment of a new kind of political organization based on rational grounds. These voluntary organizations would abandon "a struggle for immediate power with no one having any idea of what is to be done with the power if it is gained—except to use it again in the next election" (LW 6:162) that was prominent in the current two-party system and address themselves to the resolution of the problems of society.

Dewey was personally involved with all sorts of such voluntary organizations, the most significant of which were three primarily educational quasi-political organizations: the League for Industrial Democracy, the People's Lobby, and the League for Independent Political Action.[93] Since he was particularly closely related to the League for Independent Political Action—serving as its national chairman as well as its spokesman—it will be worthwhile to take a closer look at it.[94] The LIPA was, Dewey writes, "not a party and has no ambition to become a party." Rather, the LIPA was a kind of *pre*-party, an organization whose aim it was "to promote education

---

[92] Cf. Walter E. Weyl: "our political forms are not a last will and testament of a dead sovereign, but are themselves as mutable as the things which they regulate" (*The New Democracy,* 119; cf. George Herbert Mead, Review of Jane Addams's *The Newer Ideals of Peace,* 126).

[93] For Dewey's activities for these various organizations, see: Dykhuizen, *The Life and Mind of John Dewey,* 223–24, 229–30, 251–54; Westbrook, *John Dewey and American Democracy,* 443–52; Rockefeller, *John Dewey,* 447–48; Richard J. Brown, "John Dewey and the League for Independent Political Action"; Edward J. Bordeau, "John Dewey's Ideas about the Great Depression."

[94] Cf. Karel Denis Bicha, "Liberalism Frustrated: The League for Independent Political Action"; Eugene M. Tobin, *Organize or Perish: America's Independent Progressives,* 203–44.

and organization looking toward the organization of the desired new alignment" (LW 9:67). While it had long-term intentions "to encourage and assist the ultimate formation of a new political party," he writes that its immediate goals were more centrally educational. "The League intends to discover and to cooperate with liberal groups and individuals throughout the country; to bring them into conscious contact with one another and to promote that sense of solidarity among them which is the condition of further effective political action." The LIPA was thus "a clearing house for liberal sentiment and ideas" that hoped to "carry on the work of research and of education in order to build up that body of positive and constructive political policies which can alone give unity and endurance to a progressive party movement." Dewey consequently calls for "a campaign of steady and continuous organization which shall effect contact and unity among the now scattered and largely inarticulate liberal persons and groups in our country" and "development of a unifying body of principles and policies adapted to present conditions" (LW 5:348, 347). He never thought that the sort of educational work of the LIPA that served as "a necessary preparation for the formation of a solid and enduring new party movement" (LW 6:151) would be easy or itself sufficient.

Dewey was also involved with several other attempts to advance democracy as a cooperative experiment by means of voluntary institutions. Some of these were brief episodes, like his involvement while in Ann Arbor with the *Thought News* project, a collaboration with Franklin and Corydon Ford that aimed at producing an intellectual journal full of scientifically prepared, socially relevant information. Dewey had a life-long commitment to write for the popular press. He believed, as we have seen in 4.1, that knowledge is a social achievement and that since public opinion results "from free exchange and communication of ideas, from teaching and from being taught" (MW 10:404) a more informed and effective public opinion could result from the increased availability of information. A major contribution to this availability would be media that were not dependent upon commercial advertising. As he writes, "the assembling and reporting of news would be a very different thing if the genuine interests of reporters were permitted to work freely" (LW 2:349). Such a paper, freed from dependencies upon narrow special interests and dedicated to advancing the common good would be able to take as its goal, not the selling of the papers, but the informing of its audience.[95] Other voluntary attempts to advance democracy as cooperative experiment were ongoing, like his involvement with the settlement movement, particularly with Jane Addams's Hull House. This relationship began before he moved to Chicago in 1894 and lasted beyond his departure for New York City in 1904.[96] Dewey was particularly drawn by the educational possibilities inherent in the settlement houses' democratic integration of various segments of society and by its commitment to address the social ills of the neighborhood as problems amenable to inquiry rather than as known evils to be extirpated and replaced with 'proper' conduct.[97]

5.9. Education and Democracy

Dewey understood the American situation to be full of possibilities —including possibilities contained in the insights of other thinkers —and he understood a rich and effective adjuvant democracy to be something approached in the future. Education is a key element in creating this adjuvant democracy because full democracy is impossible "without first freeing the mind" (MW 15:51). The intimate connection that Dewey sees between democracy and education can be recognized in such passages as the following: "Democracy has to be born anew every generation, and education is its midwife" (MW 10:139). The relationship between the two is a "reciprocal" or "mutual" one, since democracy "is itself an educational principle" (LW 13:294) that makes possible growth through involvement with

---

[95] For discussions of Dewey's involvement with the *Thought News,* see: Dykhuizen, *Life and Mind of John Dewey,* 71–72; Westbrook, *John Dewey and American Democracy,* 51–58; Rockefeller, *John Dewey,* 172–98; Coughlan, *Young John Dewey,* 93–108; West, *The American Evasion of Philosophy,* 80–83; Feffer, *The Chicago Pragmatists and American Progressivism,* 82–86; Lewis S. Feuer, "John Dewey and the Back to the People Movement in American Thought," 548–53; Willinda Savage, "John Dewey and 'Thought News' at the University of Michigan."

[96] For Dewey's involvement with the settlement movement, see: Dykhuizen, *Life and Mind of John Dewey,* 104–5; Rockefeller, *John Dewey,* 207–8, 228–29; Feffer, *The Chicago Pragmatists and American Progressivism,* 107–16; Allen F. Davis, *Spearheads for Reform,* 41, 58–59, 77–78.

[97] Cf. George Herbert Mead: "It is the privilege of the social settlement to be a part of its own immediate community, to approach its conditions with no preconceptions, to be the exponents of no dogma or fixed rules of conduct, but to find out what the problems of this community are and as a part of it to help toward their solution" ("The Social Settlement: Its Basis and Function," 110).

the problems of society.[98] "Full education comes only when there is a responsible share on the part of each person, in proportion to capacity, in shaping the aims and policies of the social groups to which he belongs" (MW 12:199). The mention of 'capacity' here should not be read as a commitment on his part to some system for ranking citizens, but rather as a claim that in a democracy citizens must receive an education sufficient to function as adequate critics of proposed values. As he puts it: "the cause of democracy is bound up with development of the intellectual capacities of each member of society" (LW 7:364). Consequently, for Dewey, "the unsolved problem of democracy is the construction of an education which will develop that kind of individuality which is intelligently alive to the common life and sensitively loyal to its common maintenance" (MW 11:57).[99]

The effectiveness of the social criticisms of the moral prophets in influencing the larger community will be increased by efforts on the part of the community to prepare an audience for such critical insights. For this reason, a central theme in all of Dewey's work on social reconstruction is the theme of education. As he writes early and late, "education is the fundamental method of social progress and reform" (EW 5:93), "the most far-reaching and the most fundamental way of correcting social evils and meeting social issues" (LW 5:297). The plasticity of the individual has a social correlate: society is shaping itself. "Since the young at a given time will at some later date compose the society of that period, the latter's nature will largely turn upon the direction children's activities were given at an earlier period" (MW 9:46; cf. EW 5:94). If a society hopes to progress, to overcome the actual and potential ills that it has inherited from its past and to pass something better on to the future, it must focus on education. Initially, we need to think differently about what 'education' is to mean and to determine what it is that our children will need to enable them to face the modern world better prepared to fulfill their roles. We also need to rework our institutional practices for reaching these intended educational goals.

---

[98] Cf. Ralph Waldo Emerson: "Our institutions, of which the town is the unit, are all educational, for responsibility educates fast. The town-meeting is, after the high-school, a higher school" ("The Fortune of the Republic," *Complete Works*, vol. 11, 527).

[99] Cf. MW 12:185; LW 13:297.

In such "progressive communities," Dewey writes, there is the ongoing endeavor "to shape the experiences of the young so that instead of reproducing current habits, better habits shall be formed, and thus the future adult society be an improvement on their own" (MW 9:85; cf. 126).

This consideration of the possibilities of education ought not to suggest that Dewey thought improvement was guaranteed. He emphasizes, much more so than critics tend to realize,[100] the practical limits in the educational process. "'Education' even in its widest sense cannot do everything," he writes (LW 9:110); and the school, although it is often treated as "the willing pack-horse of our social system" (MW 10:191), is only "one educational agency out of many" (LW 11:414). Schools are "not the ultimate formative force," he continues. "Social institutions, the trend of occupations, the pattern of social arrangements, are the finally controlling influences in shaping minds" (LW 5:102). Still, educational reform is essential as a way to break free from the unthinking reproduction of outdated institutions. "The reconstruction of philosophy, of education, and of social ideals and methods thus go hand in hand," Dewey writes (MW 9:341); and, if this sort of fundamental reconstruction is our goal, the contribution of the schools is essential. As he continues, "while the school is not a sufficient condition, it is a necessary condition of forming the understanding and the dispositions that are required to maintain a genuinely changed social order" (LW 11:414).[101]

The role of education and of the school in social reconstruction has two distinguishable aspects. The first of these, built upon Dewey's analysis of human nature that we have examined in 2.4, is to help the students develop as problem-solvers in the new and difficult situations of the new world, to help them to learn *how to think* rather than to simply fill them with whatever we think that they will need in later life. Instead of turning out students "possessed *merely* of vast

---

[100] Cf., for example, George Novack: "At the bottom of Dewey's naive and almost magical belief in the omnipotence of education in relation to the rest of social life was the implicit assumption that progressive education could find everything necessary to realize its aims entirely within the existing social system" (*Pragmatism versus Marxism*, 237).

[101] Cf. Darnell Rucker: "The true ethical function of the school is the development of intelligent, self-reliant, socially oriented individuals capable of acting in their own interests in full awareness of the relations between their individual interests and those of their society" (*The Chicago Pragmatists*, 100).

stores of information or high degrees of skill in specialized branches," Dewey writes, our goal as educators should be to produce students with "that attitude of mind which is conducive to good judgment in any department of affairs in which the pupils are placed" (LW 8:211).[102] The ultimate goal of education in his work is thus to produce adults capable of "sound judgments," people who are able "to pass judgments *pertinently* and *discriminatingly*" on the problems of human living (LW 8:211). We can do this, he believes, by fostering "the habits of mind and character" (LW 11:44) that he refers to as 'the scientific attitude'. Teachers should insist that "education means the creation of a discriminating mind, a mind that prefers not to dupe itself or to be the dupe of others," and they should "cultivate the habit of suspended judgment, of scepticism, of desire for evidence, of appeal to observation rather than sentiment, discussion rather than bias, inquiry rather than conventional idealizations" (MW 13:334).

Fostering this kind of mental attitude requires that we abandon what Dewey calls our "systematic, almost deliberate, avoidance of the spirit of criticism in dealing with history, politics, and economics" (MW 13:332)—a weakness in our educational system that he attributes largely to the "dominant economic interests" (LW 9:110) —so that we can give the students "some unified sense of the kind of world in which they live, the directions in which it is moving, and the part they have to play in it" (LW 11:164). Our schools must become more politically conscious and must make the students familiar with what he calls "the underlying tendencies and problems they must meet in government, local, state and national" (MW 15:161). Only in this way will these children be able "to discriminate, to make distinctions that penetrate below the surface" (MW 13:329), and only in this way can each child "take charge of himself" and "not only adapt himself to the changes which are going on, but have power to shape and direct those changes" (EW 5:60). It is only in this way, Dewey writes, that each child will be capable of "effective self-direction" (MW 1:20).

The focus of education on judgment rather than on knowledge reminds us again of Dewey's emphasis on *wisdom* rather than on *intelligence* that we saw in 3.4, and of his position that wisdom is "a moral term" (MW 11:44) related to evaluation and criticism of

---

[102] Cf. MW 9:153; LW 8:327.

choices for a better future world. Because of our need for ongoing evaluation and criticism, he emphasizes the need to foster ongoing inquiry. "The most important attitude that can be formed," he writes, "is that of desire to go on learning" (LW 13:29; cf. 8:139). Consistent with his view that "life is growth," a process that is understood better as *"being* an end" rather than as *"having* an end" (MW 9:56, 55), is the view that education "is a process of living and not a preparation for future living" (EW 5:87; cf. MW 12:185). As a consequence, we need to cultivate in students not the love of idle information or the amassing of random knowledge. "The criterion of the value of school education," Dewey writes, "is the extent in which it creates a desire for continued growth and supplies means for making the desire effective in fact" (MW 9:58; cf. LW 5:297). Democratic education is thus to be seen "as a freeing of individual capacity in a progressive growth directed to social aims" (MW 9:105). The aspects of experience that underlie Dewey's ideas here, as we saw in 4.4, are continuity and interaction. Continuity must be emphasized because only when there is continuity will students be able to build effectively upon what has gone before. Interaction must be emphasized because only when there is a rich interaction between the individual and his or her situation, however complex, can there be growth. In this way students will be able to make more sense of their lives at present and make a more ordered entry into the future.

The second aspect of education and schooling in social reconstruction, built upon the social analysis of the self considered in 2.3, is the importance of helping students learn to live more cooperatively and to work together to accomplish tasks that cannot be done individually. Educators thus play a central role in socializing the student or, as we saw in 4.2, in "saturating him with the spirit of service" (MW 1:20). "Education should create," he continues, "an interest in all persons in furthering the general good, so that they will find their own happiness realized in what they can do to improve the conditions of others" (LW 7:243). This need for "the definite substitution of a social purpose . . . for the traditional individualistic aim" (LW 9:180), is especially important now when we are attempting to fill out the broader possibilities that our social situation has given us. "In a complex society, ability to understand and sympathize with the operations and lot of others is a condition of common purpose which only education can procure" (MW 10:139). The school has long been the social tool most able to advance the goal of community. It should remain "the shuttle which has carried the threads across and woven the otherwise separate threads into a coherent pattern" (MW 15:150).

It is perhaps necessary to consider further two elements of Dewey's call for socialization. One is that in his call for saturating the students with the spirit of service Dewey is not attempting to eliminate or prevent the development of individuality. His goal is, rather, to increase individuality by preparing the students to become "good citizens, in the broadest sense," citizens who are capable of "recognizing the ties that bind them to all the other members of the community, recognizing the responsibility they have to contribute to the upbuilding of the life of the community" (MW 15:158).[103] Secondly, although Dewey calls for the development of "public-mindedness, a sense of public service and responsibility" (MW 10:183), this 'public-mindedness' is to be, as we have just seen, a critical one and in no way the same as a simple-minded promulgation of the *status quo*. "If our public-school system merely turns out efficient industrial fodder and citizenship fodder in a state controlled by pecuniary interest," he writes (LW 5:102), we are not building good citizens. Education must make the students better able to recognize values and more conscious of the nature of possibilities of social progress. They must grow in the "ability to judge men and measures wisely and to take a determining part in making as well as obeying laws" (MW 9:127). They must have the ability "to take their own active part in aggressive participation in bringing about a new social order" (LW 9:182; cf. MW 8:412).

Dewey believes that these students' abilities to participate and evaluate could be fostered by democratic school procedures. Another way to phrase this point would be to say that the means used in our attempts at the "preparation of free individuals for intelligent participation in a free society" (LW 13:297) cannot be divorced from the goal. Dewey writes, "[w]hether this educative process is carried on in a predominantly democratic or non-democratic way becomes therefore a question of transcendent importance not only for education itself but for its final effect upon all the interests and activities of a society that is committed to the democratic way of life" (LW 11:222). Schools in which all of the decisions are made for students, in which the individual and collective responsibility of the

---

[103] Cf. MW 15:190; LW 11:192, 205–7.

youngsters is not developed, will not foster an inquiring democratic citizenry. It is foolish to expect that our schools will be able to turn out "young men and women who will stand actively and aggressively for the cause of free intelligence in meeting social problems and attaining the goal of freedom," he writes, "unless the spirit of free intelligence pervades the organization, administration, studies, and methods of the school itself" (LW 11:254). Such a school would not divorce the ends of socialization from the means of its attainment. "The only way to prepare for social life is to engage in social life," Dewey writes (EW 5:62); and, if that social life is to satisfy the human needs "to lead and to follow" (LW 13:286), schools must provide opportunities for both.

We must attempt to create in our schools "a projection in type of the society we should like to realize, and by forming minds in accord with it gradually modify the larger and more recalcitrant features of adult society" (MW 9:326). In such a community-oriented school, Dewey writes, the child will be stimulated "to act as a member of a unity, to emerge from his original narrowness of action and feeling and to conceive of himself from the standpoint of the welfare of the group to which he belongs" (EW 5:84). By means of providing an education in a school organized along the lines of the "principle of shared activity" (MW 9:18), we could hope for more socially conscious citizens. Such a communal school atmosphere would have a very different overall impact from the isolating one in which "for one child to help another in his task has become a school crime" (MW 1:11). It would rather make each individual "a sharer or partner in the associated activity so that he feels its success as his success, its failure as his failure" (MW 9:18; cf. EW 5:88) and give rise to shared meanings of the sort that would make fuller community life possible.

In all of this consideration of the socializing possibilities of education, it is necessary to remember Dewey's reminder that "the school is primarily a social institution" (EW 5:86). When schools function as "genuine community centres," their influence "ramifies to take in the main interests of the community in such things as nutrition, health, recreation, etc." (LW 9:185). Thus, understanding the school as a social center means "the active and organized promotion of this socialism of the intangible things of art, science, and other modes of social intercourse" (MW 2:93; cf. LW 11:408–17). This wider availability of these social goods through the schools draws upon the model that he saw in the settlement houses. "What we want," he writes, "is to see the school, every public school, doing something of the same sort of work that is now done by a settlement or two scattered at wide distances through the city" (MW 2:91; cf. 15:157).

Dewey takes seriously the importance of education as guidance; and, although he recognizes the potential for manipulation in the "social engineering" of educational practice (LW 5:20), he rejects the possible identification of all education that attempts to guide with manipulation. He emphasizes the need to steer between the extreme positions of releasing the students from all control on the one hand and of attempting to bring them under the control of rigid direction on the other.[104] In his rejection of the extreme form of freedom, he cites the question Emerson poses to himself: "would you leave the young child to the mad career of his own passions and whimsies, and call this anarchy a respect for the child's nature?" (MW 9:57).[105] Historically, of course, the tendency of education, especially about values, has been at the other extreme, towards indoctrination. The young child begins as a highly plastic individual; but, to many educators, this plasticity has signified "not capacity to learn liberally and generously, but willingness to learn the customs of adult associates, ability to learn just those special things which those having power and authority wish to teach." Such a conception of education makes it "the art of taking advantage of the helplessness of the young; the forming of habits becomes a guarantee for the maintenance of hedges of custom" (MW 14:70, 47). Dewey maintains that this sort of "external imposition" *is* manipulative and has nothing to do with guidance, which he defines as *"freeing the life-process for its own most adequate fulfillment"* (MW 2:281). Guidance in this sense, he continues, is "an aid to freedom, not a restriction upon it" (LW 13:46).

Dewey thus believes that enhancing the abilities of students to participate in and evaluate social life can be accomplished without indoctrination. He rejects the view that all education entails indoctri-

---

[104] Cf. MW 1:90; 2:279–83; LW 5:319–25; 13:8–10.

[105] Dewey continues, quoting from Emerson's answer: ". . . keep his *naturel,* but stop off his uproar, fooling and horse-play; keep his nature and arm it with knowledge in the very direction in which it points" ("Education," *Complete Works,* vol. 10, 143–44; cf. MW 9:121; 10:136; Eames, *Pragmatic Naturalism,* 216–19).

nation and that we are consequently justified in inculcating as correct a traditional answer to questions of how to address our social problems, like the answer of capitalism or that of communism. He maintains, on the contrary, that it is possible for teachers to guide their students through a consideration of what he calls "the underlying social problems of our civilization" (LW 5:102) while still remaining politically neutral.[106] He writes that "the essence of indoctrination" is to be found in a relationship in which "those educated do not have an opportunity to make the choice [of tradition] or to share in making it." He believes that the teacher's focus should not be on a "pre-selected" tradition but on "the rapidity of social change and shifting of aims and methods in society . . . the various methods urged for dealing with [our situation] and the various traditions related to it." In this way, the tradition that the student eventually adopts "would be from each one's own choice and through his own participation in the processes which lead up to choice and not because of inculcation of a choice made by others" (LW 6:142–44; cf. 13:306–7).[107]

Guidance, thus conceived, admittedly relies upon some understanding of what would constitute human fulfillment. Students would not need to be guided if they spontaneously sought their good. And this conception of fulfillment must of necessity be chosen by the teachers, the school board, the PTA, and other groups of

---

[106] Cf. George S. Counts: "Neutrality with respect to the great issues that agitate society, while perhaps theoretically possible, is practically tantamount to giving support to the most powerful forces engaged in the contest. You will also say, no doubt, that I am flirting with the idea of indoctrination. . . . the word does not frighten me. We may all rest assured that the younger generation in any society will be thoroughly imposed upon by its elders and by the culture into which it is born. For the school to work in a somewhat different direction with all the power at its disposal could do no great harm" ("Dare Progressive Education Be Progressive?," 263; cf. Counts, *Dare the School Build a New Social Order?;* Counts, "Freedom, in Relation to Culture, Social Planning, and Leadership"; John L. Childs, "Democracy, Education, and the Class Struggle"; Childs, "Dr. Bode on 'Authentic' Democracy.")

[107] Cf. John L. Childs: "Dewey's concern was not whether adults had the right to transmit their beliefs and moral standards to the young, but rather that this should be so done that the young would understand the elements of fact and value embedded in them, and thus be prepared to reconstruct them without undue emotional strain whenever subsequent developments made such reconstruction necessary" (*American Pragmatism and Education,* 293; cf. Childs, "John Dewey and Education," 160–63; LW 8:75–76; Alfonso J. Damico, *Individuality and Community,* 37–38).

adults.[108] From Dewey's point of view, however, the defense of the goal of social service should not be attempted on the basis of the untutored wishes of children or their parents any more than upon the whimsy of well-educated, reform-minded adults. The only justifiable defense of the possible goals toward which the teachers and others are guiding the students is that they are likely to result in the advancement of the common good. "The educator's part in the enterprise of education is to furnish the environment which stimulates responses and directs the learner's course" (MW 9:188).[109] The educator's duty is to guide this course toward fulfillment as social creatures. The role that the teacher plays in the school is, for Dewey, similar to the role that the expert plays in the larger society; and, although the students are as yet only partially developed, they are learning to fulfill their later role in society as suggesters and evaluators of experts' suggestions.

Dewey's emphasis upon the relationship between democracy and education is not just a point about schooling, of course, but about the ongoing education of engaged citizens. He writes that "freedom of thought in inquiry and in dissemination of the conclusions of inquiry is the vital nerve of democratic institutions" (LW 11:375). This emphasis upon the sharing of knowledge in a democracy requires once and for all the abandonment of the "purely individualistic notion of intelligence" and of "our ingrained habit of regarding intelligence as an individual possession" (LW 11:38, 47). Such knowledge as our society possesses is gained through the cooperative efforts of human beings living together. "Knowledge cooped up in a private consciousness is a myth, and knowledge of social phenomena is peculiarly dependent upon dissemination, for only by distribution can such knowledge be either obtained or tested" (LW 2:345). Dewey's assumptions about the social nature of intelligence and about adjuvant democracy lead to his belief that

> native capacity is sufficient to enable the average individual to respond to and to use the knowledge and the skill that are

---

[108] Cf. Richard Hofstadter: "the ideal of social reform was, after all, an adult end, and . . . to realize it the cooperation of children could not be automatically counted upon. . . . it was impossible to impute to [the child] a natural interest in the reconstruction of society or in having his mind 'saturated' with 'the spirit of service'" (*Anti-intellectualism in American Life,* 381, 387).

[109] Cf. EW 5:95; LW 13:36–37.

embodied in the social conditions in which he lives, moves and has his being. There are few individuals who have the native capacity that was required to invent the stationary steam-engine, locomotive, dynamo or telephone. But there are none so mean that they cannot intelligently utilize these embodiments of intelligence once they are a part of the organized means of associated living (LW 11:38).[110]

But, for adjuvant democracy to succeed, this cooperative interaction must take place over the broad range of shared activity.

---

[110] Cf. LW 2:366–67; 11:48–49.

CHAPTER 6

Criticisms and Responses

IN THIS CHAPTER and the next, I want to explore in a more critical fashion the potential value of Dewey's philosophy of social reconstruction through a direct comparison of his work with other views. There are two general lines of criticism that I believe are important enough to consider in detail. The first, the subject of this chapter, challenges his work on the general question of its practicality or workability. The relevant critics here do not so much disagree with Dewey over such fundamental questions as the values of democracy and participation, or of the importance of cooperation and efforts to advance the common good. Their challenge focusses instead on the question of whether his particular approach is likely to succeed in our contemporary situation. The second line of criticism, to be addressed in the final chapter, questions whether we should adopt Dewey's social approach as our fundamental stance. Instead of his social system of cooperative values, others would propose an individualistic system that emphasizes the cluster of personal choices and private goods, all conceived in ways that emphasize individual freedom.

This chapter examines the criticisms of a series of thinkers who accept in general Dewey's social vision but who maintain that his belief that we can attain it by a social method of cooperative inquiry is unfounded. In the place of our ever present temptation to enact predetermined solutions, he advocated social action as a kind of cooperative experimentation in which we envision society as made up of interacting clusters of democratic individuals seeking the common good and in which the political life of the community is seen as the basic forum for social education. Some critics suggest, however, that people are not sufficiently interested in the political processes of communal life to maintain a level of familiarity with the material to render sensible judgments. Others suggest that people are not intelligent enough to offer sensible judgments. Still others suggest that people are too selfish to be able to overcome their own narrow interests and advance the common good.

I think that these lines of criticism can be countered, initially at least, by Dewey's reminder that his positions were not based upon the assumption that the conditions of his situation were permanent. Rather, his positions on the possibility of a cooperative, experimental political life were based upon the assumption of our continued attempts to improve the nature and practice of a broad conception of education in society as a concomitant of our efforts to change society. Individuals, he reminds us unceasingly, can become better able to act with intelligence to address the problems that we face. This clearly opens up the consideration of the political question of the efficacy of education as a means to social reconstruction; and, again here, Dewey's meliorism cannot be rejected in advance. A more serious issue, I believe, is the line of criticism developed especially by C. Wright Mills, who suggests that Dewey's approach to the recon-struction of society is not adequate because it does not 'fit' the way that our political activities work. Cooperative social interaction between social units with different goals and differing amounts of social power will result, according to this criticism, in exploitation of the weak by the strong. It is important to notice that this criticism is not an *individual* criticism: there is no necessary claim here that the citizens of the democracy do not measure up to the personal challenges of self-government or that the leaders of the various organizations are personally engaged in social sabotage. The point is that they are attempting to advance the interests of certain subgroups within the larger society and they fail to recognize or they feel obligated to overlook the interests of others.

6.1.   Can We Meet the Demands of Democracy?

Returning now to the first line of criticisms—that the aim of Dewey's writings on social reconstruction is perhaps ideally sound but that his method will not succeed—we can begin with a criticism that is based in citizen apathy. Presented in the form of a fantasia, this criticism proceeds as follows: Are people really that concerned about social problems? Are they really interested in this kind of cooperative democratic community? In a world of overwork and overworry, in a world that drives us toward diversionary entertainment and compen-satory recreation, can we expect people to be concerned about engaging in social action? Society has always been a field of corruption and pain; there have always been suffering and injustice. And there have always been dreamers. Dewey, another in this long line, offers us a method of social reconstruction that at best has only the slimmest hope of working, and that only if it can generate a high level of selfless involvement on the part of the citizenry. Given what Dewey himself has written about the American situation with which he was familiar, noninvolvement on the part of the citizenry would not seem to be an irrational response. People have been systematically miseducated and propagandized, alienated in their working lives and exploited in their economic relations. They might well believe that a personally rational reaction to a nonresponsive, atrophied political system is noninvolvement. People have reason to worry about their families and themselves. People are justified in their attempts to distract themselves, to relax and have fun. They are justified to complain when possible, and protest when necessary, to obtain 'little' victories. They are not justified, however, to hope that by cooperative social inquiry the situation might be made fundamentally better. It would be nice if the situation were otherwise, if social action were a viable option and the citizenry were engaged and effective; but, for now, no such expectations are realistic. And so on.

Thus runs the first criticism of Dewey's method of social reconstruction. He, of course, does not deny the fact of apathy nor that such apathy demonstrates a kind of short-range 'rationality' on the part of those who adopt it. He does, however, dispute the fatalistic assumptions that underlie this criticism. For him, this kind of political apathy is grounded upon a complex interrelationship of various facts. Our long history of general social stability and progress fostered the rise of a confident self-sufficiency and moral privateness. In the absence of clearly recognized and delineated problems, the critical examination of our social situation lost out to diversions; and, as long as whatever social interest that could be generated was wasted on nonissues like Prohibition, hunting for various kinds of witches, and opposing the teaching of Darwinism in schools, the addressing of more serious issues could not gather sufficient support. Even the developing series of crises in Dewey's day was not sufficient to shake people out of their apathetic stance because, he writes, their apathy was due "fundamentally to mental confusion arising from lack of consciousness of any vital connection between politics and daily affairs" (LW 5:96). So few potential voters even bothered to cast a ballot because they were convinced that "nothing happens of public significance in consequence of approval of one party rather than another" (LW 6:182). All of this constituted a prescription for still more apathy, a situation in whose continuation he found the two national parties to be "eager accomplices" (LW 5:96), as we saw in 5.8.

Dewey believes that this apathy can be overcome and citizens can be drawn to take an active part in the much more demanding democratic running of their own lives, but only if they can be convinced that this involvement has a chance of succeeding and if they discover from personal experience the compelling nature of political involvement. While recognizing that political democracy is grounded in "the assumption that with the widening of the franchise there would also go a wholesome widening and deepening of watchfulness, concern, and activity" (LW 6:185), he maintains that the failure of this involvement to materialize does not spell the end of political democracy, much less that of democracy as a way of life. Even such ills as the mindless pursuit of diversions that we considered in 5.3, the short-sighted toleration of political corruption, and the dangerous spread of totalitarianism should not be interpreted as indications of the end of democracy. What the failure of spontaneous involvement does point to, however, is the end of political democracy as we have inherited it: the combat of two distant and self-serving national political parties for positions from which to distribute the spoils of victory. All along, as Dewey writes in 1939, his point has been the need to side-step or transcend the established party system and to use heightened involvement on the part of members of the community, working in "voluntary associations," to directly address social problems: "the ultimate way out of the present social dead end lies with the movement these associations are initiating. Individuals who have not lost faith in themselves and in other individuals will increasingly ally themselves with these groups. Sooner or later they will construct the way out of present confusion and conflict" (LW 14:96–97). If they continue their efforts to uncover the facts of our current social situation and continue to demonstrate the social meaning of these facts, they will increasingly involve people in the cooperative inquiry necessary to address our social ills.

Two additional aspects of Dewey's position need to be stressed here. The first is that serious effort needs to be addressed to making cooperative inquiry and its fruits, as discussed in 5.8, more attractive to potential participants. He disputes the assumption that the majority of the public is uninterested "in learning and assimilating the results of accurate investigation," and that consequently the fruits of expert inquiry will not be taken up by the community but will remain "in secluded library alcoves . . . studied and understood only by a few intellectuals" (LW 2:349). While he admits that many styles of presentation of such material will "appeal only to those technically high-brow" (LW 2:349), there is no necessary commitment on the part of the inquiry process to such styles. As Dewey writes, "ideas are effective not as bare ideas but as they have imaginative content and emotional appeal" (LW 13:169). This is so because "intelligence does not generate action except as it is enkindled by feeling" (LW 11:38).[1] His recognition leaves open the possibility as well that we might be able to foster an "intense emotional allegiance" to the method of intelligence (LW 13:54; cf. 11:38). Consequently, as we saw in 5.8, we need to develop a better manner for presenting the materials of expert inquiry. The way to do this, he believes, is by enlisting the contribution of artists. "The function of art," he writes, "has always been to break through the crust of conventionalized and routine consciousness." This power could be applied beyond what has been traditionally seen as the realm of art. By offering our artists, who "have always been the real purveyors of news," the task of publicizing this important social material and our need to address it, Dewey believes we could create a flood of engaging and compelling exchanges that would carry public discourse forward. "The freeing of the artist in literary presentation," he writes, "is as much a precondition of the desirable creation of adequate opinion on public matters as is the freeing of social inquiry" (LW 2:349–50).

We thus come to recognize that, for Dewey, overcoming apathy will require efforts to make the material of expert inquiry and the activity of inquiry itself more attractive. A second requirement is equally important. Our attempts to overcome apathy will demand in addition some changes in ourselves, in how we educate and prepare ourselves and our children for citizenship. Democracy in Dewey's conception is based upon, as we have seen in 5.5, "faith in the capacity of human beings for intelligent judgment and action if proper conditions are furnished" (LW 14:227). When, on the

---

[1] Cf. MW 14:136–37; LW 9:52–53; 13:70.

contrary, citizens' "mental habits are formed under conditions which render their minds unfit for accepting the intellectual responsibilities involved in self-government" (LW 7:353), we can expect little spontaneous involvement. Thus, as discussed in 5.9, the requirement of 'proper conditions' indicates that for Dewey "faith in democracy is all one with faith in experience and education" (LW 14:229), with faith in the cooperative, problem-solving efforts of an engaged and informed public. If we cannot become such a community of cooperative inquirers, then apathy and its resulting ills will continue to plague us.

As a means of attempting to evaluate the likelihood of this pair of changes and the consequent likelihood that apathy can be overcome, I would like to turn to two additional criticisms of Dewey's view that are often used to support the apathy criticism by suggesting that the citizenry is not likely to rise above it. These two criticisms emphasize the intellectual and moral hurdles to be surmounted in our attempts to carry on cooperative social inquiry. An excellent introduction to these two lines of criticism of Dewey's attempt to transcend popular disinterest and foster cooperative inquiry can be found in the following passage drawn from Joseph Wood Krutch:

> man's ingenuity has outrun his intelligence. He was good enough to survive in a simple, sparsely populated world, where he was neither powerful enough nor in sufficiently close contact with his neighbors to do them or himself fatal harm. He is not good enough to manage the more complicated and closely integrated world which he is, for the first time, powerful enough to destroy.[2]

We find in this passage, and in many discussions directly critical of Dewey's method of social reconstruction, two themes: that we are neither smart enough nor good enough to engage in cooperative social inquiry. Although these two themes are closely related, it will be beneficial to examine them separately as our second and third criticisms of Dewey's position.

If we attempt to formulate this second criticism—that people are, in some sense, too 'stupid' for the kind of cooperative social inquiry that will lead to successful social reconstruction—the result would be something like the following. Dewey offers, the critics say, a nice *theory;* but, realistically speaking, are the citizens with whom we are

---

[2] Krutch, *The Measure of Man,* 25; cf. LW 13:54.

familiar *smart* enough to play such an involved role in their political lives? Human beings simply do not demonstrate a level of intelligence sufficient to keep pace with the increasing complexity of our social existence. In the narrower sense of 'politics', we can consider the level of current political debate. There we find, for example, political candidates required to demonstrate high levels of 'toughness', religious orthodoxy, and nationalism—and little else—before they can be considered seriously for public office. There we find as well little interest in addressing the central issues of national, international, and global import, but a great willingness to engage in symbolic activities designed to demonstrate the politicians' patriotism and to endear them to the voters. Do examples like these demonstrate that our intelligence is just a thin veneer, insufficient for self-government? Do they serve to undermine the belief that we can think our way through the complexities of our modern situations? While these examples do give strength to those who fear that if the people ever get involved in the day-to-day workings of the government there will be chaos and who maintain that political apathy is a positive good, does this mean that we should attempt to remove government from the hands of the people?

One figure who emphasized what he saw as a lack of intelligence on the part of the voting public was Walter Lippmann (1889–1974). Taking as a paradigm of American democratic action the Scopes Trial of 1925, Lippmann maintains that it shows us the absurdity of our democratic faith. Believers in democracy have always assumed that "even if the majority is not wise, it is on the road to wisdom, and that with sufficient education the people would learn how to rule." But, he continues, "in Tennessee the people used their power to prevent their own children from learning, not merely the doctrine of evolution, but the spirit and method by which learning is possible." They had thus "used the prerogatives of democracy to destroy the hopes of democracy."[3]

Lippmann's own proposal, to be found in such volumes as *Public Opinion* (1922) and *The Phantom Public* (1925);[4] was to relegate the citizenry to a more spectatorial stance, a role of choosing the leaders who would then be able to make intelligent choices based on their

---

[3] Lippmann, *Men of Destiny*, 48–49.

[4] Dewey discusses these volumes in MW 13:337–44 and LW 2:213–20, 308, 334 respectively.

personal abilities and their access to expert knowledge. At the base of Lippmann's criticism are the beliefs that we live in what he calls "a pseudo-environment" of facts and dreams, illusions and prejudices, and that we live by what he calls "casual opinion" rather than inquiry. Such individuals cannot hope to fulfill the role of "omnicompetent citizen" that is required of them in our complex social situation.[5] Given this recognition, yielding a central role in politics is a realistic response: we sacrifice our demand for *self*-government in hopes of attaining *good*-government. Public opinion then becomes "a reserve of force brought into action during a crisis in public affairs," he writes. "To support the Ins when things are going well; to support the Outs when they seem to be going badly . . . is the essence of popular government."[6]

For Dewey, in response, there is always a distinction to be made between the conditions in our present transitional situations and what these conditions might become. In particular, there is the need for faith in the intellectual possibilities that might be actualized through education. We must be careful not to accuse him of extreme views that he does not hold: for example, that intelligence is "the power in man which can guide him toward the resolution of any problem" or that he claimed to know "how schools could save society."[7] He readily admits that it is too much to expect of "the average citizen" that he or she be individually intelligent enough to be able to make sense of social events when "even superior minds are distracted and appalled by the intricacy and extent of the problems which confront society." But as we have seen in 5.8, his claims about intelligence are not about the intellectual level of various individual members of the general population, even if their level of intelligence were assumed to be—an assumption he does not share—"as low as those assume who talk glibly about morons, boobs, and persons with eleven-year-old mentality" (LW 6:185; cf. 5:48).[8] His point is rather about the efficacy of cooperative inquiry using shared intelligence.

---

[5] Lippmann, *Public Opinion*, 15, 254, 273; cf. 364–65, 398–410.

[6] Lippmann, *The Phantom Public*, 69, 126; cf. 40–44, 63–70, 124–30, 197–99; cf. Lippmann, *The Method of Freedom*, 74–79.

[7] Edwin A. Burtt, "The Core of Dewey's Way of Thinking," 418; Joseph Featherstone, "John Dewey," 29.

[8] One such figure is H. L. Mencken, who writes of the typical citizen whom he calls "Homo boobiens": "The whole life of the inferior man, including especially his so-called thinking, is purely a biochemical process, and exactly comparable to what

For Dewey, there is often a sharp difference between the high level of intellectual insight necessary to make a discovery, and the normal level of intelligence necessary to make use of it. "Not many intellectual workers are called to be Aristotles or Newtons or Pasteurs or Einsteins" (MW 13:300; cf. LW 11:38), he writes; but, when working in cooperation with others to address problems with which they are familiar, even those individuals who are not so intellectually gifted can attain high levels of success. Consequently, while he grants that "our physical knowledge has far outrun our social or humane knowledge" (LW 6:52) and that to a certain extent "[i]t is inevitable that genuine knowledge of man and society should lag far behind physical knowledge" (LW 4:216; cf. MW 10:62–63), this does not mean for him, as it does for Krutch, that our 'ingenuity' has outrun our 'intelligence'. It means, rather, that we have fallen behind in our attempts "to employ our physical knowledge and physical technologies for social ends." With an education that was more cooperative and problem-oriented, however, this distance could be reduced. And with this change could come more interest in, and success at, addressing social problems. Thus, when people begin to "collectively organize their knowledge for social application, and when they systematically use scientific procedures for the objective control of social relations," and when they begin to act "with faith in the possibility of dealing scientifically with social changes and with the stern and courageous determination to make that faith effective in works" (LW 6:52), the complaint that people are too stupid to lead lives of cooperative intelligence will have to be re-evaluated.

Recognizing that this is an initial response to the criticism that people are too stupid for democracy rather than a final answer, let us continue on. If we turn to the third criticism—that people are, in some sense, too 'evil' for successful cooperative social inquiry—we will find something like the following. Dewey offers, the critics say, a nice *theory,* but people simply are not *good* enough to play such a role in their shared lives.[9] Their inherited selfishness is simply too strong. People—and, as in the other two cases of apathy and stupidity, the

---

goes on in a barrel of cider" (*Notes on Democracy,* 45, 59–60).

[9] Even as sympathetic a commentator as John J. McDermott writes: "Dewey had an enormous trust in rationality, good will, and the distribution of intelligence. Unfortunately, he had an undeveloped doctrine of evil, the demonic, and the capacity of human beings *en masse* to commit heinous crimes against other human beings" ("Introduction" to LW 11:xxxii).

'people' here means *us*—are simply incapable of the level of *impartiality* that is necessary for the life of cooperative social inquiry that Dewey proposes, and to expect it of them—of us—is utopian.

Reinhold Niebuhr (1892–1971) was perhaps the most influential exponent of this view. "In the liberal world," he writes, "the evils in human nature and history were ascribed to social institutions or to ignorance or to some other manageable defect in human nature or environment."[10] In fact, however, he maintains that the trouble with our social world is neither ignorance nor lag; it is that the basic human material is not good enough to sustain cooperative attempts to reach a common good. He continues:

> The most persistent error of modern educators and moralists is the assumption that our social difficulties are due to the failure of the social sciences to keep pace with the physical sciences which have created our technological civilization. The invariable implication of this assumption is that, with a little more time, a little more adequate moral and social pedagogy and a generally higher development of human intelligence, our social problems will approach solution.

For Niebuhr, this rosy understanding that he finds an essential element of the Deweyan response to the second criticism overlooks "the complexities of human behavior" which result from conflicts between the objectives of reason and "those of the total body of impulse, rationally unified but bent upon more immediate goals than those which man's highest reason envisages." As a result, while some modest advances in the direction of selflessness may be achieved over time, "there are definite limits in the capacity of ordinary mortals which makes it impossible for them to grant to others what they claim for themselves."[11]

In consequence, Niebuhr maintains that we need to recognize that, instead of the possibilities for cooperative inquiry held out by Dewey, "relations between groups must therefore always be predominantly political rather than ethical, that is, they will be determined by the proportion of power which each group possesses at least as much as by any rational and moral appraisal of the comparative needs

---

[10] *The Irony of American History,* 4; cf. 80–84.
[11] *Moral Man and Immoral Society,* xiii, 35, 3; cf. ix, 9.

and claims of each group." Niebuhr thus emphasizes "the brutal character of the behavior of all human collectives, and the power of self-interest and collective egoism in all intergroup relations" in the place of Dewey's emphasis upon attempting to develop impartial cooperative inquiry.[12] "Not a suspicion dawns upon Professor Dewey," he continues, "that no possible 'organized inquiry' can be as transcendent over the historical conflicts of interest as it ought to be to achieve the disinterested intelligence which he attributes to it." People are simply too selfish to rise to the high level of impartiality that would be required to be truly disinterested. Moreover, one aspect of our excessive self-regard is our ability to convince ourselves that a sufficient level of impartiality has been reached. "The worst injustices and conflicts of history arise from these very claims of impartiality," Niebuhr concludes; and Dewey's failure to recognize this makes his purported solution "an incredibly naive answer to a much more ultimate and perplexing problem than he realizes."[13]

For Dewey, again, there is the need for faith in possibilities of expanding our cooperative social horizon that will be developed through education. While admittedly his expectations are higher than Niebuhr's, he is surely correct to maintain that we cannot know in advance the limits of selfless action. Moreover, he is also correct that social existence shapes us with regard to the level of selfishness in action that is appropriate. We *learn* the limits of the self; we *learn* what to consider 'other'. From here, it is no great jump to the claim that higher levels of selflessness are possible through education. Thus, although Niebuhr is no doubt correct that "there are definite limits" to selflessness, we have no way of knowing how close we are to these limits at any given time.[14]

6.2. Can We Rely on Cooperative Inquiry?

We have now considered a series of three related criticisms of Dewey's method of social reconstruction. They suggest, in order,

---

[12] *Moral Man and Immoral Society*, xxiii, xx; cf. 4, 44. For Niebuhr, patriotism "is simply another form of selfishness" (*Ibid.*, 48; cf. 91).

[13] *Nature and Destiny of Man*, vol. 1, 111.

[14] For related criticisms of Niebuhr, see also: Tufts, *Selected Writings*, 292–93; Morton White, *Social Thought in America*, 247–64, 277–80; Rockefeller, *John Dewey*, 459–66.

that 'the people are not *interested* enough to make his method of social reconstruction work' or that 'the people are not *intelligent* enough to do it' or that 'the people are not *selfless* enough to do it'. The Deweyan response in each case is to assert that, although at the present time such criticisms may be very persuasive, none of them should be seen as eliminating future possibilities or as rendering present efforts toward these possibilities futile. To maintain this is completely consistent with the assumptions about the existence of a common good, democracy, and the educational nature of social reconstruction that we saw in chapter 5. In our present "backward" state, he writes, "we are not even aware of what the *problems* are" (LW 16:415); and, further crippled by our assumption that our difficulties are based in our evil and our stupidity (cf. LW 15:55–59; 16:416), we are not even looking for answers. With better presentations and fewer diversions, with increased participation and more cooperative inquiry, and with more emphasis upon social morality rather than individual salvation, we stand a much better chance of being able to make the method work. In any case, it would be foolish to give up now when the possibilities are still realizable. Therefore, it is necessary to have faith in our fellow citizens and in the power of democracy as an educational and socializing way of life, and to work to bring a higher level of democratic practice into existence in the future.

I now want to turn to a different and what I believe is a more fundamental line of criticism, one that is aimed not at the members of our society for failing to measure up to the challenges of involvement and intelligence and morality that accompany Dewey's method of social reconstruction. This line of criticism is aimed rather at the method itself. Dewey offers, these new critics say, a nice *theory;* but when we stack the various *assumptions* that he is making about political life up against the political *reality* that we face, we recognize that his method simply does not 'fit'. All that Dewey writes about the common good and collective social progress, about expanding cooperative participation within growing communities infused with trust, about experimenting toward the communal development of a program to advance the common good, about possibilities that will be developed through education, and so on, constitute in the words of C. Wright Mills (1916–1962) — my focus in this section — "a set of images out of a fairy tale: they are not adequate even as an

approximate model of how the American system of power works."
Mills continues: "The issues that now shape man's fate are neither
raised nor decided by the public at large. The idea of a community of
publics is not a description of fact, but an assertion of an ideal, an
assertion of a legitimation masquerading . . . as fact."[15] Dewey's
method, therefore, simply does not fit the kind of political life that
we experience. In most cases, Mills contends, individuals, voluntary
associations, local groups, and the other key aspects of Dewey's view,
matter little; and, in the really significant political, economic, and
military decisions of our society—decisions, Mills writes, that "carry
more consequences for more people than has ever been the case in the
world history of mankind"—they matter not at all. Such "key
decisions," he continues, are made by "an elite of power."[16]

Instead of seeing ourselves as living in a society in which 'publics'
interact to form opinions and collaborate to enact decisions, Mills
believes that it is more accurate to describe our situation as one of "a
society of masses." Such a society he describes as one in which the
number of "givers of opinion" is much smaller than the number of
opinion "receivers," in which these receivers have little possibility for
"freely answering back," in which their opinion is ineffective "in the
shaping of decisions of powerful consequence," and in which
"institutional authority" chokes off autonomous discussion.[17] In
such a mass society, the commitment to faith, cooperation, and so on
is certainly futile and may even be counterproductive for those who
maintain it.

Because my aim in this chapter is a critical examination of
Dewey's social thought, I will not attempt here a full-scale consideration of the work of Mills, or even of the relationship between Mills
and Dewey.[18] I will limit myself instead to an examination of Mills's
discussion of Dewey as it fleshes out his criticism of Dewey's method

---

[15] *The Power Elite*, 300; cf. *Power, Politics and People*, 37, 357; *The Causes of World War Three*, 31–55.

[16] *The Power Elite*, 28; cf. 18.

[17] *The Power Elite*, 302–3; cf. 304, 321; *White Collar*, 149–60; *Power, Politics and People*, 353–55.

[18] Readers wishing to pursue the relationship between the work of Dewey and Mills should see: Rick Tilman, *C. Wright Mills: A Native Radical and His American Intellectual Roots*, especially 172–202; Irving Louis Horowitz, *C. Wright Mills: An American Utopian*, 117–47; and Horowitz "The Intellectual Genesis of C. Wright Mills."

of social reconstruction, and then attempt to evaluate the importance of this criticism. Mills's most explicit commentary on and criticism of Dewey is found in his posthumously published doctoral dissertation, *Sociology and Pragmatism: The Higher Learning in America*[19]; but the particular theme that I will be emphasizing carries throughout most of his work. This theme is his criticism of Dewey's method of social reconstruction as a kind of cooperative inquiry based in the belief that it demonstrates a misunderstanding of the nature of social action. In fact, social action is, Mills maintains, neither *cooperative*— in the sense of shared efforts to advance the common good—nor even *inquiry*—in the sense of a serious attempt to discover what ought to be done. Social action is rather politics; and, as politics, it "is a struggle for power," Mills writes. Power, in the sense that he is using the term, "has to do with whatever decisions men make about the arrangements under which they live, and about the events which make up the history of their times."[20] Using this competing understanding of social action, Mills develops a serious fundamental challenge to the approach found in Dewey's method of social reconstruction.

The challenge to Dewey's understanding of social action as cooperative *inquiry* is a rejection of his attempts to replace the squabbling and deal-making of partisan politics with cooperative attempts at fostering scientific methods and attitudes. It will be recalled that it was this very aspect of Dewey's position that Dewey offered as a defense against the criticism that people were too stupid for successful democracy.[21] For Mills, however, Dewey fails to see that "the attempt to carry this laboratory technique over into social data precipitates methodological and political problems." Dewey's understanding of social problems, Mills writes, is grounded in what Dewey sees as "a social situation whose integration can occur by means of liberal individuals heavily endowed with substantive rationality."[22] Such individuals, not locked into the mechanical pursuit of

---

[19] The dissertation itself, *A Sociological Account of Pragmatism,* was completed in 1942. Mills revised it somewhat and it was edited and published in its present form in 1964 by Irving Louis Horowitz after Mills's death.

[20] *The Power Elite,* 171; *Power, Politics and People,* 23; cf. *Power, Politics and People,* 408; *The Causes of World War Three,* 155.

[21] Cf. Mills's favorable presentation of Lippmann's exposure of the "woefully utopian, rational psychology" of liberalism in *White Collar,* 325.

[22] *Power, Politics and People,* 466; *Sociology and Pragmatism,* 393.

previously chosen values but possessed of broad social perspectives and able to transcend their immediate situations, undertake careful and self-conscious actions to integrate past and future. "Adjustment is the term," Mills writes.

> It is not brute action because that would be blind, unintelligent. It is not violence, for that is "wasteful." It is not repetition of "tradition," for that would be sluggish and lazy. It is not abruptly discontinuous with what has been and is, for that would be utopian, unrealistic, or, again, by divorce of ends and means, it would be "unintelligent" action. It has to go slowly in order to squeeze the meaning and values from events it encounters. It is careful. It is intelligent action.[23]

The problem, as Mills sees it, is that such an analysis of social action as inquiry has nothing at all to do with political action as it occurs in our modern industrial society. Dewey's method is simply inappropriate to our situation. "His conception of action is *of an individual,*" Mills writes. What Dewey has in mind are the actions of "of a member of a free profession" like an architect or a lawyer or a physician. Because Dewey's understanding of social action as cooperative inquiry is "rooted in a liberal desire to save or to reconstruct individuality," it finds itself well suited to a situation like Hull House; but it is not "very well suited for action, *e.g.,* of revolutionary scale, nor indeed for the large scale planning of a society."[24] And it is this latter sort of action, in which conflicting powers attempt to get their way, that comprises the most important part of politics.

As we saw in 5.6, Dewey believes that cultural lag is at the root of our failures to adopt necessary changes: "Lag in mental and moral patterns provides the bulwark of the older institutions" (LW 11:54). Mills writes, however, that using the notion of cultural lag veils choice: "To state problems in terms of cultural lag is to disguise evaluations."[25] Mills is not suggesting here that Dewey was attempting, for example, to claim some kind of 'scientific' objectivity while hiding some sort of pro-capitalist bias. Nor does Mills fail to recognize that Dewey explicitly maintains that social inquiry always

---

[23] *Sociology and Pragmatism,* 393.

[24] *Sociology and Pragmatism,* 392–93, 432.

[25] *The Sociological Imagination,* 89.

involves evaluation. His point is rather that to adopt the model of cultural lag, and its correlative method of "adjusting groups and individuals to one another" (LW 2:355) as the proper method of social action, is itself an evaluation that is disguised by Dewey's assumption that the biological model is appropriate for action in the social realm. By maintaining that a kind of educative social inquiry modeled upon a pattern of inquiry that was itself derived from individual action is the rational method of social action, in conformity with his belief that aspects of society lag behind and that there must be adjustments, Dewey has prejudged—Mills would say *mis*judged—how politics is to be carried out. In Dewey's approach, Mills continues, "value-decisions as value-decisions are assimilated into the biological and hidden by formality."[26]

This criticism of the relationships that Dewey believes exist among politics, science and education has been explored by several other commentators as well. On the one hand, as Gail Kennedy notes, Dewey's idea of political democracy is "framed on an analogy to the community of scientists" in its ability to combine authority and freedom and to balance individual desires with probable common good. On the other hand, the ideal of political democracy postulates, as does education, a situation of common growth through the solution of social problems. In the minds of critics like Mills and Kennedy, both of these assumed relationships are suspect. With regard to the first relationship, between democratic political procedures and science, the belief that political problems can be solved in the same way as scientific problems is challenged initially by stressing the fact that the scientist works with interested and informed colleagues and in a controlled and simplified situation. Moreover, as Kennedy continues, for scientists "the issues are definable in objective terms, and there are (in the political sense) no interest groups, factions, or social classes passionately asserting their antagonistic claims."[27] The political figure, however, faces a com-

---

[26] *Sociology and Pragmatism,* 380.

[27] "The Process of Evaluation in a Democratic Community," 256. Cf. Albert William Levi: "The formulation of a social problem assumes the kind of agreement upon values and coincidence of interests which a heterogeneous society (however democratic) seems to lack. . . . To assimilate social problems to the form of scientific inquiry (as Dewey constantly does) is perhaps to overestimate the extent of social rationality, and to underestimate the dilemma of partisanship, political and economic, in a democratic society" (*Philosophy and the Modern World,* 323; Damico,

pletely different kind of situation where diverse groups present conflicting demands, and where political power depends more on the practical ability to continually re-establish a coalition than on the intellectual validity of one's position.[28] With regard to the relationship between political action and education, Niebuhr writes that Dewey's belief that intelligent social action is possible betrays what he calls "the natural bias of the educator."[29] Those who would defend the educational aspects of our present political situation, Mills and Niebuhr maintain, need only consider whether citizens come together to examine issues and attempt to reach an objectively common good or whether groups make use of available power in their attempts to achieve as much as possible of their predetermined and self-serving goals. Here the issue is not the theoretical question that we considered in 5.7 of whether social inquiry is science. It is, rather, whether what passes for social inquiry is inquiry at all.

Rather than understanding social action as inquiry, Mills suggests that a more realistic analysis would be to see social action as struggle. We thus return to his analysis of social action as power-oriented politics, and hence to a consideration of the role of political parties. "Parties," Mills writes (after Max Weber), "live in a house of power. They are organizations for social fighting."[30] Their purpose is not inquiry but action, not the uncovering of truth but the enactment of policies; and their weapon is not the intellect, but the emotions.[31] Dewey, as we have seen in 6.1, understood the importance of emotion to social action. He writes, for example, that "no movement

---

Individuality and Community, 93–96; Kaufman-Osborn, "Pragmatism, Policy Science, and the State," 835–45; "John Dewey and the Liberal Science of Community," 1154–59).

[28] Not only do some critics reject the analogy of political action to the problem-solving process that Dewey elaborates, others reject even the relationship of scientific practice itself to this pristine ideal. Cf. Sidney Hook, "John Dewey and the Crisis of American Liberalism," 226; Hofstadter, *Anti-Intellectualism in American Life,* 197–229; Featherstone, "John Dewey" 32.

[29] *Moral Man and Immoral Society,* xiv.

[30] *Sociology and Pragmatism,* 394. Cf. Edward Sutherland Bates: "The League for Independent Political Action . . . [was] . . . self-condemned by its very name, since independent action is no action" ("John Dewey: America's Philosophic Engineer," 396; cf. Richard J. Brown, "John Dewey and the League for Independent Political Action," 157–58).

[31] Cf. Reinhold Niebuhr: "Contending factions in a social struggle require morale; and morale is created by the right dogmas, symbols and emotionally potent oversimplifications" (*Moral Man and Immoral Society,* xv).

gets far on a purely intellectual basis. It has to be emotionalized; it must appeal to the social imagination" (LW 6:175). The aspect of social imagination to which Dewey wishes to appeal, however, is the desire to participate in the intellectually driven advance of the society toward the common good. Political parties, on the other hand, attempt to excite less universal group loyalties and less intellectual mass followings, their focus upon victory and rewards; and this is what caused Dewey to want to minimize their role.[32] For Mills, on the contrary, if what is wanted is "a chance at power," what is needed is a political party.[33] This kind of party—short on inquiry and long on emotion and action—is the kind of tool that Mills believes will be effective in the social struggle.[34]

The first aspect of Mills's challenge to Dewey's method of social reconstruction considers whether social action is to be seen as cooperative *inquiry*. The second aspect of this challenge, to which we now turn, considers whether it is to be seen as *cooperative* inquiry. It was this very aspect of Dewey's position that Dewey offered as a defense against the criticism that people were too selfish for successful democracy. Mills writes that Dewey's view of intelligent action assumes the existence of "a 'common ground', a point of mediation." This common ground is, for Dewey, the locus of our cooperation; for Mills, it is a mirage. Mills writes:

> Underlying and sustaining the cogency of this ethical and metaphysical endeavor is the assumption of a relatively homogeneous community which does not harbor any chasms of structure or power not thoroughly ameliorative by discussion. Always there must be the assumption that no "problems" will arise that will be so deep that a third idea-plan would not unite in some way the two conflicting plans.

---

[32] Dewey does at times write in a more supportive fashion of a power conception of politics. See, for example: "politics is a struggle for possession and use of power to settle specific issues that grow out of the country's needs and problems" (LW 9:68; cf. MW 10:271)

[33] *Sociology and Pragmatism*, 394.

[34] Cf. John Herman Randall, Jr.: "Can men oppose intolerance and power with the tentative, inquiring, searching, provisional temper of mind, the temper that has abandoned certainty, finality, and the burning faith that human feeling and action so deeply demand?" ("Liberalism as Faith in Intelligence," 260; cf. 254; George R. Geiger, "Dewey's Social and Political Philosophy," 365).

But, as Mills continues, "this model of problem posing does not concern itself with two social interests in a death-clutch."[35] As an indication that Dewey has no clear recognition of such ultimate confrontations, Mills cites Dewey's claim from *The Public and Its Problems* (LW 2:245) that "every serious political dispute turns upon the question whether a given political act is socially beneficial or harmful."[36] To recall another passage cited in 5.6, we can consider Dewey's view that our aim should be to bring conflicting social purposes into the open "where their special claims can be seen and appraised, where they can be discussed and judged in the light of more inclusive interests than are represented by either of them separately" (LW 11:56). In both of these cases, and in others, Dewey uses as a means of attempting to resolve the problem the central point of contention: the existence of community. For Mills, the questions of whether a political act is simply "socially beneficial or harmful" and whether there are these "more inclusive interests"— questions of whether a community exists—must be answered first. For Dewey, they are questions to be answered in the process of cooperative inquiry: "all the serious conflicts and struggles that occur in society grow out of different conceptions, expressed or implicit, of what society is and should be" (LW 11:177).

Emphasizing the complexity of our social interactions and the prevalence of the exploitation of some by others, Mills asks "what is *not* done in the name of the public interest?" His aim here is to drive home the point that 'we' is "the most tricky word in the vocabulary of politics."[37] For him, a more accurate analysis of our circumstances realizes that one person's or group's good is often another's evil. Dewey, on the contrary, "never seriously questioned a fundamental and ultimately communal homogeneity of society," he contends. "What is a 'problem' to one 'group' is not at all problematic to another; it may well be a satisfactory 'solution'."[38] Because different

---

[35] *Sociology and Pragmatism*, 395, 405.

[36] *Sociology and Pragmatism*, 438.

[37] *Power, Politics and People*, 333; *The Marxists*, 19; cf. "Comment on Criticism," 243.

[38] *Sociology and Pragmatism*, 412; cf. *The Sociological Imagination*, 76; *Power, Politics and People*, 396; Coughlan, *Young John Dewey*, 86; Nirmal C. Bhattacharyya, "John Dewey's Instrumentalism, Democratic Ideal and Education," 64–66; Howard Selsam, *Socialism and Ethics*, 121–22; George Novack, *Pragmatism versus Marxism*, 204–7.

social groups have vastly different values, they want to go to "different 'places' ":

> they encompass and pivot around different systems of objects which their activities are striving to realize and which guide their directions and hence furnish the guiding thread for the emergence of their problems. It is here that "problems" arise and obviously they often involve deep conflicts of value. Dewey's theory of value is not capable of really handling such situations. The concept of the problem aids in this process of masking.

However, because of his "biological model of action and reflection," Mills continues, Dewey tends to minimize "the cleavage and power divisions *within society,*" and ultimately to locate "all problems between *man and nature,* instead of between *men and men.*"[39]

In a fashion similar to the suggestion in my earlier comments on cultural lag and the possibility of disguised evaluation, I do not believe that Mills thinks that Dewey is attempting to slant the problem to benefit one particular group. Mills's point is rather that, just as analyses in terms of 'lag' imply the need for 'adjustment', so do discussions of *a* problem or *the* problem, and correspondingly of *a* solution or *the* solution, imply the existence of a common good. In a view expressed in *The School and Society* in 1899 and only slightly modified throughout his life,[40] Dewey writes that a society "is a number of people held together because they are working along common lines, in a common spirit, and with reference to common aims" (MW 1:10). We have seen the importance that Dewey places in ongoing efforts to mediate social transitions. But critics like Mills are more skeptical than Dewey, who can write as late as 1939, that it is "obvious" that the knowledge that a certain social arrangement benefitted "a small group or special class" to the harm of others would result in a "revaluation of the desires and ends that had been assumed to be authoritative sources of valuation." Even to allow

---

[39] *Sociology and Pragmatism,* 412–13, 382. Cf. Joseph Featherstone: "Applied to social life, the biological metaphor was misleading . . . because it pictured a cooperative struggle against nature, building bridges or fighting epidemics. Most social situations lack the unity of purpose given by a common natural enemy: the social 'problem' is the exploitation of some people by other people" ("John Dewey," 27; Dicker, "John Dewey: Instrumentalism in Social Action," 228–31).

[40] We have seen in 5.6 his re-identification of the common good with the interests of *the vast majority* of citizens rather than the interests of *all.*

Dewey his qualification that such a revaluation would not necessarily take place "immediately" (LW 13:244) is not enough for Mills, because barring fundamental changes he does not expect such a revaluation to occur at all. In a community, where the advance of the common good was of central importance, such a revaluation would take place, of course; but, for Mills, the whole push behind his criticism that Dewey's method is inappropriate is his belief that we do not have such a community.[41]

For Mills, the political activity of our society is neither *cooperative* nor *inquiring*. It is a romantic, fairy-tale understanding of our democracy, he continues, to assume that 'the people' discuss issues, formulate opinions, and decide social policy in a democratic fashion. The truth, he maintains in 1956, is that the United States is "now in considerable part more a formal political democracy than a democratic political structure."[42] A powerful elite in our society—the central figures in our vital "political, economic, and military circles" —are the actual determiners of events. "In so far as national events are decided, the power elite are those who decide them." Consequently, the issues that "shape man's fate are neither raised nor decided by the public at large."[43] Whether these elites decide issues in terms of their own private interests, or what they believe to be good for the community or humankind in general, is irrelevant here.[44] The point is that decision-making about the pivotal issues of our society is out of the hands of 'the people'. In addition, underneath the level of the power elite, Mills believes that our centralized and myopic mass society is increasingly home to massive institutions and to the

---

[41] Consider the following statement by Dewey in support of the American Association of University Professors: "the term trades unionism has been used to suggest a fear that we are likely to subordinate our proper educational activities to selfish and monetary considerations. I have never heard any one suggest such a danger for the American Bar Association or the American Medical Association. Pray, are the aims of college teachers less elevated?" (MW 8:102). In this passage, we find Dewey maintaining that professors as a group are no less communally-minded than lawyers or physicians. The central point, however, according to Mills, is whether any of these groups are adequately communally-minded.

[42] *The Power Elite*, 274; cf. *The Sociological Imagination*, 188–89. Cf. Quentin Anderson: "in Dewey one finds the last gasp of the American faith in democracy" (John Dewey's American Democrat," 157).

[43] *The Power Elite*, 18, 300.

[44] Mills's use of the term 'power elite', rather than 'ruling class', was intended to overcome the latter term's implied economic determinism. See: *The Power Elite*, 277; *The Marxists*, 117–19.

bureaucratic rationalization of procedures, both of which preclude any attempts on the part of the citizenry to break through and reassume democratic control. Mills continues:

> social, technological, or bureaucratic rationality is not merely a grand summation of the individual will and capacity to reason. The very chance to acquire that will and that capacity seems in fact often to be decreased by it. Rationally organized social arrangements are not necessarily a means of increased freedom — for the individual or for the society. In fact, often they are a means of tyranny and manipulation, a means of expropriating the very chance to reason, the very capacity to act as a free man.[45]

The reason why average individuals do not gain the capacity to act as free citizens is that they do not participate in decision-making. Dewey also emphasizes that this problem must be overcome. Mills continues, however, that the problem is exacerbated because these average citizens are outsiders; and, as outsiders, they will never come to understand events. "Only from a few commanding positions or — as the case may be — merely vantage points, in the rationalized structure," he writes, "is it readily possible to understand the structural forces at work in the whole which thus affect each limited part of which ordinary men are aware." In general, however, "history is made behind men's backs."[46]

Mills hopes that the impact of his more 'realistic' analysis will cause people to question whether all of the participants in a social decision actually ought to focus on an overall solution. Is social action a realm where we attempt to gain a clearer understanding of social issues or to get our way, where we attempt to advance equality and justice or to force a compromise from a position of strength? Mills is more concerned than Dewey with keeping clear the difference between political romanticism and political realism. For him, the heart of political democracy is power. For Dewey, on the other hand: "The very heart of political democracy is adjudication of social differences by discussion and exchange of views. This method

---

[45] *The Sociological Imagination,* 168–69; cf. 115–16; *The Causes of World War Three,* 21; *Power, Politics and People,* 27–35.

[46] *The Sociological Imagination,* 169; *White Collar,* 350; cf. *The Power Elite,* 244, 322.

provides a rough approximation to the method of effecting change by means of experimental inquiry and test: the scientific method" (LW 15:273). Mills's response here is to question whether this is an accurate description of our democracy or an embellished account modelled on Dewey's ideal. It may even be that the rhetoric of romantic democracy—of open participation in discussions on street corners and issues being fully and fairly presented in the media—is not only *false* but also *harmful*. That is, the communal glow of romantic democracy may leave such open-minded and cooperative citizens unprotected and unprepared for the 'realistic' democracy of party and interest-group politics. To help make citizens open-minded and cooperative may thus undermine their already limited chances for fuller democracy.

In the place of Dewey's call for cooperative inquiry to make democracy work, Mills calls for a 'realistic' assessment of "[t]he engineering of consent" and of attempts "to manage and to manipulate the consent of men"[47] that are such an essential element of our current democratic practice. By 'manipulation' Mills means "the 'secret' exercise of power, unknown to those who are influenced."[48] Such manipulation, which Mills believes is "more insidious than coercion precisely because it is hidden,"[49] cannot be totally eliminated from our social lives. The reason why Mills believes that manipulation will remain a danger is that he is operating with a social theory of the self—a theory that he held in common with such figures as Dewey and George Herbert Mead[50]—and he does not believe that we can live free or independent of the contributions of our groups. "None of us stands alone directly confronting the world of solid fact," Mills writes; as social creatures, "men live in second-hand worlds."[51] People rely upon others. Attempts at persuasion or guidance are central to social life, to politics and education, a point that we have seen Dewey defend in 5.8 and 5.9. Mills too asserts the central role that such interaction plays in individuals' lives: "The quality of their lives is determined by meanings they have received

---

[47] *White Collar*, 110; *The Sociological Imagination*, 40.

[48] *The Power Elite*, 316; cf. *The Sociological Imagination*, 41; *Power, Politics and People*, 23; *White Collar*, 109; *The Causes of World War Three*, 34.

[49] *White Collar*, 110; cf. *The Power Elite*, 317.

[50] Cf. *Power, Politics and People*, 426.

[51] *Power, Politics and People*, 375, 405.

from others."[52] If the meanings we receive are tainted and we do not recognize it, however, then we will be manipulated. Consequently, it is necessary to stand up and question, to recognize that "manipulation feeds upon and is fed by mass indifference," and to resist, for example, the attempts of the media to "expropriate our vision."[53]

Again, Mills's point is not that Dewey was intending to manipulate the American populace.[54] Rather, Mills is maintaining that, because of Dewey's emphasis upon cooperative inquiry and because of assertions such as his claim that American democracy was using or at least approximating "the method of discussion" rather than "the method of coercion" (LW 13:153), the effect of his work has been to

---

[52] *Power, Politics and People*, 405; cf. *The Power Elite*, 310–16.

[53] *White Collar*, 349, 333; cf. *Power, Politics and People*, 381–82.

[54] A number of other critics, however, have suggested that some manipulation was an essential element of the educational work of Dewey and others. See, for example, Clarence J. Karier: "The condescending role of the intelligent expert advising the relatively ignorant masses on how to manage their lives has been a continuing problem of American liberal reformers throughout the twentieth century" ("Making the World Safe for Democracy," 42; cf. Feinberg, "The Conflict between Intelligence and Community in Dewey's Educational Philosophy"; Nirmal C. Bhattacharyya, "Demythologizing John Dewey.")

One particular instance is that of Dewey's *Confidential Report of Conditions among the Poles in the United States* and two related confidential memoranda of 1918 (MW 11:248–330) that he wrote during World War One. Here Dewey is seen by some to demonstrate the combination of manipulating people for their own good (some of the critics would say *against* their good but for the good of American industry) and secretive procedures to prevent the manipulation from being discovered. See, for example, Karier: "Is it not reasonable to suggest that at this historic point, John Dewey, the philosopher of American democracy, was, within the context of calling for more democratic representation, at the same time calling for the 'manipulation' of Polish affairs so that the American government might achieve its 'end in view?'" ("John Dewey and the New Liberalism," 427; Karier, "Liberalism and the Quest for Orderly Change"; Karier, "Making the World Safe for Democracy").

One need not be taken as an apologist for Dewey who suggests that this is a clouded issue at best, as is much else of Dewey's understanding of and actions before and during the Great War. Consider, for example, Dewey's clearly atypical position at one point that democracy is satisfied when the "governing group . . . [achieves] . . . the assent and support of large masses of people," even if this assent and support is obtained through "the expert manipulation of men *en masse* for ends not clearly seen by them, but which they are led to believe are of great importance for them" (MW 10:271). Whether or not these are still instances of guidance in his mind, they can clearly be seen to be contrary to the overall spirit of Dewey's thought. Cf. MW 11:241–47, 398–408, 421–25; Oscar Handlin and Lilian Handlin, "Introduction" to MW 11:xii–xvii; Westbrook, *John Dewey and American Democracy*, 214–21; Charles L. Zerby, "John Dewey and the Polish Question"; J. Christopher Eisele, "John Dewey and the Immigrants."

predispose people to be manipulated. Although the "moral force" of such a liberal position may be strong, it does not demonstrate a "theory of society adequate to its moral aims." As a result, Mills maintains, the overall position of liberal democracy has misled the people and has helped ultimately to sustain the domination by the power elite.[55]

6.3   A Deweyan Response

I want to consider initially the extent to which Mills's presentation of Dewey is correct.[56] Unfortunately, Mills complicates the situation by placing Dewey in what he considers to be the bankrupt political perspective of liberalism.[57] It is perhaps best to begin with a clear recognition of Mills's imprecise usage of the term 'liberalism', an imprecision that allows him to lump Dewey-as-liberal in with such unlikely allies as John Locke, John Stuart Mill and Herbert Spencer, as well as with various New Dealers and Cold Warriors.[58] Part of Mills's imprecision may result from his belief that the term 'liberalism' is itself imprecise, or at least that liberalism was functioning in 1952 imprecisely as "the official language for all public statement."[59] Still, on occasion, Mills does indicate that he finds in liberalism some specifiable content: the support of a market system and private property capitalism, an emphasis upon the primacy of individual freedom, an understanding of society as best when allowed to exist in a kind of spontaneous equilibrium, and so on.[60] Liberalism is, for

---

[55] *Power, Politics and People*, 191; cf. 303; *The Marxists*, 29; *The Power Elite*, 336.

[56] Other parts of Mills's criticisms of Dewey, not considered here, are clearly wrong. Consider, for example, his discussion of "Dewey's pupil, John Watson (who became an advertising expert" with whom "in [the] matter of 'control' [Dewey] agrees completely" (*Sociology and Pragmatism*, 380).

[57] In 1962, a decade after Dewey's death, Mills writes of this bankruptcy that the liberal approach to political action had become "increasingly divorced from any historical agencies by which they might be realized" and consequently "liberalism is now more of a rhetoric than anything else" (*The Marxists*, 28).

[58] See: *The Sociological Imagination*, 91–92, 167; *White Collar*, xix–xx; *The Power Elite*, 215, 334; *Sociology and Pragmatism*, 447; *Power, Politics and People*, 189–95; cf. West, *The American Evasion of Philosophy*, 102.

[59] *Power, Politics and People*, 189; cf. *The Marxists*, 20.

[60] Cf. *Power, Politics and People*, 191, 263, 537; *The Marxists*, 24, 28; *The Power Elite*, 242, 299, 336.

Mills, "the firm ideology of one class inside one epoch—the urban and entrepreneurial middle class."[61] However, it should be clear that the more we elaborate Mills's understanding of liberalism, the less it has to do with Dewey, who as we saw in 5.6 was a radical liberal in no way committed to a market economy or to a belief in the spontaneous success of social living as long as individual freedoms are maximized.[62]

Perhaps a consideration of another aspect of Dewey's position would be helpful here, especially one that would allow for a close comparison to Mills's analysis of manipulation that we have just seen. What I have in mind here is Dewey's consideration of the topic of propaganda. Although we find Dewey in what might be called good 'liberal' fashion expressing great appreciation for the comment of Oliver Wendell Holmes, Jr., that "the best test of truth is the power of the thought to get itself accepted in the competition of the market" (LW 3:177),[63] we do not find Dewey either praising the assaying powers of his current intellectual market place or claiming that all ideas that have won popular acceptance are therefore true. Dewey, as a witness to numerous governmental and corporate attempts at "manufacturing public opinion and sentiment" (LW 3:141), was cognizant of the power of propaganda. As he writes in 1918, the World War offered "a remarkable demonstration of the possibilities of guidance of the news upon which the formation of public opinion depends" (MW 11:118). This demonstration was not lost on those with an interest in control; and in 1932 he writes of "a multitude of agencies which skilfully manipulate and color the news and information, which circulate, and which artfully instill, under the guise of disinterested publicity, ideas favorable to hidden interests" (LW 7:360–61). The existence and growth of such agencies were directly related to their perceived manipulative success. This success in turn was due in part to the fact that, as we have explored in 5.1, people were being asked to make decisions about complex issues that were largely beyond their direct familiarity. Dewey believed that another source of this success was the fact that,

---

[61] *The Marxists*, 29; cf. *Power, Politics and People*, 191.

[62] Cf. Rick Tilman: Mills's "interpretation is not an adequate view of Dewey as a political thinker, but it is a compelling criticism of present-day liberal doctrine and practice" (*C. Wright Mills*, 172; cf. 124, 144–49).

[63] *Abrams et al. v. United States*, 250 US 616, 630.

as discussed in 5.8, people were unable to organize and evaluate the flood of information that reached them, and thus were easy targets for those who would attempt manipulation. Technological developments have "multiplied the means of modifying the dispositions of the mass of the population" (LW 13:90) and thus afforded "an organ of unprecedented power for accomplishing a perversion of public opinion" (LW 7:361).[64] 'Perversion' is, to Dewey's mind, exactly the term to be used: "The very agencies that a century and a half ago were looked upon as those that were sure to advance the cause of democratic freedom," he writes, "are those which now make it possible to create pseudo-public opinion and to undermine democracy from within" (LW 13:168; cf. 2:340–41).

With the end of the days "when the few did not have to go through the form of consulting the opinion of the many," Dewey writes (LW 3:141), went also the end of rule without consent. "The days are past when government can be carried on without any pretense of ascertaining the wishes of the governed," he continues (LW 2:348; cf. MW 11:118). However, while in some technical sense popular consent must still be secured, ascertaining the wishes of the populace has too often given over to molding and creating them. In consequence, we cannot assume any great overlap between the acquiescence of the public and vibrant democracy. While in a democracy there is a focus on the development of the citizens and a requirement of participation in the definition of the common good, he writes that frequently in his situation there is neither. What we have in the United States instead, he notes in 1928, is "enough government by public opinion so that it is necessary for the economic powers that govern to strive to regulate the agencies by which that opinion is created" (LW 3:142; cf. 6:178). Instead of an attempt to foster the development of an informed popular opinion, "there is a premium put on the control of popular opinion and beliefs" (LW 3:141). The manipulation of the society is the goal of the few, and they recognize that "[t]he smoothest road to control of political conduct is by control of opinion" (LW 2:348; cf. MW 10:271). Consequently, the fact that we ultimately have a democracy and can re-assert control, and the fact that "democracies are con-

---

[64] Dewey's emphasis is on the power of the press and radio. See: LW 9:309; 11:344.

trolled through their opinions" (MW 11:119) and not by violence or threats, are not enough for the existence of a vibrant democracy. We must also live in active, inquiring communities.

It is no defense of the 'democracy' of such a managed situation to assert that the citizenry does not complain or that they are 'getting what they want'. Dewey admits, for example, that "it is probably true by-and-large that the press is a fair reflection of the state of the public mind" (LW 11:272). Democracy remains, however, a matter of much more than the reckoning of actually expressed wishes; it has to do with the reality of a developed intellectual freedom operating in a dynamic public arena. Our usual sense of discussing the dangers to freedom of the media is, as we saw in 5.4, with other questions of freedom, "based on the assumption that the government is the chief enemy to be dreaded." Consequently, we often overlook the economic side to the matter. When we glorify freedom of the press, Dewey continues, what is often being praised is not the demonstrated effectiveness of our media as a means to intellectual freedom but rather "the power of the business entrepreneur to carry on his own business in his own way for the sake of private profit" (LW 11:270). And, if it turns out that the economically powerful media giants are not troubled by other instances of centralized economic power—"Capital in one form is naturally friendly to capital in other forms," Dewey writes (MW 11:118)—and that these giants "carry on a vast and steady indoctrination in behalf of the order of which the press is a part" (LW 11:343),[65] we should not be surprised.

These sorts of questions are only secondary aspects of the matter of intellectual freedom. As he writes in 1935, the primary question that he wants to explore is the question of "how far genuine intellectual freedom and social responsibility are possible on any large scale under the existing economic regime" (LW 11:270; 17:45–49). And this, of course, is an open question, a question whose resolution is to be determined in the future and whose resolution can be influenced by efforts like his various public attempts to arouse the populace. "Propaganda can be attacked and its force weakened only by one agency—informed publicity," Dewey writes. "A free circulation of the pure air of intelligence is a prerequisite in any attempt to cleanse society of its corruptions and

---

[65] Cf. LW 11:271–73; 13:168.

enable it to lift its load of oppression" (LW 6:178). He did not believe that such changes were likely under our present economic organization, in which "[t]he gathering and sale of subject-matter having a public import is part of the existing pecuniary system" (LW 2:349). Moreover, he did not anticipate that these necessary changes will be easy to bring about because "the system that nourishes these evils is such as to prevent adequate and widespread realization of the evils and their causes" (LW 11:272). However, we still do ultimately have a democracy, he maintains, and we have the means of public inquiry—even if they are atrophied. Revitalizing them was part of his motivation for his involvement with the *Thought News* project and with the LIPA that we considered in 5.8. He continues to believe that our efforts to advance inquiry further stand a chance of limited, but growing, success.

Here again, as we have seen so frequently, Dewey's emphasis returns to education as the most likely key to positive social reconstruction. In the face of the tidal wave of propaganda that American citizens faced in the mid-1930s, Dewey writes that the schools can give students an "intelligent understanding of social forces" and that "unless the schools create a popular intelligence that is critically discriminating, there is no limit to the prejudices and inflamed emotion that will result" (LW 11:344; cf. 14:373). Dewey continues a few years later that the future success of democracy is "allied with spread of the scientific attitude" which he sees as "the sole guarantee against wholesale misleading by propaganda" (LW 13:168; cf. 11:408–17). With the self-conscious stance made possible by the methods and goals of cooperative inquiry fostered in the schools, Dewey looks forward to a time when a public has "located and identified itself" (LW 2:348) and is moving forward to advance the common good.

If we take Dewey's discussions of the possibilities of propaganda and manipulation seriously, we surely cannot consider him to be—as Mills suggests—a naive proponent of a romantic sense of democracy.[66] It would also be a mistake, however, to see Dewey as a

---

[66] Even the works like *Freedom and Culture* (LW 13:65–188) and "Creative Democracy—The Task Before Us" (LW 14:224–30), that when read out of their social context of totalitarianism and war appear somewhat romantic in their appreciativeness toward the American democratic tradition, were far too critical of their situation to appear as celebrations of current democratic practices.

hard-boiled realist along the lines of Mills's occasional posturing.[67] What shines through Dewey's critical stance toward his democracy is a sense of idealism. For example, although it is clearly too simple to suggest, as we saw Mills do in 6.2, that Dewey sees all problems as being "between *man and nature,* instead of between *men and men,*"[68] there is a sense in which this claim is not false. In the final analysis, Dewey does think there is a common good whose approximation will increasingly benefit the real interests of all. His reminder that we cannot overlook "the extent to which that life which we call social has been organized and arranged for private and conflicting purposes, rather than for a common and public end" (MW 11:74),[69] is not a claim that such a system must continue. The fundamental point to emphasize behind his condemnations of social conflicts in which the participants seek "no common ground, no moral understanding, no agreed upon standard of appeal" and in which "each side treats its opponent as a wilful violator of moral principles, an expression of self-interest or superior might" (MW 14:59) is that such conflicts allow for no resolution other than through the repeated use of power. Dewey continues to maintain, however, that in a processive world, to hope and to act for social betterment is worth a try even if it contains the danger of potential failure. Although it certainly is 'fairy-tale' thinking to see what Dewey himself called our "rather poor embodiment of democracy" (LW 11:416) as one of fully participatory democracy, it is not delusional thinking to hope to approximate participatory democracy more closely by means of serious cooperative work in the future. And clearly, Dewey's vision is directed ahead, not behind, as Mills suggests it is.[70]

Understood in this way, Dewey demonstrates several key similarities to Mills himself, similarities that would seem to be worth exploring. One such similarity is in their conceptions of the ideal of democracy. Dewey's sense of 'democracy' we have considered in 5.5.

---

[67] See, for example, the following: "there comes a point when any solution of any 'value problem' becomes: Who can kill whom? Or in peaceful civilized countries: Who can have whom put in jail?" (*Power, Politics and People*, 168).

[68] *Sociology and Pragmatism*, 382.

[69] Cf. MW 11:104; 13:310; Veblen, *The Theory of the Leisure Class*, 226–45.

[70] Thus I would maintain the irrelevance to Dewey of Mills's attack on those who use "the images of classic democracy . . . as the working legitimations of power in American society" (*Power, Politics and People*, 357; cf. 580–81).

Mills's sense of democracy refers to a social situation in which "those vitally affected by any decision men make have an effective voice in that decision." Democracy of this sort is constituted by "the power and the freedom of those controlled by law to change the law, according to agreed-upon rules—and even to change these rules." Such a democracy requires that "all power to make such decisions be publicly legitimated and that the makers of such decisions be held publicly accountable." Democracy thus means ultimately "some kind of collective self-control over the structural mechanics of history itself."[71] In comparing Mills to Dewey here, it is important to emphasize that both stress the participatory and egalitarian aspects of democracy and play down the often overly stressed equation of democracy and freedom. For Dewey, again as we have seen above in 5.4, effective freedom is a matter of the distribution of power in situations of social interaction. For Mills, freedom means the chance to play a role in the processes of one's social life: "Freedom is, first of all, the chance to formulate the available choices, to argue over them—and then, the opportunity to choose." The goal of freedom within a democracy is therefore not "independence" but rather "control over that upon which the individual is dependent."[72]

A second similarity between Mills and Dewey can be seen in their generally negative evaluation of American democratic practice. Dewey, as we have seen in 5.6, spoke repeatedly of the need to establish democracy in America. In 1959 Mills offers a similarly negative evaluation, writing that the United States is "generally democratic mainly in form and in the rhetoric of expectation. In substance and in practice it is very often non-democratic, and in many institutional areas it is quite clearly so." Indicating this failing is not for Mills, just as it is not for Dewey, the end of the story. On the contrary, it is simply the first step in his attempt to increase the level of democratic involvement by making use of the "legal forms" that our society provides, and "formal expectations" that our democracy raises, "to make the society more democratic." Mills, sounding almost Deweyan, is here relying upon the potential effectiveness of "acting as if we were in a fully democratic society"

---

[71] *The Sociological Imagination*, 188, 116; cf. *The Causes of World War Three*, 118–19.

[72] *The Sociological Imagination*, 174; *Power, Politics and People*, 191; cf. 297; *White Collar*, 58–59.

for removing "the 'as if'."[73] He thus hopes, on the one hand, to engage more of those who presently are politically "inactionary," and, on the other, to contribute to the development of "parties and movements and publics" that will debate "ideas and alternatives of social life" and that will "have a chance really to influence decisions of structural consequence."[74]

A third aspect of similarity between Dewey and Mills can be seen in their call for efforts on the part of dedicated individuals from the intellectual world to advance the common good. Because of their stated objections to the use of slanted and partial information to manipulate political processes, both Dewey and Mills call for the use of the independent and socially responsible intellectuals as guides for more adequate education and fuller democracy. Dewey's consideration of the role of philosophical criticism in society we have examined in 3.4; and a comparison to Mills's work is in order. "The intellectual ought to be the moral conscience of his society, at least with reference to the value of truth," Mills writes. They should be absorbed "in the attempt to know what is real and what is unreal." Following the life of what he calls "the politics of truth" requires that, in addition to attempting to *know* the truth, intellectuals must also attempt to *tell* the truth: to present their fellow citizens "with genuine alternatives, the moral meanings of which are clearly opened to public debate."[75] And, whether this appeal to intellectuals is addressed primarily to 'philosophers' (as in Dewey's case) or to 'social scientists' (as in Mills's) is surely irrelevant.

Mills, like Dewey before him, maintains that intellectuals must challenge their social situation by "criticizing or debunking prevailing arrangements and rulers." In our role as intellectuals, he continues, "we should conduct a continuing, uncompromising criticism of this established culture." The difficult task of the liberating educator thus begins with attempts "intellectually to transcend the milieux in which he happens to live."[76] There then

---

[73] *The Sociological Imagination*, 188, 190–91, 189; cf. *The Causes of World War Three*, 136, 141.

[74] *Power, Politics and People*, 24; *The Sociological Imagination*, 41, 190; cf. *Power, Politics and People*, 408.

[75] *Power, Politics and People*, 611, 235; *The Sociological Imagination*, 178; *Power, Politics and People*, 338.

[76] *The Sociological Imagination*, 80; *Power, Politics and People*, 233; *The Sociological Imagination*, 184; cf. *The Causes of World War Three*, 118, 124–30.

begins the intellectual's dual "public role." One part of this dual role is to try to help individuals mired in aspects of our social ills that they see only as personal troubles to attain what he calls "adequate definitions of reality." What the intellectual can do for individuals "is to turn personal troubles and concerns into social issues and problems open to reason—his aim is to help the individual become a self-educating man, who only then would be reasonable and free."[77] The second part of the intellectual's public role is on a broader scale. It is to join with others to establish "a creative minority" that "might prevail against the ascendancy of the mass society, and all the men and apparatus that make for it."[78] Writing in a mood reminiscent of Dewey's call for "a minority having the requisite courage, conviction, and readiness for sacrificial work" (LW 6:189) that was cited at the end of 5.7, Mills writes that it is part of the intellectual's public role "to combat all those forces which are destroying genuine publics and creating a mass society—or put as a positive goal, his aim is to help build and to strengthen self-cultivating publics. Only then might society be reasonable and free."[79]

6.4.   Meliorism and Commitment

We have been considering a Deweyan response to the criticism, drawn largely from C. Wright Mills, that Dewey's method of social reconstruction through cooperative inquiry is inappropriate to our social lives because it misunderstands the pervasive aspects of power in social action. The essence of Mills's criticism is not that those who refused to adopt Dewey's method are not interested enough to care about, or intelligent enough to see, or selfless enough to do, what ought to be done, and that, in consequence Dewey's method will not work. Rather than putting forward these individual-oriented criticisms, Mills offers a fundamentally social criticism: to see social action as cooperative inquiry is simply to misunderstand how the political process works. Moreover to adopt the stance of a coopera-

---

[77] *The Sociological Imagination,* 186; *Power, Politics and People,* 373; *The Sociological Imagination,* 186; cf. *Power, Politics and People,* 367–70; *The Power Elite,* 318–19.

[78] *Power, Politics and People,* 372.

[79] *The Sociological Imagination,* 186; cf. 191; *Power, Politics and People,* 367, 373; *The Power Elite,* 318.

tive inquirer in a society that has only skeletal common goods and scarcely any inquiry, and to advocate that others do the same, is to adopt a self-defeating stance. On the contrary, what we need to do, Mills suggests, is to keep constantly before our minds a realistic evaluation of our situation and never confuse how we want our social interactions to work with how they do work. This criticism is, I believe, an absolutely essential contemporary criticism of any liberalism that might be inclined toward a naive romanticism. I also believe, as I have suggested, that this criticism is in no way an adequate criticism of Dewey's position.[80] When applied to the Dewey we have been considering, it should be obvious that Mills offers us not a refutation of his method of social reconstruction but rather a constant challenge to those who might adopt the method that they remember the importance of entering into cooperative inquiry with both eyes open. Of course, Dewey's method does not fit the normal sort of social situation with which we are currently familiar—his work does not comprise a handbook for contemporary political practice. The point of the realistic analysis that Dewey developed, however, is that, if we ever hope to break out of our current political situation, we need to try to reconstruct our social situation to make something like the method he is proposing fit.

To interpret his criticism of Dewey in this way is not to discount all that Mills writes about the political ills of our society: about the replacement of publics by masses, about the inaction of the citizenry and the excessive power wielded by the elite, about intellectuals who avoid practical work to help society, and so on. It is rather to place these problems, as I believe Mills himself does, in the category of the potentially meliorable. Why challenge intellectuals and social scientists to play a role in overcoming the ills of mass society if the problems are completely intractable? Why write about participatory democracy and the evils of a society in the control of a power elite if not in the hope that such actions will contribute to a social situation in which cooperative inquiry will be the appropriate method? Why not simply enjoy the spectacle of human futility and the wonder of human naivete?[81] Mills's answer, and Dewey's, is that human life can be improved.

---

[80] Dewey cautions us, as we saw in 3.3, against presenting an improved version of "existence" as "reality."

[81] Cf. H. L. Mencken: "I enjoy democracy immensely. It is incomparably idiotic,

Under the proper conditions—that is, as long as we know the limitations on cooperation and on inquiry in our current situations, and have some sense of our fellow citizens, and see cooperative inquiry as a deliberate choice to be pursued beyond guarantees, and take account of other possible factors—it will not harm us greatly to have faith in the possibilities of self-conscious cooperative inquiry and to act with some expectation that we will succeed. Although Mills himself is in no way overly confident of success,[82] he came increasingly to believe that the effort is worthwhile. If our focus is upon the long-range goals of society, we must try to rise above the limitations of our current situation. "No one knows the limits of possible human development," he writes. "What men might become, what kinds of societies men might build—the answers to such questions are neither closed nor inevitable." And, while he realizes that such considerations introduce what "so-called practical men of affairs" see as "utopian ideals," Mills is proud to admit such ideals as his own.[83] To say this, however, is simply to say that for Mills, as for Dewey, efforts to make our society the sort of place where social action could be carried on as a kind of cooperative inquiry require faith in future possibilities.

Dewey repeatedly points out the existence of inherent limits on our problem-solving abilities. We live, as we saw in 3.2, in a world that intermixes support and frustration. "All action," he writes, "is an invasion of the future, of the unknown" (MW 14:10). In consequence, all action leads to results that could not have been anticipated: "Men always build better or worse than they know" (MW 14:143). Moreover, there are many sorts of problems that we encounter where "adaptation" is impossible and where our "adjustment" is limited to "accommodation" (LW 9:12).[84] We know as well that new struggles and new failures are inevitable because "problems

---

and hence incomparably amusing. . . . In the long run, it may turn out that rascality is necessary to human government, and even to civilization itself—that civilization, at bottom, is nothing but a colossal swindle. I do not know: I report only that when the suckers are running well the spectacle is infinitely exhilarating" (*Notes on Democracy*, 211–12).

[82] And, at times, Mills is explicitly pessimistic. See: *The Sociological Imagination*, 193; *Power, Politics and People*, 338.

[83] *The Causes of World War Three*, 94; *Power, Politics and People*, 233; cf. 254, 402; *The Causes of World War Three*, 134.

[84] Cf. MW 4:141; 9:51–52; Eames, *Pragmatic Naturalism*, 9–16.

will recur in the future in a new form or on a different plane" (MW 14:197). As a result, "when all is said and done, the fundamentally hazardous character of the world is not seriously modified, much less eliminated" (LW 1:45). Our natural world remains a "precarious and perilous" place, a place where there is "no preference for good things over bad things" (LW 1:42, 93). And, on the social side, there arc similar difficulties arising from the fact that, as he writes, we humans are aspects of our own problems. In many ways, "man is naturally or primarily an irrational creature" because "impulse and habit, not thought, are the primary determinants of conduct" (MW 13:247; 14:153; cf. 155). And, while changes can be made, "there are some limits to modifiability of human nature and to institutional change," limits that must be determined "by experimental observation" (LW 6:38). Consequently, we have the ongoing task of attempting to develop, out of our impulsive and habitual selves, more intelligent inquirers—rational prophets to take up the task of contemporary Jeremiahs—with "the social sensitiveness" (MW 12:165) to recognize and address the significant problems and issues of the present and future.

Given this as our situation, we cannot allow ourselves to be blindly optimistic. Nor can we claim, Dewey admits, either that "intelligence will ever dominate the course of events" or that "it will save [us] from ruin or destruction" (LW 1:325–26). He writes this, moreover, not just in the cause of greater accuracy, but also because he believes that any softer conclusions lead us away from the ever necessary "task of reconstruction and direction" (LW 5:110). The moral life requires, Dewey writes, "a certain intellectual pessimism, in the sense of a steadfast willingness to uncover sore points, to acknowledge and search for abuses, to note how presumed good often serves as a cloak for actual bad" (MW 5:371). Still, although we should not be blindly optimistic, neither should we allow ourselves to sink into pessimism. We should not reject the world which at times fails us because there always remains "the possibility of constructive social engineering" (MW 10:241), of positive social reconstruction to solve our problems. How much success we will have if we try our best remains to be determined.

It should consequently be clear that it would be a mistake to consider Dewey to be an optimist. His understanding of human action emphasizes, in the words of John Herman Randall, Jr., "the better, not the perfect."[85] It is *melioristic,* not *optimistic*[86]; or, if it is optimistic at all, it is what he calls "optimism of *will*" (MW 5:371). His assumption is not a belief in the eventual triumph of reason in history, but in the worthwhileness of efforts to try to advance the common good. "Meliorism is the belief," Dewey writes, "that the specific conditions which exist at one moment, be they comparatively bad or comparatively good, in any event may be bettered" (MW 12:181–82).[87] Meliorism thus encourages intelligent action, which pessimism cannot, and arouses confidence and hopefulness without relaxing us into optimistic passivity. Only a meliorism can underlie a philosophy of action that allows for the possibility of reform and progress through human effort.

Dewey writes that "progress is not inevitable, it is up to men as individuals to bring it about. Change is going to occur anyway, and the problem is the control of change in a given direction" (LW 14:113). Existence presents us with a mixture of goods and evils, with an evolving process of potential benefit and harm. It is our social task to try to direct this process collectively toward an increased common good: "reconstruction in the direction of the good which is indicated by ideal ends, must take place, if at all, through continued cooperative effort" (LW 9:32). Without the hopeful tone of meliorism, the call to this cooperative inquiry will fall victim to the laziness of optimism or the paralysis of pessimism.

Undergirding Dewey's meliorism is a faith, a willingness to try, to take a chance. He sees this kind of faith as a tendency toward action still rooted in "the dumb pluck of the animal" (MW 14:200); and, as William James notes, it is a basic aspect of human living: "We cannot live or think at all without some degree of faith."[88] It is this faith that makes it possible for us to act in the face of uncertainty, to live in an evolving world bereft of guarantees. In this kind of world we need an

---

[85] Randall, "Dewey's Contribution to Scientific Humanism," 136.

[86] Dewey's use of the term 'melioristic' derives from James's use of it to emphasize possibilities and the need for our efforts to attain them (Cf. *Pragmatism,* 60–61, 137–38).

[87] Cf. John J. McDermott: "the attitude of meliorism acknowledges both sin and possibility. Dewey is adamant in his conviction that nothing will go totally right in either the short or the long run. He is equally convinced that all problems are malleable and functionally, although not ultimately, resolute, even if they are sure to appear in another guise at another time" (*Streams of Experience,* 118).

[88] *The Will to Believe,* 79.

experimental philosophy, one which can guide us as we move onward into the unknown. There are, as James indicates, "cases where a fact cannot come at all unless a preliminary faith exists in its coming"[89]; and, with regard to our social problems, this point is of extreme importance. As Dewey writes, because "we are part of the causes which bring them about in what we have done and have refrained from doing" (LW 9:131), our actions can influence the severity of these ills. For him then, moral courage requires effort beyond guarantees,[90] effort based upon faith:

> Hope and aspiration, belief in the supremacy of good in spite of all evil, belief in the realizability of good in spite of all obstacles, are necessary aspirations in the life of virtue. The good can never be demonstrated to the senses, nor be proved by calculations of personal profit. It involves a radical venture of the will in the interest of what is unseen and prudentially incalculable (MW 5:371).

Our efforts are both definitely necessary and possibly efficacious. Dewey therefore maintains that these efforts—to foster democratic faith in the possibilities of cooperative inquiry as a means for advancing the dual goods of fulfilled individuals and of enriched community life—must be carried forward. He writes that *"the problem of our day and generation"* is demonstrating that there is no *"inherent"* incompatibility "between individual human beings integrated in themselves and a community life marked by diversity of voluntary groups representing different interests" (LW 14:40). This demonstration must take place in the process of social inquiry.

Is there, then, no situation conceivable within which Dewey would be forced to admit that his faith in the possibilities of cooperative action was misguided? If the emphasis is upon 'forced', the answer to this question must be negative: there is no set of circumstances that would force him to consider his faith in democracy to be mistaken. There are many different possible circumstances that might cause him to suggest a reconstruction of our conceptions of key political terms or of political institutions. There are particular constellations of events that might cause some individuals in the

---

[89] *The Will to Believe*, 29.

[90] Rejecting the conservatism of 'realistic' politicians, Dewey writes, "I am not, thank God, what is called a practical politician" (LW 6:151).

future, as they have in the past, to tire "of the responsibilities, the duties, the burden that the acceptance of political liberty involves" (LW 13:294), to "sag, withdraw and seek refuge" and even to "cave in" (MW 14:200),[91] and as a result abandon their personal faith in the possibilities of democracy. But there are no circumstances that would force him to have to abandon democracy as having been finally repudiated. Regardless of what may have happened in any instance of failed democratic practice to throw doubt on the possibilities of cooperative inquiry, the next time things might turn out differently. As Dewey puts it:

> The objection that the method of intelligence has been tried and failed is wholly aside from the point, since the crux of the present situation is that it has not been tried under such conditions as now exist. It has not been tried at any time with use of all the resources that scientific material and the experimental method now put at our disposal (LW 11:37).

The open-endedness of these strong qualifications should not suggest that this faith is without any sort of potential verification. This faith, however unproven in terms of *past* experience, may still be justified in terms of *future* experience; and, for Dewey, this melioristic faith is forward looking. As he writes, a philosophy should function as "a social hope reduced to a working program of action" (MW 11:43). In exactly this way, "[a] philosophic faith, being a tendency to action, can be tried and tested only in action" and its realization if it is to occur at all, "is in the future" (LW 5:278). The democratic ideal, he writes, is "that each individual shall have the opportunity for release, expression, fulfillment, of his distinctive capacities, and that the outcome shall further the establishment of a fund of shared values." Like other ideals, democracy thus "signifies something to be done" through the "constant meeting and solving of problems" rather than signifying "something already given, something ready-made" (LW 7:350). Democracy, as something to be worked toward, is "an ideal in the only intelligible sense of an ideal: namely, the tendency and movement of some thing which exists carried to its final limit, viewed as completed, perfected" (LW 2:328). Democracy is thus, of necessity, never to be fully attained. Still, it can always be more closely approximated.

---

[91] Cf. LW 7:359; 15:170–72, 251–52.

It is possible to examine the reasons Dewey offers for his acceptance of this faith. The first is that faith is a necessary element of democratic social practice if that practice is ever to succeed. As he writes, "all endeavor for the better is moved by faith in what is possible, not by adherence to the actual" (LW 9:17). Faith in democracy will increase the possibility of its success; and pessimistic anticipation of failure will definitely contribute to failure. As long as our faith is not without some foundation, it is as justified as it can be. His second reason is that, if we want to advance the common good, we really have no other choice: "The task is to go on, and not backward, until the method of intelligence and experimental control is the rule in social relations and social direction. Either we take this road or we admit that the problem of social organization in behalf of human liberty and the flowering of human capacities is insoluble" (LW 11:64). Thus, insofar as it is sensible to talk at all of "salvation" in our limited and uncaring world, Dewey writes, "[f]aith in the power of intelligence to imagine a future which is the projection of the desirable in the present, and to invent the instrumentalities of its realization, is our salvation" (MW 10:48). This melioristic sense of salvation through advancement of the common good—a salvation that is hypothetical and tentative, cooperative and active—is what Dewey offers us.

Dewey concentrates throughout on the long-term possibilities. Our goal, under his approach, is not simply to get by from day to day by meeting and addressing problems and issues as they appear, in whatever way we can and with whatever means are handy. "Experimental method," as we saw in 5.8, "is not just messing around nor doing a little of this and a little of that in the hope that things will improve" (LW 11:292–93). Our goal is to move to a new kind of social interrelation that would be alive to the concern that we were not just solving our present problems by bringing on new ones. For Dewey, the present is always pivotal—"Any present always offers itself as a transition, a passage, or becoming" (LW 5:363; cf. 53)—we are always beginning here and now, and moving one step at a time with our eyes on the long-run for humankind. He believes that, by an increased emphasis upon the use of the method of intelligence and the development of a community, we could realize the long-term development of a common good. From this point of view, the criticism that this is a 'fairy-tale' understanding of our society must be reinterpreted to stress, as Mills eventually did, that the real fantasy is the expectation of a fulfilling existence in society without personal contribution. There is little more that can be said at this point to convince those who find this commitment misguided. What response is possible to an individual such as Morris Cohen, when he writes that "Dewey puts the Golden Age in the future rather than in the past. Such hope strengthens men, and it cannot be refuted. But the philosopher who piously visits the cemetery of human hopes may well shake his head"[92]? Is it not adequate to say that human hopes are not only buried but forever reborn? If we accept as our goal Dewey's goal of democratic involvement, then our job is to attempt to advance the common good through efforts at cooperative inquiry. And, if presently available means seem inadequate to this melioristic task, then we need to try to make them better.[93]

---

[92] *American Thought*, 300.

[93] For another discussion of the theme of melioristic commitment, see my volume, *The Community Reconstructs*, 99–109.

CHAPTER 7
Human Community as a Religious Goal

IN OUR EXAMINATION of the meaning and importance of John Dewey's philosophy, there is one more critical theme to be considered: the challenge to his belief that shared experience is the greatest of human goods. This final criticism questions the *motivation for*—rather than the *rationality of*—his attempts at social reconstruction. The essence of this final criticism is that we should not pursue participatory democracy and cooperative efforts to advance the common good, that we should not seek Dewey's social sense of human fulfillment. What we should seek instead is an individual sense of fulfillment through an increase in personal freedom and initiative and expanding private goods. In responding to such a criticism, the material considered in the preceding chapter is of little use. Here, the question is not one—as it was there—of the proper method to reach the social goals that were generally accepted as worthwhile; rather, the point of any Deweyan response must be the attempt to convince the critics of the correctness of his analysis of human nature and human fulfillment. Dewey's response is two-fold. One aspect is to maintain that the life of the democratic community requires efforts and involvement on the part of the citizenry that would preclude the kind of isolated existence that this individualism advocates. Dewey emphasizes here the obligations of those who live lives of unearned, modern comfort to those who are as yet not benefitting or who are yet to come. The second aspect of Dewey's view is his emphasis upon the social sense of human nature and upon the necessity for seeing human fulfillment as social in nature rather than as individual. Much of the material for this defense must be drawn from Dewey's religious writings, especially from his Terry Lectures of 1934 published as *A Common Faith*. It is necessary for us, he believes, to overcome the political, national, racial, and economic 'sectarianism' of our contemporary world before we can build a fully human community.

7.1. Dewey and the Religious Life

In this section, I undertake an examination of the religious aspect of Dewey's work. My purpose here is not so much to consider his philosophical understanding of religion, which is admittedly limited,[1] as much as it is to consider his overall philosophy as essentially religious. His is a religious philosophy not in the sense that it is concerned with things unseen or supernatural, nor in the sense that it emphasizes such topics as guilt or grace or redemption. Dewey's philosophy is religious rather in the sense that it attempts to focus human concern upon the overarching ideal of cooperation and community, and to foster "the miracle of shared life and shared experience" (MW 12:201). As we saw in 1.2, he writes: "Social interests and problems from an early period had to me the intellectual appeal and provided the intellectual sustenance that many seem to have found primarily in religious questions" (LW 5:154). The religious spirit thus serves as the driving force of Dewey's philosophy. Taking as fundamental the importance of Dewey's confession that for him "[s]hared experience is the greatest of human goods" (LW 1:157),[2] we recognize his belief in the possibility of self-transcendence through communal life as demonstrated in the spiritually uplifting codas to so many of his volumes. Consider, for example, the last few sentences of *The Public and Its Problems*:

> There is no limit to the liberal expansion and confirmation of limited personal intellectual endowment which may proceed from the flow of social intelligence when that circulates by word of mouth from one to another in the communications of the local

---

[1] Cf. John Herman Randall, Jr.: Dewey's "whole conception of religion is Christian, Protestant, and American, with all the limitations to the restricted experience of our own present culture those adjectives imply" ("The Religion of Shared Experience," 107).

[2] Cf. George Herbert Mead: "All the things worth while are shared experiences. Even when a person is by himself, he knows that the experience he has in nature, in the enjoyment of a book, experiences which we might think of as purely individual, would be greatly accentuated if they could be shared with others" (*Mind, Self, and Society*, 385).

community. That and that only gives reality to public opinion. We lie, as Emerson said, in the lap of an immense intelligence.[3] But that intelligence is dormant and its communications are broken, inarticulate and faint until it possesses the local community as its medium (LW 2:371–72).[4]

His commitment to the cooperative life found here and in such passages as "[d]emocracy is the faith that the process of experience is more important than any special result attained" (LW 14:229) demonstrates that his philosophical perspective is fundamentally religious. In addition to making this religiousness more explicit, this section also functions in part as a response to the criticism that we considered in 2.5 that Dewey does not really understand individuality.

At a time in the history of American higher education when Christianity and philosophy were closely allied[5] and when the single undergraduate course in philosophy was conceived as the keystone in the education of a Christian gentleman, Dewey began his academic career in a traditionally religious fashion, as we saw in 1.2. He had been converted as a young man and he belonged to congregations throughout the first three and one-half decades of his life. He was active in the Students' Christian Association while at Ann Arbor,[6] and he published in various religious journals.[7] Dewey was offered the position at the University of Chicago in 1894, in part at least,

---

[3] Cf. Emerson: "We lie in the lap of immense intelligence, which makes us receivers of its truth and organs of its activity" ("Self-Reliance," *Complete Works,* vol. 2, 64).

[4] Cf. James Hayden Tufts: "Man without friendship, love, pity, sympathy, communication, cooperation, justice, rights, or duties, would be deprived of nearly all that gives life its value" (*Ethics* [with Dewey], MW 5:439).

[5] Cf. Max C. Otto's review of the 1930 two-volume set, *Contemporary American Philosophy: Personal Statements*—a volume that contains among other essays Dewey's "From Absolutism to Experimentalism" (LW 5:147–60) and Tufts's "What I Believe" (reprinted in *Selected Writings,* 1–18)—in which Otto explores the importance of the profound impact of the Christian religion on the developing philosophers (review of *Contemporary American Philosophy,* ed. G. P. Adams and W. P. Montague; cf. Bruce Kuklick, *Churchmen and Philosophers,* 230–53).

[6] Cf. for example, EW 1:61–63, 90–92; 4:3–10, 96–105, 365–70.

[7] During his years at the Universities of Michigan and of Minnesota, Dewey had published in such religions periodicals as: *Andover Review* (EW 1:48–60, 205–26; 3:14–35, 110–24, 180–90), *Bibliotheca Sacra* (EW 1:93–115), and *Christian Union* (EW 3:36–42). For a consideration of Dewey's religious life during these years, see Rockefeller, *John Dewey,* 125–68.

because of James Hayden Tufts's enthusiastic endorsement of his "religious nature."[8] He was by this time, however, losing confidence in the ability of the Church to address our temporal problems, and his break was made irreparable by his experiences of the social turmoil of Chicago. Except for the particulars, Dewey's experience of abandoning the Church while carrying on what he saw as its proper mission was not uncommon. Many of his contemporaries worked for the salvation of society outside of the Church.[9]

When Dewey presented the formulation of this critical feeling about religion and the Church in an intellectual fashion, his attack was fundamental. He maintains that religiosity or piety is an important aspect of human existence that was suffering because our religious thinking and practices had become outdated, and that in our religious lives, as elsewhere, "[r]econstruction is a periodic need of life" (EW 4:97). His intention was not to go back and recover one of the earlier stages during which the role of religion had been experienced as being correct or proper. It was, rather, to find the vital core of the historically religious life and to nurture this core in ways appropriate to our lives. To carry out this task of reconstruction, Dewey maintains that we must begin with a consideration of the history of religion and its past success. It performed at one time, he believes, a vital moral and intellectual function as "an integrating bond" in society (LW 5:72); and, in this way, religion helped make *groups* into *communities*, and *locations* into *places.*

"An individual did not join a church," Dewey writes. "He was born and reared in a community whose social unity, organization and traditions were symbolized and celebrated in the rites, cults and beliefs of a collective religion" (LW 9:41). He continues that when we consider religion's current situation we must be careful not to

---

[8] Tufts writes in part: "As a man he is simple, modest, utterly devoid of any affectation or self-consciousness, and makes many friends and no enemies. He is a man of religious nature, is a church-member and believes in working with the churches." The full text of Tufts's undated letter of 1893 or 1894 is reproduced in *John Dewey: Master Educator,* ed. William H. Brickman and Stanley Lehrer, 167–68; cf. Rucker, *The Chicago Pragmatists,* 10–11; Dykhuizen, *Life and Mind of John Dewey,* 76–77.

[9] Cf. Robert M. Crunden: the Progressives "grew up in a world where the ministry no longer seemed intellectually respectable. . . . They groped toward new professions such as social work, journalism, academia, the law, and politics. In each of these careers, they could become preachers urging moral reform on institutions as well as on individuals" (*Ministers of Reform,* ix; cf. 14–16, 52–63).

overemphasize its decline "in an outward sense," in terms of "church membership, churchgoing and so on." Religion's slippage, while undeniable, is far more important elsewhere:

> it is hardly possible to overstate its decline as a vitally integrative and directive force in men's thought and sentiments. . . . it was the symbol of the existence of conditions and forces that gave unity and a centre to men's views of life. It at least gathered together in weighty and shared symbols a sense of the objects to which men were so attached as to have support and stay in their outlook on life (LW 5:71; cf. MW 4:176–77).

Thus, the integrative function of religion was its vital core; but, Dewey concludes in 1930, religion "does not now effect this result" (LW 5:71), although he does suggest soon after that "conditions are now ripe for emancipation of the religious quality from accretions that have grown up about it and that limit the credibility and the influence of religion" (LW 9:56). He writes that, if "the naturalistic foundations and bearings of religion" were grasped, and the religious element in life emerged "from the throes of the crisis in religion," religion would then be able to take "its natural place in every aspect of human experience that is concerned with estimate of possibilities, with emotional stir by possibilities as yet unrealized, and with all action in behalf of their realization." He maintains moreover that all that is significant in human experience "falls within this frame" (LW 9:38–39).

Dewey had a model here: the Emerson who nearly a century before had stood at the Harvard Divinity School and called for a return to the people of what had been "embezzled from the common store and appropriated to sectarian and class use" (MW 3:190).[10] Dewey continues that instead of the spirit of community and natural piety, what we now get from religions are too often the shell of ritual and ceremony and the credal formulas of dogma. Religion, he writes, "has been formulated into fixed and defined beliefs expressed in required acts and ceremonies"; and, as a consequence, "the office of religion as sense of community and one's place in it has been lost" (MW 14:226; cf. EW 4:3–4). Religions as a result inhibit, he writes in 1934, what they are supposed to be cultivating: "religions now prevent, because of their weight of historic encumbrances, the

---

[10] See Emerson, "An Address," *Complete Works*, vol. 1, 119–51.

religious quality of experience from coming to consciousness and finding the expression that is appropriate to present conditions, intellectual and moral" (LW 9:8). It is thus important for us to recognize the difference between religions as we usually encounter them and the religious values of experience that the religions are supposed to enhance. "Just because the release of these values is so important, their identification with the creeds and cults of religions must be dissolved" (LW 9:20). Individuals who place their emphasis upon the cooperative pursuit of the common good "have within their experience all the elements which give the religious attitude its value" (LW 14:80).[11]

Dewey's critique of the natural and social failure of religions can be seen upon analysis to contain two fundamental themes. The first is that our religions are *intellectually* bankrupt. One aspect of this intellectual bankruptcy can be found in the dogmatism contained in various religions' claims to have "special truths" to which there are only "peculiar avenues of access" (LW 9:23). While the scientific method is "open and public," Dewey writes, "[t]he doctrinal method is limited and private" (LW 9:27). While the scientific method is proud of its tentative development,[12] the doctrinal method views any such development as a falling away from the 'truth'. In fact, the search for 'open and public' proofs of religious claims is often seen, Dewey recognizes, to be itself "sacrilegious and perverse." The usual method of justifying such religious claims is intellectually "secret, not public; peculiarly revealed, not generally known; authoritatively declared, not communicated and tested in ordinary ways"; and it thus exemplifies a wholly different "standard for coming to know" (MW 4:173), a standard that is thought to be appropriate to matters of a religious sort. This method is particularly conservative, sacralizing contemporary beliefs as eternal 'Answers' (cf. MW 4:4; LW 5:273).

Another aspect of the intellectual bankruptcy Dewey found in religions can be seen by examining the specific content of the beliefs thus derived. For example, he writes that religions are far too

---

[11] Dewey writes that *A Common Faith* "was addressed to those who have abandoned supernaturalism, and who on that account are reproached by traditionalists for having turned their backs on everything religious" (LW 14:79–80).

[12] Cf. Charles Sanders Peirce: "the first step toward *finding out* is to acknowledge you do not satisfactorily know already" (*Collected Papers*, 1.13).

comfortable in claiming resolution of unanswered questions by means of some supernatural agency. He notes, for example, that the term 'supernatural' itself has changed in meaning from "that which was striking and emotionally impressive because of its out-of-the-way character" (LW 9:46) to that which explains what science is unable to explain.

> We lack, for example, knowledge of the relation of life to inanimate matter. Therefore supernatural intervention is assumed to have effected the transition from brute to man. We do not know the relation of the organism—the brain and nervous system—to the occurrence of thought. Therefore, it is argued, there is a supernatural link. We do not know the relation of causes to results in social matters, and consequently we lack means of control. Therefore, it is inferred, we must resort to supernatural control (LW 9:50–51).

In these cases, "[e]xisting ignorance or backwardness is employed to assert the existence of a division in the nature of the subject-matter dealt with" (LW 9:24). The great tragedy here, from Dewey's point of view, is that this method of separation precludes other methods of response and this method is in consequence virtually self-perpetuating. "The needed understanding will not develop unless we strive for it," he writes (LW 9:51); but, if we believe that natural "human capacities are so low that reliance upon them only makes things worse" (LW 15:55), we will be tempted to rely upon other means to solve our problems. "The assumption that only supernatural agencies can give control is a sure method of retarding this effort" (LW 9:51; cf. 31–32). As a result of the resort to supernatural 'solutions', we will be less likely to ever achieve practical answers. And this misdirection will assure that the potentially vibrant religious element in living will go undeveloped because "the religious factors of experience have been drafted into supernatural channels and thereby loaded with irrelevant encumbrances" (LW 9:19). Instead of helping to uncover the human values present in experiences and relationships—of birth and death, of fellowship and marriage—religions have projected these values "into a supernatural realm for safe-keeping and sanction" (LW 9:48).

A second and more serious theme (cf. LW 9:293) to be found in Dewey's understanding of the failure of our religions is his belief that they are *morally* bankrupt. One aspect of this criticism is that our religions have become secure and complacent. Christianity, he writes, although it began "as a demand for a revolutionary change," now has become "respectable," a defender of "established economic, political, and international institutions" (LW 5:273). Our religions he sees as being at best half-hearted opponents of "war, economic injustice, political corruption," and other social ills (LW 9:55), because their overriding otherworldly commitments undermine their efforts at temporal reconstruction. Another, more serious aspect of Dewey's criticism is that our religions themselves have actively contributed to, and continue to contribute to, factional conflicts. Instead of being the great unifiers and integraters of our society that work to create "a vital sense of the solidarity of human interests and inspire action to make that sense a reality" (LW 5:273–74), our religions are fundamentally sectarian. He writes that "the multiplication of rival and competing religious bodies, each with its private inspiration and outlook" (MW 4:175), has brought about the greatest harm to the efforts of organized religion. "It is impossible to ignore the fact," he writes "that historic Christianity has been committed to a separation of sheep and goats; the saved and the lost; the elect and the mass." While he recognizes that this element of "[s]piritual aristocracy" is not the whole story of religions, he maintains that it is central to the story: "Lip service—often more than lip service—has been given to the idea of the common brotherhood of all men. But those outside the fold of the church and those who do not rely upon belief in the supernatural have been regarded as only potential brothers, still requiring adoption into the family" (LW 9:55; cf. 5:71). Dewey maintains that before a widespread emphasis upon the religious element in experience can emerge, it will be necessary to overcome this sectarianism. He maintains as well, however, that it can be done. "Whether or not we are, save in some metaphorical sense, all brothers, we are at least all in the same boat traversing the same turbulent ocean," he writes. "The potential religious significance of this fact is infinite" (LW 9:56). If we can come to appreciate fully the commonality, we may be able to overcome religion's moral bankruptcy and recover its role as provider of a "sense of community and one's place in it" (MW 14:226).

However bad the inherited form of institutional religion may be, Dewey believes that there is still something of value to be derived from the religious life if it can be reconstructed. If we can break free from the outdated shell of current religions, we may be able to recover the vital possibilities that the religious life contains; and, if we can find new and vibrant symbols to carry the religious meaning of experience, we may be able to live the religious life. In a manner encountered in other areas of social reconstruction, the process of religious reconstruction will require both intellectual and institutional changes. We will need to determine in each area, he writes, "how much in religions now accepted are survivals from outgrown cultures" (LW 9:6). This determination, and the subsequent development of new symbols and institutions that it will engender, will no doubt bring us into a clear confrontation with the literalist defenders of the past. Religions need such symbols; but all too often, Dewey maintains, "men have been idolaters worshiping symbols as things" (MW 14:226).[13] Still, he continues, even "these symbols which have so often claimed to be realities and which have imposed themselves as dogmas and intolerances" almost always still contain "some trace of a vital and enduring reality, that of a community of life in which continuities of existence are consummated" (MW 14:226). If we are able to recognize the symbolic nature of so much of our inherited religions, and introduce "the fullest liberty of symbolic interpretation of any and all articles and items" (LW 2:166), we will be able to expand upon this meaningful trace to construct more adequate symbols for the present and future. The exact nature of the new symbols cannot of course be determined in advance.[14]

From a more philosophical point of view, the development of these new symbols involves rethinking our religious ideas. Among the conceptual changes that are necessary, Dewey believes that we need to rethink especially the meaning of the term 'religious'. The adjectival form is important in order to separate the focus of his interest from any institutional pre-commitments, especially if the institution in question, as a religion, treats the natural/supernatural distinction as revelatory. "It is of the nature of a religion based on the

---

[13] Cf. James Hayden Tufts: "The symbols which men have hitherto framed to convey what they have deeply felt, or ardently aspired to, or in great moments envisaged, were all for the most part conceived in imagery of long ago. . . . They inevitably came into conflict with advancing thought. But the symbols are not the spirit" (*Selected Writings*, 270).

[14] Cf. James Hayden Tufts: "It is no doubt an era of transition between the imagery, doctrines, and conceptions which served to interpret man's deeper life in days past, and those as yet unframed symbols and conceptions which shall both interpret and inform the deeper life of the future" (*Selected Writings*, 266; cf. 17–18, 345).

supernatural," he writes, "to draw a line between the religious and the secular and profane, even when it asserts the rightful authority of the Church and its religion to dominate these other interests." But, he continues, the situation is very different with the adjectival form:

> The conception that "religious" signifies a certain attitude and outlook, independent of the supernatural, necessitates no such division. It does not shut religious values up within a particular compartment, nor assume that a particular form of association bears a unique relation to it. Upon the social side the future of the religious function seems preeminently bound up with its emancipation from religions and a particular religion (LW 9:44–45).

The adjective 'religious', in other words, "denotes attitudes that may be taken toward every object and every proposed end or ideal," attitudes, he writes, "that lend deep and enduring support to the processes of living" (LW 9:8, 12). This commitment to human well-being, as he sees it, has little or nothing to do with the supernatural. Moreover, just as he is not concerned with a separate realm of experience beyond nature, he also makes clear that he is not attempting to elaborate a separate type of experience within the natural realm. He consequently rejects the view that "there is a definite kind of experience which is itself religious," and which can be "marked off from experience as aesthetic, scientific, moral, political; from experience as companionship and friendship." For Dewey, on the contrary, "'religious' as a quality of experience signifies something that may belong to all these experiences" (LW 9:9).[15] The key element that needs to be present is support for the processes of living, striving for human good. "Any activity," he writes, "pursued in behalf of an ideal end against obstacles and in spite of threats of personal loss because of conviction of its general and enduring value is religious in quality" (LW 9:19).

A second term that stands in need of reconstruction is 'faith'. We have already seen in 5.5 Dewey's emphasis upon what he called a "working faith" in democratic cooperation (LW 14:226). This sort of faith in the potential realization of ideals he also calls "moral faith" (LW 9:15); and he believes that it is, recognizing the limitations of

---

[15] Cf. Max C. Otto: "it almost seems as if Mr. Dewey were saying that every activity in the world may take on a religious character, excepting religion" (Review of *A Common Faith*, 496; cf. Hook, *John Dewey*, 219).

the present situation that we considered in 6.3, legitimate. He writes, however, that faith is illegitimate when it becomes an "anticipatory vision of things" or "a substitute for knowledge" (LW 9:15) and thus comes into conflict with scientific inquiry. Religion's attempts to combat science, he writes, are misguided and wasteful: "It is probably impossible to imagine the amount of intellectual energy that has been diverted from normal processes of arriving at intellectual conclusions because it has gone into rationalization of the doctrines entertained by historic religions" (LW 9:23–24). If, however, we are able to abandon the intellectual pretensions of this sense of faith and thus avoid the intellectual rationalizations it requires, Dewey believes that we can develop our moral faith. This moral faith is a faith that "signifies being conquered, vanquished, in our active nature by an ideal end" and then working to bring that ideal end into existence "as far as lies in our power" (LW 9:15–16; cf. 23).[16] He believes that our chance to recover the values of the religious life is dependent upon our ability to develop a faith "in the possibilities of human experience and human relationships that will create a vital sense of the solidarity of human interests and inspire action to make that sense a reality" (LW 5:273–74).[17]

Still another religious term that Dewey believes needs to be reconstructed is 'God'. If we keep the term at all—and, as we shall see, whether we should keep it remains an open question for Dewey—we need to adopt a conception of it that conveys a meaning appropriate to the world of our experience. He is convinced, therefore, that we need to abandon any conception of 'God' as *omnipotent king* or *master of nature* or *arbitrary tyrant*. This conception may make perfect sense in the world of historical aristocracy (or of religious fundamentalism); but it is not appropriate to the world of cooperative democracy. In fact, because developments in our knowledge of ourselves and our world have forced the abandonment of the older conception of a personal God (cf. LW 9:213–22), he maintains that we need to turn away from any meaning that connects the term with "a particular Being" (LW 9:29).

---

[16] Cf. John Herman Randall, Jr.: "Religious faith is not belief in a supernatural deity, nor in values transcending human life; it is the organized direction of man's life in devotion to the ideal possibilities discerned in imagination" ("The Religion of Shared Experience," 128).

[17] For a further discussion of the role of faith in Pragmatic social thought, see my volume, *The Community Reconstructs*, 91–109.

The suggestion that Dewey offers is that we might adopt a sense of the term 'God' (or 'the divine') that denotes "the unity of all ideal ends arousing us to desire and actions." He continues: "Suppose for the moment that the word 'God' means the ideal ends that at a given time and place one acknowledges as having authority over his volition and emotion, the values to which one is supremely devoted, as far as these ends, through imagination, take on unity" (LW 9:29). He writes that these ideals are rooted in nature and in society and that they are advanced by human actions. "It is this *active* relation between ideal and actual to which I would give the name 'God'" (LW 9:34).[18] While such a use of the term 'God' may initially be puzzling to many, Dewey finds such a conception of the unifying of ideals to be powerful: "It can unify interests and energies now dispersed; it can direct action and generate the heat of emotion and the light of intelligence" (LW 9:35). Of course, he is not *requiring* that we use the term this way; he does, however, want to proscribe uses that refer to supernatural personages. *"Either then the concept of God can be dropped out as far as genuinely religious experience is concerned,"* he writes, *"or it must be framed wholly in terms of natural and human relationship involved in our straightaway human experience"* (LW 9:224). If we find the term to be unsalvageable under any conception, as he himself finally did, he is willing to reformulate the whole discussion in terms of 'the divine' instead of 'God' to avoid misleading conceptions" (LW 9:34).[19]

There are other religious terms whose meanings could be considered here, as well as the critical responses of those individuals who remained wedded to past meanings.[20] Let us rather pass on to the

---

[18] Cf. Addison Webster Moore: "Does the concept 'God' mean an eternally completed, all-inclusive, unmoved, and immovable sum or unity of being, or does it mean active, working being engaged in real struggles with real problems?" (*Pragmatism and Its Critics,* 22).

[19] For the controversy that arose over Dewey's use of the term 'God', see: LW 9:213–28, 294–95, 412–40; Milton R. Konvitz, "Introduction," to LW 9:xxi–xxiii; Corliss Lamont, "New Light on Dewey's *Common Faith*"; Horace L. Friess, "Dewey's Philosophy of Religion," 210–12; Rockefeller, *John Dewey,* 321, 328, 512–27; Jo Ann Boydston, "Introduction" to *The Poems of John Dewey,* lx–lxii.

[20] Cf. Henry Hazlitt: "Is not Mr. Dewey, in effect, attempting to exploit the traditional prestige of words that he has emptied of nearly all their traditional meaning? Certainly his religiousness will strike the orthodox as something extremely attenuated, the extract of an extract, having the same relation to old-fashioned religion as beef bullion poured through a filter has to beef" (Review of *A Common Faith,* 168).

second phase of Dewey's position. As with the other instances of social reconstruction that we have been considering, the reconstruction of religious ideas and concepts is related to the reconstruction of religious institutions and practices. Dewey is not directly concerned here with the reconstruction of what we refer to under the heading of 'institutionalized' religion—that is, the reconstruction of denominations and congregations—but with the reconstruction of the habits and practices that make up the religious life. He admits, of course, that religious bodies have played an important role in human history, and he recognizes the possibility of a fundamental reconstruction by means of which "the churches would indeed become catholic" (LW 9:55); but his central interest remains in the habits and practices. Much of the work that he sees necessary here will be destructive: eliminating relics inherited from religion's past. Because we are dealing with important human matters such as expanding patterns of reconciliation and developing methods for the reaffirmation of social value and the creation of social goods, however, reconstruction is necessary as well. And, while Dewey believes that the reconstructive proposals will need to be developed in their specific and incomplete situations, the general aspects of this new religious life can be adumbrated.

One major aspect of the new religious life is that it would need to be careful about avoiding the intellectual troubles of current religions. This would mean, first of all, that the religious life must be naturalistic rather than supernaturalistic, hypothetical and inquiring rather than dogmatic and catechetical. He emphasizes here that there could thus be no room for dualisms that play off science against religion, or natural against human understanding (cf. LW 9:37). Neither could there be room for claims about religious 'knowledge' —gospels, prophecies, guarantees of various sorts—or for the discord that such knowledge-claims bring about when they encounter the inevitable 'heresies' of other-minded individuals. This new religious life "would surrender once for all commitment to beliefs about matters of fact, whether physical, social or metaphysical" and leave such matters to be determined by "inquirers in other fields" (LW 4:242).

Secondly, to move to the more important question of overcoming the moral troubles of our current religions, the new religious life would need to emphasize increasingly democratic and cooperative, rather than individualistic, values. In this way, reconstructed religion could hope to foster efforts to advance the common good by turning away from "the other-worldliness found in religions whose chief concern is with the salvation of the personal soul" (LW 4:219–20). In Dewey's understanding of religious life, as we have seen, there can be no separation between sheep and goats, the saved and the damned, those gifted with the revealed truth and those left in 'darkness'. Of the many possible forms of divisive human pride, he writes that the pride of those "who feel themselves learned in the express and explicit will of God is the most exclusive" (LW 4:245). What the religious life must advocate in the place of this polarization, he maintains, is an integrating sense of community:

> Within the flickering inconsequential acts of separate selves dwells a sense of the whole which claims and dignifies them. In its presence we put off mortality and live in the universal. The life of the community in which we live and have our being is the fit symbol of this relationship. The acts in which we express our perception of the ties which bind us to others are its only rites and ceremonies (MW 14:227; cf. LW 5:272–75).

Community is essential, for Dewey, both to human fulfillment and to successful society; and, if we are able to better ground our ideals of human community in concrete relations to our fellows, we will improve our level of fulfillment.[21] Rejecting the pride of the 'elect' who are convinced of their individual sanctity, he writes explicitly that "[t]he things in civilization we most prize are not of ourselves." They exist, on the contrary, "by grace of the doings and sufferings of the continuous human community in which we are a link" (LW 9:57).[22] The proper response to our situation is thus not conceit but indebtedness.

> Ours is the responsibility of conserving, transmitting, rectifying and expanding the heritage of values we have received that those who come after us may receive it more solid and secure, more widely accessible and more generously shared than we have received

---

[21] Cf. William James: "Our nation had been founded in what we may call our American religion, baptized and reared in the faith that a man requires no master to take care of him, and that common people can work out their salvation well enough together if left free to try" (*Essays in Religion and Morality,* 66).

[22] Cf. MW 9:42; 14:19; Tufts, *The Real Business of Living,* 9–10.

it. Here are all the elements for a religious faith that shall not be confined to sect, class, or race.

Dewey believes that such a communal stance has always been "implicitly the common faith of mankind." What remains to be done is to make it "explicit and militant" (LW 9:57–58).[23]

A third aspect of this reconstructed religious life is the fostering of piety toward nature. Although it is difficult to separate this natural or ecological theme from the moral theme we have just considered,[24] the contemporary importance of ecological questions makes separate mention worthwhile. For Dewey, unification with our fellows is not to be seen as a means to the more systematic plundering of our environment. On the contrary, his advocacy of human community yields a sense of pious interaction within the natural world where, as we saw in 3.2, the lives of all of us are rooted. He thus rejects the "essentially unreligious attitude" (LW 9:18) found in many proponents of what he calls "militant atheism" who he believes are "affected by lack of natural piety." In such individuals, he writes, "[t]he ties binding man to nature that poets have always celebrated are passed over lightly. The attitude taken is often that of man living in an indifferent and hostile world and issuing blasts of defiance" (LW 9:36). This unreligious attitude "attributes human achievement and purpose to man in isolation from the world of physical nature and his fellows." Our long-term collective possibilities of success, he contends on the contrary, are "dependent upon the cooperation of nature" (LW 9:18). This kind of natural piety recognizes the limitations on human possibility and emphasizes that, as we have seen in 6.3, while some of our attempts at adjustment of natural

---

[23] Cf. James Hayden Tufts at the laying of the cornerstone of the Chapel at the University of Chicago: "It is, then, our hope that in our chapel the spirit of service to mankind in its special forms will find reinforcement in common purpose and feeling; that our partial interests and sympathies will be broadened and deepened by contacts with those of like minds and hearts; and that the common purpose will find renewed vitality and ampler range as the ties which bind mankind are felt to be but manifestations of the larger life in which we share" (*Selected Writings*, 273; cf. *Ethics* [with Dewey], LW 7:453; Geiger, *Philosophy and the Social Order*, 98–99).

[24] Cf. John Herman Randall, Jr.: "These two unifying ties, the bond with one's fellows and the bond with nature, are alike capable of producing intense religious satisfactions in human experience. Dewey has woven them so closely together, in his imaginative feeling and emotion as well as in his thought, that he never speaks of one without the other" ("The Religion of Shared Experience," 123; cf. Rockefeller, *John Dewey*, 74–75).

situations do allow for adaptation, often our sole recourse is to accommodate ourselves to the demands of nature (cf. LW 9:12).

The reconstructed religious life that Dewey is advocating brings us to clearer consciousness of the fundamental place of humankind in nature, of our roots and flowerings in a world that we share with others. It thus fosters piety toward our abode and concern for our fellows. Nature, he writes, "including humanity, with all its defects and imperfections, may evoke heartfelt piety as the source of ideals, of possibilities, of aspiration in their behalf, and as the eventual abode of all attained goods and excellencies." At the same time, these ideals connect back with the realities of a daily living: "Religious faith which attaches itself to the possibilities of nature and associated living would, with its devotion to the ideal, manifest piety toward the actual" (LW 4:244; cf. MW 4:176). Moreover, he maintains that the possibilities contained in these ideals, although necessarily the products of human imagination, are not themselves imaginary. As we saw in 4.4, it is his belief that "[i]nfinite relationships of man with his fellows and with nature already exist" (MW 14:226). It is our human task to attempt to bring these relationships to consciousness so that they might inform conduct. In this way, the religious life of human cooperation and piety toward nature might move closer toward the common good.

———

I suggested initially that Dewey's philosophy cannot be understood or appreciated without an understanding of the American Experience of which his life was a part. If, however, his work is of only provincial or historical importance, it hardly matters whether it is studied or not. I hope that I have shown, on the contrary, that approaching his work through the American Experience does not isolate his philosophical perspective, because the flow of experience that he elaborated is the flow of experience that all humans face. His story-line, his idioms, his sense of possibility and his ideals are all American and all of his time; but the life of which he speaks is not. Our situation is the current pivot of history and our efforts at reconstruction will fundamentally affect the future of human existence. Human beings are natural creatures who face, day-in and day-out, a full range of problems. Some of them are momentous, others merely momentary; some of them are of our own making, others have been thrust upon us. But how we understand and address these problems will make a difference in how well we deal with them, and our dealings with these problems thus can benefit from Dewey's work. His ongoing call for evaluation, for testing of the goods we experience and for searching for better goods, reminds us of the inadequacy of our past responses and the stakes at present. And his emphasis upon our life within the group, that our likeliest successes come from cooperative efforts and that our deepest fulfillment comes from full participation in the social processes, recalls us to the recognition that an upward future lies in social democracy. This is why Dewey's work is worthy of study, adaptation, and application.

Appendix

The thirty-seven volume critical edition of *The Works of John Dewey*, edited by Jo Ann Boydston, appeared between 1969 and 1990. This edition—divided into *The Early Works* (EW), *The Middle Works* (MW) and *The Later Works* (LW)—contains all of Dewey's books, articles, encyclopedia entries, and reviews, along with occasional reports, letters, syllabi, etc.; and it represents the only adequate source for research into Dewey's work. I have consequently adopted this critical edition as my only form of citation in this volume. I recognize, however, that many readers may still want some more immediate indication of the location of some theme in Dewey's original books. I have therefore provided the following summary of the contents of the critical edition that indicates where Dewey's books appear. When page numbers have not been listed, the book comprises the entire volume in the critical edition.

EW 1 (1882–1888)	*Leibniz's New Essays Concerning the Human Understanding* (pp. 251–435)
EW 2 (1887)	*Psychology*
EW 3 (1889–1892)	*Outlines of a Critical Theory of Ethics* (pp. 237–388)
EW 4 (1893–1894)	*The Study of Ethics: A Syllabus* (pp. 219–362)
EW 5 (1895–1898)	
MW 1 (1889–1901)	*The School and Society* (pp. 1–109)
MW 2 (1902–1903)	*The Child and the Curriculum* (pp. 271–91)

MW 3
(1903–1906)

MW 4　　　　　　　*Moral Principles in Education* (pp. 265–91)
(1907–1909)

MW 5 (1908)　　　*Ethics,* with James H. Tufts

MW 6　　　　　　　*How We Think* (pp. 177–356)
(1910–1911)

MW 7　　　　　　　*Interest and Effort in Education* (pp. 151–97)
(1912–1914)

MW 8 (1915)　　　*German Philosophy and Politics* (pp. 135–204);
　　　　　　　　　　Schools of To-Morrow, with Evelyn Dewey
　　　　　　　　　　(pp. 205–404)

MW 9 (1916)　　　*Democracy and Education*

MW 10
(1916–1917)

MW 11
(1918–1919)

MW 12 (1920)　　*Reconstruction in Philosophy* (pp. 77–201)

MW 13
(1921–1922)

MW 14 (1922)　　*Human Nature and Conduct*

MW 15
(1923–1924)

LW 1 (1925)　　　*Experience and Nature*

LW 2　　　　　　　*The Public and Its Problems* (pp. 235–372)
(1925–1927)

LW 3
(1927–1928)

LW 4 (1929)　　　*The Quest for Certainty*

LW 5　　　　　　　*Individualism, Old and New* (pp. 41–123)
(1929–1930)

LW 6
(1931–1932)

LW 7 (1932)　　　*Ethics,* with James H. Tufts, revised edition

LW 8 (1933)　　　*How We Think,* revised edition (pp. 105–352)

LW 9 (1933–1934)	*A Common Faith* (pp. 1–58)
LW 10 (1934)	*Art as Experience*
LW 11 (1935–1937)	*Liberalism and Social Action* (pp. 1–65)
LW 12 (1938)	*Logic: The Theory of Inquiry*
LW 13 (1938–1939)	*Experience and Education* (pp. 1–62); *Freedom and Culture* (pp. 63–188); *Theory of Valuation* (pp. 189–251)
LW 14 (1939–1941)	
LW 15 (1942–1948)	
LW 16 (1949–1952)	*Knowing and the Known*, with Arthur F. Bentley (pp. 1–294)
LW 17 (1885–1953)	

Works Cited

Addams, Jane. *Democracy and Social Ethics.* New York: Macmillan, 1905.

Alexander, Thomas M. *John Dewey's Theory of Art, Experience and Nature: The Horizons of Feeling.* Albany: SUNY Press, 1987.

Allport, Gordon W. "Dewey's Individual and Social Psychology." In *The Philosophy of John Dewey,* 2nd ed., ed. Paul A. Schilpp, 265–90. Vol. 1 of The Library of Living Philosophers. La Salle, IL: Open Court, 1951.

Anderson, Quentin. "John Dewey's American Democrat." *Daedalus* 108, no. 3 (Summer 1979): 145–59.

Angell, James Rowland, and Addison Webster Moore. "Reaction-Time: A Study in Attention and Habit." *Psychological Review* 3, no. 3 (May 1896): 245–58.

Baldwin, James Mark. *Handbook for Psychology.* Vol. 2: *Feeling and Will.* New York: Henry Holt, 1894.

Bannister, Robert C. *Social Darwinism: Science and Myth in Anglo-American Social Thought.* Philadelphia: Temple University Press, 1979.

Bates, Edward Sutherland. "John Dewey: America's Philosophic Engineer." *Modern Monthly* 7, no. 7 (August 1933): 387–96, 404.

Beard, Charles A., and Mary R. Beard. *America in Midpassage,* 2 vols. New York: Macmillan, 1939.

Benson, Lee. "The Historical Background to Turner's Frontier Essay." *Agricultural History* 25 (1951): 59–82.

Bernstein, Richard J. *Praxis and Action: Contemporary Philosophies of Human Activity.* Philadelphia: University of Pennsylvania Press, 1971.

——. *Philosophical Profiles: Essays in a Pragmatic Mode.* Philadelphia: University of Pennsylvania Press, 1986.

Bestor, Arthur. "John Dewey and American Liberalism." *New Republic* 133 (29 August 1955): 18–19.

Bhattacharyya, Nirmal C. "John Dewey's Instrumentalism, Democratic Ideal and Education." *Educational Theory* 18, no. 1 (Winter 1968): 60–72.

——. "Demythologizing John Dewey." *Journal of Educational Thought* 8, no. 3 (December 1974): 117–25.

Bicha, Karel Denis. "Liberalism Frustrated: The League for Independent Political Action, 1928–1933." *Mid-America: An Historical Review* 48, no. 1 (January 1966): 19–28.

Blanshard, Brand. "Can the Philosopher Influence Social Change?" *Journal of Philosophy* 51, no. 24 (25 November 1954): 741–53.

Blau, Joseph L. *Men and Movements in American Philosophy*. Englewood Cliffs: Prentice-Hall, 1952.

———. "John Dewey and American Social Thought." *Teachers College Record* 61, no. 3 (December 1959): 121–27.

Boisvert, Raymond D. *Dewey's Metaphysics*. New York: Fordham University Press, 1988.

Bordeau, Edward J. "John Dewey's Ideas about the Great Depression." *Journal of the History of Ideas* 32, no. 1 (January-March 1971): 67–84.

Boring, Edwin G. *A History of Experimental Psychology*. New York: Century, 1929.

Bourne, Randolph S. *War and the Intellectuals: Essays by Randolph S. Bourne, 1915–1919*. Edited by Carl Resek. New York: Harper Torchbooks, 1964.

Boydston, Jo Ann. Introduction to *The Poems of John Dewey*, ix–lxvii. Carbondale: Southern Illinois University Press, 1977.

Brickman, William H., and Stanley Lehrer, eds. *John Dewey: Master Educator*. New York: Atherton Press, 1966.

Brodbeck, May. "The Philosophy of John Dewey." In *Iowa Publications in Philosophy*, Vol. 1, *Essays in Ontology*, 188–215. Iowa City: University of Iowa Press, 1963.

Brown, Richard J. "John Dewey and the League for Independent Political Action." *Social Studies* 59, no. 4 (April 1968): 156–61.

Buchler, Justus. *Charles Peirce's Empiricism*. New York: Harcourt, Brace, 1939.

Buck, Paul H., ed. *Social Sciences at Harvard, 1860–1920: From Inculcation to the Open Mind*. Cambridge: Harvard University Press, 1965.

Burke, Kenneth. "Liberalism's Family Tree." *New Republic* 86 (4 March 1936): 115–16.

Burtt, Edwin A. "The Core of Dewey's Way of Thinking." *Journal of Philosophy* 57, no. 13 (23 June 1960): 401–19.

Campbell, James. "Rorty's Use of Dewey." *Southern Journal of Philosophy* 22, no. 2 (Summer 1984): 175–87.

———. "Dewey's Understanding of Marx and Marxism." In *Context over Foundation: Dewey and Marx*, ed. William J. Gavin, 119–45. Dordrecht: Reidel, 1988.

──────. "Buchler's Conception of Community." In *Nature's Perspectives: Prospects for Ordinal Metaphysics,* ed. Armen Marsoobian, Kathleen Wallace, and Robert S. Corrington, 315–34. Albany: SUNY Press, 1991.

──────. *The Community Reconstructs: The Meaning of Pragmatic Social Thought.* Champaign: University of Illinois Press, 1992.

──────. "Ayer and Pragmatism." In *The Philosophy of A. J. Ayer,* ed. Lewis E. Hahn, 83–104. Vol. 21 of The Library of Living Philosophers. La Salle, IL: Open Court, 1992.

──────. "Du Bois and James." *Transactions of the Charles S. Peirce Society* 28, no. 3 (Summer 1992): 569–81.

Childs, John L. "Democracy, Education, and the Class Struggle." *Social Frontier* 2 (June 1936): 274–78.

──────. "Dr. Bode on 'Authentic' Democracy." *Social Frontier* 5 (November 1938): 40–43 [reprinted in LW 13:384–90].

──────. "John Dewey and Education." In *John Dewey: Philosopher of Science and Freedom,* ed. Sidney Hook, 153–63. New York: Dial, 1950.

──────. *American Pragmatism and Education: An Interpretation and Criticism.* New York: Henry Holt, 1956.

Cohen, Morris Raphael. "Later Philosophy." In *The Cambridge History of American Literature,* Vol. 3, ed. William P. Trent, John Erskine, Stuart P. Sherman, and Carl Van Doren, 226–65. New York: Macmillan, 1917–1921.

──────. "Some Difficulties in Dewey's Anthropocentric Naturalism." *Philosophical Review* 49, no. 12 (March 1940): 196–228 [reprinted in LW 14:379–410].

──────. *A Preface to Logic.* New York: Henry Holt, 1944.

──────. *American Thought: A Critical Sketch.* Edited by Felix S. Cohen. Glencoe, IL: Free Press, 1954.

──────. "Scientific Method." In *Encyclopedia of the Social Sciences,* Vol. 9, ed. Edwin R. A. Seligman, 389–96. New York: Macmillan, 1933.

Conkin, Paul K. *Puritans and Pragmatists: Eight Eminent American Thinkers.* Bloomington: Indiana University Press, 1976.

Connolly, William E. *The Terms of Political Discourse.* 2nd ed. Princeton: Princeton University Press, 1983.

Coughlan, Neil. *Young John Dewey: An Essay in American Intellectual History.* Chicago: University of Chicago Press, 1975.

Counts, George S. "Dare Progressive Education Be Progressive?" *Progressive Education* 9, no. 4 (April 1932): 257–63.

──────. "Freedom, in Relation to Culture, Social Planning, and Leadership." In *Theses on Freedom*, 3–6 Washington, DC: National Education Association, 1932 [reprinted in LW 6:445–49].

———. *Dare the School Build a New Social Order?* New York: John Day, 1932.

Creighton, James Edwin. "Darwin and Logic." *Psychological Review* 16, no. 3 (May 1909): 170–87.

Croly, Herbert. "A School of Social Research." *New Republic* 15 (8 June 1918): 167–71.

Crunden, Robert M. *Ministers of Reform: The Progressives' Achievement in American Civilization, 1889–1920.* Urbana: University of Illinois Press, 1984.

Curti, Merle Eugene. *Probing Our Past.* New York: Harper & Bros., 1955.

Damico, Alfonso J. *Individuality and Community: The Social and Political Thought of John Dewey.* Gainesville: University Presses of Florida, 1978.

Darwin, Charles. *The Origin of Species by Means of Natural Selection, or the Preservation of Favored Races in the Struggle for Life* [1859], and *The Descent of Man and Selection in Relation to Sex* [1871]. New York: Modern Library, 1936.

———. *The Autobiography of Charles Darwin, 1809–1882.* Edited by Nora Barlow. New York: Norton, 1969.

Davis, Allen F. *Spearheads for Reform: The Social Settlements and the Progressive Movement, 1890–1914.* New York: Oxford University Press, 1968.

Dewey, Jane M., ed. "Biography of John Dewey." In *The Philosophy of John Dewey*, 2nd ed., ed. Paul A. Schilpp, 3–45. Vol. 1 of The Library of Living Philosophers. La Salle, IL: Open Court, 1951.

Dewey, John. *The Early Works of John Dewey, 1882–1898.* Edited by Jo Ann Boydston. 5 vols. Carbondale: Southern Illinois University Press, 1969–1972.

———. *The Middle Works of John Dewey, 1899–1924.* Edited by Jo Ann Boydston. 15 vols. Carbondale: Southern Illinois University Press, 1976–1983.

———. *The Later Works of John Dewey, 1925–1953.* Edited by Jo Ann Boydston. 17 vols. Carbondale: Southern Illinois University Press, 1981–1990.

———. *The Poems of John Dewey.* Edited by Jo Ann Boydston. Carbondale: Southern Illinois University Press, 1977.

Dewey, John, and Arthur F. Bentley. *A Philosophical Correspondence, 1932–1951.* Edited by Sidney Ratner, Jules Altman, and James E. Wheeler. New Brunswick: Rutgers University Press, 1964.

Dicker, Georges. "John Dewey: Instrumentalism in Social Action." *Transactions of the Charles S. Peirce Society* 7, no. 4 (Fall 1971): 221–32.

Dorfman, Joseph. *Thorstein Veblen and His America*. New York: Gollancz, 1935.

Dykhuizen, George. *The Life and Mind of John Dewey*. Carbondale: Southern Illinois University Press, 1973.

Eames, S. Morris. *Pragmatic Naturalism: An Introduction*. Carbondale: Southern Illinois University Press, 1977.

Eisele, J. Christopher. "John Dewey and the Immigrants." *History of Education Quarterly* 15, no. 1 (Spring 1975): 67–85.

Eiseley, Loren C. *Darwin's Century: Evolution and the Men Who Discovered It*. Garden City: Anchor, 1961.

_____. *The Unexpected Universe*. New York: Harcourt, Brace, Jovanovich, 1969.

Emerson, Ralph Waldo. *The Complete Works of Ralph Waldo Emerson*. Edited by Edward Waldo Emerson. 12 vols. Boston: Houghton, Mifflin, 1904.

Evans, Rand B. "Introduction: The Historical Context." In the critical edition of William James's *The Principles of Psychology*, Vol. 1, xli–lxviii. Cambridge: Harvard University Press, 1981.

_____. "The Origins of American Academic Psychology." In *Explorations in the History of Psychology in the United States*, ed. Josef Brozek, 17–60. Lewisburg, PA: Bucknell University Press, 1984.

Faulkner, Harold Underwood. *The Quest for Social Justice, 1898–1914*. New York: Macmillan, 1931.

Fay, Jay Wharton. *American Psychology before William James*. New Brunswick: Rutgers University Press, 1939.

Featherstone, Joseph. "John Dewey." *New Republic* 167, no. 2 (8 July 1972): 27–32.

Feffer, Andrew. *The Chicago Pragmatists and American Progressivism*. Ithaca: Cornell University Press, 1993.

Feinberg, Walter. "The Conflict between Intelligence and Community in Dewey's Educational Philosophy." *Educational Theory* 19 (Summer 1969): 236–48.

Feuer, Lewis S. "John Dewey and the Back to the People Movement in American Thought." *Journal of the History of Ideas* 20, no. 4 (1959): 545–68.

Fisch, Max H. *Peirce, Semeiotic, and Pragmatism*. Edited by Kenneth Lane Ketner and Christian J. W. Kloesel. Bloomington: Indiana University Press, 1986.

Flower, Elizabeth, and Murray G. Murphey. *A History of Philosophy in America*. 2 vols. New York: Putnams, 1977.

Fontinell, Eugene. *Toward a Reconstruction of Religion: A Philosophical Probe*. West Nyack, NY: Cross Currents, 1979.

Forcey, Charles. Introduction to *The Promise of American Life*, by Herbert Croly, vii–xxii. New York, Dutton, 1963.

Frankel, Charles. "John Dewey's Legacy." *American Scholar* 29, no. 3 (Summer 1960): 313–31.

Franklin, Benjamin. *The Writings of Benjamin Franklin*. Edited by Albert Henry Smyth. 10 vols. New York: Macmillan, 1907.

Freud, Sigmund. *Civilization and Its Discontents*. New York: Norton, [1930] 1961.

Friess, Horace L. "Dewey's Philosophy of Religion." *Guide to the Works of John Dewey*, ed. Jo Ann Boydston, 200–217. Carbondale: Southern Illinois University Press, 1970.

Gabriel, Ralph Henry. *The Course of American Democratic Thought: An Intellectual History since 1815*. New York: Ronald, 1940.

Geiger, George Raymond. "Dewey's Social and Political Philosophy." In *The Philosophy of John Dewey*, 2nd ed., ed. Paul A. Schilpp, 337–68. Vol. 1 of The Library of Living Philosophers. (La Salle, IL: Open Court, 1951.

———. *Philosophy and the Social Order: An Introductory Approach*. Boston: Houghton Mifflin, 1947.

———. *John Dewey in Perspective: A Reassessment*. New York: McGraw-Hill, 1964.

Ginger, Ray. *Six Days or Forever? Tennessee v. John Thomas Scopes*. Boston: Beacon Press, 1958.

Gouinlock, James. *John Dewey's Philosophy of Value*. New York: Humanities, 1972.

———. *Excellence in Public Discourse: John Stuart Mill, John Dewey, and Social Intelligence*. New York: Teachers College Press, 1986.

———. "Dewey." In *Ethics in the History of Western Philosophy*, ed. Robert J. Cavalier, James Gouinlock, and James P. Sterba, 306–34. New York: St. Martins Press, 1989.

Greene, John C. *The Death of Man: Evolution and Its Impact on Western Thought*. Ames, IA: Iowa State University Press, 1959.

Grimes, Alan Pendleton. *American Political Thought*. Rev. ed. New York: Holt, Rinehart & Winston, 1960.

Hall, David D. *Worlds of Wonder, Days of Judgment: Popular Religious Belief in Early New England*. New York: Knopf, 1989.

Handlin, Oscar, and Lilian Handlin. Introduction to *The Middle Works of John Dewey, 1918–1919*, Vol. 11, ed. Jo Ann Boydston, ix–xx. Carbondale: Southern Illinois University Press, 1982.

Hayek, Friedrich. *The Road to Serfdom*. Chicago: University of Chicago Press, 1944.

Hazlitt, Henry. Review of *A Common Faith*, by John Dewey. *Yale Review* 24, no. 1 (September 1934): 166–68.

Herbst, Jurgen. *The German Historical School in American Scholarship: A Study in the Transfer of Culture*. Ithaca: Cornell University Press, 1965.

Herrick, Genevieve Forbes, and John Origen Herrick. *The Life of William Jennings Bryan*. Chicago: Buxton, 1925.

Hickman, Larry A. *John Dewey's Pragmatic Technology*. Bloomington: Indiana University Press, 1990.

Hofstadter, Richard. *Social Darwinism in American Thought*. Rev. ed. Boston: Beacon, 1955.

———. *The Age of Reform: From Bryan to FDR*. New York: Vintage, 1955.

———. *Anti-intellectualism in American Life*. New York: Vintage, 1963.

Holmes, Oliver Wendell, Jr. *Abrams et al. v. United States*, 250 US 616, 624–31 (1919).

———. *Justice Oliver Wendell Holmes: His Book Notices and Uncollected Letters and Papers*. Edited by Harry C. Shriver. New York: Central, 1936.

———. *Holmes-Pollock Letters*. Edited by Mark DeWolf Howe. 2 vols. Cambridge: Harvard University Press, 1941.

Holmes, Robert L. "John Dewey's Moral Philosophy in Contemporary Perspective." *Review of Metaphysics* 20, no. 1 (September 1966): 42–70.

Hook, Sidney. *John Dewey: An Intellectual Portrait*. New York: John Day, 1939.

———. "The Desirable and Emotive in Dewey's Ethics." In *John Dewey: Philosopher of Science and Freedom*, ed. Sidney Hook, 194–216. New York: Dial, 1950.

———. "John Dewey and the Crisis of American Liberalism." *Antioch Review* 29, no. 2 (Summer 1969): 218–32.

———. *Pragmatism and the Tragic Sense of Life*. New York: Basic Books, 1974.

Horowitz, Irving Louis. "The Intellectual Genesis of C. Wright Mills." In *Sociology and Pragmatism*, by C. Wright Mills, 11–31. New York: Oxford University Press, 1966.

———. *C. Wright Mills: An American Utopian*. New York: Free Press, 1984.

James, William. *The Principles of Psychology*. 3 vols. Cambridge: Harvard University Press, [1890] 1981.

———. *Psychology: Briefer Course*. Cambridge: Harvard University Press, [1892] 1984.

———. *The Will to Believe and Other Essays in Popular Philosophy*. Cambridge: Harvard University Press, [1897] 1979.

———. *Pragmatism: A New Name for Some Old Ways of Thinking*. Cambridge: Harvard University Press, [1907] 1975.

———. *The Meaning of Truth: A Sequel to 'Pragmatism'*. Cambridge: Harvard University Press, [1909] 1975.

———. *Some Problems of Philosophy: A Beginning of an Introduction to Philosophy*. Cambridge: Harvard University Press, [1911] 1979.

———. *Essays in Radical Empiricism*. Cambridge: Harvard University Press, [1912] 1976.

———. *Essays in Religion and Morality*. Cambridge: Harvard University Press, 1982.

———. *The Letters of William James*. Edited by his son, Henry James. 2 vols. Boston: Atlantic Monthly Press, 1920.

Journal of Philosophy: Fifty-Year Index, 1904–1953. New York: Journal of Philosophy, 1962.

Kallen, Horace M. "Individuality, Individualism, and John Dewey." *Antioch Review* 19, no. 3 (Fall 1959): 299–314.

Karier, Clarence. "Liberalism and the Quest for Orderly Change." *History of Education Quarterly* 12, no. 1 (Spring 1972): 57–80.

———. "John Dewey and the New Liberalism: Some Reflections and Responses." *History of Education Quarterly* 15, no. 4 (Winter 1975): 417–43.

———. "Making the World Safe for Democracy: An Historical Critique of John Dewey's Pragmatic Liberal Philosophy in the Warfare State." *Educational Theory* 27, no. 1 (Winter 1977): 12–47.

Kaufman-Osborn, Timothy V. "John Dewey and the Liberal Science of Community." *Journal of Politics* 44, no. 4 (November 1984): 1142–65.

———. "Pragmatism, Policy Science, and the State." *American Journal of Political Science* 29, no. 4 (November 1985): 827–49.

Kennedy, Gail. "Science and the Transformation of Common Sense: The Basic Problem of Dewey's Philosophy." *Journal of Philosophy* 51, no. 11 (27 May 1954): 313–25.

———. "The Hidden Link in Dewey's Theory of Evaluation." *Journal of Philosophy* 52, no. 4 (17 February 1955): 85–94.

———. "Pragmatism, Pragmaticism and the Will to Believe—A Reconsideration." *Journal of Philosophy* 55, no. 14 (3 July 1958): 578–88.

———. "The Process of Evaluation in a Democratic Community." *Journal of Philosophy* 56, no. 6 (12 March 1959): 253–63.

Kesselman, Steven. "The Frontier Thesis and the Great Depression." *Journal of the History of Ideas* 29 (1968): 253–68.

Knight, Frank H. "Pragmatism and Social Action." *International Journal of Ethics* 46, no. 2 (January 1936): 229–36.

Konvitz, Milton R. Introduction to the *Later Works of John Dewey, 1933–1934,* Vol. 9, ed. Jo Ann Boydston, xi–xxxii. Carbondale: Southern Illinois University Press, 1986.

Krutch, Joseph Wood. *The Modern Temper: A Study and a Confession.* New York: Harcourt, Brace and World, [1929] 1956.

———. *The Measure of Man: On Freedom, Human Values, Survival and the Modern Temper.* Indianapolis: Bobbs-Merrill, [1953] 1962.

Kuklick, Bruce. *Churchmen and Philosophers from Jonathan Edwards to John Dewey.* New Haven: Yale University Press, 1985.

Lamont, Corliss. "New Light on Dewey's *Common Faith.*" *Journal of Philosophy* 58, no. 1 (5 January 1961): 21–28.

Levi, Albert William. *Philosophy and the Modern World.* Bloomington: Indiana University Press, 1959.

Levy, David W. *Herbert Croly of 'The New Republic': The Life and Thought of an American Progressive.* Princeton: Princeton University Press, 1985.

Lewis, Clarence Irving. Review of *The Quest for Certainty,* by John Dewey. *Journal of Philosophy* 27 (1930): 14–25.

Lincoln, Abraham. *The Collected Works of Abraham Lincoln.* Edited by Roy P. Basler. 9 vols. New Brunswick: Rutgers University Press, 1953.

Lippmann, Walter. *Drift and Mastery: An Attempt to Diagnose the Current Unrest.* New York: Mitchell Kennerley, 1914.

———. "The Basic Problem of Democracy: I. What Modern Liberty Means." *Atlantic* 124 (November 1919): 616–27.

———. *Public Opinion.* New York: Macmillan, 1922.

———. *The Phantom Public.* New York: Harcourt, Brace, 1925.

———. *Men of Destiny.* New York: Macmillan, 1927.

———. *The Method of Freedom.* New York: Macmillan, 1934.

May, Henry F. *The End of American Innocence: A Study of the First Years of Our Own Time, 1912–1917.* Chicago: Quadrangle, 1964.

Mayerhoff, Milton. "A Neglected Aspect of Experience in Dewey's Philosophy." *Journal of Philosophy* 60, no. 6 (14 March 1963): 146–53.

McCaul, Robert L. "Dewey, Harper and the University of Chicago." In *John Dewey: Master Educator,* ed. William W. Brickman and Stanley Lehrer, 31–74. New York: Atherton, 1966.

McDermott, John J. *The Culture of Experience: Philosophical Essays in the American Grain.* New York: New York University Press, 1976.

———. "Josiah Royce's Philosophy of the Community: Danger of the Detached Individual." In *American Philosophy,* ed. Marcus G. Singer, 153–76. Cambridge: Cambridge University Press, 1985.

———. *Streams of Experience: Reflections on the History and Philosophy of American Culture.* Amherst: University of Massachusetts Press, 1986.

———. Introduction to *Later Works of John Dewey, 1935–1937,* Vol. 11, ed. Jo Ann Boydston, xi–xxxii. Carbondale: Southern Illinois University Press, 1987.

Mead, George Herbert. Review of *The Newer Ideals of Peace,* by Jane Addams. *American Journal of Sociology* 13, no. 1 (July 1907): 121–28.

———. "The Social Settlement: Its Basis and Function." *University [of Chicago] Record* 12 (1908): 108–10.

———. "Bishop Berkeley and His Message." *Journal of Philosophy* 26, no. 16 (1 August 1929): 421–30.

———. *The Philosophy of the Present.* Edited by Arthur E. Murphy. Chicago: University of Chicago Press, [1932] 1980.

———. *Mind, Self, and Society from the Standpoint of a Social Behaviorist.* Edited by Charles W. Morris. Chicago: University of Chicago Press, 1934.

———. *Movements of Thought in the Nineteenth Century.* Edited by Merritt H. Moore. Chicago: University of Chicago Press, 1936.

———. *The Philosophy of the Act.* Edited by Charles W. Morris, John M. Brewster, Albert M. Dunham, and David L. Miller. Chicago: University of Chicago Press, 1938.

———. *Selected Writings.* Edited by Andrew J. Reck. Chicago: University of Chicago Press, 1981.

Mencken, Henry Louis. *Notes on Democracy.* New York: Knopf, 1926.

Metz, Joseph G. "Democracy and the Scientific Method in the Philosophy of John Dewey." *Review of Politics* 31, no. 2 (April 1969): 242–62.

Miller, Perry. *The New England Mind.* Vol. 1, *The Seventeenth Century.* Vol. 2, *From Colony to Province.* Cambridge: Harvard University Press, 1939, 1953.

———. *Errand into the Wilderness.* Cambridge: Harvard University Press, 1956.

Mills, C. Wright. *The Power Elite.* New York: Oxford University Press, 1956.

———. *White Collar: The American Middle Classes.* New York: Oxford University Press, 1956.

———. *The Causes of World War Three.* New York: Simon & Schuster, 1958.

———. *The Sociological Imagination.* New York: Grove Press, 1961.

———. *Sociology and Pragmatism: The Higher Learning in America.* Edited by I. L. Horowitz. New York: Oxford University Press, 1966.

———. *Power, Politics and People: The Collected Essays of C. Wright Mills.* Edited by I. L. Horowitz. New York: Oxford University Press, 1967.

———, ed. *The Marxists.* New York: Dell, 1962.

———. "Comment on Criticism" [1957]. In *C. Wright Mills and the Power Elite,* ed. G. William Domhoff and Hoyt B. Ballard, 229–50. Boston: Beacon Press, 1969.

Moore, Addison Webster. *Pragmatism and Its Critics.* Chicago: University of Chicago Press, 1910.

Morris, Charles W. *The Pragmatic Movement in American Philosophy.* New York: Braziller, 1970.

Murphy, Arthur E. "Dewey's Theory of the Nature and Function of Philosophy." In *The Philosopher of the Common Man: Essays in Honor of John Dewey to Celebrate His Eightieth Birthday,* ed. Sidney Ratner, 33–55. New York: Putnam, 1940.

———. "John Dewey and American Liberalism." *Journal of Philosophy* 57, no. 13 (23 June 1960): 420–36.

Murphy, Gardner. *An Historical Introduction to Modern Psychology.* New York: Harcourt, Brace, 1930.

Myers, Gerald E. "Introduction: The Intellectual Context." In the critical edition of *The Principles of Psychology,* by William James, Vol. 1, xi–xl. Cambridge: Harvard University Press, 1981.

———. *William James: His Life and Thought.* New Haven: Yale University Press, 1986.

von Nardroff, Ellen. "The American Frontier as a Safety Valve—The Life, Death, Reincarnation, and Justification of a Theory." *Agricultural History* 36 (July 1962): 123–42.

Nathanson, Jerome. *John Dewey: The Reconstruction of the Democratic Life.* New York: Scribners, 1951.

Nettels, Curtis. "Frederick Jackson Turner and the New Deal." *Wisconsin Magazine of History* 17 (1934): 257–65.

Niebuhr, Reinhold. *Moral Man and Immoral Society: A Study in Ethics and Politics.* New York: Scribners, [1932] 1960.

————. *The Nature and Destiny of Man: A Christian Interpretation.* Vol. 1, *Human Nature.* New York: Scribners, [1941] 1964.

————. *The Irony of American History.* New York: Scribners, 1962.

Novack, George. *Pragmatism versus Marxism: An Appraisal of John Dewey's Philosophy.* New York: Pathfinder, 1975.

Ogburn, William Fielding. *Social Change with Respect to Culture and Original Nature.* New York: Huebsch, 1922.

Orwell, George. *The Collected Essays, Journalism, and Letters of George Orwell.* Edited by Sonia Orwell and Ian Angus. 4 vols. New York: Harcourt, Brace, & World, 1968.

Otto, Max Carl. *The Human Enterprise: An Attempt to Relate Philosophy to Life.* New York: Crofts, 1940.

————. Review of *A Common Faith,* by John Dewey. *Philosophical Review* 44, no. 5 (September 1935): 496–97.

————. Review of *Contemporary American Philosophy: Personal Statements,* ed. George P. Adams and William P. Montague. *International Journal of Ethics* 41, no. 2 (January 1931): 230–34.

Parker, William Belmont. *The Life and Public Services of Justin Smith Morrill.* Boston: Houghton Mifflin, 1924.

Paxson, Frederic L. "A Generation of the Frontier Hypothesis, 1893–1932." *Pacific Historical Review* 2, no. 1 (1933): 34–51.

Peirce, Charles Sanders. *The Collected Papers of Charles Sanders Peirce.* Edited by Charles Hartshorne, Paul Weiss, and Arthur W. Burks. 8 vols. Cambridge: Harvard University Press, 1931–1958.

Perry, Ralph Barton, ed. *The Thought and Character of William James.* 2 vols. Boston: Little, Brown, 1935.

Philosophical Review: Index to Volumes I–XXXV. New York: Longmans Green, 1927.

Price, David E. "Community and Control: Critical Democratic Theory in the Progressive Period." *American Political Science Review* 68, no. 4 (December 1974): 1663–78.

Randall, John Herman, Jr. "Liberalism as Faith in Intelligence." *Journal of Philosophy* 32, no. 10 (9 May 1935): 253–64.

————. "The Religion of Shared Experience." In *The Philosopher of the Common Man: Essays in Honor of John Dewey to Celebrate His Eightieth Birthday,* ed. Sidney Ratner, 106–45. New York: Putnam, 1940.

————. "Dewey's Interpretation of the History of Philosophy." In *The Philosophy of John Dewey,* 2nd ed., ed. Paul A. Schilpp, 77–102. Vol. 1 of The Library of Living Philosophers. La Salle, IL: Open Court, 1951.

———. "John Dewey, 1859–1952." *Journal of Philosophy* 50, no. 1 (1 January 1953): 5–13.

———. "Dewey's Contribution to Scientific Humanism." *Humanist* 19, no. 3 (1959): 134–38.

Randall, John Herman, Jr., and Justus Buchler. *Philosophy: An Introduction.* New York: Barnes & Noble, 1942.

Reck, Andrew J. "The Influence of William James on John Dewey in Psychology." *Transactions of the Charles S. Peirce Society* 20, no. 2 (Spring 1984): 87–117.

Rockefeller, Steven C. *John Dewey: Religious Faith and Democratic Humanism.* New York: Columbia University Press, 1991.

Rodgers, Daniel T. *Contested Truths: Keywords in American Politics since Independence.* New York: Basic Books, 1987.

Roosevelt, Franklin Delano. *The Public Papers and Addresses of Franklin Delano Roosevelt.* Edited by Samuel I. Rosenman. 13 vols. New York: Random House, 1938–1950.

Rorty, Richard. *Philosophy and the Mirror of Nature.* Princeton: Princeton University Press, 1979.

———. *Consequences of Pragmatism (Essays: 1972–1980).* Minneapolis: University of Minnesota Press, 1982.

Ross, Earle D. *Democracy's College: The Land Grant Movement in the Formative State.* Iowa City: Iowa State College Press, 1942.

Ross, Edward Alsworth. *Sin and Society: An Analysis of Latter-Day Iniquity.* Boston: Houghton Mifflin, 1907.

Royce, Josiah. *The Philosophy of Loyalty.* New York: Macmillan, 1908.

Rucker, Darnell. *The Chicago Pragmatists.* Minneapolis: University of Minnesota Press, 1969.

Ruse, Michael. *The Darwinian Revolution.* Chicago: University of Chicago Press, 1979.

Russell, Bertrand. "Dewey's New *Logic.*" In *The Philosophy of John Dewey,* 2nd ed., ed. Paul A. Schilpp, 137–56. Vol. 5 of The Library of Living Philosophers. La Salle, IL: Open Court, 1951.

Sandburg, Carl. *The Complete Poems of Carl Sandburg.* New York: Harcourt, Brace, Jovanovich, 1976.

Santayana, George. "Dewey's Naturalistic Metaphysics," *Journal of Philosophy,* XXII (3 December 1925), 673–88 [reprinted in LW 3:367–84].

———. *The Genteel Tradition at Bay.* New York: Scribners, 1931.

Savage, Willinda. "John Dewey and 'Thought News' at the University of Michigan." *Michigan Alumnus Quarterly Review* 56, no. 18 (Spring 1950): 204–9.

Schneider, Herbert Wallace. "William James as a Moralist." *In Commemoration of William James,* ed. H. M. Kallen, 127–39. New York: Columbia University Press, 1942.

Selsam, Howard. *Science and Ethics.* 2nd. ed. New York: International, 1945.

Sleeper, Ralph W. "Dewey's Metaphysical Perspective: A Note on White, Geiger, and the Problem of Obligation." *Journal of Philosophy* 57 (1960): 100–115.

———. *The Necessity of Pragmatism: John Dewey's Conception of Philosophy.* New Haven: Yale University Press, 1986.

Smith, Henry Nash. *Virgin Land: The American West as Symbol and Myth.* Cambridge: Harvard University Press, 1950.

Smith, John E. *Purpose and Thought: The Meaning of Pragmatism.* New Haven: Yale University Press, 1978.

———. *The Spirit of American Philosophy.* Rev. ed. Albany: SUNY Press, 1983.

Sokal, Michael M. Introduction to the critical edition of *Psychology: Briefer Course,* by William James, xi–xli. Cambridge: Harvard University Press, 1984.

Stern, Sheldon M. "William James and the New Psychology." In *Social Sciences at Harvard, 1860–1920: From Inculcation to the Open Mind,* ed. Paul H. Buck, 175–222, 299–305. Cambridge: Harvard University Press, 1965.

Suckiel, Ellen Kappy. *The Pragmatic Philosophy of William James.* Notre Dame: University of Notre Dame Press, 1982.

Sumner, William Graham. *The Challenge of Facts and Other Essays.* Edited by Albert Galloway Keller. New Haven: Yale University Press, 1914.

Taylor, George Rogers, ed. *The Turner Thesis: Concerning the Role of the Frontier in American History.* Rev. ed. Boston: Heath, 1956.

Thayer, H. S. *The Logic of Pragmatism: An Examination of John Dewey's Logic.* New York: Humanities Press, 1952.

———. *Meaning and Action: A Critical History of Pragmatism.* Rev. ed. Indianapolis: Hackett, 1981.

———. "John Dewey, 1859–1952." In *American Philosophy,* ed. Marcus G. Singer, 69–89. Cambridge: Cambridge University Press, 1985.

Thwing, Charles Franklin. *The American and the German University: One Hundred Years of History.* New York: Macmillan, 1928.

Tiles, J. E. *Dewey.* London: Routledge, 1988.

Tilman, Rick. *C. Wright Mills: A Native Radical and His American*

Intellectual Roots. University Park: Pennsylvania State University Press, 1984.

Tobin, Eugene M. *Organize or Perish: America's Independent Progressives, 1913-1933*. Westport, CT: Greenwood, 1986.

Tufts, James Hayden. "Recent Sociological Tendencies in France." *American Journal of Sociology* 1, no. 4 (January 1896): 446-56.

———. "On Moral Evolution." In *Studies in Philosophy and Psychology by Former Students of Charles Edward Garman*, ed. James Hayden Tufts, Edmund Burke Delabarre, Frank Chapman Sharp, Arthur Henry Pierce, and Frederick J. E. Woodbridge, 3-39. Boston: Houghton Mifflin, 1906.

———. *The Real Business of Living* (New York: Henry Holt, 1918).

———. *America's Social Morality: Dilemmas of the Changing Mores*. New York: Henry Holt, 1933.

———. *Selected Writings of James Hayden Tufts*. Edited by James Campbell. Carbondale: Southern Illinois University Press, 1992.

Tufts, James Hayden, and John Dewey. *Ethics* (the 1908 edition appears as volume 5 of *The Middle Works of John Dewey;* the revised 1932 edition appears as volume 7 of *The Later Works of John Dewey*).

Turner, Frederick Jackson. *The Frontier in American History*. New York: Holt, Rinehart & Winston, [1920] 1962.

United States Statutes at Large, XII (1863).

Veblen, Thorstein. *The Theory of the Leisure Class: An Economic Study of Institutions*. New York: Macmillan, 1899.

———. *The Engineers and the Price System*. New York: Huebsch, 1921.

———. *Absentee Ownership and Business Enterprise in Recent Times: The Case of America*. New York: Huebsch, 1923.

Webb, Walter Prescott. *Divided We Stand: The Crisis of a Frontierless Democracy*. New York: Farrar and Rinehart, 1937.

West, Cornel. *The American Evasion of Philosophy: A Genealogy of Pragmatism*. Madison: University of Wisconsin Press, 1989.

Westbrook, Robert B. *John Dewey and American Democracy*. Ithaca: Cornell University Press, 1991.

Weyl, Walter E. *The New Democracy: An Essay on Certain Political and Economic Tendencies in the United States*. New York: Macmillan, 1913.

White, Morton G. *The Origins of Dewey's Instrumentalism*. New York: Columbia University Press, 1943.

———. *Social Thought in America: The Revolt Against Formalism*. Rev. ed. Boston: Beacon Press, 1957.

————. *Science and Sentiment in America: Philosophical Thought from Jonathan Edwards to John Dewey.* New York: Oxford University Press, 1972.

————. *Pragmatism and the American Mind: Essays and Reviews in Philosophy and Intellectual History.* New York: Oxford University Press, 1973.

White, Howard B. "The Political Faith of John Dewey." *Journal of Politics* 20 (1958): 353–67.

Wiebe, Robert H. *The Search for Order, 1877–1920.* New York: Hill and Wang, 1967.

Wiener, Philip P. *Evolution and the Founders of Pragmatism.* Cambridge: Harvard University Press, 1949.

Wilson, Daniel J. *Science, Community and the Transformation of American Philosophy, 1860–1930.* Chicago: University of Chicago Press, 1990.

Wirth, Arthur G. *John Dewey as Educator: His Design for Work in Education (1894–1904).* New York: John Wiley, 1966.

Woodward, William R. "William James's Psychology of Will: Its Revolutionary Impact on American Psychology." In *Explorations in the History of Psychology in the United States,* ed. Josef Brozek, 148–95. Lewisburg, PA: Bucknell University Press, 1984.

Zerby, Charles L. "John Dewey and the Polish Question: A Response to the Revisionist Historians." *History of Education Quarterly* 15, no. 1 (Spring 1975): 17–30.

Index